POWER, POLITICS AND TERRITORY IN THE 'NEW NORTHERN IRELAND'

POWER, POLITICS AND TERRITORY IN THE 'NEW NORTHERN IRELAND'

Girdwood Barracks and the
Story of the Peace Process

ELIZABETH DEYOUNG

LIVERPOOL UNIVERSITY PRESS

First published 2023 by
Liverpool University Press
4 Cambridge Street
Liverpool
L69 7ZU

This paperback edition published 2026

Copyright © 2026 Elizabeth DeYoung

Elizabeth DeYoung has asserted the right to be identified as
the author of this book in accordance with the Copyright, Designs and Patents
Act 1988.

All rights reserved. No part of this book may be reproduced, stored in a retrieval
system, or transmitted, in any form or by any means, electronic, mechanical,
photocopying, recording, or otherwise, without the prior written permission of
the publisher.

British Library Cataloguing-in-Publication data
A British Library CIP record is available

ISBN 978-1-83764-467-4 (hardback)
ISBN 978-1-80596-818-4 (paperback)

Typeset by Carnegie Book Production, Lancaster

Contents

List of Abbreviations	vii
Acknowledgements	ix
Preface	xiii

Introduction: Planning, Politics and Contested Space	1
The Girdwood Community Hub	1
From Army Barracks to Community Hub	8
Space, Place and Power in the Urban Landscape	14

1	The First Step: Musings on History, Ethnography and Methodology	21
	A Note on Methods	21
	A Field Guide to Belfast: Walking as Methodology	26
	An Ode to Cliftonpark Avenue	32
	'A Fine History of Walls': North Belfast and the Troubles	35

2	Politicking and Peacebuilding in Northern Ireland: The Good Friday Agreement and Its Prescriptions	41
	The Good Friday Agreement	41
	Ethnic Entrepreneurs: Sinn Féin and the DUP	45
	Backroom Dealings in Northern Ireland	50

3	'Frictions, Factions and Fractions': Identity and Territory in North Belfast	55
	'A Protestant State': Demographic Change in Belfast	56
	Community Development and the Dunlop Report	64
	A 'New Northern Ireland'	68

4	'Unlocking the Potential': Grassroots Advocacy and the Girdwood Draft Masterplan	77
	'A Beautiful Patchwork Quilt?'	77

	Avoiding Equality at Girdwood	86
	The Girdwood Residents' Jury	92
5	Ethnic Champions and the Zero-Sum Game: Political Dynamics of the Northern Ireland Assembly	97
	Nixing a Shared Future	98
	Pork Barrels and Hidden Transcripts	102
	Tit for Tat: A Zero-Sum Approach to Governance	108
6	Carve-up or Compromise? The Bid for the Girdwood Community Hub	113
	From Contested to 'Shared': The European Union (EU) PEACE III Programme	114
	The Masterplan and the Maze	123
	The DSD, the DUP and 'Differential Deprivation'	130
7	The Trouble with 'Community': Paramilitaries and the Peace Industry in Northern Ireland	141
	Rhetorical Fluff: The Language of Community	142
	The Peace Industry	145
	Paramilitarism in Northern Ireland: 'They Haven't Gone Away, You Know!'	151
8	'Shenanigans and Skullduggery': Community Engagement and Argument at Girdwood	161
	How Can It Be 'Shared Space' When You're Wrangling Over the Whole Planning Process?	162
	'Have You Heard about Girdwood?': Building the Hub	167
	'The True Spirit of Girdwood' and the Race to the Finish Line	173
9	'Better' at Girdwood Community Hub: The Legacy of the Girdwood Development	183
	Opening Day	183
	Better than Nothing?	186
	'These Civil Wars Are Only Ever Over on Paper!'	191

Epilogue	195
The Assembly Collapses	195
Brexit and the Protocol	198
The Assembly Collapses … Again!	202

Bibliography	209
Index	247

Abbreviations

CAJ	Committee on the Administration of Justice
CEP	Community Empowerment Partnership
CCRF	Cliftonville Community Regeneration Forum
DCAL	Department of Culture, Arts and Leisure
DETI	Department of Enterprise, Trade and Investment
DOE	Department of the Environment
DSD	Department for Social Development
DUP	Democratic Unionist Party
ECNI	Equality Commission for Northern Ireland
EQIA	Equality Impact Assessment
IRA	Irish Republican Army (in this book, used to refer to the Provisional wing)
IRC	Independent Reporting Commission
INLA	Irish National Liberation Army
LOCA	Lower Oldpark Community Association
LSCA	Lower Shankill Community Association
MLA	Member of Legislative Assembly (Stormont)
NAMA	National Assets and Management Agency
NBCAP	North Belfast Community Action Project
NBCAU	North Belfast Community Action Unit
NICVA	Northern Ireland Council for Voluntary Action
NIHE	Northern Ireland Housing Executive
NIO	Northern Ireland Office
NISRA	Northern Ireland Statistics and Research Agency
OFMDFM	Office of the First Minister and Deputy First Minister
PPR	Participation and the Practice of Rights
PSNI	Police Service of Northern Ireland
RHI	Renewable Heat Initiative
RUC	Royal Ulster Constabulary

SDLP	Social Democratic and Labour Party
SEUPB	Special European Union Project Board
SIF	Social Investment Fund
TBTC	Take Back the City
TUV	Traditional Unionist Voice
UDA	Ulster Defence Association
UFF	Ulster Freedom Fighters (connected to the UDA)
UUP	Ulster Unionist Party
UVF	Ulster Volunteer Force

Acknowledgements

I would never have started my doctorate or written this book without Professor Marianne Elliott, to whom this book is dedicated. Thank you, Marianne, for believing in me.

I am thankful for the support of the Institute of Irish Studies, University of Liverpool, and to my doctoral supervisors Professor Peter Shirlow and Dr. Kevin Bean, who helped shape my conceptual framework and ability to articulate Girdwood's broader relevance. Professor Kimberly Jones, an incisive and deeply empathetic scholar, was also an early steward of this work. During my doctorate, I received financial support from the Liverpool Doctoral College, British Association of Irish Studies (BAIS) and the European Federation of Associations and Centres of Irish Studies (EFACIS)'s Werner Huber bursary. These funding opportunities allowed me to conduct extended fieldwork in Belfast and to meet and learn from scores of people along the way. EFACIS also provided me with the chance to workshop and present my research as part of the International Doctoral Seminar cohort of 2016 – a group of wildly thoughtful and brilliant scholars that I appreciate to this day.

Gratitude for reading, editing and stewarding this project goes to Christabel Scaife and the editorial team at Liverpool University Press and to the anonymous readers who provided much-needed and welcome critical feedback. Sincere thanks are also due to photographer Thomas McMullan, who has long chronicled the Girdwood story, for generously lending his work to the cover.

To my wonderful friends in Ireland – Adam and Laura, for providing a literal and figurative home over the many years of our friendship, through ups and downs and walks along the promenade by the Irish Sea. Amy and Megan, dynamic duo, friends and hosts extraordinaire – Amy in particular provided generous insight on various iterations of this book over the years, and taught me how to hail a black taxi. Thanks to Niamh T. for your scintillating wit and verve, and a friendship that has endured since our first nervous class at Cluain Árd. Deirdre – *anonn 'gus anall*, from Boston to the Gaeltacht and everywhere in between, deepest thanks for buoying me up and for sharing all the good tunes. Sinéad, *a chara*, from our first encounter at Áras Mhic Reachtain to our adventures in Philadelphia, your alacrity and brilliance continue to enliven. And I fondly remember Niamh R.'s patient tutelage as Gaeilge, much laughter, music and miso.

I am deeply grateful to the people of Belfast – those who agreed to be interviewed, dear friends and acquaintances who contributed to the research and to my life there in ways large and small. My virtuosic musician friends welcomed me into the sessions and their lives over many years, and my friends at the pub warmly accepted me into the fold. Particular thanks are due to those who participated in the research project and graciously shared their worlds, their time and expertise with me. It was a tremendous privilege to work with the people and community organisations in these pages, all of whom played a part in writing Girdwood's story. *Míle buíochas*, too, to Dr Barbara Graham for your counsel in the last part of the writing. And to Paweł, thank you for sharing your unparalleled knowledge of Belfast with me, for all our long walks together that shaped my path and my practice as a researcher.

Tá mé thar a bheith buíoch daoibhse, a chairde Gael, as bhur gcineáltas agus bhur gcairdeas ó'n chéad lá agus mé in mBéal Feirste. B'iomaí lá a chaith muid ag an Cumann Chluain Árd agus thart fa Gaoth Dobhair, ag deánamh ár gcaint's ár gcomhra ó oíche go maidin. Is mor domh an am a chaith mé in bhur gcuideachta.

To my postgraduate community in Liverpool and the friendly camaraderie at the Institute, thanks are due for companionship, conversation and commiseration. I am particularly indebted to Dr Anna Walsh for lending her intellectual dynamism and creativity to the materials that became this book. Thank you for emboldening me in moments of doubt, for being there every step of the way through the PhD, for your steadfast friendship and ready humour. Thanks also to Dr James Gallacher for a long tradition of scholarly conversations that alternately inspire and challenge, and for your advice and impeccable music taste over the years. Finally, to Dr Ellie Perrin for contributing critical insight to this work and for your unwavering commitment to justice that years later continues to inspire me.

Friends across time zones and countries provided constant encouragement over the years. Johanna, Robin and Sarah – your love has sustained me, pulled me through the most difficult times of my life and illuminated my best moments. *Merci bien aux filles folles*.

Unbounded gratitude goes to Rosemarie and Maura, my oldest friends, for your grace and generosity of spirit. Special thanks to Maura for her feedback on various materials which informed this book. And during lonely moments of the pandemic, dear friends Ciara, Nabilla and Alana in Philadelphia fortified me and kept my spirits high.

ACKNOWLEDGEMENTS

To Lauren, my kindred spirit, for her deep empathy, for long car rides and honest conversations, for unconditional love.

To my friends and colleagues at Penn who supported this project and offered consistent encouragement, thank you for your wisdom. It is a joy to work with and learn from you on a daily basis. Many thanks also go to Stephanie Rivera-Kumar, who jumped in with generosity and great patience at the final hour to lend her GIS expertise to the project.

Dr Shelly Ronen shared astute comments and helped me rethink critical parts of the introduction. Her insistent commitment to integrity and her example as a scholar and friend have been invaluable.

An enormous thank you to my family. My mum and dad, who have nurtured my curiosity from the very beginning, who have been inexpressible and inexhaustible sources of comfort, advice and love all my life. Mum, your irrepressible spirit and *joie de vivre* have guided me throughout my travels and my trials. Dad, in research and in life I have attempted to emulate your commitment to honouring others with dignity. To my brother Greg, my first and closest confidante, whom I trust and admire completely. Thank you for being there, always, *le chéile go deo*. Thanks to Alex, my sister-in-law, for your honest counsel and friendship, and to Thomas and Patrick, perpetual sources of joy.

Lastly, thanks are due to Brendan, my partner in all things. It is a delight and a privilege to walk alongside you in this life.

There are many other friends, family members and neighbours who inquired about the book and offered advice and support, and to whom I owe a debt of gratitude. *Go raibh míle maith agaibh uilig.* I am lucky to have you all.

Preface

My decision to conduct research on the Girdwood Barracks was a fortuitous accident.

The first time I arrived in Belfast, I was 20 years old and travelling by myself on a university exchange. I had been hired for a six-month internship at a peacebuilding organisation. That was the idea, anyway. But Belfast is a funny place. It gets deep under your skin. Alone in the city, I found myself walking for hours on end in strange neighbourhoods, past concrete barriers and tall steel walls and through graveyards. Far away from the city centre and far removed from my internship, the landscape was bleak and oddly absorbing.

I haunted the pubs. I struck up conversations with strangers and became friends with the regulars. I had 'the craic' (an all-encompassing, hard-to-define term for fun, gossip, hijinks). I ran around with musicians, traversing the city. We talked over kitchen tables in far-flung housing estates and stumbled out of secret drinking holes when the birds began their mornings. I moved among social clubs and music venues, attended loud smoky parties and traditional sessions and warehouse raves. I was fondly referred to as a 'wee hallion', or a 'rocket', in the parlance of the city.

Belfast is full of sharp edges and prone to extremes, not all of them pleasant. At the time, I was renting a room from an elderly couple who lived in a house by the university. They were not pleased by my youthful indiscretions. After I broke house rules, I was asked to leave. My belongings were dumped unceremoniously in garbage bags. The internship ended badly, too, after that, like a bad relationship. I had to meet with my university counsellors and make a case for why I still deserved the course credit, why I'd ventured so far and foolishly from the safety of my neat student life. Belfast had almost taken me down, but I loved the city still. I loved it completely (still do) and I hated to leave.

When I got back to Boston and got myself together again, I started researching the walls I'd passed and the many neighbourhoods I'd spent time in. I compared murals and memorials, committed bombings to memory and became familiar with a long list of deaths. The city and its history wholly fascinated me. It captured my imagination in a way nothing in my life had before. I tried to figure out a way to get back.

And I did. A few years later, I was accepted to the MA programme at Queen's University Belfast. Those intervening years had given me some perspective on my 20-year-old self. One day, I left the Queen's library and walked over to my former landlords' house. Shame bubbled in me but I lifted the door knocker anyway, meaning to apologise for my old antics. The woman didn't recognise me at first. She ushered me in and offered me a cup of tea. We sat awkwardly in her sitting room, and I told her about my university course. I was glad her husband wasn't in. I remembered him saying once, 'The last thing the world needs is another academic researching Northern Ireland'.

'What are you writing your thesis on?' she asked. It was early in the semester. I didn't know. She paused thoughtfully and said, 'They're doing up the old Girdwood Barracks in North Belfast. It might be a good topic for you, I don't know of anyone that's ever looked at the place'. I Googled the name and found nothing on Girdwood. Not a single article. I wasn't sure what it was. I returned to my coursework and forgot about the Barracks.

Later in the year, I found myself lost on my way to a meeting on the Cliftonville Road in Catholic/Nationalist North Belfast. This was an unfamiliar place to me, although it was located only 15 minutes' walk from the outskirts of the city centre. Intending to cut through a side street, I found instead a dead end, closed off by a solid wall of metal sheeting. It looked like an interface barrier ('peace wall'). This was perplexing to me. I had been told that this was a solidly Catholic/Nationalist area, and so there was no logical reason a peace wall should be there. It was out of place. I gave up on my route, shoulders slumping, sweating and frustrated and hoping no one had noticed my small failure. I backtracked and walked up the Crumlin Road, still unsure of where I was. A Union Jack flag fluttered farther down, signifying the approach to a Protestant/Unionist neighbourhood. That was definitely not Cliftonville. I asked a harried-looking woman for directions. She sent me up a street to the right, saying it took a funny turn at the end.

The first thing that struck me about Cliftonpark Avenue was all the empty space. It looked like a residential street at first glance, but with a number of gaps where houses should have been (I later found that during the Troubles, much of Cliftonpark Avenue's housing stock was abandoned or burned out, and later bulldozed). Although it was situated between two main roads, and despite its proximity to the city centre, the neighbourhood was quiet and still. It was eerie. The same metal sheeting ran all the way along the street. I wondered what its purpose was. I peeked through a gap in the wall – just a derelict lot, with trash and trees dotting the ground and a pile of tangled plastic bags. On the left side of the street, another interface barrier I had never seen before started from the pavement and snaked past clusters of houses. I did not know it then but I had literally stumbled across my MA dissertation and PhD thesis.

The metal sheeting turned out to be the perimeter wall of the demilitarised Girdwood Army Barracks, and Cliftonpark Avenue, along which it ran, was an interface between highly segregated neighbourhoods. Over the subsequent four and a half years, I became deeply invested in piecing together the story of Girdwood and its transition from army barracks to community hub in real time. I followed the redevelopment process as it unfolded, thanks in large part to the generosity of community workers, activists and residents in the neighbourhoods around the site.

Belfast offered myriad possibilities for *flânerie*, the act of aimless strolling and 'reading the street' first popularised by Baudelaire and, later, Benjamin (1997). Along thousands of walks through Belfast's housing estates and liminal spaces, I chronicled the city's divided geography. I saw broader sociopolitical and economic forces writ in the built environment and observed exclusion and inclusion (Bairner 2006, 2012). In doing so, I realised the fractious processes around Girdwood and its environs were a microcosm for the peace process itself, and the ways in which post-Agreement politics had failed to deliver a 'shared future' for the people of Northern Ireland.

In the years between that fieldwork and this book, I moved back to the States and walked there, too. I found the same forces that shaped the army barracks in different forms. Here, segregated neighbourhoods are legacies of intentional and deeply rooted policy and planning practices. The ubiquity of division and deprivation, private development and displacement shapes spaces as durably as it did in Belfast. There is a conspicuous lack of quality affordable housing. Around the world, there are thousands of other stories like Girdwood, other contests over the right to space and other movements for equitable distribution of resources.

The following recounts my adventure as a wayward *flâneuse*. It is a tribute to all those I met along the way. But it is also an attempt to write Girdwood with an eye to the struggles over space, place and territory that occur daily in cities globally. While the fate of the barracks clearly mirrors the Northern Irish peace process run aground, this book's indictments of power, policymaking and planning resonate on a broader scale.

INTRODUCTION

Planning, Politics and Contested Space
The Girdwood Community Hub

On the bitterly cold morning of 15 January 2016, two hundred-odd people congregate across from a large steel wall on Cliftonpark Avenue in Belfast, Northern Ireland. This wall, painted bright blue, is alternately referred to as a peace wall, a peace line or an interface barrier. It divides a Protestant/Unionist/Loyalist neighbourhood from a Catholic/Nationalist/Republican one, zigzagging behind houses and along vacant fields. A relic of the conflict colloquially known as the 'Troubles' in Northern Ireland, the wall bears witness to decades of intense ethnosectarian violence and the lingering suspicion, fear and threat that remains between elements of the two groups.

Across from the wall, a brand-new building is opening its doors to the public for the first time. This is the Girdwood Community Hub. It sits on a space which had formerly been the Girdwood Barracks, the main army barracks in North Belfast and a central site of conflict. During the Troubles, this part of North Belfast was characterised by sniper battles and sectarian murder, riots and petrol bombs and raids. After the ceasefires, the Girdwood Barracks were demilitarised. They sat vacant for years, an abandoned monument to the conflict.

On this January day, though, the Hub is full of people. The 'state-of-the-art' building is all brick and glass, surrounded by streetlights and tasteful stone piazzas. Inside, community development workers, Belfast City Council representatives, politicians and journalists are gathered in groups around the wide, clean foyer. The high ceilings begin to fill with the buzz of conversation. People file into a massive auditorium for the opening ceremony. Politicians take their turns crossing the stage to the podium, each one dotting their speeches with the feel-good aphorisms of 'community' and 'shared space'. There is applause.

The Girdwood Community Hub was the product of £11.7 million of funding from the Department for Social Development (DSD),[1] Belfast City Council

---

[1] The DSD was dissolved and replaced by the Department of Communities in 2016. At the time of the Girdwood development it was still referred to as the DSD and so this book will do the same.

Fig. 1.1

and the European Union PEACE III programme: the artefact of 11 years of negotiations and trade-offs, stalemate, contention and an eventual agreement between politicians and community groups in North Belfast. From the outset, its development was hailed as an internationally significant 'symbol of hope' for Northern Ireland. It was a major investment in an area that had been ravaged by conflict and an opportunity to both promote peacebuilding and tackle economic deprivation and housing needs.

Over the years, the Girdwood Barracks site was alternately envisioned as a social and economic catalyst for North Belfast; a space to promote reconciliation across the divide; and a resource for a multiply disadvantaged population. It also offered 27 acres of land on which to build housing – a documented need in North Belfast. The final Community Hub featured 'shared space': meeting rooms, a youth space, an auditorium, a gym and sauna and an outpost of Belfast Metropolitan College (hereafter referred to as Belfast Met). Nearby was a new football pitch and a small housing development.

Even by Northern Ireland's standards, Girdwood's location is incredibly contentious. It serves effectively as a buffer zone between four neighbourhoods that are highly segregated by ethnonational identity and political allegiance. On one side of the barracks, the Protestant/Unionist Lower Oldpark is divided by an interface barrier from the Catholic/Nationalist Lower Cliftonville. On the other side is the Catholic/Nationalist New Lodge and the Protestant/Unionist Lower Shankill, which are divided by the Carlisle Circus roundabout. These neighbourhoods all experience high levels of poverty and unemployment and low levels of mental and physical health.[2] These neighbourhoods also experienced intense violence during the Troubles. Cliftonpark Avenue, which runs along the front of the Girdwood Hub, was once named the deadliest street in Northern Ireland (*Irish News* 1993c). Yet the area is located within walking distance of Belfast city centre, one mile away on the other side of the motorway.

In the wake of the 1998 Belfast Agreement (hereafter referred to as the Good Friday Agreement or the Agreement), a normalisation of security arrangements took place consistent with a 'normal, peaceful society' (Northern Ireland Office (NIO) 1998a: 25).[3] Along with other sites, the Girdwood Army Barracks were demilitarised in 2005, during a time of relative political and economic optimism. Formerly, Girdwood had been the largest army base in Northern Ireland and one of the most 'battle-scarred' during the conflict (*Irish Times* 2005; Archer 2016). The location therefore offered enormous opportunity for a symbolic transformation of a conflict site: a clean slate to put the ideals of the Good Friday Agreement into practice. It was also a major investment opportunity. Politicians and planners saw its proximity to the city centre as ideal for reconnecting North Belfast to the main consumption and investment arena of the centre.

The regeneration of the Girdwood Barracks was a test of the Agreement's promise of equality where there had been discrimination, reconciliation where there had been division and a 'peace dividend' for those areas most affected by the Troubles (NIO: 1998a). It was an opportunity for the new power-sharing government to realise the legal duties and obligations of the Northern Ireland Act. The redevelopment offered a new future for a society (and a neighbourhood) previously mired in sectarian politics and violence. Policy and planning rhetoric around the regeneration of the site had promised, in turn, a space which provided

---

[2] For instance, the area with which this study is concerned comprises the Super Output areas of New Lodge_1, Shankill_2 and Crumlin_2. These ranked fifth, sixth and seventh respectively on the Multiple Deprivation Measure out of 890 areas in 2010, the most recent year available when the research was undertaken (NIMDM 2010: 27). The NIMDM evaluates seven domains of deprivation: income, employment, health, education, proximity to services, living environment and crime. Measures are updated every seven years (NIMDM 2010: 5). For more information see: https://www.nisra.gov.uk/sites/nisra.gov.uk/files/publications/NIMDM_2010_Report_0.pdf.

[3] The way people refer to the Agreement itself can serve as a marker of ethnonational allegiance. Those from Protestant/Unionist backgrounds tend to refer to the Belfast Agreement and Catholics/Nationalists refer to the Good Friday Agreement because it was reached on Good Friday, 10 April 1998.

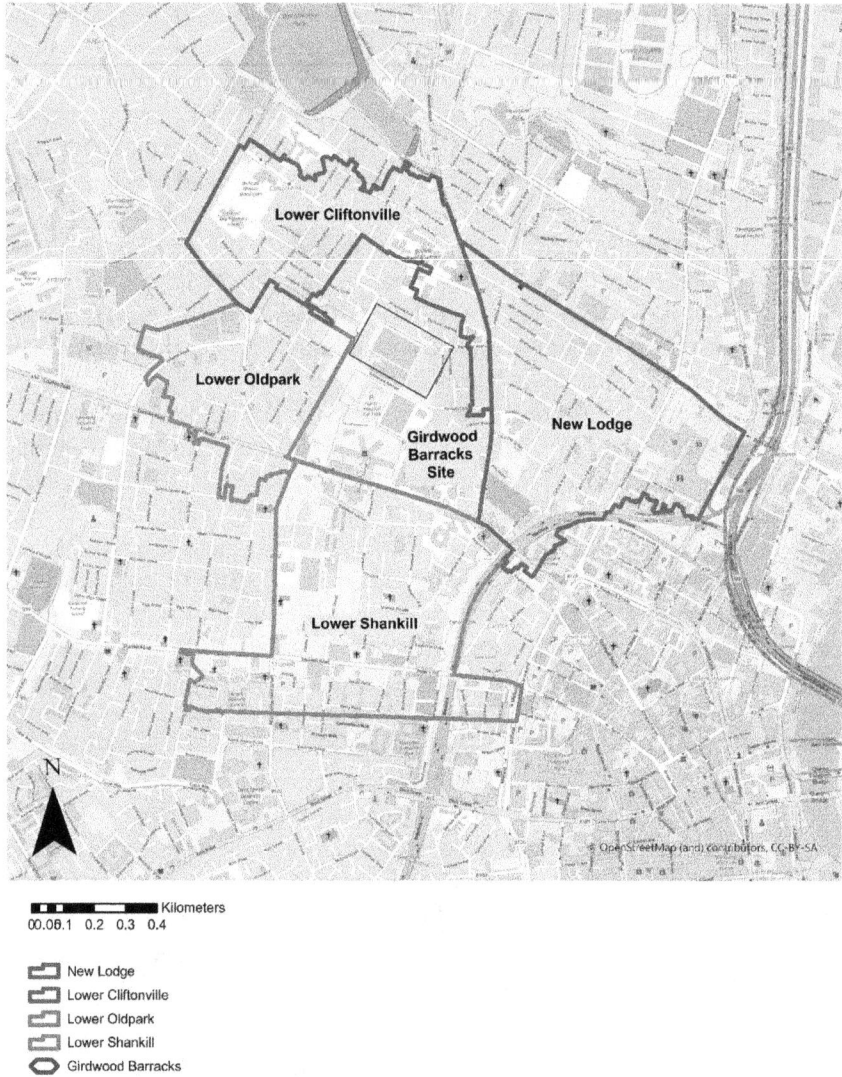

Fig. 1.2 This map was created using Census Super Output Areas, which do not take into account the subtle boundaries of socially constructed and contested space. Therefore, each neighbourhood's boundaries as delineated by the map may vary slightly from colloquial knowledge. I have taken pains to hew as closely as possible to both geographical accuracy and locally recognised boundaries, but allows that for a reader with knowledge of the area, the GIS software's boundaries may look slightly different.

'maximum economic, social and environmental benefit to the local and wider community' (BDP 2007b: 4) and promoted 'shared space', 'good relations' and 'peacebuilding' in a deeply divided society emerging from violent conflict (Cogent Management Consulting[4] 2010: 6). Indeed, it was asserted that, 'if there is anywhere in Northern Ireland and the six border counties that can physically symbolise our transition to a normal society – it will be a new, shared, welcoming and open space at Girdwood' (Cogent Management Consulting 2010: 4).

Unfortunately, this has not occurred. A familiar suite of 'isms' – sectarianism, territorialism and clientelism – continue to shape space and society. On the neighbourhood level in some areas, paramilitary flags still wave from terraced houses and charged political murals constitute a barometer of local opinion. The continued existence of the interface barriers that separate Protestant/Unionist and Catholic/Nationalist areas are testament to lingering feelings of mistrust and fear. On a broader level, competing claims of 'needs', 'rights' and 'truth' between the two main ethnonational groups colour governance and thwart social justice.

This is particularly evident in issues around housing provision. The Agreement had also promised equitable distribution of resources and the protection of vulnerable groups. This was enshrined in law in the subsequent Northern Ireland Act. The Girdwood site provided 27 acres of public land on which to build badly needed social housing for North Belfast. Yet plans for housing on the site were blocked time and time again by political, paramilitary and community development elites because of ethnosectarian interests and territorial claims, as the following chapters will demonstrate.

Today, as Foucault accurately framed it, inverting Clausewicz, 'politics is now the continuation of war by other means' (1980: 123). Conflict is being reproduced in the arenas of policy and planning, in the corridors of Stormont and in spaces like the Girdwood Community Hub (Wilford and Wilson 2006; Planning for Spatial Reconciliation Research Group 2016: 106).[5] The power-sharing framework intended to transform government and society has instead managed and, indeed, reified the two-group dynamic of Protestants/Unionists and Catholics/Nationalists, 'setting antagonism in aspic' (Wilford and Wilson 2006: 24). In the post-Agreement period, the two most ethnically intransigent political parties, the Democratic Unionist Party (DUP) and Sinn Féin, the political wing of the former IRA, have come to hold power in the Northern Ireland Assembly.[6] Under their leadership, the Unionist versus

---

[4] Cogent Management Consulting was the external evaluator of Belfast City Council's bid for the Girdwood Community Hub.
[5] Stormont is the seat of the Northern Ireland Assembly, where the Parliament Buildings are located.
[6] This book examines Sinn Féin and the DUP as the main actors of political power

Nationalist antagonism framed by history and forged in violence relocated itself into an unstable power-sharing arrangement.

In turn, these divisive forces have shaped the physical landscape of post-Agreement Northern Ireland. Murtagh and Ellis note that 'the strategic advantages of ethnic segregation, the manipulation of territory by sectarian politics, the fear of, and policing by, paramilitaries all dictate the regeneration agenda in divided places' (2011: 362). The constitutional question – Irish or British? – is played out at the micro level in contests over territory, and electoral and demographic shifts fuel tensions around space, place and belonging. The redevelopment of the Girdwood Barracks is a microcosm of these fractious dynamics – funded, ironically, by European Union PEACE III funding.[7]

Although Girdwood has been mentioned in other scholarship, it has never been examined and analysed as robustly as herein. Certainly, there have been many studies to date which document the ways that division is inscribed in urban space, and which detail the impact of segregation and the legacy of violence on people and place in Northern Ireland (see, as a small sample, Bryan 2000; Byrne et al. 2012; Gormley-Heenan et al. 2013; Jarman 1997, 2004, 2008; Lysaght and Basten 2003; Mulholland 2002; Murtagh 2002; Nic Craith 2003; Shirlow and Murtagh 2006). In contrast, the significance of the decision-making processes at the political level which continue to reproduce segregation in the post-ceasefire period has remained relatively underexplored. So, too, has the significance of those community and activist elements, however fringe, that have mounted challenges to the status quo.

And it is critically important we do explore these decision-making processes. It is important we strip away all the rhetorical fluff and state clearly that at Girdwood, only 60 houses were built on 27 acres of land in the midst of a housing crisis. The development did not adhere to legal obligations set forth in the Northern Ireland Act. It ignored documented housing needs. It is important to understand why those decisions were made, and what they say more broadly about the state of post-Agreement Northern Ireland. An enormous opportunity has been squandered. This book demonstrates that the regeneration of the

---

in post-devolution Northern Ireland. The Northern Ireland Assembly, or 'Assembly', is the Northern Ireland government, also referred to as Stormont. Within the Assembly, the Executive refers to the First Minister and Deputy First Minister, and eight departmental ministers.

[7] As part of the peace process, the European Union, among other bodies, committed to funding peace and reconciliation programmes in Northern Ireland and the border regions. As its name suggests, PEACE III was the third round of this funding, with €333 million total expenditure; it focused on projects based around building positive relations, creating shared space and reconciliation. See Chapter Four for further detail.

Girdwood Barracks was fundamentally a failure, and if that is all this book achieves, then it has done its job.

But there is more to discuss. This volume sheds light on the 'darker realities' of planning practice in Northern Ireland (Bou Akar 2018: 4–5); the gaps between rhetoric and reality in policymaking; and, ultimately, how these machinations have tangible (and negative) impacts for poor and working-class neighbourhoods. The Girdwood redevelopment offers both an indictment of the Northern Irish peace process and a broader meditation on the intersection of power, politics and urban space. I hope, therefore, that the following chapters will add not only to the body of work on conflict transformation and contested space, but to urban studies more generally. After all, Girdwood is but one example of the ways in which disparate claims to place and belonging collide within urban spaces. It is one of many buildings constructed on a foundation of political wrangling and territorial contest.

When I moved back home to the United States, I saw clear parallels in the way our cities are shaped to exclude some and privilege others, and the means that have been used over the years to legitimise and excuse racial division and white supremacy. This took on a new urgency as the COVID-19 pandemic exposed these fault lines, and as the health and economic crises had an outsized impact on the same zip codes most afflicted by poverty, unemployment and the legacy of racial segregation. The murders of George Floyd and other unarmed Black people have further highlighted the devastating consequences of redlining, economic exclusion and targeted policing in American cities. It feels important to explore the phenomenon of segregation and marginalisation in Belfast, knowing that there are parallels with divided cities across the globe. Belfast is not the only city divided by historical narratives of violence and exclusion, where broader social, political and economic systems reinforce and reconstitute those divisions in the present day.

Understanding cities and their economic and social systems requires more than observation or description alone but a critical analysis of process. Drawing from an extensive range of primary and secondary resources, some of the former uniquely available to me, the following chapters chart not only the nuances of the redevelopment of the Girdwood space, but that of post-ceasefire governance in Northern Ireland as well.[8] They argue that neither is fit for

---

[8] These include a complete set of original meeting minutes and discussion documents from the 2006 Girdwood Advisory Panel; the 2010 independent economic appraisal of Belfast City Council's application for a Community Hub, prepared for SEUPB; and transcripts from PPR's 2012 Girdwood Residents Jury. All of these were furnished to me by contacts involved in different stages of the Hub's development and have not, to my knowledge, been previously available to researchers.

purpose as defined by their own legal obligations and duties. If, as rhetoric around the site has suggested, the regeneration of Girdwood Barracks was an opportunity to test the idea of a 'new Northern Ireland', then it has been far from convincing.

From Army Barracks to Community Hub

In 1998, the Good Friday Agreement brought an official end to the violence of the Troubles, a miserable conflict which had been waged for over 30 years in Northern Ireland, though its roots go back much further. It is beyond the scope of this book to give a comprehensive background of the Troubles (see, for instance, Bardon 1992; Bell 1993; Bew and Gillespie 1999; McKittrick 2000; Whyte 1991). The starting point of the Troubles is often cited as 1968, though the tensions that sparked them stretch back to the plantation of Ulster by Britain in the 1600s (and, indeed, further still to the colonisation of Ireland by Great Britain). Great Britain confiscated large tracts of land from the native Irish population and gave them to Protestant settlers, who relocated to Ulster but retained their religious distinctiveness and political loyalty to Great Britain (Connolly and McIntosh 2012a: 20; Fitzduff and O'Hagan 2009). Over the centuries that followed plantation, the British/Irish diametric was performed in different ways in Ulster and across the island of Ireland, the question of Irish or British sovereignty over land writ in sporadic rebellion, rioting and insurrection.

Pressure grew to grant independence to the island of Ireland, and after the First World War Great Britain agreed to limited independence. The Protestant population in Ulster resisted, threatening violence, and in an attempt at compromise, the island was partitioned in two in 1921. The six counties of Northern Ireland would remain part of the United Kingdom, while the other 26 counties would gain independence. The arrangement led to bitter conflict between Nationalists who supported Partition as the best possible option and those who rejected it. The former won out, and in 1923 the Irish Free State was formally incorporated (Bew, Gibbon and Patterson 1996; Boyce and O'Day 2006; Fitzduff and O'Hagan 2009).

In the following decades, Northern Ireland was ruled by a hegemonic Protestant/Unionist government, allied closely to Great Britain through trade and industry (Buckland 1981). During the 1960s, increasing evidence of discrimination against Catholics in housing, employment and electoral politics brought agitation for equal rights. Inspired by the civil rights movement in the United States and uprisings against the status quo happening elsewhere, Catholics began to take to the streets. This movement did not have a nationalist dimension at first; protestors asked only for equal rights within the framework of Northern

Ireland (Melaugh 2016a). But they drew a hostile response from the Protestant state. Police brutality became a feature of protests (Power 1972). Fear and insecurity among Protestants/Unionists in response to the protests brought further violent repression, lighting the proverbial powder keg of division, discrimination and sectarianism. A series of riots erupted. People were burned out of their homes.

The beginnings of the conflict resulted in massive displacement, a resettling of the city along sharply segregated lines. People in mixed areas fled and neighbourhoods re-emerged as Protestant or Catholic. Abandoned houses and makeshift barriers in the spaces between Protestant and Catholic areas served as the first 'interface' markers; then the British Army built temporary walls of corrugated iron as a military response to sectarian violence (Byrne 2009; Gormley-Heenan et al. 2013: 357). Local vigilante groups formed to protect their areas, leading to the resurgence of paramilitary groups. The British Army was deployed and became another actor in the conflict. Three decades of bitter warfare followed. An estimated 3,720 people were killed and approximately 47,541 injured (CAIN 2003; McKittrick et al. 2007: 1552). Though death crossed class lines and visited both rural and urban locales, much of the violence was concentrated in certain places, including the working-class terraced streets of Belfast and Derry (Gregory et al. 2013); indeed, just under half of all the deaths recorded during the conflict occurred in the Belfast Urban Area (Sutton 2002).

Over time as divisions ossified, dozens of concrete and steel-clad walls proliferated throughout the city, along with a 'ring of steel' around Belfast city centre and dozens of army barracks, fortified police stations and other defensive architecture (Gaffikin et al. 2010: 505). Chapter One explores the history of division in North Belfast, where the Girdwood Barracks are located, and how space, place, power and territory intersect both in Belfast and further afield. It sketches out the terrain on which this book focuses, through which I walked and watched the Community Hub take shape, as well as the methods I used to do so.

Chapter Two sets out the peacebuilding and legislative framework within which the Girdwood development process took place. It provides context on the Good Friday Agreement, the power-sharing government it instituted and the subsequent prescriptions for transforming conflict. In particular, Section 75 of the Northern Ireland Act was designed to enshrine 'equality of opportunity' into policymaking. The chapter then explores the ways in which these well-intentioned promises have been subverted by politicians; as in other societies, identity politics, backroom dealings and trade-offs are part and parcel of governance in practice.

Chapter Three brings us back to North Belfast, setting the scene for how identity politics around demography and territory shaped the first phase of

Girdwood's development. In Northern Ireland, and in North Belfast, the Protestant/Unionist population tends to be ageing and declining while the Catholic/Nationalist community is more demographically robust.[9] This has produced a Protestant/Unionist narrative of cultural despondency, fear and insecurity (Shirlow and Murtagh 2006: 7). In 2001, the notion of physical and symbolic Catholic/Nationalist 'growth' and Protestant/Unionist 'decline' sparked the infamous Holy Cross dispute in North Belfast. The fallout from Holy Cross resulted in a renewed push to invest in community and economic development in the area, and the North Belfast Community Action Project (NBCAP) was commissioned to address the major social and economic issues plaguing North Belfast. Among its recommendations was the development of a major site to serve as a symbol of hope for North Belfast.

Chapter Three goes on to outline how Girdwood initially fit into this vision. This was a time when the 'new Northern Ireland' was emerging: in the absence of conflict, peacebuilding money and private investment flowed into Northern Ireland, making large-scale redevelopment projects possible. Girdwood was described as a 'symbol of hope', a 'regeneration project of international significance' and a 'catalyst' for social and economic investment in North Belfast (BDP 2007b: 4). In 2006 the first phase of redevelopment commenced. The adjacent Crumlin Road Gaol and Courthouse were also included in the vision for redevelopment (Crumlin Road Courthouse Ltd. 2006: 1). Five international design firms tendered for the project, with Building Design Partnership (BDP) of London winning the bid for the Masterplan (DSD 2006). Ideas for the space ranged from a global peacebuilding centre to the new site of the Public Records Office (PRONI) and a new neighbourhood 'quarter' with shops, offices, community facilities and social housing (OFMDFM 2005c: 4; BDP 2007b: 8–10).

However, Chapter Four demonstrates how contestation over social housing brought progress to an impasse. For an area in severe housing stress, the

---

[9] According to the 2011 census data in Northern Ireland, those identifying as Irish had a younger age profile: 53 per cent of those who were or had been brought up Irish were under 35, compared with 41 per cent of those who identified as British; 18 per cent of the latter were over 65, compared to 10 per cent of Irish-identified individuals (NISRA 2011). Nolan's analysis of the 2011 census data provides further detail: using census data, he calculates that 95,000 Protestants and 46,000 Catholics died between 2001 and 2011, while there were 89,000 Protestant and 118,000 Catholic births. From 2001 to 2011, the Catholic population increased by 4.2 per cent whilst the Protestant population declined by 11.9 per cent, and the number of those identifying as 'Other' doubled. The effect is that what was formerly a Protestant-majority city is now one where the Catholic population has the largest share (Nolan 2014: 22).

Girdwood site represented a boon for social housing provision.[10] Furthermore, under Section 75, a key part of the Northern Ireland Act, the government was obligated to provide social housing according to objective need and regardless of ethnoreligious background (NIO 1998b: 38). But for sections of the Protestant/Unionist population of North Belfast, any new housing represented a 'takeover' of or 'encroachment' on the land, in that housing allocation would be overwhelmingly to Catholics/Nationalists given the level of need. Unionist politicians, and in particular the DUP, had to respond to this narrative of loss among their constituents. They also needed to maintain the electoral balance of the area – because of demographic shifts, Unionists were losing electoral clout in North Belfast. More Catholic/Nationalist residents in North Belfast potentially meant more Nationalist votes, threatening the DUP's slim lead in the constituency.

Therefore, DUP politicians and other Unionist actors of power consistently aimed to block the prospect of social housing on the Girdwood site, despite the provisions of Section 75. Chapter Four goes on to interrogate the tactics that political elites deployed to put 'good relations' over 'equality of opportunity'. They insisted that new-build social housing would, by default, be allocated to Nationalists and would therefore impinge on good relations. Other actors emerged to challenge this approach: for instance, the activist group Participation and the Practice of Rights (PPR) facilitated collaborative research with residents around alternative ways forward for the site.[11] They released two community-informed reports based on peacebuilding legislation that pointed to the need for new-build housing, but their work was ignored by both Sinn Féin and the

---

[10] Throughout the book, updated statistics on housing needs will be used where appropriate. However, since the book focuses on the decision-making processes around the Girdwood redevelopment, it feels most useful to cite housing need statistics from the time when decisions around housing for the Girdwood site were being made. Therefore, statistics from the early 2000s onward will be used in keeping with the Girdwood redevelopment timeline, rather than solely referencing more contemporary trends.

[11] PPR are based in Belfast; they support groups of marginalised local residents campaigning on social justice issues like the right to housing, employment and education. They use a rigorous international and domestic legislative framework and employ human rights-based indicators to analyse government policymaking and to hold the government to account on equality and human rights issues (PPR n.d.). Unlike some groups in Northern Ireland, PPR are not Protestant/Unionist or Catholic/Nationalist by background but rather function as an independent critic or 'watchdog'. They work with local campaign groups on both sides of the ethnonational divide. However, they are perceived as Nationalist sympathisers by some Unionist elements because their work is based on objective equality legislation, which tends to focus to Catholic/Nationalist social issues.

DUP.[12] The result was 'a zero-sum outcome of deadlock and delay' (Planning for Spatial Reconciliation Research Group 2016: 106). A political stalemate enveloped Girdwood and the site lay vacant for years.

Chapter Five unpicks the dynamics that caused the first phase of redevelopment to fail. In particular, it highlights the unhappy partnership of Sinn Féin and the DUP during this period, and the ways in which their ethnosectarian entrepreneurialism informed policy and planning on a broader scale. Zero-sum resource allocation, tit-for-tat posturing and alleged clientelism became the status quo. Chapter Six charts how the next proposal for Girdwood emerged from this political context. In 2009, Belfast City Council submitted a funding bid to the EU PEACE III programme to build a 'Community Hub' at Girdwood. Initially, Sinn Féin supported the prospect of social housing provision on the site, in line with Section 75 and the Catholic/Nationalist electorate's documented housing needs. However, the DUP continued to be unequivocally against any type of housing.

After a series of trade-offs, the DUP and Sinn Féin reached a compromise on the Community Hub. Two separate areas of social housing were planned: 60 houses on the Catholic/Nationalist New Lodge side of the development and space for housing on the Protestant/Unionist Lower Oldpark side, despite there being no documented need for the latter.[13] The decision was deemed by many to be a 'sectarian carve-up' and 'the best worst option' – better than nothing. It involved Sinn Féin giving up on social housing provision for Catholic/Nationalist North Belfast, however – and, in turn, on the equality legislation set out in Section 75 of the Northern Ireland Act.

Where previous chapters focus on the 'top-down' political elite, Chapter Seven provides background on the 'bottom-up' landscape of community development and paramilitary influence. It explores the various permutations and contradictions inherent in the notion of 'community' in Belfast. It explains how the community development sector functions in a place like Northern Ireland, critiques the role of paramilitaries within their geographic 'communities' and looks at how these various actors intersect and interact on the ground. Chapter Eight elaborates on this context with community-level ethnographic insights into the final phase of planning. Parties involved included community development groups, statutory agencies like the City Council,

---

[12] According to PPR, at the time that Girdwood was being developed, the religious composition of the North Belfast Housing Waiting List for people in housing stress was 76 per cent Catholic and 22 per cent Protestant: in 2006, for example, there were 831 Catholic applicants and 253 Protestants (PPR 2012: 2, 4). Families were (and are currently) waiting for years for a home, stuck in temporary accommodation or hostels or living with family in overcrowded conditions.

[13] This housing has yet to materialise and according to some interview respondents, a judicial review is currently underway on the space.

paramilitary groups and a private social enterprise operator, all of whom exerted varying levels of influence on the redevelopment. This chapter details the many meetings that I attended of and between these actors in the run-up to the opening of the Girdwood Community Hub. Disagreement, miscommunication and missed opportunities shaped the final phase of planning, despite the best efforts of some community groups involved in the process.

The Conclusion describes the Hub's grand opening – with a whimper, not a bang. At its launch, the development included the Hub building, parking lots, a sports pitch and 60 units of housing surrounded by stretches of empty land. It was a far cry from the internationally significant peacebuilding opportunity that had been promised with the initial demilitarisation of the barracks. Instead, it reflected the political powers that produced it and their fundamental inability to imagine transformative change. The Conclusion then attempts to recount the Hub's subsequent impact (or lack thereof) on the broader area. Ultimately, the Hub development merely 'reproduced the social and sectarian geographies' that were already present in the urban landscape (Planning for Spatial Reconciliation Research Group 2016: 106).

The story of Girdwood is, in many respects, the story of the Northern Ireland Assembly, whereby a series of competing discourses and disagreements give way to ineffectual compromise among the political elite. The Epilogue acknowledges shifts in Northern Ireland's political fortunes that have occurred since the initial fieldwork took place. The dynamics that scuppered the Girdwood development eventually caused the collapse of the Assembly. Until 2017, Sinn Féin grudgingly shared power with the DUP. Deals were made between the two parties without Sinn Féin winning its full agenda, but enough to assuage its electorate – echoing the dealings at the Girdwood Hub. Eventually, however, Sinn Féin's tactic of compromise in government began to lose the party votes. In the wake of the DUP's catastrophic mismanagement of a renewable heating initiative in 2017, Sinn Féin collapsed the Assembly. The two parties' inability to come to another shared-out compromise meant political stasis between 2017 and 2020, leaving Northern Ireland rudderless during the Brexit campaign and negotiations. A brief reunion occurred in 2020, but Unionist identity politics around the Irish border informed another collapse at the time of writing.

Whilst this book concerns itself in part with the power-sharing relationship between the DUP and Sinn Féin, it also highlights the alternative politics that emerged with PPR's work on the Girdwood site and on social justice issues. PPR drew upon the legislative framework of the Northern Ireland Act and attempted to utilise its provisions to ensure policymaking protected the rights of vulnerable groups. Their work clearly documented a housing crisis in Catholic/Nationalist North Belfast and they petitioned for an adequate social housing element to the Girdwood redevelopment, along with the Housing Executive,

Equality Commission (ECNI) and Human Rights Commission and some community elements. When Sinn Féin compromised on social housing in the name of 'good relations' with the DUP, PPR raised a critical voice of dissent. Their role indicates a reversal of ethnic politics in favour of the politics of legally defined justice, albeit on a small scale.

The Epilogue observes that years later, the 2022 elections showed the strongest ever result for the centrist Alliance Party in the Assembly, and polls show a growing number of people identifying as neither Unionist nor Nationalist, but rather as 'Northern Irish'. Perhaps as the Assembly has run out of road, so too will the sectarian dynamics that underwrote it for so long.

Space, Place and Power in the Urban Landscape

When societies are troubled by violent conflict, we need to bring into focus the complexity and diversity of struggles for power in other socio-spatial spheres.

(Svašek and Komarova 2018: 10)

On the surface, the Girdwood Barracks site feels deeply specific: two dozen-odd acres of land in a northern corner of a small island. But as a metaphor for the redevelopment of contested space, it has broad implications indeed. In order to understand Girdwood, it is worth considering the wider dynamics of urban space outside Belfast, a city that can quickly come to feel claustrophobic and parochial.

The story of the Girdwood Barracks reminds us of the negotiations over space that occur daily in cities around the world. In the words of Low and Lawrence-Zúñiga (2003: 1), 'all behavior is located in and constructed of space'. It is both social product and process: every society produces its own space in response to its own needs. And each society's spatial practices create unique rhythms and patterns of daily life (Lefebvre 1991: 26). Cities are, perhaps, the fullest and most complex expression of this exchange between behaviour and space: a complicated, multilayered and ever-changing interplay of people, buildings and environment. On the micro-level, each street and dwelling place is a site of countless small decisions and interactions, a locus for the visible and invisible sediment of time. On a broader scale, the landscape mirrors social and political relations, demographic change and economic status within the city (Vergunst 2010: 4). As a *flâneur* or *flâneuse*, one can move through and observe all these dynamics at work.

As Fullilove noted, 'cities are always growing or shrinking, hence remaking themselves. Sometimes this reordering is haphazard and sometimes it is planned, carried out according to the agendas of those paying for the improvements' (2004: 52). But every city reflects the powers that produce it. For instance, 'urban renewal' plans spread through cities in the United States, the United Kingdom and Europe in the 1950s and 1960s, heralding post-war technocrats' vision of 'progress'. Planners and government officials remade cities for cars and a growing class of suburban commuters by constructing huge motorways that sliced through or ringed around cities. Their construction displaced people and businesses in poor and working-class areas, destroying what were often tight-knit communities and pushing their denizens to isolated places far from the old schools, services and local economies which made those communities interwoven places. This is evident in Belfast, where the Westlink cut an ugly swathe through formerly vibrant neighbourhoods; now marred by vacant lots and brownfield, the fabric of the surrounding area was never rebuilt (Sterrett et al. 2012).

In the United States, urban renewal had a specifically racialised element, plans for new development targeting and destroying predominantly Black neighbourhoods and pushing Black residents into inferior public housing. And in recent times, a general urban trend towards waterfront development has seen previously industrial or public land privatised in order to provide space for high-end offices, hotels and luxury condominiums, the flow of water reflecting the flow of capital. Walking through any city, the passage of time and development trends becomes clear in the patterns of neighbourhoods, the sprawl of motorways, old buildings that have survived and buildings newly constructed. The built environment offers clues to broader questions of economics, demographics and power dynamics – who belongs and who is excluded (Harvey 1996, 2009; Massey 2005; McFarlane 2011). Therefore, the rhetoric of policymakers and the decisions of planners are writ in stone and concrete. Our cities are testament to the machinations of power from the top down.

But cities can also bear witness to the minutiae of the everyday. We can tell a lot about a society by the way citizens interact with the spaces around them, turning them into 'place'. Theories on spatial perspectives and practice have proliferated across academic disciplines, and academics studying space, place and environment all recognise the mutually constitutive relationship that humans have with their surroundings. Urban spaces are marked by overarching structures and foregrounded practices, like laws, rules, social norms and institutions (de Certeau 1984: 48). The command of this space entails 'the setting up of mental maps, norms of spatial competence, and rules of spatial performance' (Feldman 1991: 9). In navigating their surroundings, citizens are interacting with space and turning it into 'place' every day. The act of walking, too, affords the researcher (or *flâneur*) a window into the relationship between people and the places they create.

Place can be conceptualised in several different ways. Of course, there is the two-dimensional aspect of a point on a map, or the name of a place – a geographic location. But place is also the material form through which a broader context of social differences, inequalities and collective actions are shaped and manifested (Gieryn 2000: 464–465). This includes the physical 'street furniture' we walk through, sometimes unthinkingly each day, which determines – and restricts – our possibilities for movement and encounter within the landscape. Indeed, infrastructure, according to Dovey (2005, 2008), is inherently coercive, enforcing limits to action and enabling only certain forms of social practice. This becomes clear in militarised spaces, where barriers exist to control and surveil the movement of people, or on the borders between spaces of conflict, where land is claimed based on ethnic or political allegiance. For instance, in Belfast, social interactions are proscribed by the way in which places are divided. In other cases, visible and invisible boundaries, like motorways, industrial parks or even large redevelopment projects, can serve as buffers between wealthy and low-income neighbourhoods, ensuring that residents do not mix (Fullilove 2004: 64).

This way in which social relations shape space relates to an even more abstract form of 'place', a space invested with meaning through processes of classification, identification and representation (Agnew 1987; Bourdieu 1977; Gieryn 2000: 471). Here, place is an interpretive frame through which people order the world, evaluate others, assign meaning and act accordingly. It is simultaneously perceived, conceived and lived (Lefebvre 1991: 36). It is the assemblage of stories we tell ourselves to make sense of our lives and our surroundings.

In one sense, this is natural and meaningful – place is 'a hybrid product of biography and location(s), the one informing the other in a constant round of influence and interpretation' (Hall et al. 2006: 2). We create mental maps of our environment as we become familiar with it. Memories and sensory experiences link places together: the texture of a brick wall, the smell of paint, a derelict house or open field bring a host of recollections to mind. Surrounded by physical and emotional reminders that ground us, we feel a sense of belonging and rootedness in particular spaces (Rose 1995).

However, place identifications can encourage more insidious dynamics. Belonging to a place inherently suggests the presence of an 'Other' that does not belong. This can lead to discrimination against or rejection of those classified as outsiders, reinforcing perceptions of 'us vs them' (Sibley 1988). There are places in the city that one simply 'does not go', places where the 'Other' lives. Spatial practices, markers and boundaries delineate where one place ends and another begins and where there is contestation, place can become a terrain of symbolic struggle between different groups. Place can become territory – 'our place' that must be claimed and defended, something indelibly linked with a sense of identity, ideology and permanence. This is evident in walking the streets of Belfast, for instance, and the divided spaces in which the Girdwood site is located.

In every society, contestation arises over the right to space and place: how access to it is controlled and negotiated, who belongs and who is excluded. Space is key to furthering political ideologies, and the mix of political enmity, resource competition and territorialism we will see at Girdwood is reflected in cities on a global scale. Urban spaces are deliberately constructed by forms of power to advance particular agendas, fix and spatialise social identities and claim rights to access and control (Sack 1983). Boundaries can be physical, like the walls in Belfast, Israel/Palestine and Cyprus, for instance (Bollens 2000). But every city has walls that make people 'Other' and that keep us in our own neighbourhoods. This can be useful for those in power, who may bend division to their own aims, as we will also see at Girdwood.

Particularly in contested or post-conflict cities, 'competing potential centres of power may structure, use, and exploit public planning and policymaking functions in ways to assist them in establishing authority or dominance' (Bollens 2009: 82). As Yiftachel and Yacobi also observe, 'planning and development strategies reflect deep ethnocratic logic, couched in "professional," "civil" and "economic" reasoning"' (2003: 690). In cities divided by ethnonational allegiance, development, planning and usage of land are all influenced by ethnic interest and rationalisation; beneath the trappings of democracy or the rhetoric of peace agreements, ethnosectarian contestation continues to unfold. The use of discourse is a key factor in facilitating and legitimising this.

Ethnographic work conducted in Lebanon (Bou Akar 2018; Randa Nucho 2016) demonstrates the powerful implications of sectarian discourse from the top down, but also shows how sectarianism is practiced, negotiated and challenged in the spaces of the everyday. Planning has become the nexus of contest for competing political parties, non-governmental organisations and developers, and sectarian dynamics are acted out through the use and control of space by political and religious groups: 'War in times of peace is not fought with tanks, artillery and rifles but through a geopolitical territorial contest, where the fear of domination of one group by the other is played out over such issues as land and apartment sales, access to housing, zoning and planning regulations, and infrastructure projects' (Bou Akar 2018: 9). Such practices challenge the idea of planning and development as a rational means of organising space – as Bou Akar puts it, '[these practices] debunk modern narratives of peace, order and progress and they collapse distinctions between peace and war, order and chaos … progress and stagnation' (2018: 4–5). The Girdwood case study contributes to the emerging body of work on the messy realities of post-conflict planning practice.

The effects of political discourse and urban planning in sustaining division are not unique to places emerging from conflict. The United States is a notable example where systematic and racially explicit planning policies have resulted in deliberately constructed spaces of exclusion. There is ample evidence of how federal, state and local governments codified racism into the very fabric of American cities, unconstitutionally using housing policy to create and reinforce segregation (Rothstein 2017: 14). Many factors contributed. Federal public housing projects were segregated, with quality housing open only to White families. 'Urban renewal' plans targeted and destroyed hundreds of predominantly Black neighbourhoods, which were perceived by white planners and politicians as expendable. 'Redlining' occurred, where banks would not lend to businesses or insure mortgages in areas with high concentrations of African Americans. Developers would not sell homes to African Americans. If someone did sell a home to a Black family, realtors responded with a practice known as 'blockbusting', panicking white families into selling their neighbouring homes for discounted prices to speculators; Black buyers desperate for homes would purchase them at inflated prices (Rothstein 2017: 12). Segregation was not only *de facto* but intentional and pervasive. The result in American cities today is a clear spatial divide between predominantly White and Black areas, the latter often marked by poorer housing conditions and higher levels of poverty, unemployment and marginalisation.

Ethnic and racial segregation shapes cities, and segregation by class does too. In many cities, there is a marked contrast between upper- and middle-class areas and working-class and poor areas in terms of physical space and movement (Till 1993). The wide, gracious streets off the Malone Road in Belfast, for example, shaded by curved trees and punctuated by gated, detached houses, have ready access to shops, services, schools and the city centre. Residents often own cars, further broadening their ability to travel across and around sectarian boundaries. Those in poorer areas, however, are cut off from the city centre by the motorway, by a patchwork of perceived 'safe' and 'unsafe' spaces and by various physical barriers. There are typically fewer public green spaces, fewer parks, and less access to quality grocery stores and services. These patterns are evident in cities globally. Certain social groups experience the city in very different ways than do others (Petty 2016). Boundaries, whether by class, ethnicity or race, place people on the peripheries, and the denial of their reality is a luxury afforded only to those not trapped by them (Jacobs and Fincher 1998: 27).

However, as Jacobs recognised, the most effective cities are based on connection, not division. Streets, buildings and the spaces between them should be tightly interwoven, encouraging lively networks of movement and flows of people. She describes the 'sidewalk ballet' of a healthy city street, where everyone has a part and place, whether itinerant or permanent. On the street, small 'partings and joinings' take place between groups of people (Vergunst 2010: 6). There is action, 'a marvelous order' beneath the chaos, routine and pattern as well as improvisation as people pass along their routes and their lives (Jacobs 1961: 50). Segregation, by imposing impenetrable borders, wrecks the function of the city and leads to a loss of 'critical functioning' (Fullilove 2014: 134). We see in Belfast, and in all cities divided by ethnicity, religion and race, an unnatural division, an amputation. Segregation causes harm to the complexly layered stories, rituals and routes that make good cities. At the time of writing, in the midst of a global pandemic and reckonings around race and belonging, it feels critical to consider how power is wielded, segregation imposed and world views shaped in our cities – and how we might undo this harm in future.

Safe, equitable space and thoughtful urban development have never been more important. How we get there is another story, rife with competing actors and aspirations, public-, private- and community-sector involvement, activists and advocates working with and against politicians and planners. Urban regeneration projects often seem to privilege profit over the needs of the population. Lip service is frequently paid to 'community engagement' and 'community input' on economic development projects, but in practice, working with community members in the conceptual phases of a project is messy and complicated. And in the community development sector itself, power struggles between and within groups for representation and funding also shape the outcome of development processes in different ways.

As Bollens notes in reference to post-conflict societies, 'the technical reworking of the city becomes a crucial test and indicator of a new social and political process' (2009: 102). In Northern Ireland, unproblematic space-sharing has only occurred with the neoliberal-influenced development of formerly industrial areas, such as those along the River Lagan and the Titanic Quarter. Regeneration projects in highly contested space, like Girdwood, have proved contentious, testing the Northern Ireland Assembly's[14] capacity for compromise and challenging the rhetoric of the Good Friday Agreement, Northern Ireland Act and subsequent policy and planning documents. It is a testament to the ways in which physical and symbolic notions of place permeate decision-making.

The following chapters take a multifaceted, place-based perspective to examining the Girdwood development. On one hand, they focus on ethnography and the small-scale – everyday observations from the field and pedestrian conversations that nod to the different interests involved in the construction of space. As Svašek and Komarova note, 'everyday strains are innate to human experience and to understand political conflict, it is necessary to explore how small-scale tensions and mundane conflict may shape broader interactions and decisions' (2018: 9).

---

[14] The Assembly refers to the power-sharing government that sits at Stormont.

On the other hand, this book is situated within a wider context of place-making, development and territorial contest. The themes that range around the Girdwood development can be overlaid on just about any city in the world, despite wildly differing geographical, historical and political contexts. I hope the reader can draw mooring lines to their own experience of place; that they can see the decisions and the divisions that actors of power have wrought in the spaces around them, too. Often, Northern Ireland can feel limiting as an interpretive framework because the peculiarities of place are insistent. But Girdwood has relevance past the limits of 'Catholic/Nationalist vs Protestant/Unionist', eliciting insight into large-scale political, economic and demographic oppositions.

Spoilers aside, the eventual Girdwood redevelopment is a disappointing farce, and this book's purpose is to recount the wasted opportunities as emblematic of a failed peace process. But it would be remiss not to note, too, moments where the power of the small-scale was in evidence, forging connection and consensus where it otherwise would not have existed. This book, although primarily a critique, also seeks to highlight instances where dedicated activists and community members saw a different path. Despite the physical infrastructure that divides, there seem always to be forces at work that interrupt discord and suggest a common way forward.

CHAPTER ONE

The First Step

Musings on History, Ethnography and Methodology

A Note on Methods

I used a qualitative framework to examine the many angles of Girdwood's redevelopment process. Qualitative research can illuminate the mechanisms that structure a particular place, the position and behaviour of the actors within that place and their daily procedures, practices and negotiations (Berg 2007; Bernard 1988; Brewer 2000). But it can also highlight how these narratives and experiences link to broader sociopolitical conditions and institutional frameworks. I wanted to explore how the 'macro' – politics, history, locality – manifests in the 'micro', everyday interaction and understanding in a particular time and place (Barbour 2008: 11). Finally, qualitative research is well-suited to revealing process: this was particularly important for capturing the transformation of the Girdwood site in full and uncovering the dynamics that shaped that transformation.

To explore both the subjective understandings of those involved in the development process and the complex context within which these were formed, I needed methods that could provide what Geertz terms 'thick description' (1973: 50). In this regard, I was drawn to an ethnographic approach. According to Charmaz, ethnographers 'seek detailed knowledge of the multiple dimensions of life within the studied milieu and aim to understand member's taken-for-granted assumptions and rules' (2006: 21). The aim is to use tools like participant observation and interviews to tell 'the story' of a place (Gray 2014: 439) – and, importantly, 'a credible, rigorous and authentic story' (Fetterman 2010:1). One of the primary aims of my research was to tell the story of Girdwood as closely and accurately as possible.

My other aim was to use the observations from the Girdwood case study to shed light on broader dynamics in Northern Ireland. In this sense, this book fits into a longer tradition of using ethnography to highlight broader social, economic and political trends in Northern Ireland (see Aretxaga 1997; Bell 1990; Burton 1978; Evershed 2018; Feldman 1991; Harris 1972; Jenkins 1983;

Kelleher 2004; McAuley 1994; Rush 2022; Sluka 1989). Many scholars have drawn wider conclusions from their detailed studies of place and people: for instance, Jenkins (1983) immersed himself as a youth worker on the outskirts of Belfast in order to document the passage from adolescence to adulthood and the parallel transition from education to the labour market during the conflict. Aretxaga's ethnography of Nationalist women's political tactics (1997), set in West Belfast, speaks to both the ordering of gender relationships in daily life and broader shifts in political consciousness within Catholic/Nationalist districts.

Many of these researchers describe the inherent challenges of being an 'outsider': situating themselves in a place, patiently forging relationships and building trust over time. Their work also reflects the opportunities afforded by ethnographic methods. These methods allow researchers to document and unpick the relationship between the macro and the micro, the ways in which each informs the other. Everyday observations reveal underlying spatial, political or gendered tensions. Broader dynamics are reinforced by the particularities of place. Perhaps most importantly, creating space for the perspectives of research participants both animates the work and grounds it in lived experience.

Lofland and Lofland (1984: 17) describe ethnography as an adventure. During my own ethnographic fieldwork in Belfast, I attempted to carry out what Toren calls 'a particularly intense way of living, a day-to-day experience in which you are simultaneously caught up and distant; at once a participant and a questioning observer of your own and other's participation in ordinary events' (1996: 103). Whilst I was based in Liverpool during my PhD, I spent much of my time in Belfast. At least once a month, I booked a foot passenger ticket on the Stenaline ferry and made the eight-hour journey over the Irish Sea, leaving behind one industrial skyline for another. Each visit to Belfast was filled with meetings, archival research, conversations and interviews. These encounters were arranged mostly in advance while also leaving room for spontaneous meetings and *flânerie*.

A key part of my research from the beginning was using walking as methodology, supported by photography, to gain an understanding of this part of North Belfast and its changes over time. These methods were chosen following Jacobs's assertion that 'the way to get at what goes on in a space is to look closely and without expectation at ordinary scenes and events and attempt to see what they mean, whether any threads of principle emerge' (1961: 13). I walked the spaces around Girdwood on hundreds of occasions. I took surreptitious photographs of graffitied walls and lampposts and paused to read memorial plaques. Noted the placement of flags and murals, and how they evolved. I got hopelessly lost and sometimes embarrassed as I followed bewildering routes and doubled back. On one of my first walks, I knocked on the door of a community group in the area, seeking to find out more about

Girdwood. There, an initial cup of tea and a chat snowballed into four years of participant observation around the site.

Although a central research method in qualitative research, participant observation is perhaps the least well-defined. It involves entering a setting, establishing a rapport with people and becoming a 'familiar face' in that setting, observing events and interactions, then contextualising the data and putting it into perspective through recording extensive fieldnotes (Berg 2007: 195). From 2013 to 2017, I attended dozens of meetings within and between community groups on both sides of the divide. Eventually, the meetings grew to include Belfast City Council and the Girdwood Community Forum, a working group of community representatives. Most of the time, I blended in quietly into the background, listening, observing and blithely scribbling notes during meetings. People were mostly used to my presence. Other times I felt my role as outsider keenly. Once at a meeting, one of the members stopped, stared at me, said sharply – 'I don't want anyone writing anything down'. I blushed scarlet, mumbling that they could read my notes if they wanted. For a minute, everyone had seen me, and I felt that momentary shift in atmosphere.

Awkward moments aside, the groups I worked with were all aware of my status as a researcher and kept me informed of upcoming events and meetings to attend. The community workers and activists I met were incredibly generous with their time and experience, and I am grateful for the access they afforded me. Towards the end of my fieldwork, I conducted in-depth, semi-structured interviews with seven of these 'gatekeepers' with whom I had worked closely over the years. These summarised previous informal conversations and themes that had arisen throughout fieldwork.[1] Within these chapters, I have also relied on the copious and detailed fieldnotes I took after each stint in the field, which included interactions, conversations and, sometimes, arguments.

My fieldwork was thus initially anthropological and documented by extensive fieldnotes (Burgess 1997; Emerson et al. 1995; Fetterman 2010). But as Jenkins (1983: 22) noted in his ethnography of Ballyhightown, participant observation alone is not enough to capture both the life-worlds within a research site and its broader social context. As the research progressed and evolved, my observations were buttressed by primary and archival research on government policies, Masterplans, Hansards,[2] newspapers and meeting minutes, as I analysed the discourses contained within. I was also fortunate to receive a trove of documents from the redevelopment process. A community

---

[1] I sent all interviewees their quotations and context to approve in advance of the book's publication. Other quotations I used came directly from fieldnotes. Not all the interviews I conducted were used in the book.

[2] Hansard is the official record of all Northern Ireland Assembly proceedings (and UK Parliamentary debates).

member passed them along to me, noting they had never been circulated before. These included a complete set of meeting minutes, discussion papers and background information provided to the Girdwood Advisory Panel during its existence from 2006 to 2007 and an economic appraisal and analysis of the City Council PEACE III bid in 2010, done for the European Union by Cogent Management Company, an independent consulting firm. I also collected various internal community group meeting minutes and documents of my own from the latter part of the process in 2014–2016.

These documents provided valuable insights into the political nuances of the redevelopment. As Prior notes, 'documents are never inert', and one must 'look at documentation not merely for its content but more at how it is produced, how it functions in episodes of daily interaction, and how exactly it circulates' (2004: 388). For instance, by reading subsequent community relations strategies, city masterplans, area-based regeneration plans, etc., it was possible to note shifting priorities, language – even word choice – which reflected the authors and the context of political decision-making at the time. So, too, much stayed the same, with continued ideological intransigence and stalemates over resources, territory and legitimacy. I contrasted the rhetoric of planning, economic and community relations policy with the reality of Girdwood and with the commitments of the Good Friday Agreement and the legislative framework of Northern Ireland Act. This allowed me to find common themes and patterns and identify their consequences on the ground. In doing so, I was able to both rigorously document the site's progress from vacant lot to construction zone to Community Hub – and highlight the underlying policy and planning forces at work.

Outside of the Girdwood research, it was important to me to spend as much time as possible learning from the city and its denizens – the history and geography of its narrow streets; the canon of murals and memorial plaques; the changing built environment along the docks and in the city centre. My first experience in Belfast as an intern laid the foundation for this. I had kept in touch with my old friends, and the regulars at the pub were still there in their usual places. People told me where to go. I hung out faithfully at the Twaddell flag protest camp (DeYoung 2016), marched in pro-choice and LGBTQ rights rallies, sat in at 'trad' sessions and samba gigs and sipped cheap pints in social clubs on both sides of the interface. In doing so, I discovered a place much richer than the stereotypical 'Protestant/Catholic' binary, but much poorer for the underlying divisions that persist.

I learned a different vocabulary – the way Belfast people string sentences together, the slang and sarcasm that first fell unintelligible upon my American ears. I memorised dozens of different acronyms.[3] I became acquainted with the

---

[3] There is a profusion of acronyms for political parties and paramilitary groups in Northern Ireland: the IRA, INLA, UVF, UDA, etc. (see Index).

complicated set of social norms known as 'telling', where in first meeting, people draw upon a variety of subtle markers to ascertain the other's ethnoreligious identity (Burton 1979: 67; Harris 1972: 148; Wilson and Donning 2006: 126). These can range from home address or school uniform to football club and favourite pub: a million different ways to guess someone's background in polite conversation, and thus pigeonhole them. I started doing it unconsciously, too.

There is also a 'minefield' of sensitive political connotations to language which have implications for a researcher (Knox 2001: 215) – for instance, learning the subtle difference between 'Northern Ireland' (the name of the political unit established by the Government of Ireland Act (1920) and preferred by Unionists) and 'the North of Ireland' or 'Six Counties' (preferred by Nationalists). Even the terms Unionist and Nationalist have different iterations (Whyte 1991: 18). Unionists broadly support the constitutional link to the United Kingdom, whilst Loyalists feel primary allegiance to Ulster. Nationalists broadly support reunification with Ireland by constitutional consent, whilst Republicans support the use of violence to achieve it.[4]

As much as I loved Belfast, there was a lot to dislike. The constant spectre of sectarianism. The politics. The paramilitaries. The poverty and unemployment. The flagrant abuses of power at work in the Northern Ireland Assembly. These were all evident at Girdwood. As a researcher, it is difficult to maintain 'objectivity', not to 'take sides' in the face of blatant inequality, where individuals and areas experience deprivation and discrimination in the context of a political and economic system (Scraton 2004: 181). Sluka noted in his own ethnography that 'no one can study a community in Belfast first-hand without becoming emotionally and morally involved' (1989: 4). This certainly resonated. My research elicited issues of zero-sum resource allocation, sectarianism, alleged clientelism and structural failures. In particular, the issue of social housing in North Belfast was emotive. Though the argument made by some Protestants/Unionists against housing made total 'sense' given the context of territorialism and communal insecurity, its consequences were unjust and cruel to those left homeless or on the waiting list.

---

[4] In general, this book will use the terms 'Catholic/Nationalist' and 'Protestant/Unionist' to denote the two ethnonational groups. Catholic/Nationalist refers to those consider themselves Irish and who support the reunification of Ireland as a 32-county sovereign country. Protestant/Unionist refers to those who consider themselves British and support union with the rest of the United Kingdom. Where you see the terms Republican and Loyalist, these generally describe those who would support the use of violence to achieve a United Ireland or preserve the union with the United Kingdom, respectively. As with all generalisations and labels, there are many exceptions and contradictions. Finally, by using the terms 'Catholic' and 'Protestant' I do not suggest that the past conflict has a primarily religious basis as there are many other factors involved, national identity and allegiance included.

I am grateful for the access and the trust that my research participants placed in me, and their willingness to share their perspectives. Specifically, I got to know many Protestant/Unionist/Loyalist community workers and community members during my years in Belfast and recognised that they indeed bore some unfair stereotypes and judgements. Working-class Loyalists are often sneered at (in popular discourse, in the media) as brutish or bigoted (Evershed 2018: 92). Like everything in Northern Ireland, I found that it was far more complex than that. Many of these communities have been left behind by their politicians and economically marginalised. And many commentators ignore elements of Unionism that are grounded in an ethos of political transformation. However, while I sought to represent all perspectives accurately in the research, the Unionist opposition to social housing provision in contested areas became an issue which I could not help but let inform my writing-up process.

It is worth noting that ethnography itself is inherently partial – the task of conveying a social world and the structures which make it up is enormous. Consequently, 'the best we can do is take snapshots' (Gray 2014: 462). As Burton put it regarding his ethnography of a Belfast community, 'there are worlds, no doubt, I never knew existed, others I caught only fleeting glimpses of. Even those I penetrated often defy easy description. Some of the last may be blind alleys' (1978: 10). As an outsider, nuances will have been lost to me, doors will have remained closed to me and my own perceptions and background are intrinsic to how data was collected and conceptualised.

In the following, I attempt to encapsulate the complexity of Northern Ireland and of North Belfast: not only describing its social, economic and political context, but also capturing the very palpable wit and character of the people who inhabit its streets. However, in the end this book is my interpretation alone, and as Aretzaga wryly notes of her own ethnography, 'it risks pleasing nobody' (1997: 23). Given the contested milieu around Girdwood, some readers will not agree with the story as I have written it. I therefore assume responsibility for my conclusions and for any inaccuracies derived from my own perspective.

A Field Guide to Belfast: Walking as Methodology

Each part of Belfast has its own distinct character. Each deserves its own book, really. In awareness of treading on tired tropes, the following sections attempt to provide a brief 'field guide' of the city as context for subsequent chapters. Without a working knowledge of Belfast's complicated geography, we cannot fully reconstruct the redevelopment of the Girdwood Barracks and its transformation into a Hub.

East Belfast is considered a predominantly Protestant/Unionist area, a legacy of its shipbuilding past. The Titanic Experience, a shiny museum about the ill-fated vessel, attests to this history. It is located on the redeveloped docks of the River Lagan. There is one small Catholic/Nationalist enclave in East Belfast, Short Strand, that sits in the shadow of St Matthew's Church on the Lower Newtownards Road. It is neatly enclosed by fencing and nets to protect it from its Protestant/Unionist neighbours. Across from Short Strand on the Newtownards Road, you pass Freedom Corner, a series of splashy Ulster Defence Association (UDA)[5] murals featuring the clenched red hand of Ulster. You might not notice the fake shopfronts camouflaging vacant properties on the main road. You might notice stencilled graffiti on other empty buildings, 'Property of UDA'. Further up the road, the area becomes leafier, the houses bigger. Up here, Stormont, the seat of the Northern Ireland Assembly, sits on a hill overlooking the city.

West Belfast, 'Up the Falls',[6] is predominantly Catholic/Nationalist. Divis Tower, an ugly Brutalist apartment block, marks the bottom of the Falls Road, a main thoroughfare. Tourists take black taxi tours up to snap photos of the 'International Wall', a rotating cast of political murals on the lower Falls, and the big mural of hunger striker Bobby Sands on the side of the Sinn Féin constituency office.[7] But there are dozens and dozens of other murals and memorials hidden in the estates that cluster off the main road. Some commemorate fallen Republican paramilitaries, others local people who died on the streets during the Troubles. Many were shot by the British Army or the Royal Ulster Constabulary (RUC);[8] many were innocent civilians, some were children. All were reduced to names carved into stone. Further up, the Springfield, Whiterock and Andersonstown roads split off the Falls and stretch all the way up to the mountains. To an outsider, the neighbourhoods in Nationalist West Belfast might bleed into each other, one small street of terraced houses indistinguishable from the next. But they are actually a patchwork of defined places, each with its own history, character and paramilitary allegiances: Divis, Beechmount, St James, 'Andytown' and so on.

---

[5] The Ulster Defence Association is one of the main Protestant/Unionist/Loyalist paramilitary groups.
[6] A popular reference to the Falls Road, one of the main arteries that runs through West Belfast and long affiliated with the Catholic/Nationalist population.
[7] Black taxi tours are political tours often run by local guides, some of whom are ex-combatants. They drive tourists around West Belfast and the murals and interfaces (Weidenhoft Murphy 2010). Black taxis, or 'people's taxis', were substitutes for official bus service during the conflict and travelled fixed routes – they were famously used on the Catholic/Nationalist Falls Road but a separate black taxi service also operated on the Protestant/Unionist Shankill (Aretxaga 1997).
[8] The Royal Ulster Constabulary, the police force of Northern Ireland during the Troubles. The RUC was widely thought of as anti-Catholic among the Nationalist community. As part of the peace process, the RUC was disbanded and replaced by a new service, the Police Service of Northern Ireland (PSNI).

I loved the Falls and spent a lot of time there, attending Irish language classes at Cumann Chluain Árd, hanging out in An Cultúrlann's café and drinking pints at the Rock and the Hawthorn.

The staunchly Unionist Shankill Road, which runs parallel to the Falls Road, is also technically considered 'West Belfast' though it is divided by interface barriers from the rest of the West. It also consists of a patchwork of different neighbourhoods off the main road and up to the mountains: Lower Shankill, Woodvale, Ballysillan. They have their own history, character and paramilitary allegiances, too. If you took away the British flags that wave from lampposts and the content of the murals and memorial gardens, which correspond to Loyalist paramilitary groups and victims, the streets would look much the same as the ones on the Falls. There are warrens of small, identical terraced houses punctuated by corner shops. The main road is lined with takeaways, hair salons, pubs and bookmakers. Halfway up the Shankill on Agnes Street, an Ulster Volunteer Force (UVF)[9] mural used to signal a change from UDA to UVF territory (it has since been painted over as part of a reimaging campaign). Halfway up the Shankill, there also used to be a fish shop. It was blown up by the IRA on a Saturday afternoon in 1993 in one of the more infamous atrocities of the Troubles. Ten people were killed, one of them the bomber. I spent time on the Shankill, too – there was a greasy spoon that I often stopped by, and I enjoyed ducking into the Lower Shankill Community Association now and again. For many months, I attended the nightly protest camp at the junction of Woodvale Avenue. And during marching season each year, I went to observe the various Orange Order parades.[10] These are both an enjoyable community spectacle and a jarring exercise in triumphalism. On 12 July, the route goes all the way to South Belfast and back to the various Orange lodges around the city.

South Belfast is home to Queens University, the Botanical Gardens and the Ulster Museum. It is widely thought of as one of the more genteel and mixed-religion parts of the city. The Malone and Lisburn roads are shorthand for the affluent and leafy Belfast, the one with a Marks and Spencer, posh coffee shops and big gated houses set back from the road. On the other side of Queens, the Holylands area, named for its peculiar streets (i.e., Jerusalem, Palestine, Damascus) is full of shabby student housing run by itinerant landlords. And the Ormeau Road has, over the years, gone from an uneasy interface area to a comparatively vibrant one. Some of my friends – musicians, artists, academics

---

[9] The Ulster Volunteer Force is the other main Protestant/Unionist/Loyalist paramilitary group.
[10] The Order, a Protestant fraternal organisation formed in 1795, is known to be anti-Catholic and pro-Union, but it also encourages place-based loyalties, creates and maintains social networks and provides a means of symbolically constructing community. A key part of this is parading through civic space (Bell 1990: 210).

– lived in Ormeau. Over the years, I saw vegan bakeries and ramen spots open up without the stereotypical smugness next to the ordinary off-licences and pubs. However, there are several pockets of beleaguered working-class neighbourhoods in South Belfast that seem to get forgotten: for instance, the Protestant/Unionist Sandy Row and Village, tucked along what is now the M1 motorway, the Catholic/Nationalist Markets area along the River Lagan and the Protestant/Unionist Annadale flats on the Ormeau Road.

Other elements seem to be forgotten sometimes in discussions of the city and its spaces. Alongside the sectarian divisions that burden Belfast, there are a multiplicity of people and perspectives navigating these streets. The city is experienced differently by different populations, and other forms of social identity – class, gender and sexuality – are inscribed into the city just as durably as sectarian divides.

As noted elsewhere in these chapters, class divisions are fundamental to the city's geography. The Westlink functions essentially as an economic interface, a buffer that cuts off the poorer environs of East, West and North Belfast from the city centre (Sterrett et al. 2012). There are stark differences between the comfortably middle-class neighbourhoods adjacent to the university and the terraced houses of Sandy Row, less than a mile away. Those who can afford a car are able to motor easily through interface areas, passing through the city in a different way than those who must make their way on foot or by public transit.

Other research examines the gendered and sexual divides in the city. Lysaght and Basten (2002) explored differing perceptions of spatial freedom by gender: men tended to limit their movements as they were perceived as a 'threat', where women tended to move more freely through space. Smyth (2009) detailed maternal experiences of public space, and how everyday carework tasks commonly left to women, like 'shopping', take place alongside and despite sectarian divides. And as part of a broader project on sectarianism in everyday life and movement in Belfast, Kitchin and Lysaght (2002) also highlighted the experiences of LGBTQ individuals, who managed and regulated the ways in which they moved through the heteronormative city. Often, these strategies were fraught with fear of homophobic intimidation and violence. This body of work reminds us that throughout the city, it is not only sectarianism that determines one's experience of Belfast. Each neighbourhood is complex and multilayered, variously perceived as safe or unsafe, welcoming or inaccessible. Those who live in Belfast depend on different 'mental maps' based not only on spatial markers of sectarian identity, but other identity configurations as well.

This story takes place in North Belfast. North Belfast is a fractious patchwork of highly segregated neighbourhoods, home to some of the most acrimonious quarrels over space in Northern Ireland. Carson describes 'an ongoing head-counting territorial dispute ... where many huddles of opposing loyalties rub up against each other in frictions, factions, and fractions' (1997: 94).

Protestant/Unionist and Catholic/Nationalist residents live 'cheek by jowl', as they say, divided by a staggeringly creative array of boundaries. There are metal walls and steel palisade fencing and barbed wire. There are countless close boundaries and fault lines both visible and invisible. Traffic roundabouts separate Unionist and Nationalist areas; different sides of the street and bus stops are considered Catholic or Protestant. An interface barrier cuts through one of the parks. Where the other parts of Belfast see some measure of tourist footfall, outsiders don't really go to North Belfast. Many times during my fieldwork I heard people say, 'There's no reason to come here unless you live here'.

It is a difficult place to get to know. I walked through the many distinct neighbourhoods hundreds of times in order to trace the history and chart the present day. Indeed, walking was the cornerstone of my fieldwork and of my life in Belfast. I wore out multiple pairs of Doc Martens and shouldered my carrier bags and laptop across the city (and up Cave Hill, once or twice). I recall with great affection and detail the many streets that formed the architecture of my time in Belfast. Given my research's focus on space, my status as an outsider, and the complexities of the city's geography, walking was literally the 'first step' in my research. Through being immersed in the surroundings, I gained a real feel for both the everyday realities of the landscape and the ways in which the past is continually present within it.

If you lace up your boots, go out and pay attention, you find that each walk brings new layers of meaning, a tension between the familiar and the strange. There are many dimensions to a seemingly mundane act: the body as it moves through space, the meaning and memory attached to physical objects or sites, the choices one makes between different paths (Edensor 2010; Ellidge 2017; Gustafson 2001). Geography also changes from street to street, and this can only be felt on foot (Middleton 2010: 582). One encounters Jacobs's 'sidewalk ballet' of movement, the spatial and temporal patterns of people that enliven a space. Shopfronts and developments might signal broader economic shifts and trends. A shift from one street to another can reflect racial or ethnic divides. Street signs, cemeteries and statues situate the past in plain sight.

Walks can evoke different memories: perhaps of a long-defunct grocer or pub; old neighbours and friends; the site of a first kiss, a fistfight, a riot or a murder (de Certeau 1984: 108). But the very materiality of a place – concrete, kerbstones, a patch of grass – means memory is not left to mental processes but rather inscribed in the landscape (Cresswell 2004: 85). Over the years, I made my own memories in the streets of Belfast. I found them again on subsequent walks. I saw plaques that inscribed other people's memories in space and that bore witness to past violence. As de Certeau put it, 'there is no place that is not haunted by any spirits hidden there in silence, spirits one can "invoke" or not' (1984: 108).

In all cities, space functions as a platform for historical and collective narratives and a repository for meaning. In the context of Belfast, for instance, one observes the breadth of murals, memorial plaques, flags and territorial markers that delineate neighbourhoods and reaffirm ethnosectarian identity. These reflect the relative clout of actors of power, whether it be government officials, community development elites or paramilitaries, and speak to the discourses that they circulate about place (DeYoung 2018). But like the ever-evolving city, identity is not fixed, but continually performed, practiced and reshaped. The physical environment can also signal contesting or dissenting perspectives. Walking in Belfast, I often observed the ways in which top-down power dynamics were expressed, negotiated and subverted at the street level. Graffiti on the side of a building site, the splatter of a paint bomb on the Orange Hall, a new paramilitary mural painted over a peace-themed one – these were clues as to who held power in a place, and denoted small acts of resistance against those actors, too.

My walks allowed me to track minute and major changes in the environment, to record territorial demarcations over time and to observe how people used and perceived the space. Some of this was pedestrian: walking past children playing on a rope swing or passing a football around; kicking up discarded crisp packets; peering through the iron bars surrounding the Girdwood Barracks site. I took photos of a field of acronyms – 'KAH', 'KAT',[11] 'Property of UDA', 'Israel/USA, How many kids have you killed today?' I observed piles of debris scattered across a vacant lot, waiting to be stacked and burned on Bonfire Night. There was one incongruous chicken coop which sat outside a house by an interface. More insidious – a paramilitary flag positioned above the 'peace wall' to taunt the other side. I noted chunks of cement missing from the pavement, erstwhile missiles. A brick had punched a neat half-moon through one house's window.

As an outsider, my nationality facilitated mobility between contested spaces, the crossing of boundary lines where locals might never pass. I could be transient and anonymous. This freedom was usually an asset to my walks, particularly in the strange liminal spaces around the interfaces between Catholic/Nationalist and Protestant/Unionist areas. At times, however, I felt painfully self-conscious during my wanderings – an obvious outsider in an out-of-the-way area, photographing fencing and electrical boxes with a studied air of nonchalance. I wondered if my presence was odd or noticed. The neighbourhoods are so insular. I disliked the feeling of being a voyeur, walking around housing estates before going back to my tidy university life to write up notes. At times, I felt as if all the information I had compiled was divorced from the realness of being on the ground, in a space where I was alien but

---

[11] Graffiti tags which stand for 'Kill all Huns' (sectarian slang for Protestants) or 'Kill all Taigs' (sectarian slang for Catholics) respectively.

where other people lived their daily lives. These people had to deal with the harsh realities of poverty and segregation every day, and I was merely writing about it. But I kept walking. It got me out of the confines of the university, out of the 'ivory tower' atmospheres that I disliked. It got me into pubs and corner shops and community centres, got me into conversations, helped me make connections. These adventures informed my practice as a researcher and shaped my experience as a resident of Belfast.

To understand how this all becomes relevant to the story of Girdwood, it bears exploring the history of the area around the site, the connotations of place and the ways in which these have influenced residents' perspectives and experiences. From the conflict to the present day, the built environment has been directly linked to the reproduction of segregation, mistrust and fear. It is a platform for political and paramilitary power and a space for meaning-making. This became clear with Girdwood's redevelopment, where logical planning proposals were subverted by territoriality and fear of the 'Other'. This trajectory can be traced to the way in which notions of space, place and belonging developed over the course of the Troubles.

An Ode to Cliftonpark Avenue

The area around the Girdwood Barracks suffered heavily from sectarian violence during the conflict. It is still, in some ways, a no man's land. Before we delve into politics and planning, we have to start with the first step, which is forming a mental snapshot of the landscape. Setting the stage for everything else to come, lacing up the figurative boots and traipsing around this strange part of North Belfast.

I often cut through the Lower Shankill estate *en route* to Girdwood before and during its redevelopment. The estate was the last stop on 'black taxi tours', and sometimes clusters of tourists would be out taking photographs of the murals on gable ends. One of the most famous was a masked gunman whose rifle end seemed to follow you wherever you went.[12] There were big stretches of open space throughout the estate, which came in handy when the community bonfire went up in June. It also made walking feel peculiarly exposed at times, a lone figure tracing a long route. Past a memorial mural to Stevie McKeag,[13] past rows of small houses festooned with British flags and bunting, I would

---

[12] The 'Mona Lisa' was razed in 2016 as part of a reimaging campaign to remove paramilitary-themed murals from housing estates.

[13] McKeag was a commanding officer of the UDA. Nicknamed 'Top Gun' and one of the UDA's most 'important' assassins, he was rumoured to be responsible for the murder of at least 12 Catholics. Many were civilians (Moriarty 2021).

finally pop out onto the Crumlin Road and the abandoned courthouse. The Crumlin Road Courthouse had been slated for economic development at one point along with the Girdwood site, but lay totally irreparable, surrounded by piles of rusting refuse and weeds. The site was secured with iron bolts and signs warning against breaking and entering. But people did it anyway, and in addition to graffiti, there had been several arson attacks on the property. It was a colossal shame: once-handsome windows long-shattered, high ceilings caved in and roof ruined by fire.

Directly across from the courthouse was the former Crumlin Road Gaol. The two were famously connected by an underground tunnel, where prisoners would be conducted from their cells into the courtroom and back. Around the time I conducted fieldwork on the Girdwood site, the gaol was redeveloped with some success into a tourist attraction: one could take a tour of the prison and its grounds, dine at the café and restaurant, and hire the space for conferences, functions and (perversely) weddings. In the wake of demilitarisation, the Girdwood Barracks, Crumlin Road Gaol and Courthouse were meant to be redeveloped together as one integrated whole; subsequent chapters will explore the many complications that thwarted this vision.

Continuing down the Crumlin Road, I would take a right onto Cliftonpark Avenue, sometimes stopping in the petrol station on the corner for a packet of crisps or rolling papers. At first glance, Cliftonpark Avenue looked like any ordinary street. At the top of the road, on both sides, were large patches of green space, surrounded by black metal fencing and studded with skinny young trees. There was a path through, but no benches or flowers or landscaping, no public art to admire, no one using the space at all.[14] On the left-hand side of Cliftonpark Avenue was a Baptist church. Behind it, the Lower Oldpark housing estate was screened partially by a cluster of shrubbery and a tall black gate. You could just make out a pigeon coop in someone's back garden.

Cliftonpark Avenue was a long, straight street lined by stretches of red-brick houses and large expanses of green space. The left-hand side of the street marked the edge of Lower Oldpark. Fenced-in front gardens, mostly tidy and well-kept, set the houses back from the road. On the right-hand side of the street, many of the apartments looked older, with elaborate brickwork and arched doorways. One could imagine them in another, more well-to-do life as hotels or doctors' and solicitors' chambers. Garish faux floral arrangements towered in windows. Some front gardens were carefully swept of gravel and debris. Others had been overtaken by creeping vines and undergrowth, empty bottles and shards of clear glass.

---

[14] As of June 2021, Google Street View shows construction happening at the top of the street. The Baptist Church is now called the Ark.

It was always quiet on Cliftonpark Avenue, noticeably devoid of foot traffic save for the odd cluster of children or a solitary dog walker. During the conflict, this street was a war zone, 'the worst street to live in Ireland'. Many buildings were abandoned or burnt out in times of tension and became derelict (author fieldnotes 2014). This accounted for the empty land at the top and bottom of the street where homes once stood but were later demolished. Halfway down Cliftonpark Avenue on the right, a stretch of green sheet metal announced the vacant Barracks site. Later, this wall was dismantled and a road was built into the eventual Girdwood Community Hub. Across from the Barracks site in Lower Oldpark, a children's playpark was encircled by a tall black fence, and a wide swathe of green space ran up to the 'peace wall' on Manor Street.

From across the street, the view of the Manor Street interface barrier, which physically divides Protestant/Unionist Lower Oldpark from Catholic/Nationalist Lower Cliftonville, was always striking. The empty green space next to the Lower Oldpark playpark contrasted with the Cliftonville side, where houses were crammed right up to the wall. It was a vivid reminder of the demographic tensions in the area: the blight and population decline in Protestant estates and the urgent housing need among Catholics/Nationalists. The wall is made of metal sheeting and over the years of my fieldwork, it was painted a benign yellow and then bright blue. Unlike other interface barriers, which completely impede movement back and forth, it is possible to walk straight past this wall and cross the boundary from Lower Oldpark to Lower Cliftonville.

Fig. 1.3

There were few territorial markings on Cliftonpark Avenue during my fieldwork except for one blacked-out mural. One could just make out 'Free J Adair' in block letters, a reference to a Loyalist paramilitary who had held sway in the area decades ago. However, during marching season, paramilitary flags, Union and Scottish and Northern Irish flags were typically taken out and affixed to every lamppost. One resident observed that the local UDA puts them up, and if anyone says anything they risk their windows ('windies') being put in (author fieldnotes 2014).

Cliftonpark Avenue was always eerie. Healthy city sidewalks pulse with people, paths intersecting and offering myriad routes from here to there. But this area was forlorn: although only a ten-minute walk from the bustling city centre, it felt miles away. My fieldwork ended around the time that the Girdwood Community Hub opened, but I visited the street several times afterwards and it felt similarly empty. Anecdotally, at least, the Girdwood Community Hub didn't seem to have impacted the footfall or energy of the area. Instead, the blight of economic marginalisation and the legacy of the Troubles continued to find expression on Cliftonpark Avenue and the neighbourhoods around it in North Belfast.

'A Fine History of Walls':[15] North Belfast and the Troubles

North Belfast suffered disproportionately from the impact of violence during the Troubles. Within one square mile of the New Lodge Road (which encompasses the area where this research takes place) over 635 civilians were killed and over 2,500 injured during 30 years of conflict (New Lodge Six Time for Truth Committee 2002: 11). *The Irish News* called the corner of the New Lodge Road and Antrim Road, just steps from Girdwood, 'the most unsafe place to stand in Northern Ireland' (1993b: 7). As previously noted, Cliftonpark Avenue had a similar reputation. Unionist/Loyalist paramilitaries committed random sectarian murders in order to strike fear into Catholic/Nationalist neighbourhoods and undermine support for Republican paramilitaries. Often, a 'tit-for-tat' pattern emerged whereby every atrocity committed by the IRA would see Loyalists retaliate (Southern 2008: 72; Dillon and Lehane 1973: 24). Catholic civilians were shot dead whilst walking down the street, at their doorstep, waiting for a taxi or delivering milk. Bodies were found dumped on the cricket grounds, on street corners, on wasteland (*Irish News* 1993a; Sutton 2002).[16] There have also been allegations and some substantiated cases of collusion between Loyalist paramilitaries and the security forces (Dillon and

---

[15] J. P. Lederach in Cosstick (2015: 1).
[16] Sutton (2002) counts 713 sectarian killings by Loyalists from 1968 to 1993.

Lehane 1973: 26; Stevens 2003; *Belfast Telegraph* 2015). On the other side of the divide, Republican attacks on the Shankill Road led to the Protestant civilian population also experiencing multiple shootings and a number of devastating bombings over the years.[17] Furthermore, the IRA targeted and assassinated police, soldiers and prison officers – often brutally, in their homes or at work – most of whom were Protestant/Unionist and some of whom lived in North Belfast.

Intra-community violence occurred as well: civilians were killed by the organisations that purported to defend them, whether that be accidental casualties, feuding factions or shooting informers (O'Duffy and O'Leary 1990). The British Army and RUC also surveilled, intimidated and periodically attacked civilians, particularly though not exclusively in Catholic/Nationalist areas.[18] Hundreds of people within North Belfast alone were interned without trial, arrested and/or sent to prison (including at the Crumlin Road Gaol) during the Troubles. Many of these people were interrogated at the Girdwood Army Barracks (Kennally and Preston 1971), and there were substantive allegations that torture and human rights abuses took place there (Conroy 2001; Faul and Murray 1972; McDonald 2018b; O'Tuathail 1971).

As conflict turned into a permanent feature of life, the streets of the city became battlefields (McDowell and Switzer 2011: 83). Places like North Belfast were under systematic threat – over the course of the Troubles, neighbourhoods were patrolled, raided and regularly attacked by the British Army, RUC and/or paramilitary groups.[19] In Belfast, nearly one-third of victims were murdered within their home or a few metres from it, furthering a sense of 'assault upon community' and strengthening communal narratives of suffering (Shirlow and

---

[17] In 1975, five Protestants were killed when a bomb exploded at the Mountainview Tavern on the Shankill Road, followed by the Bayardo Bar bombing on the same road, which killed a further five Protestant civilians. In 1993, on a busy Saturday afternoon on the Shankill, the IRA blew up Frizzell's Fish Shop, ostensibly targeting an alleged meeting of Loyalist paramilitaries taking place on the second floor. No such meeting occurred but ten people died in the blast – nine Protestant civilians and one IRA member. For many, the targeting of civilian-frequented establishments calls into question the IRA's contention that their violence was never sectarian in nature (Southern 2008; McKenna and Melaugh 2016).

[18] From August through December 1971, 1,981 people were detained by the state; 1,874 were Catholic/Republican, 107 Protestant/Loyalist (Melaugh 2016b). Most were civilians, not Republican paramilitaries. This was the period called 'internment' whereby under the Special Powers Act, the state had the power to intern people without trial. Ironically, internment led to an upsurge in IRA recruits whilst contributing to a sense of onslaught, siege and fear of the state within Catholic/Nationalist communities.

[19] 80 per cent of deaths in Belfast occurred within areas that were either over 90 per cent Catholic or over 90 per cent Protestant (Bairner and Shirlow 2003: 209).

Murtagh 2006: 74). Within this context, a sense of common purpose, cohesion and solidarity often prevailed. People shared the experience of being under threat on a daily basis in an enclave and, for many, this contributed to a sense of collective experience and attachment to place, usually constructed in opposition to the 'Other' ethnonational group. As Shirlow and Murtagh observed, 'loyalty to place unites atheist with godly, male with female, leftist with right-winger. It has the capacity to disguise differences through achieving a sense of value and attachment to a struggle over the maintenance of places that must remain unique' (2006: 17). Of course, seeing the world through the lens of place can lead to exclusionary or reactionary behaviour and bigotry – the notion that 'our place is threatened and others have to be excluded' (Cresswell 2004: 11). During the conflict, the physical environment both reflected and reinforced the dual senses of siege and threat, territoriality and place-identity.

Belfast became a city of walls and enclaves. As the violence worsened and the British state imposed direct rule in 1972, temporary boundaries between Protestant and Catholic neighbourhoods were replaced by permanent, large-scale barriers and gates, reifying ethnic segregation and creating a city of statis (Gormley-Heenan et al. 2013: 363). These became known as 'interfaces': 'the topographic-ideological boundary sector that physically and symbolically demarcates ethnic communities in Belfast from each other' (Boal and Murray 1977: 364). Because of their location in the liminal space between neighbourhoods, interfaces bore particular 'grim witness to bitter sectarian animosities', as Gaffikin and Morrissey (1999: 167) describe, from petrol bombings to gun battles to murder.[20] The fear and violence these barriers represented, and the division and parochialism that they encouraged, thus actually became self-perpetuating.

The resulting cocktail of place-attachment, boundary maintenance, fear and threat was a potent one for those actors seeking power over communities. With the formation of interfaces came the first attempts by paramilitary groups to control space in working-class residential areas of Belfast (Bryan 2012: 324). A process of 'ethnosectarian enclaving' brought new relationships and power dynamics to the fore (Shirlow 2003a: 83). Republican and Loyalist paramilitaries policed crime and anti-social behaviour; protected their respective areas from attack by the 'Other' (whether that be other paramilitaries, the army or police forces); and mounted offensive attacks that were ostensibly based on their ideological beliefs but often brutal and inhumane. In doing so, paramilitary groups exercised some degree of control in segregated neighbourhoods, converting a 'sanctuary space' into a base for operations (Feldman 1991: 41).

---

[20] One-third of politically motivated murders occurred within 250 metres of an interface, and around 85 per cent within a kilometre (Shirlow 2003a: 82).

From the conflict to the present day, space has been used as an important platform for political and paramilitary agendas. In addition to interfaces, a variety of territorial markers, symbolic imagery and discursive practices emerged to mark the boundaries of segregated neighbourhoods and distinguish the 'safe spaces' within. Common sights include(d): paramilitary flags waving from lampposts and bunting strung across terraced streets; memorial gardens to Republican or Loyalist paramilitary dead; and murals enforcing political ideology and, sometimes, overt sectarian hostility through imagery. Kerbstones used to be painted red, white and blue or orange, white and green to mark territory, though this practice has faded over time. Parades and protests also mark(ed) out territorial claims through the assemblage of bodies and movement. Space was (and remains) seen as a platform for historical 'truths' and collective discourses, imbued with mythology, story and symbolism. This has underlined the sense of territorial belonging and historical continuity that can bind individuals and groups to places.

Markers like murals, memorials and flags also functioned as a tool of control for both paramilitaries and political elites. They reinforce(d) a particular collective narrative and imagined space of a British Ulster or United Ireland, respectively (Shirlow 2006b: 232). As Feldman puts it in his own ethnography, paramilitaries 'exploited the inherited mythic link between micro-territorial iconography (the confessional community) and the macro-territorial icons of a "United Ireland" or "British Ulster" to secure their legitimacy' (1991: 42). But their utility was twofold: ethnonational markers also serve(d) to support a polarised discourse of 'us vs them', a binary opposition where the 'pure space' of the 'home enclave' becomes morally superior to the 'Other' (Bairner and Shirlow 2003: 210).

Paramilitaries constructed a sense of fear through this use of urban space (Shirlow 2006b: 229). By emphasising the boundary between in-group and out-group, 'us and them', paramilitary groups could consolidate power bases, claim territory and silence internal opposition. They deployed the language of 'community' to mobilise support for violence and establish wider hegemony over areas (Bean 2007: 14). In one sense, paramilitaries drew on people's sense of attachment to place, communal identity and solidarity in relation to the 'Other'. In another sense, they exploited the fear and threat which existed against that 'Other' to legitimise their presence. Communities became hostage to their protectors and the barriers and boundaries that surrounded them (Feldman 1991: 31).

The intersection of power and space always impacts to some extent on the behaviour and beliefs of people who live in that space. As Brand observes, 'the built environment, the shape of buildings, certain street patterns, territorial markers, et cetera tend to exert an intended or unintended pull or push upon people's perception and behaviour' (2009: 37). In contested places, boundaries and territorial markers are taken as a natural part of the spatial fabric, inevitable and permanent backdrops to daily life. Furthermore, the plethora of ethnonational symbols, representations and sites of remembrance within the landscape reaffirm a sense of identity and reinforce a collective narrative whilst 'silencing, degrading or ridiculing contesting cultures or perspectives' (Nagle 2009a: 330; Yiftachel and Ghanem 2004). Walls become not only physical but mental – and these mental divisions can, over time, produce structures preconditioned to identify against the 'Other'. In Belfast, one commentator noted, 'we create mental images of different groups of people, and we don't like these being disturbed. Many Republicans view all Loyalists a certain way and vice versa' (Hall 2015b: 9).

This must be qualified, however: there are a great heterogeneity of opinions and experiences within segregated areas. The violent acts and ethnonational imagery that aid the reproduction of segregation are not supported by all residents of these places, and neither are these residents automatically sectarian, political or in agreement with paramilitary control (Shirlow 2006b: 227). It is easy to flatten Northern Ireland into the 'Orange and Green' binary,[21] especially thanks to its political elites, but daily life defies those constraints. In my own fieldwork, I encountered a wide spectrum of opinion. Chapter Seven will further highlight how a variety of ideologies, identities and relationships can be found within supposedly 'homogenous' communities, even those under the control of political elites or paramilitaries.

---

[21] 'Orange and Green' popularly denotes the Protestant-Unionist/Catholic-Nationalist binary in Northern Ireland.

CHAPTER TWO

Politicking and Peacebuilding in Northern Ireland

The Good Friday Agreement and Its Prescriptions

The Good Friday Agreement

The 1994 paramilitary ceasefires brought the conditions for the peace process to Northern Ireland. After protracted negotiations between political parties in Northern Ireland and the British and Irish governments, the Troubles officially came to an end with the signing of the Good Friday Agreement in 1998 (MacGinty 1998; Breen-Smyth 2008). The Agreement promised a future in which 'partnership, equality and mutual respect' would form the basis of political decision-making within Northern Ireland, between North and South, and between Northern Ireland and Great Britain (NIO 1998a: 2). All parties committed 'to the protection and vindication of the human rights of all' (NIO 1998a: 2). They also promised to work towards 'reconciliation and rapprochement' within a democratic framework, including the European Convention on Human Rights (NIO 1998a: 3, 7). These commitments were ostensibly made in 'good faith' and 'a spirit of concord' (NIO 1998a: 3). Negotiators also promoted the idea of a 'peace dividend': that an improved political situation would attract economic investment to the region and that a devolved government would facilitate a more equal society by targeting resources to the most disadvantaged (Knox 2014: 485). High-quality jobs and social and economic development were promised for marginalised areas in the 'new Northern Ireland' (O'Hearn 2008: 105). For those most affected by violence and social exclusion, it seemed that better times were ahead.

The Agreement put into place a consociational framework of governance for Northern Ireland, better known as power-sharing. Consociationalism, most famously theorised by Lijphart (1971), has been used in societies with ethnic cleavages, some emerging from conflict: for instance, Lebanon and Bosnia-Herzegovina, in addition to Northern Ireland (Bogaards et al. 2019). It theoretically allows for democracy in deeply divided societies through four main prescriptions. It calls for a 'grand coalition' of elite representatives from the ethnic groups concerned; ensures that each ethnic group is represented proportionally in public institutions and receives an equal share of resources; assures autonomy in self-governance; and enshrines a mutual veto where each group may protect its vital interests (Dixon 2011: 310; McGarry and O'Leary 2006a: 44). Bogaards, Helms and Lijphart (2019) note that, 'consociationalism is, at its very heart, about power sharing between political elites'. The aim is to promote equality and find mutual accommodation via 'political bargaining' between these elites (Higson 2008: 2). In the following chapters, the term 'power-sharing' will be used to refer to this consociational arrangement.[1]

In the Northern Ireland Assembly, the architecture of power-sharing between Protestants/Unionists and Catholics/Nationalists included safeguards to assure proportionality and balance. The First Minister and Deputy First Minister are selected one each from the two main ethnonational political parties.[2] They, along with eight departmental ministers, make up the Northern Ireland Executive. Members of the Assembly have to designate an identity – 'Nationalist, Unionist, or Other' – to measure cross-community support in voting. The passage of key legislation requires parallel consent, in which a majority of Unionist and Nationalist designations are present, or a weighted majority (60 per cent of members present including 40 per cent each of Unionists and Nationalists) (NIO 1998a: 8).[3] Allocations of Committee chairs and members and ministers are made using the D'Hondt system, in reference to the number of each party's seats in the Assembly (NIO 1998a: 8). Therefore governance – and policy outcomes – rests on sharing power equally between the two groups (Mitchell et al. 2009: 408).

The Agreement instituted a range of new bodies, including a North/South Ministerial Council and British/Irish Council to address issues of common concern between Ireland and the United Kingdom (NIO 1998a: 15, 17). The Agreement also stated that 'an essential aspect of the reconciliation process is the promotion of a culture of tolerance at every level of society, including initiatives to facilitate and encourage integrated education and mixed housing'

---

[1] This clarification is necessary as power-sharing and consociationalism tend to be treated as overlapping concepts, despite consociationalism having specific prescriptions and power-sharing in general being defined much more broadly (Bogaards 2000; Guelke 2019).

[2] In this book, the term Office of the First Minister and Deputy First Minister (OFMDFM) is used to describe the two roles. The OFMDFM was dissolved and replaced by the 'Executive Office' in 2016 but still existed during the time of the Girdwood development.

[3] In the latter case, a 'petition of concern' comes into effect – essentially a mutual veto where one group of at least 30 members can block a decision of the Assembly by requiring 'cross-community support' – a majority of Unionists and Nationalist votes – rather than a simple majority (Schwartz 2015; Northern Ireland Assembly 2016).

(NIO 1998a: 23), thus committing to dismantling the wider environment of segregation in work, schools and housing (Murtagh and Ellis 2011: 350). It affirmed a variety of human rights, including 'the right to equal opportunity in all social and economic activity, regardless of class, creed, disability, gender or ethnicity' and 'the right to freely choose one's place of residence' (NIO 1998a: 20). Essentially, the rhetoric of the Agreement envisioned total transformation: a move from direct rule to a devolved government, and from an ethnically divided society to one based on reconciliation and equality. Political decision-making and resource allocation would be primarily concerned with targeting inequalities and promoting equality of opportunity as defined by subsequent legislation (NIO 1998a: 23).

The Agreement became the Northern Ireland Act, which forms the legislative basis of the power-sharing government in Northern Ireland. Section 75 of the Act enshrines the duty to promote equality, irrespective of ethnic or religious background, as a cornerstone of governance. It reads:

1) A public authority shall in carrying out its functions relating to Northern Ireland have due regard to the need to promote equality of opportunity:

   a) between persons of different religious belief, political opinion, racial group, age, marital status or sexual orientation

   b) between men and women generally

   c) between persons with a disability and persons without

   d) between persons with dependents and persons without

2) *Without prejudice to its obligations under subsection (1)*, a public authority shall in carrying out its functions relating to Northern Ireland have regard to the desirability of promoting good relations between persons of different religious belief, political opinion or racial group. (NIO 1998b: 39, emphasis added)

Section 76 adds that, 'it shall be unlawful for a public authority carrying out functions in relation to Northern Ireland to discriminate, or to aid or incite another person to discriminate against a person or class of person on the grounds of religious belief or political opinion' (NIO 1998b: 39). These are legally binding and enforceable by judicial review or the ECNI (ECNI 2018: 2).

Section 75 is incredibly important to the Girdwood case study: it is the foundational piece of legislation that should have shaped the development. Although sifting through pages of policy documents was not always the most engaging of exercises during my fieldwork – sometimes it was downright dull – the implications of ignoring this legislation on the ground were startling. Section 75 was not intended to be a footnote, but a sea change in how 'equality' was perceived and practised in Northern Ireland. According to the Equality Commission, 'Section 75 of the Northern Ireland Act 1998 was intended to be transformative. Its aim was to change the practices of government and public authorities so that equality of opportunity and good relations are central to policy making, policy implementation, policy review and service delivery' (ECNI 2010: 5).

To monitor the implementation of Section 75, the Northern Ireland Act established the Human Rights Commission and the ECNI (ECNI 2010: 5). These two bodies were charged with ensuring that an equality perspective and 'parity of esteem' was mainstreamed through all levels and stages of policy development (ECNI 2012b: 3).[4]

However, in the context of post-Agreement Northern Ireland, the concept of 'equality' has been perceived and manipulated by both sides in different ways. Unionism, in the guise of the DUP, has remained suspicious of the Agreement's 'equality agenda' – according to an interview respondent, 'equality is bad for Unionism' ('Liam', interview with author 2016). Indeed, Hayward and Mitchell identified the perception among some elements of Unionism that political change and the 'equality agenda' in Section 75 is 'inherently biased towards Catholics and thereby opposed to the interests of Protestants' (2003: 303). As the largest Unionist party, the DUP cannot be perceived as 'giving ground' to Catholics/Nationalists if it is to keep its electoral majority.

Sinn Féin's rhetoric around equality has, at times, seemed to confirm these fears. In a memorable public address in 2014, then-party leader Gerry Adams responded to queries about the bigotry of the DUP by saying:

> The point is to actually break these bastards – that's the point. And what's going to break them is equality. That's what's going to break them – equality. Who could be afraid of equality? Who could be afraid of treating somebody the way you want to be treated? That's what we need to keep the focus on – that's the Trojan horse of the entire republican strategy is to reach out to people on the basis of equality. (BBC News 2014a)

For the DUP – and Unionism more broadly – the concept of 'equality' can be perceived as a broader strategy for Catholics/Nationalists to dismantle Unionist claims to belonging. So, despite the rhetoric of Section 75, the DUP remains

---

[4] The term 'parity of esteem' has become something of a buzzword in the post-Agreement period and was initially conceptualised as affording equal standing, respect and recognition to both traditions regardless of majority/minority dynamics. It was initially designed to supplant the zero-sum language of majority rule or self-determination with the language of equilibrium and pluralism (Hennessey and Wilson 1997).

leery of 'equality' and intransigent on issues that concern it: equal marriage, the Irish language, abortion rights and resource allocation by objective need, for instance.[5] Because of the way the Assembly is structured, they have been able to block democratic decision-making on these issues through mechanisms like the 'petition of concern' built into governance.[6] In other cases (like at Girdwood), the DUP has used the discursive tactic of 'good relations' to get around equality obligations, arguing, for instance, that that building social housing in response to objective need prevents an area from being 'shared' by both communities.

Whilst it may seem like a small distinction, it is important to note that Section 75 states that good relations, although important, must *not* take precedence over equality (NIO 1998b: 38). During the Girdwood redevelopment, the notions of 'good relations' and 'equality' were clearly and fundamentally at odds with each other, but discourse that centred good relations over equality was allowed to win out. This tension characterised not only the Girdwood process but post-Agreement policy and planning more generally. The legislative framework of Section 75 is critical to keep in mind throughout these pages since its implementation at Girdwood effectively tests whether the 'new Northern Ireland' is fit for purpose.

Ethnic Entrepreneurs: Sinn Féin and the DUP

Despite the aspirational rhetoric of the Act and Agreement and the laudable cessation of violence, little has changed structurally in Northern Ireland. The concern of democratic governance with citizenship and individual rights sits uncomfortably with a power-sharing framework. Power-sharing is fundamentally based on communalism, rather than individualism; it has been defined as 'an association of communities … that is the outcome of formal or informal bargains or pacts between the political leaders of ethnic or religious groups' (O'Leary 2001: 49). Practically, this institutionalises a 'two-bloc' framework of communalist politics, rather than emphasising the potential for individual choice found in typical democracies.

---

[5] The collapse of the Assembly in 2017 and the resultant power vacuum meant that the British government was able to legalise same-sex marriage and decriminalise abortion in 2019, bringing Northern Ireland's laws in line with the rest of Great Britain (Yeginsu 2019).

[6] The Petition of Concern (PoC) is a mechanism whereby 30 MLAs can petition to require a matter is passed on a cross-community rather than a majority basis. It is one of the 'safeguards' in the Agreement 'to ensure key decisions [in the Assembly] are taken on cross-community basis', but has been flagged for its overuse (NIO 2022a).

Consociationalist theory was originally based on a primordial interpretation of ethnicity and identity – that these were fixed, homogenous and unchanging (Dixon 2011: 310). Lijphart contended that, 'because good social fences may make good political neighbours, a kind of voluntary apartheid policy may be the most appropriate solution for a divided society' (1971: 11). But critics respond that this reinforces ethnic division and segregation by legitimising the existence of two 'obstinate and mutually exclusive' ethnonational groups, or 'ethnic pillars' as a means of managing conflict (Higson 2008: 2). This arguably ossifies divisions rather than transforming them. And in doing so, it closes down the space for challenging the status quo or imagining new political futures (Taylor 2006: 223). Whereas in the past, sectarian division was seen as 'something to be worked against, confronted and challenged', power-sharing takes as inevitable that a 'two-tribe' framework is the only workable political future, and this is reflected in the systems and structures of the Northern Ireland Assembly (Jarman 2002: 17).[7] The idea of equality of opportunity is called into question by a government and society based on ethnicity: why would politicians work within a legislative framework and moral accord based on equality and rights when it would compromise their electoral mandate? Instead, politics is a perverse balancing act of ensuring that one side does not get more than the other.

So whilst the rhetoric of the 1998 Agreement and Act committed to promoting a culture of tolerance, equality of opportunity and human rights, the structure of government established also accommodated and legitimised – indeed, institutionalised – the existence of 'two communities', Unionism and Nationalism, and a dynamic of group difference and communal division. Power-sharing has effectively managed the conflict, bringing it into the political arena, rather than effecting genuine transformation. Instead of working towards a 'shared future', as official rhetoric has promised, informal political machinations tend to reproduce an 'us vs them' mentality. Zero-sum resource competition and territorialism are symptomatic of this.

As it has unfolded in Northern Ireland, power-sharing feels more like a new dispensation of ethnocracy. Yiftachel and Yacobi define an ethnocracy as a regime whereby 'ethnicity, and not citizenship, forms the main criteria for distributing power and resources' (2003: 689). Politics are polarised, revolving around competition for space, power and economic resources. Planning is

---

[7] For instance, in the electoral registration for Assembly members as 'Unionist, Nationalist or Other', designating 'Other' does not carry political weight in decision-making; parties must designate as Unionist or Nationalist in order to have any influence in a voting system based on cross-community consent (Bryan 2006: 610). Politicians are not incentivised to move beyond their respective blocs. Furthermore, as ministers are selected based on the D'Hondt system, a two-party monopoly can exist in practice, leading to 'individual ministerial fiefdoms' that are 'basically accountable to no one' (Wilford and Wilson 2006: 30–31).

used to 'manipulate ethnic spatial relations' rather than deliver social justice (Yiftachel 1998: 400). Territorial control is of key physical and symbolic importance, as reflected in ethnic segregation (Ghanem 2009; McDowell 2012; Yiftachel and Yacobi 2003). Ethnocracies can feature democratic principles and legislative frameworks, yet these are only employed insofar as they do not harm the interests of the ethnic group(s) in power (Bollens 2009: 82).

The ethnocratic regime has typically afforded preference to a dominant ethnic group over others in the population. This type of regime can be found worldwide: in Sri Lanka (McDowell 2012), Israel/Palestine (Ghanem 2009; Ní Cheallacháin 2010; Yiftachel 1995, 2006) and Bosnia (Howard 2012), for instance, as well as the pre-conflict hegemonic Unionist regime in Northern Ireland.[8] Unlike the typical definition, post-Agreement Northern Ireland does not have one majority ethnic group ruling over a minority group, but rather two competing ethnonational blocs within a power-sharing government. However, it fits the other criteria for ethnocratic states laid out by scholars: resource allocation and territorial contest are framed through ethnosectarian logic, politics are polarised and prevailing legal and economic frameworks are only employed to the extent they do not harm the interests of power (in this case, Sinn Féin and the DUP). Rather than holding to the rhetoric of equality, transformation and reconciliation espoused in the Agreement, political actors are instead more concerned with competition over resources and territory. In turn, these dynamics are reflected in the way space is used and developed: how policy around land use is interpreted, how planning decisions are negotiated and how resources are allocated. As Murtagh and Keaveney explain it, 'group rights were asserted in the political settlement but, in prioritising the claims of the old sectarian order, local politics became more competitive, especially around access to resources, not least land and housing' (2006: 190).

Territoriality and contestation over communal 'rights' to space have become endemic to post-ceasefire policy and planning. From the top down, actors of power, whether they be political elites, paramilitaries or community development elites, often continue to attempt to enforce control over specific geographical areas. In practice, this means policy and planning reflects sectarian interests rather than legislative frameworks. Indeed, the Equality Commission noted that Section 75 is 'regularly flouted [by politicians] to the extent the duties are currently ineffective in key policy' (ECNI 2018: 2). This became clear during

---

[8] The Northern Irish state, founded in 1921, was constructed to have a Protestant/Unionist majority and a Catholic/Nationalist minority, resulting in Protestants/Unionists in a position of political power in the government, and allowing for the discrimination of Catholics in jobs, housing and electoral rights (Breen-Smyth 2008: 2; Bew et al. 1996: 57).

the Girdwood Barracks redevelopment. Concerns over loss of territory and of electoral clout from elements of Unionism subverted the prescriptions of Section 75, stalling the provision of social housing in North Belfast. The rhetoric of 'good relations' (ensuring 'shared space' through Unionist access to the site) was deployed over equality (documented Catholic/Nationalist social housing need). This is despite the Northern Ireland Act's proviso that a public body cannot hide behind the idea of 'good relations' in order to avoid statutory equality duties, nor practise discrimination in policymaking (NIO 1998b: 38–39).

Consociational theorist Sartori warned that 'if you reward divisions and divisiveness ... you increase and eventually heighten divisions and divisiveness' (1997: 72). The rise to power of the DUP and Sinn Féin, who control the devolved Assembly and whose politics are described by some community members as 'tribal' (Hall 2015b: 13), has made for increasingly puerile decision-making. Before the Assembly collapsed in 2017, Sinn Féin and the DUP controlled 62 per cent of the vote in Stormont, allowing for 'brute majoritarianism' and the 'crowding out' of smaller parties (Nolan 2014: 142; BBC News 2017c). Both parties also regularly used the Assembly's 'petition of concern' mechanism to block decisions they disagreed with, garnering claims of abuse (Smyth 2016).[9] The day-to-day operation of Stormont was often characterised by 'stalemate and inertia' (Cochrane and Dunn 2002: 4) as the two parties battled for an 'equal' share of resources and, in turn, political legitimacy.

Legitimacy in Northern Irish politics is derived from within, rather than across, communities (Hayward and Komarova 2014: 788). This runs counter to the Agreement's stated aims of 'rigorous impartiality' in governance on behalf of all the people, across diverse identities (NIO 1998a: 4). It also undermines typical concepts of democracy, whereby citizens are seen as individuals to be wooed by a variety of competing political parties. Instead, most political parties draw their support from a specific ethnic group: by representing the exclusive interests of 'their community', they maintain political authority and gain electoral support. Any move towards intergroup cooperation or compromise could be seen as capitulation by their electorate, resulting in a loss of political power. This has led to what is termed 'ethnic outbidding', whereby parties will 'almost always' draw on an identity-based framework, portraying themselves as

---

[9] The petition of concern has been used in the past to block equality initiatives, like equal marriage. It was used on a regular basis: a *Detail* investigation found that the petition of concern was used 115 times in the period 2011–2016, 86 times by the DUP and 29 times each by Sinn Féin and the SDLP. Abuse of this power can occur since there is no criterion for tabling a petition of concern other than the signatures of 30 MLAs. Subsequent promises to reform the practice have culminated in the New Decade, New Approach (2020) deal's commitment to reduce the use of the petition (ECNI 2018: 31; Northern Ireland Executive 2015: 52; NIO 2022a; Smyth 2016; Walker 2017).

the 'true defenders' of a particular ethnic group and calling into question the ability of intra-group rivals to do so (Gormley-Heenan and MacGinty 2008: 44; Moore et al., 2014: 163).

The rise of Sinn Féin and the DUP as partners in government heightened this dynamic. These 'ethnic entrepreneurs' have come to understand that making an effort to appeal to the opposing bloc, or to deliver on the peacebuilding rhetoric of 'sharing' and 'integration', is counter-productive to their power base (Evans and Tonge 2009: 1012; Murtagh 2013: 2). As one community worker stated: 'Look at the DUP and Sinn Féin. Their expertise is in the politics of division, and that is where they get their votes. Why would either of those parties be committed to change, if it could have a detrimental impact on their electoral base?' (Hall 2015a: 13). Indeed, Bean notes that 'a society whose politics and consociational institutions are structured around communal division will ensure that the politics of actors in the region will ... continue to revolve around resource allocation and the recognition of identities' (2007: 7). In practice, this actually counteracts the principles set out in the Good Friday Agreement and the Northern Ireland Act, which are based on the rhetoric of equality, reconciliation and peacebuilding in governance.

These dynamics can be found, increasingly, in other societies – and not simply those divided along ethnosectarian lines. The same toxic cocktail of place-based identity politics and resource entitlement is evident in other places. For instance, as politics grows more polarised in the United States, the same sense of 'outbidding' exists. If politicians fail to adhere to the accepted script or move outside the liberal/conservative divide towards a sense of compromise, they risk not only losing face but losing power. Divisions are thus reinscribed and entrenched between two intrinsically polarised communities. The 2016 elections in the United States for instance, saw Donald Trump's discourses playing on the insecurities of people in places with little economic opportunity by placing them in relation to a pernicious 'Other'. Identity politics and the politics of division makes sense for those in power.

In all of this, in Belfast and further afield, the material welfare of the people on the ground, those who support the politicians and those who don't, is forgotten in the squabbles. Unemployment, deprivation, poor mental and physical health persist. Elite-level bickering over territory and power occurs in government, but politicians do not deliver basic services. The result is that good policy and planning isn't realised. Resources remain an abstract to be battled over, whilst constituents don't see the tangible resources they need to live good lives. Very little changes for people on the ground, whether in Belfast or the Rust Belt, despite their ostensible political allegiances. Discourse around identity, territory and belonging obfuscates the fact that political decision-making among elites is often not concerned with improving the everyday.

Backroom Dealings in Northern Ireland

Wherever it takes place, governance involves both formal and informal systems of decision-making and implementation:

> The formal systems are embodied in constitutions, commercial codes, administrative regulations and laws, civil service procedures, judicial structures, and so on. Their features are readily observable through written documents, physical structures ... and public events (e.g., elections, parliamentary hearings, state-of-the-union addresses, city council meetings, legal proceedings).
>
> The informal systems, by contrast, are based on implicit and unwritten understandings. They reflect socio-cultural norms and routines, and underlying patterns of interactions among socio-economic classes and ethnic groups. Their manifestations are less easily noticed and identified. (Brinkerhoff and Goldsmith 2002: 1)

A closer look at the formal system of governance in Northern Ireland – based on the consociational model and reinforced by a wide array of equality, good relations and anti-poverty legislation – reveals the influence of the informal, which is more concerned with ethnocratic politics and ethnosectarian contests over space, resources, power and authority. As Komarova observes, in Northern Ireland, 'political discourse is underscored by hidden transcripts of private and public deals, favours, cultural traditions, and demagogic posturing' (2008: 24).

All politics and planning share this tendency for 'up-front' rationality and a 'backstage' where decisions inconsistent with 'public posturing' prevail (Dixon 2002: 733). Flyvbjerg notes that, 'a rationalised front does not necessarily imply dishonesty. It is not unusual to find individuals, organisations, whole societies actively believing their own rationalisations' (1998: 228). So, too, all societies to some extent rely on informal machinations, covert relationships and backroom dealings in the exercise of power. In the case of urban planning, certainly, any new development must deal with the intertangling of local and national agendas, public and private actors and the interests of both developers and residents in order to arrive at a final consensus (Forester 2001: 72). Negotiation, compromise and agreement are always part of the practical exercise of power.

This influences how resource competition works. In Northern Ireland, there is clear evidence of 'zero-sum' politics where a perceived gain for one side is a loss for the other, and resources must be divvied up equally between the two main groups. However, politics must also concern the 'forging of relationships' between actors, bringing about a 'convergence of interests so that the government can function' (Finlayson 2007: 545). These relationships are conditional, contingent and continually responding to changing interests in the name of political expediency. For example, whilst Sinn Féin and the DUP have radically different ideological aims and political aspirations, they must come to some kind of grudging consensus to maintain power, ensuring smaller parties and other agents (like PPR) do not gain political traction. Plöger notes that 'actors do not have to share substantial ideals, values or preferences, but they have to negotiate and reach a consensus as a common platform for the process to move on' (2004: 78). This can be achieved through tactics including partnership, trade-off, contract or 'tug of war'. Therefore, within the framework of post-ceasefire legislation, a series of 'backroom' standoffs, trade-offs and agreements have occurred in relation to policy and planning.

These dynamics can be observed in the Assembly's different approaches to the redevelopment of formerly militarised sites in the post-Agreement period. The handover of military bases and sites from the British government to the Office of the First Minister and Deputy First Minister (OFMDFM) initially occurred in 2003 and 2004 under the Reinvestment and Reform Initiative. This was on the proviso that these sites would be used to benefit the peace process. In addition to Girdwood, sites like the former Maze/Long Kesh prison and Ebrington, Malone and Magherafelt Army Barracks became available for investment and development. In practice, the economic and social regeneration envisioned for these spaces has been uneven, with some spaces falling prey to sectarian stalemate and others pushing ahead in response to both favourable economic conditions and political expediency (Donnelly 2011: 2; Rutherford 2011).

Recalling elements of the Girdwood redevelopment, the Maze/Long Kesh prison site was a symbolic battleground for a series of zero-sum trade-offs that eventually ended in stalemate. Proposals for the largest publicly owned regeneration site in Northern Ireland had initially centred on a multi-sport stadium and events venue and an 'International Centre for Conflict Transformation' (ICCT) situated around some of the old prison buildings (OFMDFM 2006: 6). This was interpreted as 'political horse-trading' whereby Unionist economic interests were set to balance Republican interests in preserving part of the prison, including the hospital where hunger striker Bobby Sands died and an H-block that housed Republican prisoners (*Belfast Telegraph* 2013; Flynn 2011: 390).[10] Initially the OFMDFM published a Masterplan for the 'shared-out' compromise and tasked a development corporation with realising the plan. However, ire among some elements of Unionist at the ICCT, perceived as a 'shrine to terrorism', scuppered any form of development. Today, the 347-acre site hosts an agricultural fair once a year and otherwise lies unoccupied – a poor use of a historic and potentially transformational

---

[10] These are pivotal events and spaces in the Republican collective narrative of the Troubles.

parcel of land. According to the development corporation's website during my fieldwork – and still, at the time of writing six years later – 'development of the site is currently subject to Ministerial agreement on the way forward'.[11] In this case, negotiation fell through to sectarian stasis.

The former Ebrington Barracks, in Derry, has arguably fared better in its regeneration. The 26-acre site, including 14 listed buildings, formerly oversaw military command of a quarter of the province during the Troubles (BBC News 2012a). The OFMDFM and the DSD passed ownership of the site to the Ilex Urban Regeneration Company in 2003 (Donnelly 2011: 15). In an analysis of former sites, the Northern Ireland Audit Office noted that using an independent regeneration company meant that clearly defined business plans, measurements and objectives for the site were in evidence (Donnelly 2011: 30). It also meant increased emphasis on private sector involvement in the site.

Ebrington's redevelopment benefited from Derry's designation as UK City of Culture in 2013 and the opening of the 'Peace Bridge', part of an ambitious effort to extend civic space by connecting the largely Catholic/Nationalist 'Cityside' area with Ebrington Barracks and the Protestant/Unionist 'Waterside' area across the river (Hocking 2015: 144). Derry's City of Culture award inspired an emphasis on culture-led regeneration as a means to promote peacebuilding *and* economic development (Boland et al. 2016), and Ebrington was at the centre of this vision.[12] Hocking optimistically refers to this Barracks site as 'an example of the evolving Northern Irish public sphere and the vision of citizenship it may encourage', and in reference to the emphasis on culture-led economic regeneration, 'an arena where citizenship is increasingly defined by hierarchies of cultural and material productions and consumptions' (2015: 20, 144) rather than by ethnicity alone.

On the one hand, as the following chapters will indicate, the results of this culture- and consumption-led approach to regeneration can be piecemeal and uneven. However, the Ebrington Barracks have played host to the opening concert for the City of Culture programme, contemporary art installations, the BBC Radio Rock Festival, the 'Peace One Day' concert, the Turner Prize awards and the 2013 All-Ireland Fleadh Cheoil na hÉireann, an internationally renowned Irish traditional music festival. These events all brought huge public involvement and thousands of people into the Barracks space across the ethnosectarian divide (Hocking 2015: 148; Keenan 2013; McLaughlin 2012). In 2016, planning permission was granted for housing, offices, cafés and restaurants on the site (Stewart and Deeney 2016; McKeown 2017a). And

---

[11] See mazelongkesh.com.
[12] Derry was awarded the first-ever title of 'UK City of Culture' in 2013 after a highly competitive bidding process. It involved a calendar year's worth of events and 'cultural regeneration' (Derry City and Strabane District Council 2014).

although the COVID-19 pandemic caused delays in construction, work began in 2022 on The Ebrington, a £15 million, 152-bedroom hotel (McKinney 2022; BBC News 2020a). These developments speak to some measure of social and economic regeneration facilitated by the private sector and, perhaps, by the Barracks' location in Derry, where the issue of territoriality is arguably less acute than in the highly divided and demographically vulnerable spaces of North Belfast.

The OFMDFM sold off two other barracks sites in the wake of demilitarisation. The first, Malone Barracks, was initially valued at up to £5 million due to its desirable location in South Belfast. Its sale attracted controversy when a 2011 Northern Ireland Audit Office report revealed the site had been sold by the OFMDFM for £1.2 million less than its initial valuation, without planning permission, and was resold on the same day to a private development company (Public Accounts Committee 2012; Rutherford 2011). The Audit Office was unable to establish the sale price of the latter. By 2005, this private developer had been granted planning permission for luxury apartments and penthouses, setting 'a new high for property pricing per square foot' in Belfast (Donnelly 2011: 21). The Magherafelt Barracks in mid-Ulster were also sold, this time to the North Eastern Education and Library Board for a new primary school. In contrast to the former sale, this time the OFMDFM considered that 'under government accounting rules' it would not be possible to give the school the site in exchange for the sale of the old school's land (Rutherford 2011). A lengthy process of deliberation and valuation of the land resulted, with the final sale completed in 2010. The delay of the process was critiqued for negatively impacting the local area and wasting public-sector funds (Donnelly 2011: 26). It is unclear why the OFMDFM allowed the former site's sale to go ahead while the latter's dragged on for close to seven years. According to the 2011 Audit Office report, it is also unclear how the proceeds from both sales have been used to benefit the peace process, given that this was one of the original caveats of the Reinvestment and Reform Initiative. One can only speculate as to the 'backroom' dealings and negotiations behind these sales.

The same Audit Office report highlighted deficiencies that these demilitarised sites, the Girdwood redevelopment and broader policymaking and planning had in common. Auditors experienced difficulty in obtaining records from the OFMDFM, eliciting wider concerns about transparency and inefficiency in service delivery. They recommended that high standards of accountability be enforced so that departments might allocate resources effectively and enact 'robust, evidence-based policy' (Donnelly 2011: 6). The report also recommends clear, specific and attainable targets and objectives when designing draft Masterplans: for instance, the Audit Office pointed out that the Maze/Long Kesh draft Masterplan offered poor value for money and that aspirational rhetoric like 'the creation of 6,000 new jobs and 1,000 dwelling units' was never translated into formal delivery targets or a clear project plan by government (Donnelly 2011: 40). Unfortunately, these lessons were not taken to heart in subsequent iterations of a Masterplan for Girdwood. The following chapters will demonstrate the power-sharing government's explicit failure to adhere to these recommendations during the Girdwood process, indicting broader political dynamics in post-Agreement policymaking and planning.

All these redevelopment projects required some measure of negotiation and compromise among actors, but those delivered in contexts that were politically expedient or influenced by the private sector survived, while those that were territorially sensitive and politically contentious did not. What types of conversations, arguments, private deals and favours and other hidden transcripts occurred to shape the fate of each? The following chapters delve into these as they occurred during the Girdwood Barracks regeneration, charting the complex dynamics of formal and informal systems of decision-making that became physically inscribed into the site. The ultimate question, however, is how these dynamics undermined the rationale of the Agreement as it concerns the delivery of social justice that is blind to sectarian head-counting and demands.

CHAPTER THREE

'Frictions, Factions and Fractions'

Identity and Territory in North Belfast

In Belfast, space is controlled, claimed and imagined in countless creative and deeply divisive ways. But the city's geography has not always been so segregated. Belfast traditionally had concentrations of Protestant and Catholic populations and intermittent periods of sectarian tension, but people tended to mix freely and associate among and between neighbourhoods (Hepburn 1996; YouTube 2007). People spoke of going from the 'Catholic' Falls Road to the neighbouring 'Protestant' Shankill Road to do their shopping. The streets of North Belfast, in particular, were mixed: there were pockets of affluent doctors and lawyers; a Jewish and an Indian population;[1] and neighbourhoods of shipyard and dockworkers of both religious backgrounds. Mulholland (2019: 7) notes that Cliftonpark Avenue and adjoining 'river' streets like Roe, Avonbeg and Annalee had residents from mixed backgrounds. Further afield in North Belfast, the Housing Trust (predecessor of the Northern Ireland Housing Executive, NIHE) also built estates like White City that exemplified stable cross-community relations (Elliott 2017).[2]

In the wake of the Second World War, deindustrialisation and new plans for economic development began to reshape the geography of the city. This had a disproportionate impact on the Protestant/Unionist population, many of whom left Belfast for surrounding towns. It was not simply the Troubles, then, that created and exacerbated a sense of communal loss and territorial dissolution among elements of the Protestant population. This sense of loss shapes the way that many working-class Protestants/Unionists in Belfast, and North Belfast in particular, perceive space and territory in the present day. It shapes a sense of belonging and attachment to place and legitimises the fear

---

[1] Former president of Israel Chaim Herzog was born on Cliftonpark Avenue in 1918. His birthplace, now the headquarters of the Cliftonville Community Regeneration Forum (CCRF), was marked by a blue historical plaque until 2014, when it was taken down following several vandalism attempts.
[2] For further detail on White City pre-Troubles, see Elliott (2017).

of being pushed out of that place. And it is reflected in vitriolic territorial disputes. For instance, notions of loss and threat informed the infamous Holy Cross dispute of 2001, an example of violent clash over space in North Belfast that became the catalyst for the Girdwood redevelopment. This chapter explores the collective narrative of loss within elements of Protestant/Unionism, how it is expressed in North Belfast and how it became so instrumental to shaping discourses around 'needs', 'rights' and equality at Girdwood.

'A Protestant State': Demographic Change in Belfast

A vital centre of industry for the United Kingdom in the nineteenth and early twentieth century, Belfast bore more similarities to places like Liverpool and Glasgow than it did to the rest of Ireland. After the partition of the North from the South of Ireland in 1921, a one-party Protestant Unionist government was installed.[3] The Official Unionist party consisted of wealthy Protestant businessmen and landowners, who owned the shipbuilding and linen industries on which the economy was based. Their power was contingent on working-class support. This was achieved through preserving jobs and houses for working-class Protestants to the exclusion of Catholics. The Harland and Wolff shipyards, Mackie's textiles and munitions and the Sirocco factory were major employers: 'back then, sons stepped into their father's trade and would get a job pretty much automatically'. As one Protestant worker put it, 'you walked out of school and into the shipyard' (McKay 2000: 93). Orange Order membership further ensured cross-class cohesion and affirmation of a shared identity through Twelfth of July parades and marching season (Jarman 1997: 76). It is important to note that the advantages enjoyed by working-class Protestants were relative: days at the shipyard were dangerous and exhausting, and in general housing quality was poor. However, these advantages also fostered a sense of perceived ascendency through shared Protestant/Unionist identity to the exclusion of Catholics. Though working-class Protestants may have been in a similar economic situation to their Catholic counterparts, there was a sense of being 'ahead'. This type of shared identity rests on its opposition to the 'Other', where a sense of solidarity and civic spirit emerges from seeing the 'in-group' in relation to the 'out-group' (Catholics/Nationalists).

The decline of Unionist hegemony and the Protestant status quo in Belfast came post-Second World War. Belfast's shipbuilding, manufacturing and heavy engineering industries began a severe decline that would leave thousands

---

[3] James Craig, then-Prime Minister, is quoted as saying in 1934, 'All I boast is that we are a Protestant Parliament and Protestant State' (Bardon 1992: 538–539). This is popularly paraphrased as 'A Protestant State for a Protestant People'.

redundant in the space of a few years (Weiner 1976: 32). This disproportionately affected the Protestant working class, who accounted for the majority of skilled workers (Shirlow and McGovern 1996: 386). Between 1950 and 1994 there was a 58.4 per cent decline in manufacturing employment, and a resultant collapse in 'established, long-term intergenerational labour markets' in the sector (Shirlow and McGovern 1996: 388; Purvis et al. 2011: 11). Historically, the 'jobs for life' mentality in industrial labour followed a lack of emphasis on formal education and for some elements of the Protestant/Unionist working class, education has remained both undervalued and underappreciated (Purvis et al. 2011: 11).[4] This left them ill-equipped for the labour market, as jobs began to shift towards the public and service sectors and raised educational requirements. On the other hand, anti-discrimination legislation, including the 1976 and 1989 Fair Employment Acts (and the 1998 Northern Ireland Act), meant that a greater share of total jobs began to go to Catholics than had been the case under the hegemonic Unionist state, and trends of increasing Catholic and declining Protestant representation in the labour market look set to continue (Evershed 2018: 105). This socio-economic imbalance became one contributing factor to the narrative of collective Protestant/Unionist decline over the years.

The issue of housing also came to affect the Protestant working-class after the Second World War. A ring of ancient, decayed terraced housing circled the city centre, crammed with a high-density population (Boal 1995: 36). There was rising public dissatisfaction with the Northern Irish government's lack of action on not only housing conditions, but industrial mobilisation, widespread social deprivation and unemployment post-war (Elliott 2017: 24–25). Meanwhile, in the rest of the UK, there was a wave of modernisation, a move towards creating 'the cities of the future'. These were the days when Le Corbusier's 'streets in the sky' were in fashion and British technocrats dreamed of casting a new world in Modernist concrete. Influenced not only by trends in the rest of the UK, but by electoral considerations, Prime Minister Terence O'Neill's government commissioned Scottish architect Robert Matthew to devise a regional plan for Belfast. Like other development schemes taking place in the UK, the 1962 'Matthew Plan' called for widespread slum clearance to make way for a motorway and new housing. The Lower Falls, Shankill and Sailortown areas were slated to be razed and rebuilt. The plan laid out 'growth towns' outside of Belfast city to locate new types of industry and to decentralise the urban population; residents from slum clearance zones were encouraged to move

---

[4] High levels of unemployment among the Protestant/Unionist working class are compounded by low levels of educational attainment: using the standard measure of five 'good' GCSEs, Protestant boys with free school meal entitlement achieve less than any of the other main groups in Northern Ireland and hover near the very bottom when compared with groups in England (BBC News 2014).

there (Matthew 1962: 16; Weiner 1976: 39). This included places like Antrim, Bangor, Ballymena, Carrickfergus, Newtownards and Larne. A new 'super-city', Craigavon, was also planned between Portadown and Lurgan (Matthew 1961: 1).

In practice, the plan broke up tight-knit neighbourhoods of cramped terrace housing and old social networks. A process of depopulation began as people moved or were forced to move from their homes. Catholics tended to crowd into enclaves elsewhere in inner Belfast. The majority of those who moved outside Belfast into 'growth towns' were Protestants, and the first to move were the socially mobile – usually skilled workers with young families and higher incomes who sought to take advantage of the opportunities that property outside the city offered (Weiner 1976: 40). People were also moved to 'growth towns' with the promise they would be moved back to their former neighbourhood when the new housing was done. But by that time, people had settled in, and they didn't come back. This left an increasing residual proportion of elderly people and those without the financial or social capital to move from Protestant/Unionist neighbourhoods. One Loyalist commentator from the Lower Shankill bluntly stated, 'Anyone with any go about them got up and went. It started in the sixties and it's never stopped. If you had a decent job and could get a mortgage, would you hang about here and have your car nicked …? What's left is the poor, the defeated, the pensioners and the scumbags' (Bruce 2004: 506).

This phenomenon of deindustrialisation, migration and residualisation is no different from other industrial cities in the United Kingdom and internationally, where global economic shifts and urban redevelopment impacted local planning practices and changed the context and the skill set for employment (Murtagh 2013: 3). A knowledge- and service-based economy has replaced heavy industry. Information technology and communications have become core industries globally, along with a service economy clustered around leisure, travel and tourism (Lash and Urry 1994: 17). In the wake of deindustrialisation, cities have been redeveloped in a new way to promote these types of production and consumption (Clarke 2003: 29). In England, Scotland and Wales, for instance, widespread slum clearance took place to facilitate the building of motorways, private speculative development and sites to locate new industry. Residents in urban neighbourhoods zoned for slum clearance were moved out to council estates scattered miles from the city, with the result that social relationships were dismantled and reconfigured (Hanley 2007: 84–85). The United States, too, engaged in post-war 'urban renewal', targeting poor neighbourhoods (often those of colour) to raze and build motorways through. In this respect, and during this time, Belfast is not a city apart.

In Belfast, however, the beginnings of the Troubles in 1969 coincided with the renewal plans, and they compounded the exodus from the city. In North Belfast, perhaps the area where people once mixed most, RUC police officers were often the first to leave in response to the violence; their Protestant neighbours would then begin to drift away (*Irish News* 1993c: 9). At the same time, a young Catholic/Nationalist demographic in North Belfast continued to grow and expand, moving into formerly mixed or Protestant areas. From 1969, North Belfast has had the biggest demographic switch of any constituency from Protestant to Catholic (*Irish News* 1993c: 10). And in my fieldwork, people often estimated that the Shankill area alone had lost 50,000 people over 35 years (see Northern Visions n.d.).

In terms of housing, this created a situation of two extremes in Belfast. On the one hand, Protestant/Unionist areas tend to have low housing demand and high numbers of empty homes (DOE 2004b: 21). Areas have eventually grown derelict and blighted: in some places, whole rows of houses have been shuttered, streets strewn with debris and paramilitary graffiti. In other places, properties have been demolished, leaving wasteland or open fields. This has resulted in cultural pessimism and a sense of beleaguerment for those left behind. On the other hand, Catholic/Nationalist areas like Ardoyne, Cliftonville and New Lodge have experienced high social housing demand and higher levels of housing stress, in particular among young families.[5] By 2000, four out of five applicants classified as being in urgent housing need were from the Catholic community and also experienced higher waiting times than their Protestant counterparts (NIHE 2000: 18).[6] One community worker related that 'families are in hostels, others are split up between relatives, mothers and fathers are sleeping on floors' (*North Belfast News* 2000a: 11). Along the interfaces, Catholic/Nationalist housing is crowded right up to the walls.

As demographics have shifted in favour of the Catholic population, this has encouraged a sense of being 'under siege' for some elements of the Protestant/Unionist population – that the decline of Protestants has resulted in the incursion or encroachment of Catholics into traditionally Protestant territory.[7] Catholics/Nationalists are thereby perceived to literally be gaining ground as boundaries between areas begin to shift. Loyalist leader Billy Hutchinson explained:

> On the one hand we have a young and vibrant Nationalist community rapidly growing and pushing towards the boundaries which divide so many areas of Northern Ireland. On the other hand, we are faced

---

[5] At the time of Girdwood's demilitarisation, young Catholic families represented 44 per cent of those in urgent need (NIHE 2000: 18; DOE 2004b: 20, 45)

[6] I use statistics from this time period to create context for Girdwood's development and to show that social housing need had been documented at crisis level for years.

[7] In the 2011 Census, for the first time, the proportion of the population describing themselves as Protestant fell below 50 per cent (NISRA 2011).

Fig. 3.1 Note the empty green space on the Unionist side of the wall, whereas on the other side, Nationalist houses have been built up to the boundary line.

with a Unionist community constantly shrinking, becoming old and demoralised. Lack of confidence, incapable leadership, fear and intimidation have driven Unionists further and further back in the North Belfast area and have helped to facilitate a rapidly dwindling population. (*North Belfast News* 2000b: 7)

Some elements of the Protestant/Unionist population perceived the rising Catholic/Nationalist population to be a Republican conspiracy to drive them from their areas (Heatley 2004). People were afraid that they would be forced out of places they had long considered home. The fate of the Torrens estate in North Belfast, for example, is a touchstone in Protestant/Unionist collective memory. Many people I conversed with in the course of my fieldwork cited Torrens when they spoke of their fears for North Belfast – 'we don't want another Torrens happening' was the consensus.

Torrens was a Protestant/Unionist enclave of about 100 families within a largely Catholic/Nationalist area of North Belfast. Tensions in the estate had been high during the 1996 Drumcree riots, where struggles around Unionist parading and the right to space were played out at the micro-level. Forced evictions, violence and intimidation on both sides ensued (Jarman 1996). A campaign of sectarian intimidation of the Protestant families in Torrens followed, including offensive graffiti, verbal abuse, physical assault and petrol bombs (Simpson 2004). In 2004, the last ten families departed the estate – a symbolic exodus. 91-year-old Protestant resident Betsy McClenaghan told one reporter at the time: 'I have come through the [Second World War] blitzes and the 1932 riots but I've never known an upheaval like it' (McCartney 2004). In collective memory, the loss of Torrens remains palpable.

The peace process compounded the sense of dispossession for many working-class Protestants. In the wake of the Agreement, the Northern Ireland Life and Times Survey found that only 1 per cent of Protestants believed that the Agreement benefited Unionists more than Nationalists and an increasing number, nearly two-thirds, felt that it benefited Nationalists more than Unionists (ARK 1998, 2001). From their perspective, the negotiations had brought political gains for Catholics/Nationalists but had led to their own marginalisation (Hayward and Mitchell 2003; Shirlow and Murtagh 2006: 7). According to a 2000 *North Belfast News* feature, the prevailing attitude at that time was that '[Protestant/Unionist] Loyalists are increasingly becoming more concerned at what they see as concessions towards Republicans. They see two Sinn Féin ministers in government without the IRA having handed over everything. Loyalists do not believe that Republicans have made any attempt to build trust within the Protestant community' (2000a: 2). For some, the Nationalist community was seen as 'swaggering and self-confident ... winning the political, territorial and demographic game' (*The Telegraph* 2002).

The notion of physical and symbolic Catholic/Nationalist 'growth' and Protestant/Unionist 'decline' has become the major discourse in post-Agreement Northern Ireland. The perception of Catholic 'encroachment' upon Protestant territory feeds a 'siege mentality' whereby losing territory also means a threat to culture and identity. These perspectives of alienation, displacement and fear bolstered the rise of the initially anti-Agreement DUP as the largest political party in Northern Ireland post-ceasefire. The DUP have used discourses of exclusion to reinforce these feelings of loss and consolidate power among a disaffected electorate (Murtagh et al. 2008: 47).[8]

Discourses of fear were also deployed by some Loyalist paramilitary groups in the post-Agreement period, reinforcing dynamics of division and leading to vitriolic disputes over space. One Nationalist community worker recalled that 'North Belfast in the early noughties, with the ceasefires ... was not only traumatised [by the conflict] but heavily carved up by different paramilitary

---

[8] Murtagh et al. (2008) note that a similar discursive process has been used by the DUP's Nationalist/Republican counterpart, Sinn Féin.

factions trying to control it on a sectarian divide as well' ('Jim', interview with author 2016).

The Ulster Defence Association/Ulster Freedom Fighters (UFF) C Company paramilitary group, for instance, controlled the Lower Shankill estate, adjacent to the Girdwood Barracks and North Belfast. They are alleged to have influenced the infamous Holy Cross dispute. Holy Cross was a milestone moment in North Belfast's recent history and a critical piece in the run-up to the Girdwood Barracks' regeneration. Between September and December of 2001, Protestant/Unionist protesters from Upper Ardoyne blocked the road to the Holy Cross primary school, attended by Catholic girls aged 4–11 from nearby Ardoyne (Gallaher and Shirlow 2006: 151). The violence that the dispute caused was one of the catalysts for Girdwood's initial development, and the conflict over space and territory that Holy Cross reflected was physically expressed throughout Girdwood's later regeneration process.

The UDA's C Company was led by Johnny Adair; under his direction, they are thought to have been responsible for at least 29 murders, including 12 sectarian killings of Catholic civilians (Gallaher and Shirlow 2006: 156). Adair was also allegedly involved in widespread drug-dealing and racketeering within the Lower Shankill area. His behaviour inflamed relations with other Unionist paramilitary elements: in 2000 and again in 2002, Adair sparked feuds with the UVF and with other elements of the UDA, resulting in deaths and dozens of people forcibly evicted or burnt out from the Lower Shankill and adjacent Lower Oldpark (Wood 2006: 249). In turn, supporters of C Company were evicted from the Shankill Road and many moved to the Upper Ardoyne area of North Belfast.[9] Over 900 people were forced from their homes as a result of the feud (McDonald 2000).

The Upper Ardoyne area is predominantly Protestant/Unionist, separated from the Catholic/Nationalist Ardoyne neighbourhood by an interface barrier. Upper Ardoyne had lost half its population from about 3,000 residents in 1971 to around 1,500 in 1991 and the average age was concentrated more heavily in the over-60 group, while Ardoyne had a younger, continually growing population (Shirlow 2003b: 83; *Irish News* 1993a: 9). Again, Protestant communities were ageing and declining whilst the Catholic demographic continued to rise year on year.[10] This was a psychological blow to areas like Upper Ardoyne. Amongst

---

[9] Upper Ardoyne is a Protestant/Unionist area of North Belfast that includes the smaller micro-neighbourhoods of Glenbryn, Alliance, Hesketh and Wheatfield. Upper Ardoyne was also identified as Glenbryn during the Holy Cross dispute, as the protests started at the corner of Glenbryn Park. However, 'Upper Ardoyne' will be used in reference to the area as a whole to eliminate confusion.

[10] The Census tracked the percentage of self-identifying Catholics as 38 per cent of Belfast's population in 1981, 42 per cent in 1991 and 47 per cent in 2001, a year-on-year rise (Melaugh and McKenna n.d.).

the residents there, there was a palpable fear that the burgeoning Catholic/ Nationalist population in Ardoyne wanted to move the 'peace wall' that divided the two areas and take over Protestant homes – 'Protestants genuinely felt this was an orchestrated campaign to drive them from Ardoyne' (Cadwallader 2004: 196; Heatley 2004; McDonald 2001). The decline of the nearby Wheatfield primary school further reinforced 'a sense of cultural dissipation and betrayal' (Shirlow 2003b: 83). Unionists 'felt they were being pushed out [of North Belfast] on several different levels' ('Jim', interview with author 2016).

These feelings sparked the Holy Cross protest in 2001, where a gauntlet of Protestant/Unionist protesters lined the route that Catholic/Nationalist schoolgirls and their parents took to the Holy Cross primary school each day, just across the interface. According to participants, their protest was not directed specifically at the schoolgirls but at their parents in response to several sectarian attacks against the Upper Ardoyne area. When protesters were interviewed by the media, their reasons for participating reflected the attacks and the broader fear of territorial dissolution. One pensioner said angrily: 'I came from Ardoyne, down there and I was burned out of my house, and I moved up here, and now they want us out of here. There's no way are we moving, *no way* are we moving'.

Another woman added, 'IRA/Sinn Féin, they've stepped up their campaign to … intimidate us out of our homes … and the parents from the Holy Cross and the IRA are using their children as cover to attack the people in this area' (YouTube 2013). However, the scenes of sectarian intimidation at the protest were difficult to reconcile with this argument. For three months, the school's young pupils, accompanied by their parents and surrounded by police protection, were subject to a daily barrage of abuse by protesters: 'they were jeered at and taunted, spat on and shown lurid pornographic pictures … the protesters also threw stones, bottles, balloons filled with urine, fireworks and other projectiles (including on one occasion a homemade grenade)' (Gilligan 2009: 32). Media reports showed terrified young girls cowering from an angry crowd behind police riot shields.

There were allegations that the roots of Holy Cross lay in the expulsion of C Company members from the Lower Shankill Road, and that elements of C Company had ramped up the protest to undermine the peace process, expand their influence and provoke Republican reaction (Shirlow 2012: 117). One Ardoyne resident observed that 'last year there was a new group of people who moved into the area. We called them "new kids on the block" – they were UDA families expelled from the Shankill Road by the UVF during the loyalist feud. They are the ones behind all this trouble' (McDonald 2001).

Elements of the UDA were able to wield influence and legitimise their actions by drawing on the wider narrative of 'siege' and fear of territorial dissolution prevalent within the area. Yet other Loyalist paramilitaries and politicians in North Belfast distanced themself from the protest and officially condemned the use of blast bombs and violence (BBC News 2001).

A month before the protest ended, the DSD announced a housing redevelopment programme for Upper Ardoyne. This investment's aim was to regenerate run-down Protestant areas to attract new residents and improve poor housing, especially along the interface. However, it was seen as an attempt to persuade the protesters to end the dispute (Campbell 2003). The move was met with anger among elements of Catholic/Nationalist North Belfast. At that time, the North Belfast Housing Strategy recognised that 'Catholic communities are characterised by ... higher waiting lists and longer waiting times for housing' (NIHE 2000: 12) because of insufficient housing stock. It stated that Catholic households made up three-quarters of the waiting lists and that there was an over-representation of family applicants classified as in 'urgent need' (NIHE 2000: 17–18). Sinn Féin councillor Margaret McClenaghan remarked: 'Nationalist housing in North Belfast is chronically overcrowded and under-funded, yet here we are with [Upper Ardoyne] having millions pumped into it' (Heatley 2004). It seemed that the protestors had been temporarily placated by the investment, but the broader issues that sparked the protest were left unaddressed.

Community Development and the Dunlop Report

In another move to invest in community and economic development in North Belfast after Holy Cross, the OFMDFM commissioned the NBCAP in December 2001. According to a Nationalist community worker, this was because, 'despite the peace process, there was trouble going on, people getting killed, injured, you had the Orange marches, you had the Holy Cross dispute ... [North Belfast] was a powder keg and there was political fear that this would unravel the peace process' ('Liam', interview with author 2016).

In this context, the remit of the NBCAP was to produce a report on major social and economic issues plaguing North Belfast, like deprivation, division and unemployment, and to make recommendations to address them. The NBCAP consisted of representatives from different churches and all the main political parties in North Belfast (NBCAP 2002: 6; Girdwood Advisory Panel Secretariat 2006: 5). They submitted the Dunlop Report[11] to the OFMDFM and DSD in May 2002. The report was blunt: 'there is no substitute for visiting some of the most troubled areas and hearing and seeing firsthand what it is like to live there'. It described the poor quality of life and the stories of 'conflict, anger and stress' that Project members had encountered during their research

---

[11] The Report was named after one of its main authors, Rev. Dr John Dunlop, a Presbyterian minister.

(NBCAP 2002: 10). Its tone was urgent: 'North Belfast has the capacity to absorb resources, destroy people, impoverish children and destabilise other parts of Northern Ireland', and it must be considered a priority case for intervention (NBCAP 2002: 7). The Dunlop Report specifically addressed territoriality as 'arguably the most contentious issue in North Belfast', pointing to the overcrowding and demand for housing on the Nationalist side and the declining Protestant population with its feeling of being 'squeezed out' (2002: 60). Among its other observations were the poor physical and mental health, low educational attainment, unemployment, lack of inward investment, and lack of youth facilities in North Belfast, as well as chronic sectarian interface violence (2002: 60–61).

A key theme of the Dunlop Report was 'community capacity', defined as 'the ability and will of people who live in a locality to act collectively for their common good' (NBCAP 2002: 48). It suggested that community capacity-building in North Belfast could be achieved through empowerment, participation and partnerships (2002: 48). If the different neighbourhoods of North Belfast were introduced to sustainable funding mechanisms, cooperative networks and support for leadership development, this would improve the way in which resources were allocated and used. A Nationalist community worker observed:

> What they were saying was that local people were not only distanced and disconnected from statutory authorities, and government, but they were also not really tuning in to what was happening in communities, they thought that community groups were not accessible. So, the idea was … to try and make sure that there was a genuine participating model of community development in place. ('Liam', interview with author 2016)

The Dunlop Report recommended the establishment of 'Community Economic Partnerships' (CEPs), a new model of community development that would engage with local people and rise above inter- and intra-communal politics.

The CEPs were focused on building effective leadership, improving knowledge of funding and facilitating dialogue along the interfaces (NBCAP 2002: 76–77). There were many diverse community groups working in North Belfast at that time; the idea was to designate a key group as lead partner for each area, then all the other smaller groups in the area would amalgamate around it (author fieldnotes 2016). The lead group would distribute money to the smaller groups in the area, encouraging greater intra- and inter-community cooperation and capacity-building. There were nine geographical CEPs and four thematic CEPs around leadership, advice centres and community transformation ('Jim', interview with author 2016; Mac Bride 2008: 40).

The OFMDFM set up an overarching organisation, the North Belfast Community Action Unit (NBCAU), to oversee the CEPs. The NBCAU was an attempt to create a joined-up approach within government to deliver the Dunlop Report's recommendations. However, according to one community worker involved in the CEPs:

> It threw together civil servants from all different departments and from the Housing Executive as well to sit on one kind of joint body which would then administer this money and which would in theory go back and tweak policy delivery and strategic thinking to regenerate interface communities in Belfast. What the NBCAU became was like a palm-off where government kind of thought well, that's North Belfast sorted, we've set up that little NBCAU, they hand out money to the community, problem taken care of. ('Jim', interview with author 2016)

In another community worker's opinion, 'Basically, what they did was they gave money for diversionary-type activities and capacity-type activities and what they called "empowerment activities". However, there was no real evaluation of the impact of any of the investment, and there were no real indicators for "what does empowerment mean"' ('Maurice', interview with author 2016).

An evaluation of the CEP programme later noted that the capacity for cross-community work had been achieved to a certain extent but that some groups were more effective than others (Murtagh et al. 2009: 6). However, because the CEPs were geographically based, in some cases this increased a sense of territoriality and undermined cooperation – producing 'twelve empires' rather than one working for all of North Belfast (Murtagh et al. 2009: 2). The report further details that some CEPs were 'engrossed in a culture of territorialism, influenced by continual resource competition … and some CEPs sensed a threat from other CEPs and community groups' (2009: 20). This contradicts the Dunlop Report's rhetoric of partnership, pointing instead to continued contestation over resources and territory. It is worth noting that this occurred not only between Unionist and Nationalist areas, but within them. One respondent further explained: 'what happened in practice was that some localised groups felt vulnerable to the way the Dunlop Report was structured. And they wanted to become the dominant civil society organisation in their community. So they publicly thwarted each other and competed to undermine each other' ('Jim', interview with author 2016).

'Jim' gave the example of a training programme delivered by one of the CEPs; it was poorly attended because:

> This thwarted these localised CEPs who wanted to have control of their own training programmes. So they refused to signpost anybody from their community to [another group's] training programmes, because they didn't wait to validate this approach and they didn't want to be seen

giving recruits to [another group], because then [the other group] could get bigger funding for training programmes that they wanted to access. ('Jim', interview with author 2016)

In practice, this meant the rhetoric of improving community capacity and partnership was frustrated by 'a parochial agenda' centred on competing claims to legitimacy, representation and funding (BCDA 2013: 10). It also suggests that, despite the idea of 'community empowerment', or engaging local residents in improving their lives, this was in reality influenced by gatekeepers in some of the CEPs. The latter controlled whether people could access particular opportunities, given the impact on their own programmes and potential access to funding. Effectively, aspirational rhetoric was thwarted by the thorny reality of not only inter- but intra-group resource competition. This arguably impacted on the aims of leadership, dialogue and capacity-building on which the CEPs were premised.

Another of the Dunlop Report's key recommendations was 'to encourage Government to develop a major site involving mixed-usage to serve as a symbol of hope and economic regeneration for North Belfast' (NBCAP 2002: 83). It defined mixed usage as including housing and facilities for education, recreational and commercial pursuits that would bridge the ethnosectarian divide (NBCAP 2002: 83). The Report also recommended establishing a transformative civic space for North Belfast, like a centre for citizenship and/or peacebuilding (NBCAP 2002: 86). The Report identified the Crumlin Road Gaol and Courthouse as a potential site, along with the adjacent Girdwood Army Barracks if it was demilitarised. In 2003, the British government closed the prison and transferred ownership to the Northern Irish government under the Reinvestment and Reform Initiative. A project team was set up within the NBCAU to discuss the future of the site (NBCAU 2005: 1). The courthouse was purchased by a private developer. Discussions began around the potential these two sites to deliver on the Dunlop Report's recommendations, given their proximity to Belfast city centre and their potential as economic catalyst and tourist attractions.

As part of a process of 'normalisation', the Girdwood Army Barracks were demilitarised in 2005 and ownership passed to the DSD (Switzer and McDowell 2009: 341; NBCAU 2005: 1). Combined with the Crumlin Road Gaol and Courthouse, this represented 27 acres of public land for development (Girdwood Advisory Panel Secretariat 2006: 18). As an imagined space, the development neatly fit the rhetoric of 'economic growth' and 'place-centred investment' that characterised urban regeneration post-ceasefire. It was envisioned that a 'mixed-use space' would draw investment and create jobs for North Belfast, like redevelopments in other parts of Belfast taking place at the time. It also fit the Dunlop Report's recommendation for a major development with a transformative peacebuilding component.

However, the location was tricky. As one community worker commented, 'anywhere else in the world, [Girdwood] would be prime land but because of its location [in North Belfast], to have it work and to make everyone happy was nigh impossible' (author fieldnotes 2015).

Girdwood and the Crumlin Road Gaol functioned as an effective buffer zone between four neighbourhoods highly segregated by ethnicity: two Catholic/Nationalist areas (Cliftonville and New Lodge) with high housing need and two Protestant/Unionist areas (Lower Shankill and Lower Oldpark) with high levels of blight caused by population decline. The Cliftonpark Avenue interface wall separating Cliftonville and Lower Oldpark sat directly across from the barracks. All these neighbourhoods were economically marginalised and had experienced disproportionate violence during the Troubles. The space was a microcosm of the demographic, territorial and political tensions that characterised Belfast as a whole. In one sense, though, this presented a hugely significant opportunity to put the rhetoric of the Agreement and the Dunlop Report into practice, and to encourage a meaningful societal and spatial transformation. Deliberations around the site moved ahead.

A 'New Northern Ireland'

In March 2006, the Girdwood Advisory Panel was formed to advise on the master planning process and undertake public consultation for the Crumlin Road Gaol/Girdwood site. The aim was to produce a draft Masterplan by December 2006. Roy Adams, co-author of the Dunlop Report and Chief Executive of Building Design Partnership (BDP), an architecture firm, was chair of the Panel. Membership consisted of elected representatives nominated by the leaders of each of the four main political parties (the DUP, Sinn Féin, the Catholic/Nationalist Social Democratic Labour Party (SDLP) and the Ulster Unionist Party (UUP). There were also community representatives nominated by the Ardoyne and Marrowbone, Cliftonville, Greater New Lodge, Lower North, Upper North and Greater Shankill CEPs, and statutory representatives including the Chief Executives of the Community Relations Council and Laganside Corporation, the Director of Economic Development, Belfast City Council, the heads of the NBCAU and the Strategic Investment Board (Adams 2006a: 5). The head of the NBCAU was Tim Losty, a civil servant formerly of the Northern Ireland Bureau, who served as a 'political broker' for the Unit between the DUP and Sinn Féin, who had by this point eclipsed the more moderate UUP and SDLP as the major players in the power-sharing government. At this time in the development, the NBCAU itself had been transferred from the OFMDFM to the DSD, who had overall responsibility for developing the site.

According to the Girdwood Advisory Panel's terms of reference, the vision for the development was as follows:

> The Government believes that the imaginative and sensitive development of the Crumlin Road Gaol and Girdwood sites has the potential to create a regeneration project of international significance which can bring maximum benefits to the community in North Belfast and the wider city. The sites can become the engine for economic and social regeneration harnessing public and private sector investment. (NBCAU 2005: 2)

Initially, there were multiple expressions of interest in the space. These began to emerge as early as March 2005, when a draft Technical Feasibility and Development Potential Study was commissioned for the gaol and courthouse. The nearby Mater Hospital needed new clinical space. Directly adjacent to the Mater, St Malachy's school wanted on-site playing fields, since at the time they were transporting students to South Belfast in order to play sports. Social enterprise Bryson House submitted a bid for training facilities and meeting space (Buro Happold 2005: 31). Lastly, the Public Records Office of Northern Ireland (PRONI) put forth an expression of interest for siting their archive. This would bring considerable foot traffic – an estimated 15,500 visitors per year – to the Crumlin Road. PRONI's international reputation and potential as an 'anchor tenant' for lower North Belfast made it an attractive proposition.

In the meantime, a private developer, Cobra Estates, had bought the courthouse with the aim of turning it into a five-star hotel. The Crumlin Road Gaol and Courthouse were famously linked by an underground tunnel; the Development Potential Study noted that for maximum benefit to be realised, it was essential that the redevelopment of the two buildings be coordinated (Buro Happold 2005: 32). Discussions also began around the potential of the site given its proximity to Belfast city centre. The idea of a 'cultural corridor' from the city centre up to and beyond the gaol emerged, for example, as part of Belfast City Council's Arterial Routes programme (OFMDFM 2005c: 7). There was excitement around the opportunities the site presented; one community worker remarked that it 'was seen as being the perfect place to re-energise the whole of North Belfast *and* the whole of Northern Ireland' ('Jim', interview with author 2016).

From early on, the Advisory Panel framed the Girdwood development as an economic engine for North Belfast. At the first meeting in March 2006, Panel members discussed their initial aspirations around the site. A common theme throughout the conversations was the catalyst or 'knock-on' effect for local residential areas: that development would bring job opportunities, improved quality of life and, ultimately, community empowerment. The words 'icon', 'attraction', 'destination' and 'international' are dotted throughout the meeting minutes and there was a general sense of optimism about the potential importance and impact of the site. In advance of the second meeting, in April 2006, Adams drafted a vision and charter. He suggested framing the site as 'a catalyst for the physical, social, and economic improvement of the area' and 'a unique visitor destination … fulfilling the Gaol's potential as an anchor attraction both nationally and internationally' (Adams 2006b) These were lofty ambitions in an area that still sported the scars of inter- and intra-communal violence: shuttered buildings, paramilitary murals, territorial markers and poverty across the ethnonational divide.

Around that time, the 'Developing Leadership' CEP put forth a development bid for the site. This CEP was made up of several trade unions and Intercomm, a group set up to enable Republican and Loyalist activists to engage in community work. In line with the Dunlop Report's recommendation to foster a space for citizenship, they introduced a bid for a 'Centre for International Citizenship and Constructive Thinking', supported by the Edward DeBono Institute. The latter was based at the University of Malta but provided training internationally that focused on creative thinking, problem-solving and conflict resolution. The centre was envisioned as an attraction with global reach, offering state-of-the-art research and conference facilities whilst also involving local communities in education, training and the building's operation (Buro Happold 2005: 28; author fieldnotes 2016). Before submitting their bid, the CEP consulted with the Museum of Tolerance in Los Angeles, California, a Holocaust memorial museum, to develop expertise on creating interactive exhibits around complex conflict-related issues. As an economic and social catalyst with local and international appeal, and a centre for citizenship as recommended by the Dunlop Report, it sounded ideal on paper.

I met up with an erstwhile community worker once to discuss Girdwood. We drank bitter cups of coffee at a leafy South Belfast café and discussed sectarian politics. When they mentioned this particular bid among the ideas for the site, I was surprised – I hadn't seen any mention of it in the raft of meeting minutes, draft studies and newspaper articles I had been sifting through. They favoured me with a wry smile. Underlying competition for resources within and between local community groups, they suggested, had doomed the Intercomm bid from the start. On a grassroots level, they alleged that Intercomm's involvement as a conflict transformation group was problematic:

> The other Nationalist groups didn't want any of that to happen. Because they didn't want any contact with Intercomm[12] and they didn't want any money to be taken away from them. Unionist groups said the idea sounded

---

[12] Intercomm is perceived as Nationalist, therefore its involvement posed a potential threat to funding for other Nationalist groups.

fantastic but it was never gonna happen because they feared that anything coming from the likes of Intercomm was to reclaim that land and move the Nationalist community right out on to the Crumlin Road Gaol.

In terms of the political context at the time:

> Sinn Féin and the DUP had become the dominant political partners within the political scene ... and senior Sinn Féin people told me that privately, 'This is never gonna happen because we want to build houses on that land'. And then Unionists said, 'It's never gonna happen because we'll lose control of that land, and the Shinners[13] will come in, tear up the plans to build that centre and put housing on it'. (interview with author, 2016)

Behind the scenes, the rhetoric of the Dunlop Report and the Advisory Panel was being continually subverted and renegotiated by the influential actors involved. Each ostensibly was competing to ensure they would not lose out on the potential development. And the idea of a Catholic/Nationalist 'takeover' of the land remained a powerful qualifying force. Underlying dynamics of resource competition, territoriality and parochialism in both the government and community development sector at the time were therefore shaping – and constraining – the vision for the site. Initial optimism about the potential for the Girdwood/Crumlin Road Gaol development was, perhaps, misplaced given that the fundamentally divided structures of politics and society remained unacknowledged and unchallenged.

Instead of addressing the uncomfortable spectre of segregation and sectarianism, it was easier to latch on to the prospect of private sector-led 'economic growth' and 'job creation', language that was popular in the heady days before the 2007 economic crash. Advisory Panel members saw engagement with the private sector as a route to successful development of the site, thereby sidestepping the concerns around territory, belonging and ownership. In June 2006, they released a development brief for consultants, which envisaged:

> Engaging the private sector to invest in and profit from the opportunities that the site provides and to do so in ways that: offer sustainable social and economic benefit to the area and the city; ensure it links to the wider regeneration of the surrounding area through provision of necessary infrastructure, landscaping and public realm works; and sustainable development proposals for social, economic and physical regeneration. (Girdwood Advisory Panel 2006b: 3)

---

[13] 'Shinners' is a colloquialism used to refer to members of Sinn Féin.

The brief described a regeneration scheme with a focus on facilitating an attractive climate for investment and developing the Crumlin Road Gaol as a unique visitor destination, 'exploiting its potential as an anchor attraction both nationally and internationally' (Girdwood Advisory Panel 2006b: 3, 7).

This reflects the emphasis at that time on neoliberal-influenced policies as a panacea for peacebuilding and poverty alike. Neoliberalism was prescribed as the solution to conflict resolution – that the palliative power of the free market would better place society to move forward from conflict, delivering a 'peace dividend' (Knox 2014: 485). As in other post-industrial cities at the time, a 'trickle-down' approach to redevelopment emerged: that a 'rising tide lifts all boats', and that private investment brings benefits for high-need areas. This is evident in policy rhetoric: according to the Belfast City Masterplan released in 2004, 'facilitating investment ... is essential to the wellbeing of every citizen in Belfast ... the city cannot deal with deprivation without creating wealth' (Belfast City Council 2013: 6).

This was before the 2007 economic crash, during a period of relative optimism and prosperity. Northern Ireland had become a property hotspot, interpreted 'as both emblem and agent' of a renewed economic vitality (Baker 2012: 14; Coulter 2014: 766), and the city centre was becoming more confident and cosmopolitan. In the absence of conflict, peacebuilding money from the EU, sympathetic governments and private philanthropy flowed into Northern Ireland; private investment and large-scale redevelopment projects also began. For instance, in the wake of the peace process, the Laganside development brought offices, hotels and conference space to former industrial heartlands along the River Lagan. The soaring dome of the Victoria Square shopping centre opened in 2008, a £400 million 'cathedral of consumption' (Nagle 2009b: 173). 'Quarters' were popping up all over the city to spur tourism (there were, bizarrely, seven quarters): the old neighbourhood fondly known as the Half-Bap was renamed the 'Cathedral Quarter', the University area was labelled 'Queens Quarter', West Belfast became 'the Gaeltacht Quarter' and so forth. Adams noted, in reference to the Girdwood development, 'the economic conditions are right ... the success of Laganside, the development of Victoria Square, Cathedral Quarter and Royal Exchange show what can be achieved when the public, private and community sectors work together to a common agenda' (DSD 2006: 1).

Regarding the pervading sense of optimism, an activist remarked, 'this was a time when every area was getting its "Hub," everywhere was getting a broader tourism strategy. You have to understand this was pre-crash, there was a lot of money around, deals being done left and right' ('Eamonn', interview with author 2017). The idea of the 'peace dividend' promised by the architects of the peace process seemed to be arriving at last.

Like other post-industrial cities, one of the core strategic objectives of Belfast's policy and planning at that time was to reshape formerly industrial or vacant sites and public land into places for consumption and tourism (Buchanan et al. 2004: 104). Competition between cities for tourism and investment meant that image, branding and creating a sense of 'place' were becoming important factors in urban regeneration globally. This was increasingly accomplished through deploying 'culture' and 'heritage' as tools to shape policy and planning (Murtagh et al. 2017: 508). The Titanic Quarter development brief in East Belfast, for example, emphasised the maritime heritage of Belfast in its vision (Urban Initiatives 2004: 9). Perhaps inspired by this trend, the November 2006 Girdwood Advisory Forum document on the barracks and gaol site mentioned culture, heritage, tourism and 'creating a destination and sense of place' as essential elements to the development (Adams 2006c: 1–2).

There is little evidence that the commodification of culture or 'trickle-down' approaches to regeneration yield substantial job opportunities or widespread socio-economic transformation for those who most need it (Boland et al. 2016: 4). This rhetoric ignores the reality of unemployment, multiple deprivation and marginalisation that continues to exist in places where redevelopment has occurred. This is evident in cities internationally, like London's River Thames or Boston's Seaport District, where gentrification and private-sector waterfront development have transformed the urban fabric but have also residualised large swathes of the population or privatised formerly public land (Davidson and Lees 2005; Harvey 2012; Jacobs 1961; Shenker 2015). Yet it continues to be a popular sentiment in redevelopment practice that cutting-edge developments built for consumption and for the tourist gaze will somehow impact positively on surrounding communities (Burrows 2017; Holgersen and Baeten 2017).

The disconnect is also conspicuous in Belfast. The Titanic Experience, cornerstone of Northern Ireland's tourism strategy and symbol of the 'new Northern Ireland', sits on the east side of the Lagan on the site of the old shipyards. In its first year, it attracted more than a million visitors (Simpson 2013). The museum is indeed an experience, complete with a 'shipyard ride' and interactive exhibits. It is also a somewhat perverse exercise in commodifying the industrial heritage of Belfast through the story of the ill-fated RMS *Titanic*. I went to the Titanic Experience one afternoon with a friend. We had a good time skirting tourists and poking fun at the carefully inoffensive exhibits, which described the Belfast of old as a harmonious place full of humble workers and benevolent businessmen. We walked along the old slipways afterwards. My friend remembered when he and his friends would mess about along the abandoned docks as children and scoffed at the ticket prices we had paid. At the time, a single adult admissions ticket for the Titanic Experience was £19.50 whilst the unemployed concession rate was still £15.50.[14] The experience is not

---

[14] Ticket prices have since gone up: at the time of writing, it was £24.95 for a standard ticket and £19 for the unemployed.

priced for residents in the nearby estates of lower East Belfast, many of whom come from families that once worked in the now-defunct shipyards, and many of whom experience high levels of unemployment (Kelly 2012).[15]

For those who cannot afford to participate in the 'new Northern Ireland' symbolised by developments like the Titanic Experience, deprivation and division persist. This has been termed the 'twin-speed city' by commentators, where the social disadvantage and segregation that characterise the outskirts of the city exclude these neighbourhoods from the economic optimism of the city centre, thereby marginalising them from a place in the 'New Belfast' (Murtagh 2008: 4, Nagle 2009b: 174). The Belfast on offer to tourists is a 15-minute walk and a world away from the neighbourhoods around the Girdwood site.

The exclusion is not just symbolic. Other commentators have noted the physical lack of connectivity between the outskirts and the centre, which has been exacerbated by the motorway and the blighted spaces and car parks around it (Forum for Alternative Belfast 2009; Gaffikin et al. 2010; Martire 2017; Sterrett et al. 2012). All the pedestrian routes into Belfast's city centre (including the one from North Belfast) involve a tricky series of intersections, guesswork and quick footwork to cross. I felt this keenly many times in my fieldwork, felt a sense of outrage crossing over the motorway from West or North or East Belfast into the city centre with cars streaming in from all directions. The motorway, that great divider in cities around the world. This invisible economic interface that I observed was no less damaging than the sectarian one. The grey estates gave way to the after-work crowd in the city centre, chattering around tables at wine bars.

On the one hand, using neutral interpretations of culture and creating inoffensive spaces for consumption and leisure has been a way for Belfast to reposition itself globally by moving away from the violence of the past (Murtagh et al. 2017: 3). Yet critics note that divesting the city of traces of conflict is problematic. By reimaging Belfast to appear 'normal', policy and planning has ignored the controversies of the past and attempted to downplay the pernicious ways that segregation and social exclusion continue to be reproduced (Brett 2004: 26; Hocking 2015: 2; Switzer and McDowell 2009: 351). Essentially ignoring the elephant in the room, the official rhetoric refuses to acknowledge deeply rooted sectarianism. This only functions to a limited degree in divided cities like Belfast because space continues to be charged with meaning and contestation – 'a material and non-material resource to be claimed, fought over, won and lost ... [a] reminder of what conflict was for and how central it remains to enabling or disabling peace processes' (Murtagh et al. 2017: 3).

This is evident in the way the devolved government has enacted redevelopment

---

[15] Multiple deprivation measure for Ballymacarrett 2, East Belfast, NISRA (https://deprivation.nisra.gov.uk/MDM/Details?Id=BT4+1AB).

policy. Development has only taken place in spaces that are not contested. The Titanic Quarter, for example, received cross-party support precisely because it was located in non-contentious, formerly industrial space. Belfast city centre is another spatially unproblematic neutral zone where regeneration has been delivered across party lines. Both developments have been supported by a mix of public and private investment and have created space for consumption and leisure activities where people can mix. The idea is that consumerism and material prosperity will undermine parochial identity politics within these new spaces. The state has not challenged spatial sectarian inefficiencies here because they do not exist.

However, when contested identities and territories, ethnic and spatial division, and severe socio-economic problems come together, they can subvert the 'neutralising' tools of regeneration. This occurred as the Girdwood Advisory Panel moved forward in the regeneration process: conflict over physical and symbolic space ultimately hindered the initial rhetoric around a private sector-led space for economic growth. The cautious optimism around an internationally relevant development was tempered by ethnosectarian resource competition and discursive battles over communal 'needs' and 'rights'.

CHAPTER FOUR

'Unlocking the Potential'

Grassroots Advocacy and the Girdwood Draft Masterplan

The Advisory Panel's work on the draft Masterplan stumbled around the issue of social housing. Competing discourses around respective 'needs' and 'rights' emerged between Protestant/Unionist actors, led by the DUP, and Catholic/Nationalist ones, led by Sinn Féin. Despite the documented need for social housing in Catholic/Nationalist North Belfast, Unionists used various discursive tactics to stall agreement on housing for the site. The draft Masterplan that emerged from the negotiations was disappointingly lacking in detail on addressing not only the housing crisis, but other measures of deprivation endemic to the area.

PPR and the ECNI, two organisations outside of the traditional sectarian framework, challenged the Masterplan's failure to both deliver on Section 75 and produce a transformative scheme for North Belfast. Both parties drew attention to the lack of an equality impact assessment on the site and to other problematic trends in the devolved government's policy and planning practices. The work of PPR in particular demonstrates a different approach to the Girdwood Barracks/Crumlin Road Gaol redevelopment which relied on human rights-based indicators and genuine community engagement – a model for best practice that was ignored by Sinn Féin and DUP ministers. Despite PPR's productive community facilitation and their evidence-based recommendations for the site, the Advisory Panel's failure to agree on housing at Girdwood doomed the project. The global economic crash was the figurative nail in the coffin for the development, and the site languished.

'A Beautiful Patchwork Quilt?'

> *Only here in Northern Ireland could the religious composition of a housing list apparently generate more focus and division than the size of the list itself.*
>
> (Michael Copeland, UUP MLA, in Hansard 2014b)

By December 2006, the Advisory Panel had put out a tender for consultants for the Girdwood Draft Masterplan. Five internationally recognised firms placed costed bids, receiving a sum of money in return (DSD 2006). The winning tender came from the London-based Building Design Partnership Ltd. (BDP) (NBCAU 2007).

On 9 February 2007, BDP presented their concept plan to the Panel. They provided examples of other developments, like Paradise Street and the Ropewalks in Liverpool, Sheffield city centre, Paradise Gardens in Manchester and several university campuses, citing the mantra 'Life, spaces and buildings ... and in that order please!' (BDP 2007a). This was, perhaps, overzealous considering the former projects are sited in busy, high-footfall areas of city centres, unlike the somewhat peripheral and deprived Crumlin Road. However, it spoke to a desire to neutralise or normalise the space consistent with previous policy rhetoric on regeneration, papering over the sectarian fault lines running through North Belfast.

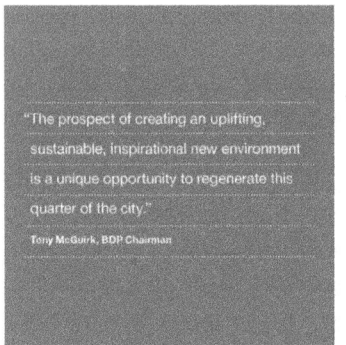
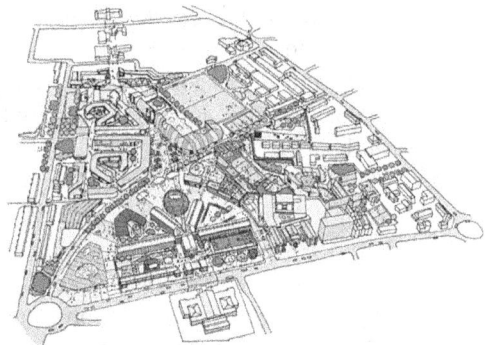

Fig. 4.1

BDP's Girdwood concept plan referred to North Belfast, unironically, as a 'beautiful patchwork quilt of communities'. The first sketches envisioned a youth club, museum, bright, airy cafés, green space and walkways, family housing and new streets lined with shops. By identifying linkages between the site and its surroundings, the plan looked to go some way towards building up the fractured urban fabric of lower North Belfast and transforming vacant and disused space. BDP also proposed four different options for siting PRONI within the Crumlin Road Gaol including reading rooms, archive storage, exhibition space, conservation and a café (BDP 2007a).

At this point in the process, Panel meetings continued to focus on the prospect of PRONI as the anchor tenant and economic catalyst of the area. It was a safe bet for a contested space. Even though most jobs in the archive would likely be staffed by existing personnel, the Advisory Panel thought that the huge numbers of visitors per year – archivists and genealogists, students and academics – would spur further development of the area. Cafés and shops would populate a vibrant streetscape, thereby creating local jobs (Buro Happold 2005: 26). The Panel had met with the Environment Heritage Service to discuss the removal of listed buildings at the front of the Crumlin Road Gaol in order to accommodate PRONI.

However, PRONI had never officially signed up to the redevelopment. On 19 April 2007, Panel chair Roy Adams received a letter from the chair of PRONI's new project board rejecting the Advisory Panel's bid. The minutes of the following advisory meeting record 'a unanimous reaction of bitter disappointment'. Panel member Carál Ní Chuilín, Sinn Féin Member of the Legislative Assembly (MLA), declared that 'the regeneration of Girdwood needs a major player and PRONI was that player'. Adams subsequently wrote panicked letters to the Department of Culture, Arts and Leisure (DCAL) and the Minister for Culture, Arts and Leisure; the new incoming ministers for the DCAL and DSD; the Secretary of State; and the First and Deputy First Ministers, citing the issue as a 'matter of urgency' (Adams 2007b). But the timing was unfortunate: the government was moving from direct rule from Westminster to devolved power-sharing for the first time since it had been suspended in 2002. It would not sit again until 8 May.[1] In August 2007, the relocation of PRONI to East Belfast was announced as part of the development of Titanic Quarter – again, an unproblematic site for regeneration ripe for investment in the pre-economic crash period (Potter 2016). This suggests, perhaps, a desire of the PRONI project board at that time to site the archives in a purpose-built space that promised a clean slate for the tourist and public gaze, rather than dealing with sectarian baggage. It reflects the failure of 'the peace dividend' to emerge in marginalised and contested spaces like North Belfast.

It was not PRONI's disappearance, however, that would pose the biggest stumbling block for the Girdwood/Crumlin Road Gaol development. It was the pernicious issue of social housing. Throughout the process, the Panel was unable to agree on housing provision for the site because of competing discourses around housing need, underlying resource competition and territorialism. The emphasis on economic development to reimage and reimagine the site was

---

[1] In 2002 Unionists pulled out of power-sharing with Sinn Féin after the latter's offices at Stormont were raided and three party members arrested on suspicion of a spy ring. The Northern Ireland Assembly was suspended until 2006, when the St Andrews Agreement was made (Northern Ireland Assembly n.d.). After the government was reformed in 2007, the DUP and Sinn Féin's more polarised brand of identity politics had superseded the UUP and SDLP, the more moderate parties that had brokered the peace process. The DUP and Sinn Féin shared power until the government collapsed again in 2017.

a convenient fix for avoiding underlying sectarian tensions around land use and the historical associations and symbolism of the gaol and army barracks (Murtagh 2011: 1123). This is despite an NIHE housing needs assessment that was provided to the members of the Panel on 12 June 2006, which described Girdwood as an 'important and unique opportunity' to address the shortfall of housing in North Belfast. The NIHE recommended building at least 100 units of social housing, 40 units of affordable low-cost housing and 60 units of private housing. These recommendations were supported by a calculated housing need projection for 2005–2010 in North Belfast, which estimated the number of applicants in housing stress at 2,414 and the projected social housing need as 1,322 units (NIHE 2006).

However, two competing sets of discourses around 'needs' and 'rights' from the political elite and local leaders twisted this objective portrait of Catholic/Nationalist housing need. On the one hand, there is a predominant narrative among some Protestants/Unionists that perceives Catholics as benefiting more from equality measures and gaining in political clout (Hall 1994; Hall 2015a; Hayward and Mitchell 2003). The latter are seen as better placed to access resources given a history of community organisation, encouraging feelings of beleaguerment and hostility among declining Protestant/Unionist areas. This has, in turn, underlined the narrative that Girdwood would not be shared and that Unionists would lose out on territory. Therefore, the 'right' to remain and the 'need' for investment in declining housing estates figures prominently in Unionist discourse on housing needs and rights.

On the other hand, Catholic/Nationalist perspectives centre around equal rights and the 'equality agenda': that past discrimination – particularly but not exclusively around housing – and continued disadvantage requires redress (Bean 2007: 6). Elite Nationalist/Republican discourse has moved from themes of suffering, victimisation and powerlessness in the colonial past to a focus on change, progress and equality for Catholics within Northern Ireland (Hayward and Mitchell 2003: 302). 'Equality of opportunity' is a rallying cry for the provision of housing and employment opportunities, as well as Irish language rights, all of which Catholics historically lacked. The 'need' for housing in areas with large Catholic populations, low social housing stock and high waiting lists, and the 'right' to shelter and to equal access to resources feature strongly in this point of view. And because perceptions of gains and loss tend to be 'relative and relational' (Hayward and Mitchell 2003: 302), these two narratives remain opposed.

Practically, this results in a zero-sum framework where everything must be 'balanced' between the two sides. If policies are perceived to favour one section of the community over another – the oft-quoted 'themmuns got more than our ones' – contestation swiftly arises (Bean 2007: 33). As Anderson and Shuttleworth observe, 'more for one side is less for the other, and vice versa, in a flawed symmetry of mutual misery' (2003: 3). This has been conceptualised as an 'either-or' rather than a 'both-and' approach to policymaking (Wilford and Wilson 2006: 6). The electorate puts pressure on their respective representatives for resources and this ensures that resource allocation remains a zero-sum enterprise. Conversely, politicians base their mandate on Unionist or Nationalist 'community rights', drawing on the nebulous spectre of 'the community' to legitimise their actions and maintain power (Shirlow 2006a: 106).

At the start of the Girdwood Advisory Forum meetings, members had participated in an initial exercise to share their aspirations for the site. Conflict over resources and claims to space can be found throughout the minutes, and most notably in regard to housing provision. Several members suggested that any housing built to mitigate the predominantly Nationalist waiting list must also take into account neighbouring Protestant areas and the opinions of those living in them, for example, 'adding value to local communities as opposed to threatening them', '[addressing] negative perceptions … and lack of confidence' and 'ensuring neighbouring communities are sustainable, attractive communities'. The underlying theme was that any new housing built for Catholics must also include investment in Protestant areas, reflecting a 'tit-for-tat' approach to resource allocation between Nationalists and Unionists. A DUP representative said:

> The two Nationalist areas around Girdwood are thriving communities. The two Protestant/Unionist areas are quite run-down communities … The two Unionist communities need regeneration. And if this is going to be developed as a shared site, they need to be regenerated before you develop the Girdwood site so that the context of it is one where it is surrounded by vibrant communities. (O'Dowd and Komarova 2011: 2023)

This idea of comparative vibrancy perhaps stems from the younger age profile of Catholics in Belfast compared to an ageing Protestant population. Yet this is polemical given that the Nationalist areas around Girdwood rank at the top of the multiple deprivation measure year on year (Northern Ireland Statistics and Research Agency (NISRA) 2005, 2010, 2017). This discourse evidences a zero-sum reading of regeneration priorities: that each group must receive an equal share of resources, despite objective need for social housing, since a gain for one side is a loss for the other.

Seven months after the Panel was first convened, the issue of housing was finally discussed in cross-community groups 'without the principle of housing on the site being accepted' (Girdwood Advisory Forum 2006c: 2). There was agreement that there was a need for housing – but differing needs in both Nationalist and Unionist communities, and thus differing discourses about what 'need' actually meant. From the Unionist point of view espoused by politicians and community development leaders, there was a 'need to balance the demand for social housing with a corresponding demand for community regeneration with a view to attracting people back to the inner city' (Girdwood Advisory Forum 2006c: 4). In other words, 'housing need' entailed tackling the dispirited environment in declining Unionist enclaves, in the hope that people would then repopulate them.

The issue over the creation of further interfaces also arose in the discussion. Protestant/Unionist members of the Advisory Panel stated that they were not against meeting Nationalist housing need but that an interface closer to Lower Oldpark and Lower Shankill would ramp up violence in the area (Girdwood Advisory Forum 2006c: 2). 'Need' thus also meant safety from potential threat or incursion, recalling shades of the 'siege mentality' among some elements of the Protestant population in North Belfast. On the other hand, Nationalist housing 'need' required new-build housing to serve a chronic and ever-expanding waiting list, in line with Section 75 equality legislation and the obligation of the state to provide housing. The latter definition of 'need' was the one underlined by a legislative framework and statutory obligations.

One community activist reflected,

> You did get a sense right from the beginning, and this was from the more Unionist-inclined CEPs as well as the politicians, like they were intent [on], they were there to stop housing being built. That was the agenda, you know? So any notion ... in terms of equality, just was anathema to them because, I mean, you couldn't avoid housing if you're talking about equality. ('Eamonn', interview with author 2017)

According to a Nationalist representative on the Panel, they were unable to reach agreement on the housing issue for the Girdwood/Crumlin Road Gaol site because:

> The DUP felt that they didn't want housing, particularly social housing on that site because the housing waiting list for North Belfast is one of the best examples you could use for structural and historical inequalities across the whole North ... it basically got down to the sectarian argument that Catholics would have got a home. (O'Dowd and Komarova 2011: 2019)

In contrast, a DUP representative said:

> That site should be given over to economic development and job creation. The site is actually surrounded by some of the most deprived communities in Northern Ireland ... The Lower Shankill community which abuts the site is the most deprived community in Northern Ireland ... residential

development is not that important and would have meant that the site could not be shared. (O'Dowd and Komarova 2011: 2019)

According to a senior member of the UDA:

> We've asked for that [Girdwood Barracks] to become work units – if you want to go cross-community let them do it through the workforce. What effectively will happen, and I can see it coming a mile off, is that if they build houses on down – you see the likes of Manor Street [across from Girdwood] that's an interface as it sits but there's a buffer, there's a big park. But if the houses come on down the road you'll lose Manor Street – and from Carlisle Circus to Hesketh will be Nationalist; there will be no loyalist Protestants on the other side of the road. The [Nationalist] plan is to take over the other side of the [Crumlin Road] I've no doubt whatsoever. (Southern 2008: 76)

The DUP's argument for mixed-use 'shared' space and economic development seems to deflect from the underlying sense of territorialism and perceived encroachment on traditionally Protestant/Unionist space suggested by the UDA member's response.

By March 2007, a year after deliberations had begun and four months after they were meant to have ended, the issue had brought the Panel to a stalemate. The chair, Adams, wrote a discussion paper for the Advisory Panel, asserting that housing would limit 'the scope for the site to be developed as space shared by both communities' but that, without housing, the site would not be 'a vibrant living space both day and night' (Girdwood Advisory Panel 2007a, 2007b, 2007c). In the discussion paper, Adams frames the quandary: 'there remain families with children in need of housing at subsidised rent. There are hundreds of them in North Belfast. They require to be catered for. But the creation of a shared future at Crumlin/Girdwood depends on a balanced approach to housing provision' (2007a: 1). But this privileges the desire for 'shared space' over housing need, in opposition to Section 75. The word 'balanced' here is notable; it unconsciously evokes the Protestant/Catholic binary that has been embedded in the process – that one side cannot get more than the other. As one commentator remarked, however, 'what I can say very simply is – equality isn't one for you, one for me' (BBC *Spotlight* 2012). The statutory duty to provide equality of opportunity for housing means that housing should have been built according to objective need and regardless of ethnic or religious background.

The Advisory Panel's disagreements also demonstrate how the discourses of 'equality' and 'shared space' were exploited by both groups as leverage. On the Unionist side, 'equality' in housing allocation was framed as impeding good relations: by building houses which would by default be allocated to Nationalists given their greater housing need, the space would not be shared, creating a new interface and impeding cross-community relations (Girdwood Advisory Panel 2006c, 2006d). The language of 'good relations' and 'shared space' was used to legitimise underlying territoriality and notions of symbolic loss within elements of Unionism. A report issued by the Equality Commission for Northern Ireland (ECNI 2018: 26) described this as a problematic trend whereby policies are assessed for their adverse impacts on good relations because they are politically contentious. This undermined the rhetoric of equality of opportunity and mutual trust set forth in the Agreement and Northern Ireland Act; Section 75 specifically notes that equality must come before good relations.

However, by establishing a particular sense of the Protestant/Unionist population's place in the lived environment of North Belfast and enforcing it through discourse, the Protestant/Unionist members of the Advisory Panel were able to retain their position. Their arguments around the possibility of Nationalists dominating the site and of a new interface played on residual feelings of territorial encroachment and symbolic loss experienced by the dwindling Protestant population in North Belfast, arguing that these were commensurate with the Nationalist need for new-build housing. Effectively, as a community activist commented, 'that's the kind of DUP strategy, to make every single site a contested area ... it has been an extremely successful strategy by the DUP and I'm confident, it wouldn't be a surprise to anybody, that's just politics and that's keeping their electoral majority in North Belfast' ('Eamonn', interview with author 2017).

On the other hand, Nationalist discourse pointed to the denial of social housing as a denial of objective need and a miscarriage of social justice, which also impeded good relations because it ignored equality legislation set out as a cornerstone of the peace process. Yet the DUP's discourses were allowed to stall the regeneration agenda. No decision on the site could go ahead without the involvement of Unionist actors because of the zero-sum nature of decision-making inherent in power-sharing.

In the end, the outcome was one of 'deadlock and delay' where each group ignored the other (Planning for Spatial Reconciliation Research Group 2016: 105). No decision on housing was finalised before the draft Masterplan was published by BDP in July 2007 (PPR 2007: 4). In a letter to Panel members before its publication, the chair went to great lengths to stress 'the draft nature of the Masterplan, the fact that its content is indicative, and the difficulties which remain across a range of issues, not least of which concerns housing' (Adams 2007d).

The draft Masterplan's rhetoric echoed the initial terms of reference, painting the site as an internationally significant benchmark for development and a symbol of 'hope and economic regeneration' for North Belfast, just as the Dunlop Report had recommended (NBCAP 2002: 14; BDP 2007b: 15). In terms of urban design, a new 'quarter' was envisioned, with an intricate maze of buildings, green spaces and roads to make the site vibrant and accessible: BDP described it as a 'carefully shaped series of activities, routes, spaces and identity areas to spatially foster new connections and thus new relationships within and between communities' (BDP 2007b: 8). The optimistic new 'quarter' echoed the neoliberal-influenced development strategies found elsewhere in the city but did not take into account that these latter spaces were unproblematic to begin with. The stalemate around housing demonstrated that dynamics around the Girdwood site were far more complex, resistant to the simple reshaping of new routes and routines when space continued to be a site of contestation and a platform for identity politics.

The Masterplan's priorities appeared to be concerned with generating employment through private investment and infrastructure – again reminiscent of the 'trickle-down' approach to regeneration at the time. However, there were no targeted strategies to facilitate job creation for local residents of North Belfast in the draft. The draft outlined extensions to the Mater Hospital and St Malachy's College, along with a sports facility. It proposed a new shared community at the centre of the site called the 'heart space', although it was not explained precisely what this 'heart space' would entail (BDP 2007b: 23). The 'international gateway', the Crumlin Road Gaol, was envisioned as a museum and boutique hotel (BDP 2007b: 24) to attract tourists to North Belfast (the courthouse is not mentioned). Mixed-use development formed the largest part of the site plan: 'local retail, housing, workshops and training facilities … integrated with new shops, restaurants and leisure facilities' (BDP 2007b: 10). It is noteworthy that housing is only mentioned in the context of offices, workshops, retail, etc. rather than as a stand-alone issue; the wording is intentionally ambiguous. While the draft Masterplan resonates somewhat with the rhetoric of economic growth and private investment, it effectively ignores the contentious issue of housing, avoiding the statistics on documented housing stress, the NIHE's recommendations and the legislative framework agreed as part of the peace process.

Given the number of Advisory Panel meetings and negotiations which took place from March 2006 to July 2007, the draft Masterplan was disappointingly lacking in detail and substance. The proposals did not include clear strategies or objectives for dealing with either housing or other social and economic inequalities around the site (PPR 2007: 5). There was also little evidence of how the aspirations of 'reconciliation' found in the Good Friday Agreement or the 'equality of opportunity' enshrined by the Northern Ireland Act might be implemented through the site's development.

Avoiding Equality at Girdwood

The publication of the draft Masterplan reflected the clash of discourses, assumptions and interests around the Girdwood site. It exemplified how post-Agreement planning and policy rhetoric was filtered through the prism of sectarian logic, how Section 75 was subverted by zero-sum readings of space and resources and how the boosterism of neoliberal-influenced economic strategies failed to offer measurable impact for places outside the gaze of the 'new Northern Ireland'. Despite the issues around housing inequality as well as the high levels of social inequality in North Belfast, the draft Masterplan's emphasis on private investment and 'trickle-down' economics as a panacea failed to consider targeted mechanisms to address poverty and unemployment. Furthermore, the troublesome issue of housing was sidestepped rather than addressed, evidencing an unwillingness to work for genuine societal transformation as envisioned by the Agreement and Act. The government was not delivering on its statutory duties or the promises of the peace process.

Other civil society actors emerged to challenge the draft Masterplan's publication. PPR, a nonpartisan human rights and advocacy group, and the ECNI, an independent body established by the Act to oversee equality legislation, both highlighted their concerns in subsequent reports. PPR also worked with local residents in order to demonstrate how the draft Girdwood/Crumlin Road Gaol Masterplan did not take into account Section 75's commitment to equality, objective need or, by extension, the right to housing. Their work, though small-scale, was an example of what could happen if alternative politics were allowed room to grow outside of the traditional sectarian divide.

PPR was founded by human rights activist and trade unionist Inez MacCormack in 2006. As part of their practice, they use indicators and benchmarks drawn from legislation to both support marginalised groups campaigning for social change and to hold the post-Agreement government to account (PPR 2013: 1). They produced a report, *Unlocking the Potential*, which unpicked the Girdwood draft Masterplan, pointing out some of the gaps between the aspirational rhetoric and the social and economic realities in North Belfast. The report concluded that government, through the draft Masterplan, had failed to consider human rights and equality obligations in a meaningful way.

One issue that PPR highlights is the omission of an Equality Impact Assessment (EQIA) in the draft Masterplan. Not only did Section 75 enshrine equality of opportunity in law, it also prefaced several other provisions in the Northern Ireland Act which aimed to transform the practice of policy implementation. An EQIA was one of them. Public authorities are required to 'assess the likely impact of their policies on the promotion of equality of opportunity' (NIO 1998b: 75) and it is recommended they do so by screening all policies through an EQIA. The EQIA is designed to determine the potential impacts of a policy upon the main groups outlined in Section 75,[2] and what measures should be taken to lessen adverse impact and best promote equality of opportunity. Also part of the process is mixed-methods data collection, consultation with affected groups and putting systems in place for ongoing monitoring of outcomes. Afterwards, the final EQIA is published (ECNI 2005: 4, 34). In 2005, the ECNI published a detailed guide on practical assistance for EQIAs; reading through it, the relatively sophisticated approach to assessment it proposed was impressive.

An EQIA was not carried out as part of the Girdwood/Crumlin Road Gaol planning process and therefore did not inform any aspect of the development priorities put forward in the draft Masterplan. This is a troubling indictment: the consultation and development process itself was not compliant with the legislative framework of post-ceasefire Northern Ireland. Indeed, if an EQIA had been carried out, it would have pointed to the statutory duty to provide adequate housing regardless of ethnic or religious identity. This calls into question the draft Masterplan's vision for a transformational scheme and negates its assurance that 'the policy context relating to the site has been carefully examined and development priorities established based on [that] analysis' (BDP 2007b: 4, 8). It also undermines the Masterplan's assertion that 'it is not easy to reconcile the differing views expressed [on housing]' and 'that it has not proved possible to reach agreement on this issue' (BDP 2007b: 6). Instead, the lack of an EQIA suggests the process was fundamentally flawed and technically illegal, for if the Girdwood site had adhered to the requirements enshrined in legislation, housing would have been a component of the site regardless of ethnosectarian resource competition or opposing discourses around housing need. This phenomenon has been described by Flyvbjerg in relation to urban planning:

> [Efforts are] made more in order to rationalise and legitimate established attitudes and prior decisions than to produce a balanced, documentary basis for making decisions. Where there is disagreement, the documentation is manipulated or left out in order to strengthen one's position or weaken that of opponents. (2008: 35)

This may explain why an EQIA was left out in the case of the Girdwood/Crumlin Road Gaol site. The DUP's rhetoric of 'economic growth' and concern

---

[2] Section 75 enshrined equality of opportunity between persons of different religious belief, political opinion, racial group, age group, marital status or sexual orientation; between men and women; between those with a disability and without; and between those with dependents and those without (NIO 1998).

over a 'new interface' was allowed to win out whilst social housing and wider social impact remained unagreed. An EQIA would have drawn attention to the matter.

In *Unlocking the Potential*, PPR observed that the DSD, who had overarching responsibility for the site, failed to carry out an EQIA; instead, the DSD claimed, 'given the conceptual nature of the draft Masterplan, DSD is satisfied, at this stage, that there are no significant implications for equality of opportunity, and therefore that an Equality Impact Assessment is not required' (PPR 2007: 14). This stance is challenged by the ECNI's guide to EQIAs, which requires a 'thorough and systematic analysis of a policy, whether that policy is written or unwritten, formal or informal, and irrespective of the scope of that policy or the size of the public authority' (2005: 3). The draft Masterplan had also stated that community engagement in the surrounding neighbourhoods would be paramount to the implementation of the project (Adams 2007c: 4). Given the language of 'community engagement', PPR (2009: 22) argued that an EQIA should have been a fundamental part of the process from the very beginning in order to consult with people in the areas around Girdwood, identify inequalities and target possible solutions through planning and policymaking. The ECNI agreed, stating that 'equality impact assessment (should be used) as part of the development process, rather than as an afterthought when the policy has been established' (2010: 13).

PPR's work questioned the DSD's excuse that the draft Masterplan was 'conceptual': 'We fail to see how a development with terms of reference, projected budgets, zoned lands, specific proposals around housing, education, health and employment provisions can be considered "conceptual"' (PPR 2007: 5). There are many possible reasons why an EQIA was not carried out at the beginning of the Advisory Panel process. It could have foiled the state's vision for a private sector-led regeneration given the context of social and economic inequality in the neighbourhoods around the site. It would have highlighted the uncomfortable housing issue by focusing attention on the statutory duty of government to provide social housing and the illegality of their failure to agree. One activist suggested that it was because the importance around equality legislation had been gradually downplayed in the wake of 1998, effectively neutering the EQIA process:

> The mainstreaming of [EQIAs] became a tick-box, bureaucratic exercise that wasn't the kind of live process that was envisaged as involving participation, promotion of equality; this kind of dedicated, systemic sort of targeting inequality ... It became this check box: 'Alright, did we look at disabled people?' – yes/no, and so forth.
>
> It became a bit of a nightmare for officials to do, so what they did was say, 'There's no equality impacts to this whatsoever' – or the classic one,

'Everyone will benefit therefore no one will be disadvantaged'. Therefore we don't need an equality impact assessment. ('Eamonn', interview with author 2017)

The latter attitude of 'everyone will benefit, therefore no one will be disadvantaged' offers a convenient means of avoiding both the inadequacy of neoliberal-influenced policy in tackling inequality and the prevalence of sectarian claims to space. A 2018 report by the ECNI terms this 'blanket impact' and it is a recurring theme of their research on government implementation of Section 75: a 'simplistic analysis' stating a policy will impact positively on everybody is made without any proper analysis of Section 75 groups (62). The report further critiques the government's approach to Section 75, finding the most common patterns for public authorities were either not conducting an EQIA screening at all on policies with clearly defined equality impacts, or conducting EQIAs 'in an inadequate manner with the purpose or effect of disguising adverse impacts' and in some cases 'studiously avoiding' equality considerations (ECNI 2018: 5). 'Disguising' or 'studiously avoiding' equality considerations defined the Advisory Panel's approach to social housing provision at Girdwood.

PPR's *Unlocking the Potential* interrogated the housing, education, health and employment proposals within the draft Masterplan for what they offered and what they failed to address. At that time, all the electoral wards surrounding Girdwood (Crumlin, Shankill, Ardoyne, New Lodge, Waterworks) were in the top 5 per cent of the most deprived in Northern Ireland in terms of unemployment; Crumlin and Shankill were second and third most deprived for employment out of 582 wards (NISRA 2005). Job creation and economic development for this part of North Belfast was therefore a major priority (Adams 2007c: 5; DOE 2004a: 59). The draft Masterplan proposed to tackle unemployment through using the site 'to accommodate a major building investment by an employer or anchor tenant'; developing social economy enterprises on the site; and providing learning and skills training, which would include involving local people in the construction industry (BDP 2007b: 19). This is not unique to the Girdwood/Crumlin Road Gaol regeneration; job creation through private investment, new infrastructure and construction-led growth was a common narrative in other cities at the time. The Advisory Panel was simply following trends that had already been established, in the hope that investment would bring 'trickle-down' benefits to the area. In an area beleaguered by high unemployment and little opportunity, it is understandable that these proposals should have been made.

The draft Masterplan also admitted, however, that 'the precise source of these investments and their nature remain to be defined' (Adams 2007c: 5). *Unlocking the Potential* notes that there was little detail in any of the proposals. There were no expressions of interest from specific employers, no feasibility studies conducted and no plans for options like a social economy enterprise, as one might expect from a draft Masterplan. This is problematic since minimum-wage or part-time labour would not have been enough to mitigate the poverty in the area, and there was no detail on how stable, quality jobs might have been created, nor a timeline for training local people to pursue qualifications. There was no provision either for other barriers faced in the workplace, such as childcare for single parents. In terms of social clauses for construction jobs, PPR observed there was no information on how contractors and sub-contractors might be regulated and monitored for compliance, what apprenticeships might involve or how recruitment would target those most disadvantaged and farthest from the labour market (PPR 2007: 8).

Clear strategies and targeted outcomes were similarly absent in the areas of health and education. At that time, the wards around the Girdwood site, again, sat in the top 5 per cent of the most deprived in Northern Ireland for health, with Shankill and Crumlin first and third respectively (NISRA 2005). Whilst the draft Masterplan cited an expansion of the nearby Mater Hospital and a 'wellbeing zone', it did not explain how this would improve health outcomes for the surrounding areas (BDP 2007b: 10). PPR suggested that an audit should have been done of specific health issues facing North Belfast – in particular, young people at risk of suicide, mental health and drug abuse, and poor housing and living conditions – so as to better target the facilities being provided on the Girdwood site (PPR 2007: 13). In terms of education, a 'Creative Knowledge Zone' and 'Children's Learning Hub' formed part of the draft Masterplan (BDP 2007b: 24, 30), but there was no detail on how these would engage young people and tackle long-term educational underattainment, especially in the context of vulnerable and hard-to-reach youth. Support for 'citizenship' and youth engagement (and the youth workers to facilitate this) as recommended by the Dunlop Report was also missing from the plan (NBCAP 2002: 14–15).

PPR found that the draft Masterplan did not adequately address the patterns of social deprivation and objective need around the site; this is unfortunate considering one of the strategies cited in its policy framework was *New Targeting Social Need* (1998). *New Targeting Social Need*'s stated aim was to 'tackle social need and social exclusion in Northern Ireland by targeting efforts and available resources on people, groups and areas in the greatest social need' (Northern Ireland Assembly Research and Library Services 2001: 2). In particular, it was meant to address unemployment and inequality in health, education and housing. Another policy document included in the draft Masterplan framework was the *People and Place Neighbourhood Renewal Strategy* (2003), which committed to economic renewal for the most deprived neighbourhoods and physical and social renewal through better-coordinated public services (DSD 2003: 29). This coordinated approach never materialised, though there were opportunities; for instance, two concurrent draft Masterplans for neighbourhood revitalisation in the immediate vicinity of Girdwood – Lower Oldpark and Lower Shankill – were not coordinated with the Girdwood regeneration.[3] This is peculiar considering their proximity to the site. Given the high levels of multiple deprivation and inequality, the opportunity to put policy into practice in 'the biggest regeneration project ever to take place in North Belfast' was underwhelming (PPR 2007: 4). At the risk of labouring the point, an EQIA from the beginning of the process could have highlighted some of these issues. PPR asserted that 'the failure of the DSD to fulfil its obligation to consider local inequalities and deprivation in the draft Masterplan represents a missed opportunity' (2007: 5).

These issues are not unique to the Girdwood site, nor to Northern Ireland. In every city, economic and community development plans are large with well-intentioned words and feel-good ideas – community engagement, economic opportunity for all, the omnipresent but over-used 'equity'. The specifics on how these laudable outcomes might be achieved are all too often absent. The most effective processes are frequently guided by the types of frameworks that PPR suggests, linking specific strategies to desired outcomes in partnership with those with lived experience. But there are a host of dynamics, from backroom political deals to economic concerns to weak civic engagement, that shape development processes and widen the gap between policy rhetoric and practical implementation.

The most glaring discrepancies between policy and practice emerged, to no one's great surprise, around the housing issue. In the draft Masterplan, the notions of both economic growth and 'shared space' took precedence over the documented housing crisis in North Belfast which the NIHE had communicated to the Girdwood Advisory Panel. This was despite the Girdwood/Crumlin Road development brief's assertion that 'human rights must be at the centre of all government legislation, policy and administrative practice', and its stated commitment to Section 75 as part of its policy framework (2006b: 5, 6). PPR helpfully pointed out that the right to housing is also protected in international treaties of which the UK is a signatory.[4] Consequently, under the framework of domestic law and international recommendations, good relations must come second to equality, the state

---

[3] In October 2009, draft Masterplans for the Crumlin Road and Lower Shankill were released by the DSD in partnership with RPS Planning and Environment and Jon Rowland Urban Design. Neither show evidence of substantive linkages with the adjacent Girdwood site; the courthouse and gaol are mentioned briefly but no detail is given as to their role in regenerating the area. The barracks site itself is only mentioned once in passing (DSD 2009a, 2009b). This is odd given both neighbourhoods are directly adjacent to Girdwood.

[4] E.g., Article 25 of the Universal Declaration of Human Rights, and Article 11 of the International Covenant of Economic, Social and Cultural Rights (United Nations 1948: 7; OHCHR 1966: 4).

has the obligation to provide adequate housing and discrimination based on political, religious or ethnic background is unlawful. The convenient privileging of 'shared space' and 'shared housing' is fundamentally unjust – a public body cannot hide behind the idea of 'good relations' in order to avoid duties to statutory equality. One observer noted:

> The whole issue is really around housing: there was this attitude of 'well we can't tackle the issue of housing equality because there is no community agreement'. Which if you were to compare that to racism or gender inequality, it would be unthinkable – if we can't deal with equality until everyone agrees, it would mean 'we can't deal with Black inequality because there's white people that don't agree' and so on … ('Eamonn', interview with author 2017)

SDLP MLA for North Belfast Alban Maginness later contended:

> Housing is an overriding need of such proportions that it requires to be satisfied as soon as is practicable. The development of the Mater Hospital, St. Malachy's College and a business park [at Girdwood] can all be accommodated in due course … I agree with those developments; they should take place, but they should not be an excuse to exclude or delay housing. Lack of consensus around those issues should not be used as a veto. (Hansard 2011: 371)

If one places the situation in any other city in the world, the refusal to build houses for a different racial/ethnic/religious group would be classed immediately as racist and/or sectarian. Equality Officer Tim Cunningham for the Committee on the Administration of Justice (CAJ), another human rights organisation in Northern Ireland, charged that: 'It is using and, very unfortunately, using and distorting this valuable idea of "good relations" and turning it on its head and trying to use it to effectively justify keeping people out of a certain area. That is racism and discrimination and should be seen as such and called as such and has no place in any society' (PPR 2008a: 25).

The Girdwood Residents' Jury

This context stands in contrast to the work of PPR, which was extremely important from an equality standpoint but tangential to the Girdwood Advisory Forum and the political parties. PPR were initially commissioned by some members of the CEPs for assistance around the Girdwood site and housing and had constructive relationships with many of the CEPs. They served as a critical (if lone) voice of reason in the Girdwood redevelopment process, but their approach contrasted with that of the NBCAU and the Advisory Forum and ultimately proved to be a 'thorn in the side' of the political system. Reflecting on PPR's relationships with political parties, one observer said:

> With Sinn Féin they would have had a proper issue-based relationship ... around social housing. Which is mixed. Sometimes, PPR tend to be critical of [Sinn Féin] when they're not doing enough as well, which [Sinn Féin] are very sensitive to ... the DUP is just notoriously bad with [community engagement], especially local levels, so PPR didn't have any relationship with them. ('Eamonn', interview with author 2017)

In 2008, PPR organised the 'Girdwood Residents' Jury' to ensure that the rights and voices of local residents were integral to the Girdwood development process (PPR 2008a: 5). It was formed in response to concerns that, despite the policy and planning rhetoric, residents had in fact been unable to participate in the decision-making around the site, and that the draft Masterplan did not adequately address local concerns around poverty and inequality. The Jury comprised residents of the five wards surrounding the site (Ardoyne, Crumlin, New Lodge, Shankill and Waterworks). They were selected to reflect a broad range of identities and to represent all the Section 75 categories: gender, religion, political opinion, marital status and disability status (PPR 2009: 8). According to one activist involved, it was 'deliberately not a 50/50 group' of Catholics and Protestants, but rather reflective of the diverse people within the area (author fieldnotes 2016). The final group comprised a variety of people from across the ethnosectarian divide. At a micro-level, then, productive exchange was taking place, challenging the framework of 'Orange and Green' within which politicians operated.

Prior to the Jury proceedings, residents took part in a development programme with PPR which considered how human rights and equality of opportunity could be integrated into the development. The residents established a set of human rights indicators to monitor whether the NBCAU and the DSD were effectively discharging their legal equality obligations, whether this constituted an efficient use of public money and whether proposals produced measurable outcomes for the deprived area, including employment, education, health and housing (PPR 2008a: 5, 7). The Jury also developed a specific framework for an outcomes-based approach to redevelopment, including proposals to train residents as data collectors and analysts; to conduct an audit of the skills base and obstacles to employment in their areas; and to create ring-fenced jobs and training opportunities for those marginalised from employment (PPR 2009: 9).

On 28 May 2008, the Jury convened for an event called the 'Residents' Jury on Regenerating Girdwood Barracks and Crumlin Road Gaol: A Human Rights Based Approach'. They heard evidence of best practices from local and international experts on human rights, community development and urban redevelopment. Participants included professors, city planners, activists and leaders involved in community-based regeneration from the UK and the US, and representatives from the Committee on the Administration of Justice, PPR and a local development association.[5] Presentations covered the themes of 'equality', 'participation' and 'accountability'. Maria Virginia Bras Gomes of the United Nations Committee on Economic, Social and Cultural Rights delivered the keynote address.

The event facilitated exchanges on the myth of the 'peace dividend' and the 'trickle-down effect' in multiply deprived areas. It highlighted the gap between rhetoric and practice in the Girdwood draft Masterplan, and featured practical recommendations gleaned from other redevelopment projects in low-income and inner-city areas. Former UN High Commissioner for Human Rights and President of Ireland Mary Robinson called the Jury's work 'innovative and exciting' and 'a pathfinder for other communities', citing the 'methodology of human rights indicators and benchmarks ... as central to the realisation of rights'. New York City Comptroller William Thompson stated that the Jury's approach to the Girdwood development 'quite literally has the potential to turn the remnants of conflict into the promise of the peace dividend' (PPR 2008a: 82).

However, the Residents' Jury's work on Girdwood – by all accounts an example of productive engagement and genuine community empowerment – was not taken into account by the government. According to PPR:

> These proposals were presented to officials in the DSD and OFMDFM with responsibility for the regeneration but were not accepted. The group in turn wrote to the First and Deputy First Minister with their proposals several times, who are ultimately accountable for human rights obligations. Finally, they received a response by the First and Deputy First

---

[5] The full list of speakers: Nicola Browne, policy officer, PPR; Tim Cunningham, equality officer for CAJ; Joe Donohoe, team leader of Fatima Groups United, Chair of the Canals Area Youth Service and Canals Area Partnership in South Inner City Dublin; Seamus Flynn, retired community worker for Markets Development Association, Belfast; Aideen Gilmore, deputy director of CAJ; Maria Virginia Bras Gomes, member of the UN Committee on Economic, Social and Cultural Rights and head of Portuguese Department for Social Research and International Relations; Tim Losty of the NBCAU; Inez McCormack, chair of PPR; Frank McMillan, volunteer at PPR; Joe McNeely, coordinator of the Central Baltimore Partnership, adjunct professor in community development at University of Baltimore and former director of the National Office of Neighbourhood Development; Ron Shiffman, city planner and architect; Richard Wilkinson, Professor of Social Epidemiology at the University of Nottingham Medical School and visiting professor at the International Centre for Health and Society, University College London (PPR 2008: 79–81).

Minister asking them not to continue writing to OFMDFM on this issue, and instead to engage with the civil servants. (2014: 4)

One might surmise that it was not politically expedient for either the DUP or Sinn Féin to highlight PPR's work because it demonstrated their own failure to adhere to statutory duties and to deliver both on the official legislation and the rhetorical promises of the peace agreement.

In 2009, the Residents' Jury produced a report entitled *The Girdwood Gamble* which criticised the government's approach to the regeneration. *The Girdwood Gamble* asserted that the draft Masterplan (and the half-hearted EQIA that eventually followed) were 'gambles', 'because the supposed benefits to the community are vague, ambiguous, undefined and uncertain. Available detailed statistics and evidence of best practice were not used' (PPR 2009: 8). PPR's Resident's Jury offered a systematic, clear-sighted approach to development based on both Section 75 and the tenets of community empowerment. It involved a representative sample of local residents who designed targeted strategies for Girdwood to address inequality and to improve quality of life. The type of work undertaken was hailed as 'innovative' and a 'showcase of best practice', involving experts, activists and residents alike. Yet it challenged the sectarian status quo and so, ostensibly, it was ignored by the government (PPR 2008a: 82).

Girdwood offered an opportunity for an internationally significant development that would deliver both social and economic benefit to the marginalised and traumatised neighbourhoods of North Belfast. But in the end, competing discourses around entitlement to resources constrained visions for the site. As pointed out by PPR, the ECNI and other actors marginal to the Advisory Panel process, there was a missed opportunity to streamline equality legislation and target social issues in an innovative way. Social housing allocation was not a meaningful part of the planning process, despite the rhetoric of the Good Friday Agreement and the legal provisions of Section 75. Instead, ethnosectarian territoriality prevailed and the issues of claims to space and competing definitions of 'needs' and 'rights' remained without agreement.

The economic crash of 2007 was the figurative nail in the coffin of the development and the site languished. This was the site that I stumbled on, several years later: a fenced-in vacant lot pockmarked by weeds, debris and graffiti. The draft Masterplan remained just that – a draft. Despite the potential of Girdwood, 'closed minds and attitudes' had prolonged the project, as one Advisory Forum member had predicted (Girdwood Advisory Panel 2006a), and they would continue to do so over the next decade.

CHAPTER FIVE

Ethnic Champions and the Zero-Sum Game
Political Dynamics of the Northern Ireland Assembly

The second phase of development of the Girdwood site took place in the context of a devolved Assembly in which the DUP and Sinn Féin held the balance of power. Rather than delivering the promises of the peace process, this government engaged in a series of sectarian trade-offs, backroom deals and negotiations to produce a weak and ineffectual compromise on the site. The final Girdwood Masterplan was reflective of the broader dynamics of the Assembly, whereby existing division and enmity is managed and reinforced, rather than transformed. It also reflected the state of relations at the time between partners in government Sinn Féin and the DUP: an uneasy alliance sustained by Sinn Féin's grudging willingness to compromise on the promises of the Agreement and the Northern Ireland Act in order to keep the government afloat and remain in power.

This chapter details the political context in which the second phase of the Girdwood development took place. Underneath the formal systems of power-sharing, underwritten by the legislative framework of the Act, politicians employed a range of informal tactics in pursuit of ethnonational advantage. As the government shifted from direct rule from Westminster to resentful partnership between the DUP and Sinn Féin, there was a tangible shift in community relations strategy from reconciliation to mutual accommodation. Political parties engaged in ethnic outbidding. Clientelism between politicians and elements of the community sector was alleged to occur. Finally, a zero-sum approach came to characterise resource allocation. These are forces which underline decision-making and planning on a broader scale, in cities globally, as actors negotiate for influence. In their own ways, these dynamics each came to powerfully inform the eventual Girdwood Masterplan.

Nixing a Shared Future

He doubted there was a more cynical electorate in the world. The average Northern Irish pleb could read between the lines of a speech better than any professional political analyst, disbelieving every treacherous word. Yet still they voted as predictably, election after election. He wondered why they didn't have a sectarian head-count every four years and be done with it.

(Neville 2009: 35)

The Northern Ireland Assembly had been suspended from 2002 to 2006, after three Sinn Féin members were arrested on suspicion of a spy ring and the Unionists pulled out of power-sharing in response. With the signing of the St Andrews Agreement in 2006,[1] a devolved Assembly was restored. By this point, the DUP and Sinn Féin had emerged as the two largest parties in the Assembly (rather than the more moderate UUP and SDLP, who had brokered the Good Friday Agreement). Soon after, the Assembly dropped the community relations strategy *A Shared Future*, which had been written under direct rule from Westminster. *A Shared Future*'s stated aim had been to facilitate a 'peaceful, inclusive, prosperous, stable and fair society firmly founded on the achievement of reconciliation, tolerance and mutual trust and the protection and vindication of human rights for all' (OFMDFM 2005a: 3). The document emphasised fostering a shared society, including sharing resources and shaping 'policy, practice, and institutions' (Todd and Ruane 2010: 6) to promote good relations (Shirlow and McEvoy 2008: 7). It was envisaged that good relations would be 'built on significant progress of the equality agenda' (OFMDFM 2005b).

However, the DUP and Sinn Féin saw little to gain from 'deconstructing their respective territorial constituency base' (Murtagh 2011: 1125). The principles of tolerance, equality and good relations set out in *A Shared Future* clashed with the ethnic entrepreneurialism of both parties, whose mandate was based on a more divisive, less pluralist platform. So, *A Shared Future* was dropped. It was not until March 2010 that the Executive released the draft community relations strategy *Cohesion, Sharing and Integration* for public consultation. This was produced after two and a half years of protracted negotiations between Sinn Féin and the DUP, 'who squabbled openly about its content' (Knox 2011: 549). It would be another three years before a strategy was actually agreed.

---

[1] The St Andrews Agreement restored devolved power-sharing governance to Northern Ireland, enshrined support for policing and the rule of law, and committed to an anti-poverty strategy, Irish Language Act and equality bill among other legislation (NIO 2006: 11).

Cohesion, Sharing and Integration was criticised as a regressive move away from the tentatively aspirational ideas of *A Shared Future*: a product of political deal-making rather than of genuine resolve to foster integration (Hayward 2012: 34). In reference to the strategy, the UUP charged that 'the DUP and Sinn Féin are more interested in sharing power between themselves rather than sharing office for the benefit of Northern Ireland, replacing the idea of a shared future with a "shared out future"' (UUP 2010: 1). The SDLP went further in their response to *Cohesion, Sharing and Integration*, suggesting that it was 'an utterly cynical exercise by two parties who do not want a strategy to deliver a shared future' (SDLP 2010: 5).

The mutual accommodation and emphasis on managing, rather than transforming, division found in *Cohesion, Sharing and Integration* is indicative of the dynamics between the DUP and Sinn Féin in the Assembly itself. *Cohesion, Sharing and Integration* envisioned a society that promotes 'pride in who we are' and 'confidence in our different cultural identities' (OFMDFM 2010: 9). The language suggests autonomous and distinct cultures that come into contact; the underlying assumption is of static identities that must accommodate each other (Todd and Ruane 2010: 15). In terms of 'shared space', *Cohesion, Sharing and Integration* notes that 'safe and secure shared community spaces should be developed in a culture of fairness, equality, rights, responsibilities and respect' (OFMDFM 2010: 22). Yet within the framework, 'shared space' comes as a short-term goal, before the long-term goal of tackling 'the multiple social issues effecting and entrenching community separation, exclusion and hate' (OFMDFM 2010: 7–9). This is nonsensical – if the root causes of division are not addressed first, how can shared space be achieved? Indeed, other scholars have noted that the strategy actually 'negated any serious commitment not only to desegregate housing, but also to reform the electoral blocs that reproduce support for both parties' (Murtagh and Ellis 2011: 351; Knox 2011; Todd and Ruane 2010). The context of political deal-making in which the strategy was produced, and the accompanying charges of a 'shared-out' rather than 'shared' future, came to be physically reflected in the Girdwood redevelopment process.

Throughout the document, there are also recurrent tensions between 'good relations' and 'equality'. For instance, one of *Cohesion, Sharing and Integration*'s stated objectives was to 'build on shared values of human rights and equality to build a society which honours rights and accepts our civic responsibilities to one another' (OFMDFM 2010: 11). It also mentions Section 75 and equality of opportunity as integral to governance (2010: 3). Yet, later in the document, it admits 'recognition that at times there are competing rights' (2010: 32). The concept of competing rights would continue to be instrumental in the shaping of space at Girdwood.

Though the Assembly was restored in 2007, the Girdwood site initially remained in limbo. This was due, in part, to the economic crash which led to the collapse of construction-led growth and the prospect of private investment as the great equaliser for the site (Murtagh 2011: 1124). But it was also due to the structure of the devolved government, which was predicated on a zero-sum game of resource competition, a 'tug of war' over political authority and legitimacy. The Girdwood planning process would become merely an expression of these difficulties inherent within the Northern Irish Assembly and society-at-large, demonstrating the failure of democratic governance in the region.

As outlined in Chapter Two, the power-sharing government in Northern Ireland has served to reinforce division by legitimising the existence of two exclusive ethnonational groups. Each is diametrically opposed to the other in terms of political ideology, ethnoreligious identity, the meaning of past conflict and the vision for the state's constitutional future. Rather than working towards some type of common agenda, most political parties remain in their 'sectarian comfort zone' (Planning for Spatial Reconciliation Group 2016: 24). The official rhetoric of a 'shared future', equality of opportunity and reconciliation is circumvented by these informal systems of power.

Moreover, political legitimacy is derived from within, rather than across, the two groups; ethnicity and identity rank higher than citizenship. And once identity has been codified as the guiding force in politics, then those professing to be 'the truest manifestation' of an identity gain credibility (Reidy 2013). These informal dynamics have informed formal systems of governance. After the Good Friday Agreement, increasingly polarised voting patterns saw the DUP and Sinn Féin outstrip the more moderate UUP, SDLP and Alliance (McGarry and O'Leary 2006b: 254; MacGinty et al. 2007: 8).[2] In one sense, this seems paradoxical: statistics suggest that the majority of people had endorsed peace, power-sharing and varying degrees of cross-community mixing in everyday life.[3] Yet they continued to return the two most ethnically intransigent – and, arguably, sectarian – parties to power. Despite voters' support of the peace process, they also wanted their ethnonational interests protected: given the nature of power-sharing and inevitable ethnic bargaining – as Kelly pithily

---

[2] According to Higson (2008: 6): 'Parties such as the DUP and Sinn Féin had massive expansions in the Westminster vote between 1997 and 2005 (+125 percent and +37.5 percent, respectively), other parties such as the UUP and SDLP, who presented a more moderate stance, have seen a significant drop in their vote (-50.7 percent and -34.7 percent, respectively)'.

[3] The Northern Ireland Life and Times Survey showed that in 2016, 77 per cent of respondent said they would prefer to live in a mixed-religion neighbourhood given the choice; 88 per cent preferred mixed-religion workplaces; and the majority of people viewed parks, shopping centres and leisure centres as 'shared and open' to both Catholics and Protestants (ARK 2016).

terms it, 'communal horse-trading' (2013: 49) – voters will want the strongest voice to represent them (Mitchell et al. 2009: 402).[4]

Rationally, citizens should vote for what the majority of them desire according to the annual Life and Times Survey – a devolved system based on equality, accountability and integration. However, even as people have rejected the violence of the Troubles and embraced power-sharing and varying levels of space-sharing, latent ethnosectarian allegiance and collective memories of past conflict have continued to hold sway. Even as people experienced ineffectual and sometimes allegedly corrupt political leadership, even if they had been marginalised from the promised 'peace dividend', they still returned the same parties to power.

In this sense, there is little motivation for moderation in politics, especially in terms of identity issues, and we see ethnic outbidding at play. This is one reason for the primacy of the DUP over the UUP and other Unionist parties, and of Sinn Féin over the SDLP and smaller splinter Republican groups, as well as the uneven support for cross-community parties like Alliance, People Before Profit and the Green Party. Parties like Sinn Féin and the DUP have been called 'ethnic tribune parties': 'simultaneously pragmatic (with regard to resources) and intransigent (with regard to identity)' (Mitchell in Gormley-Heenan and MacGinty 2008: 58). As one community worker put it, '[the DUP and Sinn Féin] are seen as being ethnic champions – "Vote for us to keep themmuns out"' (author fieldnotes 2016).

Politicians deploy discourses of fear and embattlement against the 'Other' to reinforce this primacy and to consolidate votes. In the 2017 election, for instance, DUP First Minister Arlene Foster said, 'I know other parties don't like us saying it, but the reality is that every vote for another Unionist party [other than the DUP] is a vote which is lost in the battle to make sure that Sinn Féin does not win this election' (Gordon 2017).

In past elections, Unionists and Nationalists have both been guilty of drawing on sectarianism and the 'politics of fear' to score votes and maintain power. In 2015, Sinn Féin's Gerry Kelly drew fire for 'blatant sectarian head-counting' when he released an election brochure for North Belfast, traditionally held by the DUP's Nigel Dodds. The leaflet featured the 2011 census figures for North Belfast, '46.9 per cent Catholic and 45.6 per cent Protestant', accompanied by the tag line: 'Make the change, make history' (Black 2015). This was ostensibly a reference to the rising Catholic/Nationalist population's chance to 'take over' power from the declining Unionist/Protestant presence in North Belfast. In the same election, the DUP

---

[4] After the Assembly's 2017 collapse, and as voters grow tired of the Assembly's continued inability to function in the context of Brexit and the pandemic, voting patterns have begun to change; see the Epilogue.

and UUP agreed a 'Unionist pact', fielding only one Unionist candidate in four constituencies to maximise their representation at Westminster and prevent Alliance, SDLP and Sinn Féin MPs from getting a seat (BBC News 2015; McDonald 2015).

This outbidding is particularly prevalent in North Belfast, where demographic shift has favoured the Catholic/Nationalist population and electoral power has, after many years of tension, approached a tipping point. In 2019, Sinn Féin's John Finucane narrowly beat out the DUP's Nigel Dodds by a margin of 1,943 votes in a 'showdown election' for North Belfast. Dodds had held the seat since 2001.[5] This was a significant win for Sinn Féin – North Belfast had long been a symbolic battleground and in advance of the election, the SDLP had pulled out of the constituency to give Sinn Féin the best chance of defeating the DUP (*The Journal* 2019). The loss of Dodds, who had been the DUP's leader in Westminster, was a major blow to the party.

Since 2017, Sinn Féin's vote share had increased by 5.4 per cent, while the DUP's fell by 3.1 per cent. This was exactly the type of development Unionists had hoped to avoid. During the Girdwood regeneration, the DUP still held a slim lead in North Belfast electoral demographics and the prevailing narrative was that new-build housing could potentially increase Sinn Féin's share of the vote, toppling the DUP's tenuous hold on North Belfast. This was alleged by some interview respondents I spoke with as the reason for the DUP's refusal to build social housing in the constituency and at Girdwood (interviews with author). They offered anecdotal evidence of the informal influence of territorialism and sectarian head-counting on formal, rational policy and planning.

Pork Barrels and Hidden Transcripts

Another example of the tension between formal and informal systems of power in Northern Ireland is that of alleged clientelism among political parties and the community sector. These tensions, too, emerged as part of the redevelopment process at Girdwood. Clientelism has been defined as a system of resource allocation based on 'mutual material advantage': political patron attempts to steer the maximum share of resources, like funding or jobs, to 'their group' in return for their vote and support (Brinkerhoff and Goldsmith 2002: 2). Whilst this is by no means unique to Northern Ireland – it can be found in varying

---

[5] According to the Election Office for Northern Ireland statistics, the DUP received 21,135 votes (43.1 per cent), while Sinn Féin received 23,078 (47.1 per cent) (Electoral Office for Northern Ireland 2019).

forms in most political systems – it is 'at its core a means for setting policy about "who gets what"' (Brinkerhoff and Goldsmith 2002: 2).

Clientelism is the effective opposite of democracy, as resources are allocated not based on objective need or rights, but to curry support within the grassroots, community development elite and business elite. Sometimes this is referred to as 'pork-barrel spending', whereby politicians lobby for publicly funded projects for 'their' local areas (Brinkerhoff and Goldsmith 2002: 6; Acheson and Milofsky 2008: 77). Instead of the state making a unilateral decision based on common civic interest, decisions are coloured by how they will channel funding and benefits to either the collective 'group' or the individual (Acheson and Milofsky 2008: 77). In Northern Ireland, it can be argued that this is an inevitable product of the peace process in its structural empowerment of two competing blocs. Rather than allocating resources according to democratic principles or objective need, groups engage in a contest to secure the most resources for 'their' side. Trade-offs, backroom dealings and politically expedient relationships within and between groups are all plays in the 'zero-sum' game.

The Northern Ireland Assembly has been at the centre of several scandals over allegations of corruption and clientelism. These allegations range from instances of pay-outs to family members[6] and businesses[7] connected with

---

[6] For example: Carál Ní Chuilín failed to declare in Stormont's register of interests £11,320 paid to her common-law brother-in-law, J.J. McGee, for decorating her office. This was put down to an 'administrative oversight' by Sinn Féin. The party was found to have paid £68,000 of public funds for McGee's maintenance and refurbishment services over five years (Barnes 2014). At Stormont, unlike in Westminster, there are no limits on employment of family members, and MLAs are not required to advertise or interview for staff. It was found that 'three quarters of all DUP MLAs have at least one relative on the payroll, including eight wives, and eight sons'. In accordance with Assembly rules, DUP member Robin Newton employed his wife as office manager and his son as researcher, and they earned a total of £60,831 per year. He also employed his daughter – first, as an independent contractor, and then separately, under the moniker of 'ERN Research Services' – and she received up to £13,780 for a year-and-a-half (Cromie 2013; BBC News 2014b).

[7] Sinn Féin was revealed to have paid £700,000 of public money to Research Services Ireland, a company run by its own finance managers. One MLA said they had never heard of the company, and a *Spotlight* investigation could not find evidence of any research produced. According to BBC News, 'Five years ago, the police were alerted to concerns about expenses claims made by Sinn Féin for work done by the company … at the time, the Police Service of Northern Ireland decided that an investigation was not necessary. Sinn Féin's biggest claims for payment to Research Services Ireland came after that date' (BBC News 2014b). Another instance is the Red Sky debacle. In 2011, the Red Sky maintenance firm in East Belfast – 'a key constituency for the DUP' – was informed its contract would be terminated by the Housing Executive (Young 2015). This was amid concerns about overcharging and a possible criminal investigation around suspected fraud. Red Sky subsequently went

political parties, to the NAMA (National Assets and Management Agency) scandal, in which DUP officials were accused of involvement in siphoning funds off the sale of toxic loan assets in the wake of the Great Recession in 2008.[8] Of course, these issues are not unique to Northern Ireland, but rather exemplify how those in positions of power may attempt to allocate resources for mutual political and social advantage. However, it does suggest that the formal systems of power in the post-ceasefire government (e.g., policy, procedures, laws and regulations) are perverted by informal systems of power (e.g., the underlying influence of sectarianism and the 'hidden transcripts' of alleged clientelism and private dealings) (Komarova 2008: 24). For former People before Profit MLA Gerry Carroll: 'Either there is a culture of gross incompetency in the Executive, or there is an endemic culture of corruption. Which is it?' (Hansard 2016b: 43).

Close government-community sector relationships in Northern Ireland have also attracted allegations of clientelism. This can affect the dynamics of decision-making around community development and neighbourhood regeneration programmes. In other research on the community sector, some interviewees explain that in their view,

> The political elite transfer resources into communities as a crude mechanism for buying votes and influence, or to keep 'certain individuals busy'; that may be a threat to local political stability ... in such a system, objective need and the potential impact on communities is not at the top of the list of decision-making processes for some politicians. (Ketola and Hughes 2016: 37)

Another interviewee in Ketola and Hughes's study also alleged that 'people shout in their communities and then the politicians make sure that the money is pumped in to keep people in jobs, but it's not actually making a difference

---

into administration. However, the DUP attempted to prevent the Housing Executive from cancelling the contract. The party put significant pressure on the Housing Executive and held meetings with the senior management of Red Sky, without the administrators present. The Housing Executive said, 'this raises the question of did these meetings constitute canvassing and lobbying for government contracts and in breach, not only of public procurement principles, but basic codes of conduct in public life' (McCaffrey 2012c; BBC News 2011a).

[8] The NAMA was set up to deal with toxic loans after the 2008 property crash in the Republic of Ireland. An 850-unit Northern Irish portfolio was sold off to New York firm Cerberus in 2014; two law firms were involved in the process. The former managing partner of one law firm came under investigation regarding £7m that was 'improperly diverted' to an Isle of Man bank account. It was alleged this was a 'success fee' for First Minister, at the time Peter Robinson, and four businessmen. Robinson emphatically denied involvement (O'Neill 2016).

in terms of what it was set out to do' (2016: 37). This perspective was again voiced to me by a community worker who stated that 'the politicians pay off key [community] groups. What have they done [for their areas]? Nothing! But they still get their phony baloney jobs and they can swan about the community ... and that frustrates people in the community who then become disempowered' (author fieldnotes 2016).

It seems that the hierarchical structures which characterised paramilitary groups during the conflict are now replicated in a different arena: strategists and leaders have moved into politics, those on the next rung have been rewarded with community development jobs, who then channel funding into their specific areas and provide further jobs to friends and family (Bean 2007: 98). In turn, 'closed networks of favoured interests' are created and sustained (Ketola and Hughes 2016: 37). For example, a community worker told me, in reference to development work, 'if you're not controlled by a paramilitary group, which have now kind of been demilitarised, on the Nationalist side, you're not supposed to talk about that, but you have Sinn Féin-controlled groups and they're the ones who get the money' (author fieldnotes 2016). There is a strong perception that the DUP and Sinn Féin 'split the pot', giving funding to their acolytes, and that this is how development decisions work. Like the Girdwood development, ethnosectarian interest seems to win out over resource allocation by objective need.

A blatant example is the controversy surrounding the Social Investment Fund (SIF). The £80 million fund, set up in 2011, purported to 'make life better for people living in targeted areas by reducing poverty, unemployment and physical deterioration'. Funding was given to 'projects prioritised by local Steering Groups' (Northern Ireland Executive n.d.). However, the SIF was beset by numerous issues. As far back as the 2011 consultation on the programme, the UUP recorded concerns that the First and Deputy First Minister were 'solely responsible for identifying groups and individuals' to form the steering groups (UUP 2011: 3). It was later found that these steering group members made the funding decisions amongst themselves and could award it to their own groups; there was no competitive tendering process (Bell 2016).[9] 'So you had projects that were going through, fast-tracked ... that seemed, on the face of it, to have a political agenda', one social justice activist recalled ('Eamonn, interview with author 2016). The purpose of the SIF was also questioned given

---

[9] In 2017, for example, a BBC *Spotlight* documentary found that the Speaker of the Assembly, the DUP's Robin Newton, failed to declare his role as Advisor to Charter NI whilst he sat on a steering group that awarded Charter NI a £1.7 million contract and a £226,000 payment from the SIF. Documents from Charter NI stated he had previously been involved in attending board meetings, subcommittees and lobbying for funds on the organisation's behalf (Dempster 2017).

the array of policy initiatives and funding streams already in existence to reduce poverty, unemployment and dereliction. Lastly, the fund was protected by the Executive despite cuts to the public and community and voluntary sectors. This led to allegations that the money was a 'slush fund' for the DUP and Sinn Féin (Hansard 2016a: 9; UUP 2011: 3).

In 2016, controversy reignited when it was revealed £1.7 million had been allocated to Charter NI, which is headed by alleged UDA commander Dee Stitt. The press release on the Northern Ireland Executive's website was accompanied by a cheery photograph of Stitt with the First Minister, the DUP's Arlene Foster (Northern Ireland Executive 2016; Morris 2016a). This raised fresh questions about the SIF, including a charge that it undermined a 2015 Executive action plan to tackle paramilitarism.[10] In the Assembly, a motion was tabled by the opposition parties for an independent review of the SIF's operations;[11] it was defeated by the DUP and Sinn Féin. Within the proceedings, allegations of 'secrecy and cronyism', 'elitism and patronage' and 'maximum control freakery between the DUP and Sinn Féin' were levelled by members of the opposition (Hansard 2016a: 3, 12, 15). Stuart Dickson, Alliance MLA asserted that 'the real rationale [of the SIF] seems to be to concentrate power in the hands of certain local groups favoured by the two dominant political parties, namely, the DUP and Sinn Féin'.

Claire Hanna of the SDLP remarked, 'we are building up a client state, and that should be of great concern to anyone who believes in democracy and the rule of law' (Hansard 2016a: 20). In a radio interview, Sir Alistair Graham, the former chair of the Committee on Standards in Public Life, stated that the SIF 'doesn't stand up to the principles that are generally held to be appropriate for the awarding of public contracts' and suggested it was in need of 'root and branch reform' (Bell 2016).

The SIF programme also raised questions of how funding should be 'shared-out', leading to a prolonged stalemate over releasing funds. By 2013, three years after the SIF's initial introduction, the DUP and Sinn Féin had failed to reach consensus on how to allocate the £80 million to deprived neighbourhoods. The issue of 'objective need', as at Girdwood, again reared its head because data

---

[10] *A Fresh Start for Northern Ireland*, a series of actions agreed by the Executive and British and Irish governments in 2015, committed to tackling and challenging the 'insidious influence' of paramilitarism, and set up an independent panel to provide recommendations (Northern Ireland Executive 2015: 11, 17).

[11] *A Fresh Start* also made provision for an official opposition at Stormont for the first time in the Assembly's history. Those entitled to a ministerial position under the D'Hondt formula can opt out to form an opposition (Northern Ireland Executive 2015: 35). Thus far, the UUP and SDLP have formed the official opposition, and parties outside the Executive (Alliance, People before Profit, the Green Party and the Traditional Unionist Voice (TUV)) act as the unofficial opposition.

showed that Nationalist areas suffered from greater levels of deprivation. Of the 20 most deprived wards in Northern Ireland at that time, 16 were Catholic/Nationalist (NISRA 2010: 27). Unionist areas would therefore receive a smaller share of the money if it were allocated by objective need. Instead, Unionists argued that 'pockets of deprivation' existed, experiencing specific problems like educational underattainment, and thus they deserved an equal share of funding. This delay, as an investigation conducted by *The Detail* points out, came in the face of the economic recession, high levels of unemployment and impending welfare cuts (McCaffrey 2013). This is yet another example of differing interpretations of 'need' leading to stalemate and impeding effective resource allocation, as they did during the first phase of the Girdwood development.

There are other dynamics at work between the government and community sector. A manager of a social enterprise argued that 'it's a bit more of a complicated picture than just throwing money at your favourite groups' ('Thomas', interview with author 2016). For instance, resources are allocated following a 'safe hands' mentality, where money is given to gatekeepers like larger, professional voluntary groups because there is an assurance they will deliver. In one Nationalist community worker's opinion: 'The government decide who their stakeholders are and they've built a relationship up over several years with them, but some of that relationship is built on their capacity to be able to deliver projects … to the convenience of the government. So that the government would look good, or the minister would look good' ('Maurice', interview with author 2016). This leaves smaller groups who lack the capacity to deliver programming, who are unaligned or disagree with the DUP or Sinn Féin or who are more 'democratic' and 'grassroots' in their programming at a disadvantage. Political actors thus shape the context in which groups work, lending support to some while constraining the voices of dissenters. It can be difficult for groups outside the political mainstream, or those who challenge the status-quo, to access funding. PPR, for instance, does not receive any government funding but is instead supported by independent bodies like the Big Lottery Fund, Atlantic Philanthropies and The Community Foundation for Northern Ireland (PPR n.d.).

The issue of vested interests and the 'peace industry' emerges with some established gatekeepers, whose jobs depend on delivering the programmes in question:

> Essentially all government are supposed to go out to consultation about any of their programmes, about the ideas that they're having, and those ideas should be generated from the people they serve, but for many, the clientelism comes in there as well. Depends on who they're consulting. So if they're only consulting groups whose job it is to make sure that we have capacity-building programmes, because they would be the ones to

deliver them ... then there's a bit of a conflict of interest there. You're talkin' to people who, it is in their interest, their livelihood, for jobs, to say, yeah, yeah, they're needed. Are they really needed by communities? Because if they were really needed by communities, how come ... all the people who – or all those areas in the multiple deprivation indices, have been the same areas for 20 years? ('Maurice', interview with author 2016)

In Ketola and Hughes's report, a government official suggests:

There are conflicts here which the sector probably needs to be a little bit more disciplined in managing, you are speaking to them as advocates for the people they are representing, but at the same time they can be the providers of a service and therefore there is a degree of self-interest, organisational interest, in the discussions that is not always fully transparent. (2016: 27)

The issue of the 'peace industry' has been raised regarding the billions of pounds that have been poured into multiply deprived and conflict-affected communities in Northern Ireland. While many community development organisations provide critical support in response to social issues within their neighbourhoods, their organisational stability and employment also depends on these issues existing in the first place. This strange paradox invites the question of how community 'needs' are assessed and funded.[12]

Tit for Tat: A Zero-Sum Approach to Governance

A final dynamic to consider in Northern Ireland's informal policymaking and planning is the zero-sum approach to resource distribution. The government typically allocates funding along horizontal lines: one side cannot benefit unless the other side does, equally. The Ulster-Scots dialect, for example, must receive the same amount of funding as the Irish language, despite the latter being more widely spoken.[13] A community activist reflected: 'With this talk about

---

[12] See Chapter 7 for more information.
[13] According to Conradh na Gaeilge, 'it is estimated that the 6,000 people who use the Irish education system in the North will double in the next 7 years' (2017: 5). The Irish language has a dedicated, robust and growing base of support in Northern Ireland (Northern Visions 2017). In 2019/20, 17 per cent of the adult population had some knowledge of Irish, the highest level recorded over the entire trend period from 2011/12, and this proportion increased from the previous data collection period (Communities NI 2020). Unionists often equate Irish-Gaelic with the Ulster-Scots dialect, a cultural inheritance from early Protestant settlers to the province of

objective need, equality, these types of things ... I think to such a degree that Sinn Féin went into an Executive, they talk about equality and all that, but when it comes down to having to negotiate things with the DUP, they fall into the trap of "quid pro quo"' ('Eamonn', interview with author 2017). In terms of infrastructure, one community worker remarked, 'they put £2 million into Woodvale Park [on Protestant Shankill Road] and £2 million into Dunville Park [on Catholic Falls Road]' (author fieldnotes 2016). This statement suggests that this is how politics and planning function. Resources aren't necessarily targeted – instead, one side has to get what the other side gets. Even people on the ground perceive that this is how politics works.

Within the power-sharing government, the DUP and Sinn Féin do not have to share political end goals or values, but they have to come to some kind of grudging compromise to ensure the government remains afloat. Yet they cannot be perceived as deviating too far from their accepted position by their respective constituencies – any attempt to broaden party appeal or challenge the status quo would risk alienating their electoral base. It is a fine balance to strike. There is also pressure from the bottom-up in terms of resources; as one interview respondent said, 'you've politicians who are asked by their electorate, you know, "Where is the money comin' into our area? Why are our groups not receiving money?"' ('Thomas', interview with author 2016). Politicians are 'obsessed with striking a careful balance' between themselves in order to hold on to power and support (Bean 2007: 5). Devolution has thus produced a 'deal and trade-off arrangement' rather than meaningful transformation or reconciliation. The Planning for Spatial Reconciliation Group describe this as a 'deal process' rather than a 'peace process', which has only reinforced sectarian power blocs and polarisation on the ground (2016: 22). As Nolan notes, contrary to the aspirational rhetoric of the peace process, these 'deals and side deals' only constitute a model of peace without reconciliation: a 'culture of endless negotiation has become embedded and, without a vision of a shared society to sustain it, the peace process has lost the power to inspire' (2014: 11).

A 2013 *Economist* article summarised some of these issues with governance in 'post-conflict' societies more generally:

> Power-sharing creates weak governments; nobody trusts anyone else enough to grant them real power. Poor administration hobbles business. Ethnic mafias become entrenched. Integration is postponed indefinitely.

Ulster. Linguists have argued it is a dialect, not a language (McCall 2002: 204), and commentators have suggested that its reinvention has occurred simply as an identity marker to counterbalance the revival of Irish (Nic Craith 2001: 24). Ulster-Scots can be understood by English speakers: phrases like 'Whit dae they caa ye?' (What is your name?), for instance, are cited by sceptics.

> Lacking genuine political competition, with no possibility of decisive electoral victories, public administration in newly pacified nations is often a mess.

These failures of governance can be observed in other places emerging from civil conflict, like Lebanon or Sri Lanka (Kleinfield 2005). Randa Nucho, for instance, describes the notion of the 'failed state' in Lebanon, where the provision of public service is piecemeal, infrastructure is crumbling and urban planning is indelibly shaped by sectarianism (2016: 3). In Northern Ireland, the 'deal process' marks a conspicuous gap between the rhetoric of peacebuilding and the reality of the devolved government. There has been no sense of transformation or political willingness for reconciliation. Instead, the two-bloc system has encouraged ethnic outbidding, thwarted healthy political competition and emboldened inefficient and allegedly corrupt resource allocation. As former Justice Minister David Ford (Alliance) observed during a 2016 election debate: 'Not looking forward to the future, not looking about growing our economy, not looking about growing a united community, not looking to meet the needs of our children to stop them emigrating. Instead of that, we're just into who's biggest and who's not biggest' (BBC News 2016a). It is difficult to measure outcomes for ordinary people in the political fracas. In a cross-community focus group, one participant noted in reference to politicians, 'time and time again … people's needs have become secondary to party-political ambitions [regarding Unionists]' (Hall 2015a: 7). At Stormont, the Assembly floor is an arena for political point-scoring and tit-for-tat belittling. Sinn Féin and DUP members face opposite each other, across the Assembly chamber, despite sharing power in government (BBC News 2016c). A Middlesex University study of the Assembly observed that, 'out of order utterances were frequent and confrontational; many illegal interventions were about "giving way," contesting the floor; and points of order are common to confront opponents or to get a political point into the official report' (Shaw 2013: 49).

At times, these back-and-forth arguments are almost rote – a well-worn performance where parties repeat the same tired lines. Proceedings always seem to circle back to the legacy of the past, the role of the 'Other' in perpetuating it, and the inability to agree on moving forward. Accepting the victimhood of the 'Other' would mean accepting some measure of responsibility and seeing the conflict from another's perspective (Shirlow 2006b: 235). The failure to do so from the political elite reinforces a sense of communal opposition.

Hansard can make depressing reading (if you're into that sort of thing), 'riven with sarcasm and political smear' and sly jabs slipped into sentences (Hayward 2014: 34). For instance, one December 2016 Assembly debate was focused on the controversies around the SIF. In response to legitimate queries by Alliance, the SDLP, and the UUP on the allocation of funds, DUP MLA

Christopher Stalford charged them all with 'rank political opportunism'. Fellow DUP MLA Pam Cameron said, 'I expect nothing less than such negative spin from the Alliance Party, which seeks to add further sensationalism and headline-grabbing to this already "Nolanised"[14] and anti-Assembly BBC non-issue' (Hansard 2016a: 5, 10).

Sinn Féin MLA Philip McGuigan was similarly defensive, comparing the other parties to 'a disorientated boxer swinging wildly for all his might and hoping to get lucky and land that knockout punch' (Hansard 2016a: 10). These colourful comments seem intended to obfuscate or divert attention from the issue at hand. What is clear is that such behaviour overshadows objective decision-making on pressing economic and social realities – in this case that public money for community development had been potentially mishandled, misappropriated and, in any case, delayed. This style of 'barracking' can be found in other parliaments and assemblies, like Westminster, for example. However, in Northern Ireland, it is underlined by deeper enmities, which in turn impact upon policymaking and resource allocation (Hayward 2008: 1).

This laundry list of informal political mechanisms counteracts the formal systems of legislation – the rule of law – on which the devolved government was supposed to be built. Rather than holding to the rhetoric set forth by the Agreement and Act, and by *A Shared Future*, perceived clientelism, sectarian contestation and zero-sum party politics have become the central forces in policymaking and delivery. Although the power-sharing government was set up under a consociational framework, these tactics speak to a new dispensation of an ethnocratic state, whereby resource allocation and territorial contest are framed through ethnosectarian logic, politics are polarised and prevailing legal and economic frameworks are only employed to the extent they do not harm the interests of power. This also speaks to the dynamics and relationships within and between political parties as they jostle for power and influence. The result is that 'top-down' quarrels supersede input from the 'bottom-up' and fail to efficiently target or transform social and economic deprivation. It was within this context that the second phase of the Girdwood regeneration took place, and these trends had a direct hand in both the development process and the final design for the space itself.

---

[14] Referring to BBC talk show and radio host Stephen Nolan, whose broadcasts often gleefully sensationalise or dramatise current political issues.

CHAPTER SIX

Carve-Up or Compromise?
The Bid for the Girdwood Community Hub

The first phase of development had been stymied by disagreement on housing 'needs' and 'rights' among the Advisory Panel, and then, the global economic crash. However, the subsequent stasis around Girdwood coincided with a new round of funding from the European Union's Special Programmes Body (SEUPB), 'The EU Programme for Peace and Reconciliation in Northern Ireland and the Border Region of Ireland (2007–2013)' (hereafter referred to as PEACE III). Previous PEACE Programmes I and II had been designed to 'focus on reconciling communities and contributing towards a shared society' (SEUPB 2007: 4). PEACE III was a continuation of these aims.

PEACE III seemed like a golden opportunity to secure funding for Girdwood. Belfast City Council dashed off a hasty application for a 'Girdwood Community Hub' and mixed-use site. The application required an independent economic appraisal of the project. Project appraisers recommended 500 units of housing on the site, 40 per cent of which would be social housing. This was based on an EQIA on Girdwood that was eventually conducted in 2008 and housing need statistics for North Belfast at the time. But the issue of housing remained contentious. Whilst social housing should have been a major part of the site, this, again, did not occur. Instead, another clash of opposing discourses around 'needs' and 'rights' surfaced. This time, the rhetoric of 'differential deprivation' was deployed by the DUP to refer to dereliction in Protestant/Unionist areas as commensurate to continued overcrowding and homelessness in Nationalist spaces, thereby sanctioning a skewed version of resource allocation. This narrative influenced both the development of the site and wider policy and planning. On the other hand, Sinn Féin conducted an about-face on their platform of equal social housing provision for North Belfast, agreeing to only 60 houses as part of the final plan for the Girdwood site. They deployed their own set of discourses to attempt to explain the decision. Other agents emerged to challenge Sinn Féin's relationship with their partners in power, alleging they had compromised housing in North Belfast for a backroom deal on the Maze prison site. A sense of injustice and dissatisfaction began to simmer within elements of Sinn Féin's traditional electorate in Catholic/Nationalist North Belfast.

The final Girdwood Masterplan was a simple colour-blocked map of the site. There were two areas of housing and two parking lots, one on the Nationalist side and one on the Unionist side of the development. There was space for a leisure centre and playing fields in the middle, in a neighbourhood that already had a critical mass of both. Sceptics suggested the site was a selfish 'shared-out' compromise by the DUP and Sinn Féin, rather than a meaningful move towards building a shared future.

From Contested to 'Shared': The European Union (EU) PEACE III Programme

They don't socialise, they don't mix, they don't worship [together], they don't live in a mixed environment. Why would anybody expect that if you throw millions of euros or pounds at them that they would suddenly start?

(Foley and Robinson 2004: 24)

Between 2007 and 2011, the Northern Ireland Assembly failed to produce a community relations strategy. However, a draft Equality Impact Assessment was finally conducted on the Girdwood site and put forth for consultation from October 2008 to January 2009, under DSD Minister Margaret Ritchie of the SDLP. The EQIA was supported by NBCAU, the organisation that had been tasked with the initial plans around the site (DSD 2008: 2).[1] This was the first EQIA conducted on a regeneration project in Northern Ireland (author fieldnotes 2016). The document was still predicated on the tenets of economic development and tourism for the site. It did, however, highlight Housing Executive statistics on the North Belfast waiting list for social housing at the time: in March 2008, 1,053 (self-identified) Catholic households and 421 Protestant households were in housing stress (DSD 2008: 49). The EQIA did not set out concrete recommendations, noting that disagreement on housing provision could not 'distract from the primary duty to the promotion of equality of opportunity … nevertheless one cannot ignore the need to promote good relations given the objective of shared space' (2008: 50). An activist reflected, 'I

---

[1] Chapter Three defined the NBCAU as the overarching organisation set up by the OFMDFM to oversee the CEP, made up of civil servants and the Housing Executive. The NBCAU was an attempt to create a joined-up approach within government to deliver the Dunlop Report's recommendations.

think the EQIA at the end of the day built a bit of pressure for the housing ... but didn't do much more. I mean, it was a pressure thing, as opposed to the mainstreaming of equality' ('Eamonn', interview with author 2017). Because the Catholic/Nationalist SDLP controlled the DSD at the time, they brought the need for social housing into the spotlight. Yet the DUP, as the largest party in the Assembly, still held power within the government. So, despite the prescriptions of Section 75, the same tension between equality and good relations continued to stall consensus.

Meanwhile, the Girdwood site sat empty. As one community worker drily remarked, 'Sinn Féin couldn't see any political capital from regenerating that zone if there was no houses on it, and the DUP couldn't see any political capital from regenerating that zone because there was no way they could control it' ('Jim', interview with author 2016). However, this period coincided with PEACE III, a new round of funding from the European Union to support reconciliation in Northern Ireland. The PEACE programme's definition of 'reconciliation' involves different interwoven strands including: developing a shared vision for a 'fair' society; dealing with the past; and meaningful social, attitudinal, economic and political change (Hamber and Kelly in SEUPB 2007: 29, emphasis added). The definition suggests a space where 'The culture of suspicion, fear, mistrust and violence is broken down and opportunities and space are opened up in which people can hear and be heard ... *The social, economic and political structures which gave rise to the conflict and estrangement are identified, reconstructed or addressed, and transformed*' (SEUPB 2007: 29, emphasis added). For the PEACE Programme, transformation was the end goal.

PEACE III consisted of €225 million in funding (SEUPB 2007: 5) towards these objectives, in particular addressing the 'physical segregation or polarisation of places or communities ... with a view to encouraging increased social and economic cross-community ... engagement' (SEUPB 2007: 38). The Programme priorities specifically targeted divided and marginalised areas that had missed out on economic development and suffered from high levels of sectarian tension. Perfect, on paper, for somewhere like North Belfast. Besides, the economic crash in 2007 had foiled the prospect of private investment or an 'anchor tenant' as a catalyst for redevelopment. With this in mind, Belfast City Council put forth a bid for PEACE III funding: a 'Community Hub' on the Girdwood Barracks site. One Nationalist community worker related, 'it happened at a time when the economic bubble burst ... I think there was this understanding that you know, the private sector, private money would have a big role to play [in Girdwood]. That didn't happen, and the only game in town was then European money' ('Liam', interview with author 2016).

As a result, the application was alleged to have been dashed off in a haphazard manner, without consultation. A Unionist community worker reflected that, '[it was] a grope in the dark, at the beginning – "let's get some money to put something in this site separate from housing"' (author fieldnotes 2016). According to the manager of a social enterprise:

> This was effectively an internal paper done by the City Council ... I think they stuck in three or four applications [for PEACE III capital funding]. Council officers – it was a case [of], if you were asked from above, 'What have you done for PEACE III?' they could say, 'Well, I stuck in this application'. So, I think there was a degree to which it was put in with no great expectation of success ... and so there was absolutely no consultation. ('Thomas', interview with author 2016)

As part of the Council's application, a consulting firm conducted an external economic appraisal of the bid and submitted it independently to the SEUPB. Their appraisal outlined the potential of the Girdwood site to fit PEACE III's objectives, along with detailed costings and a list of proposed facilities. In terms of the contested housing element, the appraisers consulted with the NBCAU after the EQIA was carried out. According to their findings, the Masterplan had been reshaped based on the premise 'that equality has a priority over community relations and therefore prevailing housing needs necessitate the inclusion of social housing on the site' (Cogent Management Consulting 2010: 2). The PEACE III programme had also included 'equality of opportunity' as a key part of its funding requirements, specifically mentioning Section 75 (SEUPB 2007: 45). The revised layout for the site, then, based on the EQIA and according to this appraisal document, provided for 500 units of residential development, 40 per cent of which would be social and affordable housing; mixed-use development sites; a leisure facility; playing fields; and extensions to St. Malachy's College and Mater Hospital (Cogent Management Consulting 2010: 2).

The council application for the Community Hub element of the site framed the idea of 'shared space' as congruent with PEACE III funding outlines – 'shared space' as a tool for peacebuilding and reconciliation. It assured that 'the Hub will be a true shared facility' and that the 'ethos of a shared and welcoming space is designed into the space from the outset' (Cogent Management Consulting 2010: 6). Proposed facilities and programmes for the space included: multi-purpose rooms for dialogue and town hall-style meetings; boxing facilities and changing facilities for pitches; inter-community counselling and mental health clinics; victims and survivors' workshops; community policing programmes; a multimedia suite with training programmes; and a cross-community social economy café (Cogent Management Consulting 2010: 8). Belfast Met, a regional higher education institution, was named as a project delivery partner. They would locate one of their campuses in the Hub. The peace and reconciliation outcomes listed included community and political consensus on the development of shared space and good relations; youth and community engagement; and increased ownership of the Hub as a shared community space (Cogent Management Consulting 2010: 11).

These plans contrast somewhat with the draft Masterplan and Advisory Forum's initial rhetoric about 'shared space' deriving from neutral development and economic growth. Instead, the rhetoric of the application is in line with European Union funding priorities and tailors the Hub to the PEACE III application's remit for shared public spaces. The application takes the social housing element of the EQIA into account, providing for residential development in line with Section 75. However, there is little mention of the EQIA in terms of addressing broader social inequality and long-term unemployment (e.g., targeted training programmes, social clauses or job creation). This seems like a missed opportunity. For instance, under the application's 'Proposed Staffing' section, the prospect of jobs for local residents is not discussed. A 'Shared Space Management team', city council leisure staff, Libraries NI staff and Belfast Met staff are the only positions listed (Cogent Management Consulting 2010: 15).

To comply with funding requirements, the application had to stress its potential for good relations and 'community engagement'. PEACE III required local authorities to work with community partners, noting that 'the demonstration of active partnership will be a requirement for funding' (SEUPB 2007: 47). The council's project proposal itself was for a 'Community Hub'. Yet during the course of their appraisal, the independent consultants questioned all the surrounding community groups and CEPs. Not one had received any notification or had any knowledge of the council's plans for a Hub, even those groups who had been involved in the initial Girdwood Advisory Forum (Cogent Management Consulting 2010: 44). The final Economic Appraisal, with its detailed costings and proposals for a 'shared space', was submitted to the SEUPB in April 2010, but the first community meeting was not held until 13 May 2010 (Cogent Management Consulting 2010: 44).

Reflecting on the process, community workers agreed that, in contrast to the bid's aspirational rhetoric, initial engagement with the council was 'very slow … very close to their chest' (author fieldnotes 2016). One respondent elaborated:

> In the beginning we were aware that there was some kind of proposal but it was almost like a year and a half before we were aware exactly what it was. Before we were actually engaging with the council. So at one point I decided, 'I'm not going to any more meetings, 'cos we've not been told what it's for. Why be so secretive?' So, when we did start the process with the council there was a lot of tension in the room. ('Alex', interview with author 2016)

A community worker further related:

> The Hub was a fait accompli. Basically it was Belfast City Council saw an opportunity to get money for projects, capital projects, through the PEACE programme ... and they were able to get, I think it was £9 million for that, and they basically came to the community and says, 'Look, we've got £9 million to build some sort of a Community Hub ... do you want us to go for it or do you want us to tell them to keep the money?'
>
> And we were saying, like, you know, come on, so the community sector's gonna say, 'Aw, we don't want a £9 million investment', when there were no other investments ... it was like shootin' yourself in the foot. ('Liam', interview with author 2016)

This challenges the council's repeated assurances of 'community engagement' in their application, including a statement that the proposed project 'has been informed through widespread consultation with various groups' (Cogent Management Consulting 2010: 20). Indeed, the appraiser later noted that 'there appears to be a lack of recent and relevant consultation with local communities regarding the facility' (Cogent Management Consulting: 2010: 20). The same community worker maintained that:

> The process from the start, and this is the fundamental point, and it's a very simple point ... the original concept was that it was supposed to be a bottom-up process with the community at the core of it, at the centre of it ... it was like all of these things ... it's tickin' a box and it's nice for the optics to be able to say, 'Oh look, we've the community engaged and involved and on board'. And there's no real belief to be honest with you within the community sector, community groups, that they will end up having ownership. ('Liam', interview with author 2016)

Another community worker suggested, 'you're just a token ... you think you're being a part of the process, you're carrying on as part of the process, but the decisions have been made already'. Instead, they asserted, the Hub bid came about as 'well, we already have this plan and this funding ... we want a nice, neat success story, and that was that' (author fieldnotes 2016). The rhetoric of meaningful 'community consultation' did not match the reality.

It was, perhaps, a pragmatic decision given the economic climate to shoehorn in a bid for a capital-build project. There was nothing else on offer, and a Hub was better than nothing. At the same time, however, the idea that the neighbourhoods around the site had not had any involvement in the idea of a 'Community Hub' is bizarre. How could the council have put forth priority objectives, as they did in the bid, without consultation on the specific issues facing the area and how these could be targeted as part of development? It seems like an oversight, particularly given the high levels of poverty, poor health and unemployment experienced by residents and the persistent need for social housing. A community worker drily observed:

> You have to ask yourself, how many people said that, 'Yeah, d'ya know what would actually fix our lives? If you built a building in the middle of Girdwood Barracks, that would solve all the inequalities, all our ill health, and it would all, just all evaporate … I couldn't imagine anyone would – I would be absolutely flabbergasted if as a result of a consultation, someone said, 'D'ya know the only thing that's gonna solve this, is to build a community hub in the centre of Girdwood'. ('Maurice', interview with author 2016)

In a 2012 meeting with the Assembly Personal Accounts Committee, the head of the NBCAU, Tim Losty, was tasked with an update on Girdwood and the Crumlin Road Gaol. The minutes noted that 'continued participation from communities and/or their representatives is essential in taking forward regeneration efforts on the site' (Hansard 2012a: 11). Losty responded:

> I will follow that up with some dates and an understanding of where we are. The Crumlin Road [Gaol]/Girdwood master plan was produced in 2007. We had to do an equality impact assessment, which generated substantial comment from the community. We are working closely with the Department for Social Development (DSD), which is taking the lead on that master plan. The Minister for Social Development has progressed the consultation on all aspects of that master plan, and we expect an announcement on it fairly soon. (Hansard 2012a: 34)

He described the progress made on the gaol, noting that a wing had been leased and the gaol reopened since, 'the communities were happy for us to progress work on the Gaol site while issues were being discussed and agreed on the Girdwood site' ('issues' doubtless meaning social housing) (Hansard 2012a: 35). He assured further community consultation (Hansard 2012a: 58). But throughout the update, plans for the Hub and the SEUPB bid are not mentioned, despite the bid having already been submitted and agreed upon. It is unclear what prevented the Hub from being discussed at this point. One community worker suggested that Losty 'was highly professional and he was the one who transformed Crumlin Road Gaol. But he couldn't get anything really done with Girdwood because it was out of his control and the politicians were then back into play [post-devolution] and it was more a political decision' ('Jim', interview with author 2016).

Up at Stormont, disputes around competing rights to housing continued to dominate the agenda. It was not long before fresh controversy took centre stage. Following the completion of the draft EQIA on the Girdwood and Crumlin Road Gaol site, DSD Minister Margaret Ritchie addressed the SDLP party conference on 5 February 2010, announcing:

> This area of North Belfast is deeply divided and it is difficult to find an agreed way forward for the site. But this part of North Belfast has acute levels of housing stress and more social housing is desperately needed there ... I have instructed the Housing Executive to appoint a Housing Association to commence the work to build at least 200 new social homes on the Girdwood site ... I will continue to seek consensus on the overall plan for the site, but housing will now proceed. (Hansard 2010; McCausland 2012)

The figure of 200 houses likely came from a figure mentioned in the initial Girdwood draft Masterplan and, before that, in the Housing Executive's housing needs assessment provided to the Girdwood Advisory Panel.[2]

Unionist politicians were predictably incensed by the statement. DUP politician Nelson McCausland (who would later be DSD Minister himself) alleged 'cynical electioneering', saying, 'most people, if they are honest about it, will admit that there was a connection between [Ritchie's] bid for the leadership of the SDLP and her grand announcement about the site' (Hansard 2011: 377; McCausland 2012).

The following DSD Minister (Alex Attwood, also of the SDLP) made similar promises on housing provision in March 2011, which North Belfast DUP official William Humphrey charged were a 'tactical move to outmanoeuvre Sinn Féin for the nationalist vote' while 'the community in Lower Oldpark lived in conditions akin to those during the Blitz in 1941' (Hansard 2011: 372). This opinion was echoed by a Unionist community worker, who contended that '[The 200 houses] was done politically, it was done through Margaret Ritchie when she was standing for election, and again through Alex Attwood, it was a way to gain votes. And it puts fear, it instils fear in people' ('Alex', interview with author 2016). This speaks to the narrative of siege and threat still prevalent within some sections of the Protestant/Unionist community, which in turn

---

[2] An NIHE housing needs assessment for North Belfast was provided to the members of the Girdwood Advisory Panel on 12 June 2006. The NIHE recommended 100 units of social housing: 40 units of affordable low-cost housing and 60 units of private housing. The social housing was supported by the NIHE's calculated housing need projection for 2005–2010 where the number of applicants in housing stress was estimated at 2,414 and the projected social housing need was 1,322 units (NIHE: 2006).

influences perceptions around control of space. Rather than seeing 200 houses as an attempt to address the housing waiting list, the houses were perceived as a targeted attack against Unionists in the area.

It is certainly possible that the SDLP was engaging in ethnic outbidding as a less powerful Nationalist party in the Assembly, attempting to steal Sinn Féin's thunder on the housing front. However, rational governance would support the building of housing regardless. Academic and policy research in the UK and elsewhere has overwhelmingly shown that overcrowding leads to poor quality of life, an increase in anti-social behaviour and health issues, and a decrease in children's educational attainment and health (Wilson and Barton 2021; Wallace 2015; Solari and Mare 2012; Reynolds 2005). In turn, this social burden is picked up by the state. One might infer that increased housing provision could ease some of the overall strain on state services. Further, studies have shown that stable social housing breaks the link between poor housing conditions and poverty for many low-income households (Wallace 2015: 37).

But, as Flyvbjerg observes, power exercises the rationality it wants and in doing so, power creates the reality it wants (1998: 230). Sectarianism is not rational because it privileges ethnic logic over the efficient allocation of resources. New-build social housing was anathema to Protestant/Unionist politicians despite the need for it and the measurable impact it would have for citizens' quality of life and, potentially, state coffers. Despite, too, the Ministerial Code set out in the Northern Ireland Act, which states that politicians must 'observe the highest levels of … impartiality, integrity, and objectivity in relation to the stewardship of public funds' (NIO 1998b: 66). Unionist politicians alleged ethnic outbidding to rationalise their concerns around territorial loss and symbolic Nationalist gain, recalling Flyvbjerg's observation that 'rationalisation presented as rationality is … a principal strategy in the exercise of power' (1998: 2).

So the moratorium on new-build homes in North Belfast continued. It was exacerbated when the DUP took over the DSD from the Catholic/Nationalist SDLP. The DSD is responsible for social housing provision, to which Unionists remained opposed. In order to legitimise this position in a policy context, the DUP used the familiar discourse of competing 'needs' and 'rights'. This time, the tactic was the concept of 'differential deprivation'. Differential deprivation frames overcrowding and homelessness on the Nationalist side as congruent with derelict housing and vacancy on the Unionist side. According to this differential, the two housing 'needs' are equally important. For instance, the DUP alleged that the Lower Shankill and Lower Oldpark communities had been 'seriously neglected' by SDLP DSD ministers (Hansard 2011: 377). In a particularly heated November 2011 Assembly debate, McCausland (by then DSD Minister) made reference to the Girdwood draft Masterplan where 'fundamental to obtaining community support will be ongoing commitment by government to securing the regeneration of the deprived residential areas adjacent to the site'. He said that this referred specifically to Lower Shankill and Lower Oldpark, and that he had been 'key in getting that phrase in' as part of the Advisory Panel (Hansard 2011: 377). Apparently, this phrase did not include the Lower Cliftonville and New Lodge areas also adjacent to the site, because the Lower Oldpark and Lower Shankill suffered from 'differential deprivation'. Shared deprivation was never addressed.

This manner of decision-making seemingly characterised McCausland's tenure as DSD Minister. First, Girdwood was dropped from the social housing development programme in 2011 despite clearly documented housing need. The Housing Executive sent proposals for 200 homes at the Girdwood site to the DSD, yet McCausland rejected them. Sinn Féin alleged it was a 'sectarian decision'; SDLP MLA Alban McGuinness said it was 'very disturbing news' (BBC News 2011b). The latter noted in an Assembly meeting: 'Here is land owned by DSD ... Here is a brownfield site that is completely clear, uncontaminated and free to be built upon at any time ... Yet the Minister drops this important housing scheme from the housing development programme for this year without rational explanation'. The Housing Executive wrote to the minister requesting an explanation for the decision, but no reply was received (Hansard 2011: 371). This is despite, as PPR pointed out, the fact that governments have a human rights obligation to transparency and due process; these should be the basis of decision-making (PPR 2015b).

On the ground, the North Belfast Civil Rights Association (NBCRA) went further in its response to the veto on social housing.[3] They camped out in tents on Cliftonpark Avenue for three days to protest against McCausland's decision, alleging political gerrymandering. The Irish Republican Socialist Party, Irish Socialist Network, People Before Profit, Republican Network for Unity and 'independent community activists' also supported the NBCRA protest. These groups are not allied to Sinn Féin, their parades and protests are not sanctioned by Sinn Féin and some are ostensibly linked to so-called 'dissident' Republican groups (Burns 2011a, 2011b).[4] The name of the NBCRA is a nod to the historical Nationalist struggle for housing and civil rights, suggesting that Sinn Féin has sold out on this issue. The protest was a show of strength, highlighting and

---

[3] The NBCRA was a small left-leaning activist group affiliated with the Irish Republican Socialist Party (IRSP) and other Republican groups. At the time of writing, I am uncertain of whether the NBCRA still exists as it did in 2011, given that these small groups are prone to schism and often change membership.

[4] The term 'dissident' is popularly utilised by media, pundits and politicians to label groups and individuals who reject constitutional politics as the means to a United Ireland. Although Sinn Féin agreed to participate in power-sharing as part of the Agreement, a broad range of Republican splinter groups continue to support the use of force as a legitimate tactic towards Irish independence (see Whiting 2012).

shaming Sinn Féin's failure to secure housing on the site. More broadly, it highlighted Sinn Féin's willingness to compromise on their rhetoric of 'equality' to the DUP in the name of political expediency.

The Masterplan and the Maze

In January 2012, Belfast City Council learned that their bid for the Girdwood Community Hub had been successful; the SEUPB awarded £9.6 million in funding conditional on addressing what they referred to as 'considerable risks' around the project, including the lack of an implementation plan and community buy-in. The SEUPB warned that there were 'other projects pending' and the funding would be lost if the Hub plan was not finalised by June 2012. All investment for the Hub project had to be committed and spent by 2015 (Belfast City Council 2012: 2). There was a subsequent scramble between the DUP and Sinn Féin to frame a Masterplan and make a deal – any deal – by the deadline. According to an informational pamphlet by an area community group, given the need to come up with a plan or lose the investment, 'the politicians in North Belfast came up with a plan which was a compromise. It might not be the best plan but it was the best possible plan that people could agree with at the time' (North Talks Too 2015: 10).

In May 2012, Minister McCausland announced that an agreement had been reached on the 'Masterplan Conceptual Framework' for Girdwood by the six North Belfast MLAs (PPR 2013: 51; North Talks Too 2015: 5). The Masterplan Conceptual Framework was a colour-blocked map of the site (see Fig. 6.1). The simple image it presented marked an unsettling contrast to the previous Masterplan, which for all its faults still constituted a fairly detailed 91-page document, produced by an independent architect (BDP).

I trudged through the rain one morning to the Metropolitan Art Centre (better known as the MAC), an angular building of brick and glass that sits close to the border between the city centre and North Belfast. I was meeting a well-respected planner to discuss the optics of the 2012 plan. They slid a copy of the Masterplan across the table and shook their head at the neon squares, saying, 'it looks like a three-year-old drew it, but that's an insult to a three-year-old'.

In the plan, they explained, most of the site was taken up by a sports pitch, an indoor sports facility and the proposed Community Hub. This Community Hub was billed as promoting 'shared space' and 'good relations' across the divide. Along the front of Cliftonpark Avenue, across from the interface barrier, was undefined 'mixed-use space'. Two areas of social housing were planned for opposite sides of the site: one directly next to the Catholic/Nationalist New Lodge (60 units) and the other across from the Protestant/Unionist Lower Oldpark. There were also two parking lots, one on either side of the development. This latter detail, he suggested, meant people from outside areas would be more likely to use the site, not locals, since the former had cars and could therefore move more easily around interface spaces. According to the planner, Girdwood was a 'pure sectarian carve-up, the worst example of planning ... nobody [in the area] wanted a community centre' (author fieldnotes 2017).

Criticism swiftly followed the Masterplan Conceptual Framework's release. The site was denounced as a sectarian compromise between the DUP and Sinn Féin rather than a meaningful transformation of the space. The two sections of limited housing featured on the Masterplan – one for the Nationalist side of the site and one for the Unionist side – suggested that any conciliation to Sinn Féin on housing had to include an equal share for Unionists. In response, Sinn Féin MLA Gerry Kelly said that 'Girdwood was never going to resolve all the inequalities in housing need that Nationalists face in North Belfast ... it will however play some part in addressing that need but we will continue to battle for housing developments across the constituency' (Burns 2012). Sinn Féin wanted to ensure that the party would not lose votes over the inadequate social housing; the word 'battle' suggests that they were still fighting against restrictions imposed by Unionists.

PPR submitted a query to Sinn Féin about the lack of housing in the final Masterplan. Sixty houses was very few, after all, in an area with thousands on the waiting list. The party responded that 'Sinn Féin have never suggested that Girdwood was the answer to housing need in this constituency' (PPR 2013: 53). This was an interesting about-face that contradicted Sinn Féin's previous position on the subject. In earlier statements and Assembly debates, Sinn Féin described the site as a 'unique opportunity' and a 'windfall site' (BBC News 2011b; Hansard 2011: 378). Kelly had said in 2011, regarding social housing provision, that 'leadership is needed from the political parties on the basis of objective need, and we need a strategy for that' (Hansard 2011: 374; PPR 2013: 53). Regarding another contested housing site in North Belfast, Sinn Féin councillor Michael Goodman stated: 'For Sinn Féin, need must be at the heart of these windfall opportunities when land becomes available' (Short 2015: 6). However, by 2014, they seemed to have changed their tune: during a meeting about social housing that I attended at Stormont, Sinn Féin MLA for North Belfast Carál Ní Chuilín said that 'it was good to aim high but 200 houses [at Girdwood] was just not possible'. Two hundred houses was too controversial.

The mixed messages reflect a clash between rhetoric and political expediency in regard to housing development. Sinn Féin had to give up on their platform of social housing in order to see the Girdwood site developed, but had to rationalise that position to their constituents. This is indicative of the broader functioning of the Assembly, whereby Sinn Féin were often made to compromise or make trade-offs on their platform of 'equality of opportunity' to keep the government functioning. Rather than stalemate, a grudging compromise was achieved

Building a Shared Girdwood

MISSION
VISION
OUTCOMES

Vision:
- A confident, thriving working class community.

Mission:
- To work together to create the conditions that will build a confident and thriving working class community.

Outcomes:
- Improved understanding, relationships and respect across interface communities.
- Remove the fear of living at the interface.
- Increased social, economic and physical investment into these interface communities.
- Regenerate the interface communities in Lower Shankill, Lower Oldpark and Lower Cliftonville.

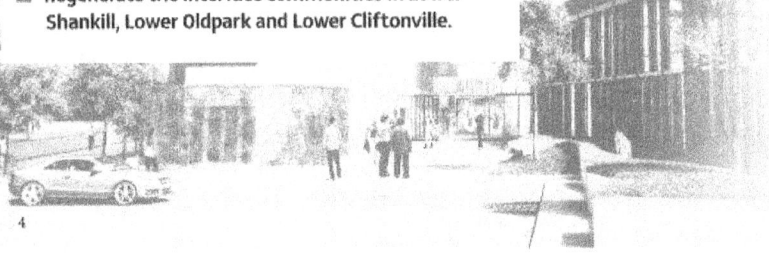

Fig. 6.1 Community group North Talks Too's leaflet on Girdwood. See the Conceptual Masterplan in top-right inset.

through informal systems of deal-making and deliberation between Sinn Féin and the DUP. This process has been described in the context of planning: 'Negotiation denotes a mix of power and influence. In negotiation, the parties involved not only maneuver for advantageous positions, as they do in conflict, they also try to understand what the other really wants, in order for example to offer what may be a cheaper satisfaction of that want than what the other is demanding' (Mansbridge in Forester 2001: 63). Applying this perspective to the Girdwood site suggests that the 60 houses in the Masterplan were a token gesture by the DUP, a 'cheaper satisfaction' than Sinn Féin's original demands. Some have also speculated that this political agreement was a 'trade-off deal' on other contested sites, raising the stakes for a potential long-term symbolic victory for Sinn Féin (Planning for Spatial Reconciliation Group 2016: 109).

In particular, it has been asserted that the former Maze/Long Kesh prison site, another hotly contested redevelopment project, was Sinn Féin's prize for the trade-off at Girdwood (author fieldnotes 2017). Maze/Long Kesh was the largest publicly owned regeneration site in Northern Ireland – roughly the size of Belfast city centre and twice the size of the Titanic Quarter (Hansard 2009: 10). Proposals initially focused on a multi-sport stadium that would host large events, and an 'International Centre for Conflict Transformation' (ICCT), which would centre around some of the old prison buildings (OFMDFM 2006: 6). One could not go ahead without the other (Flynn 2011: 390). The proposal was suggestive of 'political horse-trading', with a Unionist focus on economic interests to balance Republican interests in preserving part of the prison, including the prison hospital where hunger striker Bobby Sands had died and an H-block that had housed paramilitaries (*Belfast Telegraph* 2013). These latter spaces featured strongly in the Republican collective narrative as the site of the no-wash protests and hunger strikes for political status. The compromise solution was published as a Masterplan in May 2006 and demolition work on the site commenced in October 2006 (OFMDFM 2006; BBC News 2013b).

However, as with Girdwood, redevelopment plans eventually stalled due to a lack of political consensus. The issue of the conflict transformation centre rankled with some Unionist elements and victims' groups, who charged it a 'shrine to terrorism' (*Belfast Telegraph* 2013). There were concerns that the development would 'sanctify' Republican narrative and glorify the political violence of the IRA (McDowell 2008: 225). In 2010, First Minister Peter Robinson of the DUP and Deputy First Minister Martin McGuinness of Sinn Féin announced that a deal had been reached on the Maze/Long Kesh site. At the time of the Girdwood development in 2012, a development corporation had been established for the project (Strategic Investment Board n.d.).[5]

---

[5] As of 2021, development of the site was still paused due to ministerial disagreement (http://mazelongkesh.com/).

Some commentators have asserted that a backroom deal occurred on Maze/Long Kesh which was directly connected with the Girdwood Masterplan. SDLP MLA Dolores Kelly charged that 'some people are wondering what was the price of Sinn Féin selling out housing need ... people think the DUP rolled over on the Maze/Long Kesh conflict transformation centre in return for this deal in Girdwood' (*Belfast Telegraph* 2012).

According to the *Irish Republican News* (2012), which is not connected to Sinn Féin,[6] SDLP leader Alasdair McDonnell claimed his party had been 'misled' about the Girdwood development: 'some people were suggesting there was a trade-off here, that Sinn Féin traded off the needs of people in North Belfast, the serious housing need of 350 families, for their reconciliation centre at the Maze ... people on the ground in North Belfast are very angry'. He further observed that Sinn Féin remained 'largely silent on the matter'. It was also noted that the rhetoric of the DUP had changed from initially rejecting the centre to promoting it as a 'mecca for tourists'; at this time First Minister Robinson dismissed the 'shrine to terrorism' argument made by other elements of Unionism as 'scaremongering garbage' (*Belfast Telegraph* 2012, 2013). Dixon conceptualises this strategy of political trade-off and negotiation as 'the party that has made the concession [Sinn Féin] thereby occupies the moral high ground and wins ground in the propaganda war; it can then expect its agenda to be advanced as a reward for flexibility' (2002: 731).

Whilst the DUP and Sinn Féin cooperated on Girdwood, they were also continuing to fight behind-the-scenes for political advantage. In this case, it was Sinn Féin allegedly giving up on social housing to advance the agenda of the conflict transformation centre at the Maze. In both the Maze and Girdwood cases, decisions were determined primarily by parochial party politics and competing territorial interests (Flynn 2011: 394). Informal trade-off replaced rational decision-making on policy and planning. Again, the rhetoric of Section 75 fell victim to the reality of ethnocratic governance, which favours negotiation based on political expediency and follows democratic legislation only insofar as it does not harm ethnic interests.

Indeed, the fact that the Girdwood Masterplan granted over £9 million for a site focused primarily on leisure and sports facilities raised eyebrows, given that it was situated within two miles of four other leisure centres, and that 2,501 people in North Belfast were on the Housing Executive waiting list at the time (Black 2013). In a 2012 *Spotlight* investigation on the development, one interviewee said:

---

[6] *Irish Republican News* has an active online presence and bills itself as 'uncensored news on the struggle for a just, peaceful, united Ireland'. The group supports Republican prisoners and does not follow the party line of Sinn Féin (https://www.facebook.com/pg/IRN.IrishRepublicanNews/).

> I find it inexplicable that a party like Sinn Féin, which talks about civil rights and talks about equality and so on, is lying down on one of the very basic issues that started the whole civil rights movement, which was fair housing. The fact that Sinn Féin are agreeing to a lot less than what is needed, it is not in their interest to do that, indicates to me there is some deal. (BBC *Spotlight* 2012)

Another interviewee observed, 'what's happening here has nothing to do with Protestants and Roman Catholics together. It's an exercise where they can door knock and the DUP can say to their people, "we got houses there". Sinn Féin can say, "we got houses there"' (BBC *Spotlight* 2012).

During a community meeting, one Nationalist community worker further asserted that this was 'the nature of politics here, Sinn Féin and the DUP had a series of dirty dealings, secret meetings, and came up with the eventual plan of housing for each side of the development – one by Brucevale [for Nationalists] and one by Cliftonpark Avenue for Unionists' (author fieldnotes 2016). The result was a symbolic coup for the DUP: they had maintained electoral control of North Belfast and responded to the narrative of 'siege' and territorial encroachment that persisted in Protestant/Unionist areas of North Belfast, all under the camouflage of 'shared space' and 'good relations'.

In response to the Conceptual Masterplan, members of the Alliance Party tabled a private members' business motion on 12 June 2012 which read:

> [T]his Assembly expresses serious concern at the current segregated housing proposals in the Girdwood Conceptual Master Plan, as announced on 21 May 2012; and calls on the Minister for Social Development to conduct a landmark review of segregation in housing to inform a strategy to promote and facilitate equality and sharing in housing in order to eliminate both discrimination and segregation, and to direct the Northern Ireland Housing Executive to promote and protect all housing as mixed. (Hansard 2012b: 385)

The motion was defeated by 62 votes (Sinn Féin, DUP, UUP) to 18 (SDLP and Alliance) (Hansard 2012b: 405).

The Conceptual Masterplan underlines that space is always being used to further the interests of the dominant positions in power. The DUP's continued intransigence on the issue of social housing meant that Sinn Féin had to compromise on their platform of equality or see the site remain vacant and the PEACE III funding disappear. Sinn Féin then had to legitimise their about-turn with official discourse to assuage their electorate, while engaging in backroom trade-offs around the Maze site. This also speaks to the wider dynamic of Sinn Féin's relationship with the DUP in the Assembly. Meanwhile, this was a symbolic victory for the DUP, who had managed to maintain their electoral control of North Belfast and to appease constituents leery of Nationalist territorial encroachment. It reflects the warning made by the Planning for Spatial Reconciliation Group that 'politics in [Northern Ireland] is essentially sectarian. Thus, there is ever-present danger that development will be influenced by sectarian electoral arithmetic – how decisions impact on core partisan votes in an ethnonationally divided society' (2016: 14). These circumstances seem to have shaped the outcome of planning decisions on the site.

In response, a Catholic/Nationalist single mother who had spent 13 years on the housing waiting list launched legal proceedings against the plan, citing a breach of equality legislation. The case claimed that sectarianism on the part of Minister McCausland was the reason for his refusal to build homes. In January 2013, the DSD submitted a planning application for 60 houses on the site and the case was withdrawn just as a two-day hearing was about to begin, after 'lengthy out of court negotiations' (Black 2013; BBC News 2013a). One community worker said that the case was settled out of court before it could be heard because Belfast City Council feared losing the PEACE III funding (author fieldnotes 2017).

The figure of 60 houses – a low number given the waiting list – was deemed appropriate because it was the only option for the site to continue being developed. A social enterprise manager related:

> From the DUP side, they would rather see grass grow … than houses built, you know, so they would rather see it as a derelict site than the number of what they would perceive as Catholic/Nationalist housing units increasing … It was a very low number of houses, but it was either that or none. It was pragmatism, that rather than nothing, we move forward with something. ('Thomas', interview with author 2016)

In reference to the two separate areas of housing, another interview respondent noted:

> You know, you could sort of give a simplistic answer to that and say yeah, [it's] the DUP. But I think there was always in the background the unresolved battle here that skews everything: that the constitutional question still looms large, that the issue of territory and control of resources … is still viewed very much through a sectarian prism.

They continued:

> Girdwood's the perfect example of it. The housing need in North Belfast was massive in the Catholic/Nationalist community. And the DUP did

everything they could to ensure there was a minimal amount of houses built in that site. Because they saw this as part and parcel of the process of the growth of the Nationalist or Republican vote in North Belfast. I don't think anybody who lives in North Belfast doesn't see that, the reality of that, that that's not just a propaganda position or, you know, havin' a go at the DUP, but it's obvious.

It's blatantly obvious, if Sinn Féin for example or the SDLP had pursued that kind of line, they would have been branded, rightly so, as being sectarian. Sectarian bigots, in fact, who are interested in nothing more than holding on to territory and ensuring that the area stayed in the hands of one camp rather than the other. ('Liam', interview with author 2016)

Yet, one 'side's' view of reality is not the same as the other's. It is informed by different narratives, different senses of belonging, needs and rights. Political elites can draw upon this disparity to legitimise their decisions. As Flyvbjerg observes in relation to politics and planning:

> The decisive aspect ... is not whether one is 'correct' or 'true' but which party can put the greatest power behind its interpretation ... the interpretation with the strongest power case becomes the project's truth, understood as the actually realised physical, economic, ecological and social reality. (1998: 117)

In this way, political elites normalised resource allocation through a sectarian prism and disregarded social justice around housing in North Belfast. Against a backdrop of Unionist intransigence, it was a given that social housing at Girdwood would be curtailed and that the development would not proceed otherwise. The 'siege mentality' and 'insecurity' of Unionism was accepted as a part of the negotiation process. As one interview respondent put it, 'we move forward with something rather than move forward with nothing' ('Thomas', interview with author 2016).

The DSD, the DUP and 'Differential Deprivation'

During Nelson McCausland's tenure as DSD Minister, Girdwood was but one instance of a deeply problematic approach to social housing provision. As I pored over policy documents and newspaper articles around social housing at the time, I noticed that the concept of 'differential deprivation' kept surfacing. The argument placed the conditions of derelict and abandoned Protestant/Unionist housing estates in parallel with Catholic/Nationalist overcrowding and housing need. It was such a convenient deflection from the broader issue at hand: systemic and systematic disinvestment in social housing for Catholics/Nationalists. At the same time, it was true that derelict buildings and vacancy were an eyesore in predominantly Unionist spaces.

The concept of 'differential deprivation' and out-manoeuvring in terms of 'who deserves what' was a major force in this era of DSD policy and practice. It came to define not only the housing plans for the Girdwood site, but how social housing was framed in Belfast more broadly. In 2011, the DUP's Nelson McCausland became DSD Minister, and under his tenure, the DSD released a new strategy, *Facing the Future*. *Facing the Future* presented housing as a means of creating 'economic growth and prosperity' (DSD 2012: 4), an arguably problematic departure from the original definition of housing for shelter. One of its key tenets was 'housing-led regeneration' in once-vibrant areas experiencing 'population decline, empty homes and blight' (DSD 2012: 6). Alternatively, PPR defined this as a 'means of regenerating communities experiencing a low demand for social housing by trying to make them more attractive through measures including new housing provision' (2013: 58). Typically, these are Protestant/Unionist communities. Another objective was to reconfigure how the Housing Executive was structured and funded. This was alarming given the Housing Executive has always allocated based on objective need, not differential deprivation (DSD 2012: 6). These objectives mark a significant change in the approach to framing housing inequality at odds with previous principles and at odds with Section 75.

These considerations were raised by PPR and the Equality Commission in their consultation responses to *Facing the Future* (ECNI 2012a). Again, both groups were at the forefront of highlighting political decision-making at odds with equality legislation. PPR contended:

> [We] are deeply concerned about any move away from targeting inequality and tackling objective need. The principle of allocation on the basis of need is not only one which is deeply embedded in post-civil rights movement Northern Ireland and one which served as a building block for the formation of the Northern Ireland Housing Executive but it is also rooted in law ... (2012: 7)

Therefore, diluting the principle of housing need with other political objectives like regeneration, social mobility, economic development or job creation was problematic. Similarly, the Equality Commission noted that:

> The current housing selection scheme is designed to objectively measure housing need and allocate housing to address those identified needs. In this draft Housing Strategy, a much wider view of the functionality of housing is adopted, including as a means to facilitate regeneration of

failing areas – potentially where there is currently a low demand for housing. Housing is also viewed as a mechanism to create employment.

While these are worthwhile objectives, care should be taken that they do not divert scarce resources from the core function of social housing – to meet expressed objective housing need ... there is a clear risk that the Department may be seen to divert resources away from areas where there is very high demand for housing to areas where there is less or little demand for housing, with potential impacts on equality of opportunity and good relations. (ECNI 2012a: 8–9)

It was later found that the DSD had not conducted an EQIA screening of *Facing the Future* (ECNI 2014: 10). In April 2014, the Equality Commission launched an investigation into this failure to uphold Section 75, taking submissions from PPR, CAJ, the Equality Commission, the SDLP and Sinn Féin (ECNI 2015: 32). The Equality Commission concluded in a 'damning' report that the DSD had failed to meet its statutory duties, leading to allegations of the DUP's 'defiance or indifference' to Section 75 (ECNI 2018: 59).

Indeed, it seemed during this period that Section 75 had been compromised entirely. During a review of social housing undertaken by the DSD in 2013, the department was tasked with conducting an analysis of social housing allocation in both Northern Ireland and further afield. Northern Ireland's approach, of course, was grounded in the obligation to allocate social housing based on objective need. But in a briefing to the Assembly, a DSD official announced that a process was underway to actually 'define' what objective need was: 'One of the things that the fundamental review is very actively considering is what objective need is and how we define that. We will want to get a consensus on that and everybody's views of what they consider housing need or housing stress to be' (PPR 2013: 58). This move to redefine objective need seemed like little more than an attempt to legitimise housing investment in areas with no waiting list. Unionist elites had begun to use the language of 'needs' and 'rights' for their own constituencies' benefit, responding to the blight and abandonment of Unionist areas and the wider Unionist narrative of loss (Hayward and Mitchell 2003: 307). Unionist areas 'needed' housing investment to improve their neighbourhoods in the same way Nationalists on the waiting list 'needed' social housing. Official discourse could then redefine the meaning of 'objective need' to validate the idea of 'differential deprivation' and underline a zero-sum attitude to resource allocation.

Using the notion of 'differential deprivation' to inform housing-led regeneration was a major tenet of McCausland's tenure. A *Detail* investigation revealed that by 2012, Nationalists were estimated to make up three-quarters of the people in housing and homelessness stress in McCausland's North Belfast constituency. Yet in June 2012, after discussions between McCausland and DSD officials, 'emergency approval' had been used to add four Protestant/Unionist estates in North Belfast to the Housing Executive's social housing programme despite no evidence of homelessness or housing need. This occurred months after the initial plan had been approved and without the knowledge of the management board (McCaffrey 2012b). No EQIA was carried out on the areas of Ballysillan, Tiger's Bay, Lower Oldpark and Lower Shankill (the latter two surrounding the Girdwood site, and all four in McCausland's constituency of North Belfast) (ECNI 2015: 16).

In a statement to *The Detail*, the Housing Executive confirmed that the four estates had been added to encourage housing-led regeneration, as 'there was a requirement for new housing to play a key role in areas with very poor housing and environmental conditions' (McCaffrey 2012b). This was in line with *Facing the Future*'s key recommendations. However, it did not reflect the Housing Executive's original function, maintained over 40 years, to allocate housing based on objective need, nor Section 75's prescriptions, nor the compulsory duty of government to perform EQIAs on all policies. According to one source, 'above all else DSD and Housing Executive staff prided themselves that housing was allocated on the basis of need. How can anyone justify fast tracking these four areas for new-builds when there is clearly little or no need in three of the four areas?' (McCaffrey 2012b).

In October 2013, Minister McCausland announced a £2.5 million scheme to refurbish 26 houses in Lower Oldpark, in partnership with Clanmil Housing Association, as 'an attempt to recreate a community' (Short 2014). This estate was partly derelict, a veritable ghost town of boarded-up houses and empty land. In the Lower Oldpark Community Association's (LOCA) 2012 annual review, the chairperson wrote in advance of the refurbishments: 'Tell your friends, especially if they have moved away from the area, and encourage them to put their names on the waiting list' (2012: 3). This is effectively engineering housing need rather than responding to existing documented need.

Lower Oldpark was the first example of McCausland's new *Empty Homes Strategy and Action Plan 2013–2018*. One of its primary aims was 'to bring empty homes across Northern Ireland back into use' (DSD 2013a: 3). It referred to the refurbishment of empty homes as an opportunity to tackle housing need – a different interpretation of 'need' than that measured by the social housing waiting list. In reference to Protestant housing need, one Unionist community worker argued that:

> Regeneration is key in giving people a sense of hope, lifting the blight ... it's a challenge within this community because of the housing situation y'know, it was blighted, less than half of what it was, and we always have a challenge with the Housing Executive with the statistics saying, 'There's not any need'. But there is need ... I mean government have to appreciate

that, you know, you can't leave these places in ghettoes. There's a need on both sides, and we appreciate there's a need on the Nationalist side, but there's a massive amount of houses being developed there. ('Alex', interview with author 2016)

This respondent emphatically points to blight as a major factor in housing need, that this is also an iteration of 'objective need'. But they also allege that there is a 'massive amount' of houses being built on the Nationalist side, despite evidence to the contrary. This demonstrates the opposition that exists between the two groups, that both must exist in a horizontal relationship with one another. A gain – or indeed, a perceived gain – on one side represents a loss for the other, and each side is suspicious that the other is benefiting more.

In discussions about Protestant/Unionist decline and differential deprivation, a sense of abandonment emerges. The Protestant exodus occasioned by wide-scale redevelopment and conflict saw mostly Protestants moving to the outskirts of Greater Belfast or the new 'growth towns' further afield. Those who were left were condemned to 'watch their community die', as one housing officer put it (author fieldnotes 2015). According to a community worker, Unionist politicians at that time 'never invested in the Shankill, they never built houses in the Lower Oldpark, they abandoned those areas and left them to fester and wilt' ('Jim', interview with author 2016). Today, demographic decline, the dearth of traditional industry and educational underattainment are experienced more widely in low-income Protestant areas. There is a sense of symbolic defeat, that where Catholics suffered discrimination in the past, in the post-Agreement period it is Protestants who have been marginalised.

It is true that these places are not attractive environments in which to live, and during my fieldwork, I came to sympathise with this point of view. It was impossible not to acknowledge the pervading sense of decline that hung about the shuttered houses and empty streets. These, and the open fields where buildings once stood, were a constant reminder of physical and symbolic loss – that things weren't going well, that opportunities seemed to have passed these places by.

I visited a Protestant/Unionist community centre in North Belfast and discussed the issue with a community worker. I was ushered in, they made me a cup of tea, we sat in a little room on hard plastic chairs. When I asked about all the open space in the neighbourhood, compared to the need for housing, they said:

I think the Protestant community are actually on the back foot now. They're the ones penalised, they're the ones being said, 'You've [Unionists] got all this open space and therefore you're holding us [Nationalists] ransom 'cos we've no space on the Nationalist side', where we're [Unionists] the ones been living 40 years in blight ... I feel as though it's the Protestant community that are always seen as the bigots. We're the ones seen as, 'We've got all this land and we don't want to give it up'. But why can't we regenerate the community we once had? (author fieldnotes 2016)

Maybe it was harsh, I thought afterwards, but in practical terms, that community was gone. In all cities, in all neighbourhoods, populations shift, people leave and, for better or worse, places evolve.

But the DSD responded to these kinds of sentiments with a continued emphasis on regenerating blighted areas. A few days after the launch of the Lower Oldpark initiative, Minister McCausland rolled out the Building Successful Communities programme, which again determined 'to use housing intervention as one of the main catalysts for local regeneration' (Department of Communities 2017). Six pilot areas were selected: Lower Oldpark and Hillview, Lower Falls, Tiger's Bay and Mountcollyer, Lower Shankill and Brown Square,[7] Lenadoon and Glencolin, and Doury Road (Ballymena). Four of the six areas were Protestant/Unionist; out of these four, three were again located in or directly adjacent to McCausland's own constituency of North Belfast. There was no EQIA conducted on the programme as, according to the DSD, it was a 'pilot initiative not a policy' and thus not subject to the requirement to conduct EQIAs on all 'policies' (ECNI 2015: 16). McCausland later defended the impetus for the programme, noting,

> The role of the Department for Social Development does not include only housing; it also includes regeneration. We have areas with high levels of dereliction and decay, with empty houses boarded up, and they drag communities down. They become magnets for antisocial behaviour and dumping. They blight the lives of the residents, creating despair, and they are a lost opportunity. (Hansard 2014a: 28)

The pilot schemes were selected based on these types of criteria (blight, dereliction, etc.), found in *Facing the Future*. In reference to these criteria, PPR noted, 'it is difficult to comprehend the suggestion that areas which: "have experienced a decline in housing demand" and "are in proximity to places where there is housing need" should be prioritised for new housing provision while there are areas with proven current demand' (PPR 2013: 59).

Another report on housing inequality in Northern Ireland remarked that 'the aggregate data repeatedly suggests that applicants with lower levels of

---

[7] This is despite the draft Belfast Metropolitan Area Plan's statement that 'there is generally a high level of social housing need throughout Belfast, with the exception of the Shankill area' (DOE 2004b: 6).

housing need are allocated homes more quickly than applicants in housing stress' (Wallace 2015: 38). From a housing need perspective, it just didn't make sense. As I walked on the Crumlin Road past Lower Oldpark one afternoon in 2014, I noticed a large sign on the corner that advertised the new housing built there by Clanmil Housing Association. Later, I confirmed that houses had been offered to tenants with zero points on the social housing waiting list because, according to Housing Executive criteria, there was no 'need' in the area (author fieldnotes 2014; Short 2014).

Curiously, McCausland's keen interest in housing provision did not extend to a patch of land on Frederick Street, close to the New Lodge and to a contested Orange Order parade route. It was earmarked for social housing under the Belfast Metropolitan Area Plan (BMAP) (DOE 2004b: iv). The Housing Executive had put forth proposals to build social housing there, but the DSD removed it from the social housing programme in 2013. According to another *Detail* investigation, correspondence from the DSD to NIHE explained:

> The site is owned by UU [University of Ulster] and is on a long lease to DRD [the Department for Regional Development] for use as a car park. UU has also stated their plans for development of this site in line with the new campus. Given that the likelihood of developing social housing on the site at present is unlikely, DSD would be grateful if NIHE could remove from the current SHDP (Social Housing Development Programme). (McCaffrey 2014)

Sinn Féin MLA Carál Ní Chuilín alleged this had been a deliberate attempt by the DUP-controlled DSD to block the building of housing in a Nationalist area, saying that 'at a Planning Appeals Commission hearing, which I attended for 10 hours, DSD officials admitted that, yes, [Frederick Street] was earmarked for social housing but now it was not. More gerrymandering' (Hansard 2014b).

Then, in February 2014, plans to build houses near the Stanhope/Clifton Street junction in North Belfast, adjacent to a contested Orange Order parade route, were also jettisoned.[8] I trudged up and down Clifton Street several times a week on my walks back and forth from the Girdwood site. It links the Crumlin Road to the city centre. It also connects to an interface at Carlisle Circus: on one side of the Carlisle Circus roundabout is an entrance to the Protestant/Unionist Lower Shankill estate. On the other side is the bottom of

---

[8] As mentioned in Chapter Three, the Orange Order is a Protestant fraternal organisation. Their parades are perceived as an expression of sectarian triumphalism by Catholics, and sometimes act as a catalyst for violence on both sides. When Orange parades abut Nationalist areas like Clifton Street, counter-protests by Nationalists occur on the basis that they constitute sectarian intimidation.

the Antrim Road and the Catholic/Nationalist New Lodge. To the uninformed pedestrian, the landscape looks unremarkable: a florist, an off-license, a betting shop and a constant flow of traffic. But during the conflict, this was a no man's land. Anna Burns, in her novel *Milkman*, describes a 'ten-minute area' on the boundary of town that is very like Carlisle Circus, a little place with supposed offices and shops that no one enters or exits, a bus stop no one uses, a 'ghostly place that simply you had to get through' (2018: 81).

The Belfast Orange Hall is past Carlisle Circus on Clifton Street: a target for bored young people from the New Lodge across the road, its exterior is frequently mottled by paint bombs. Clifton Street has often been a site of tension as Orange Order parades pass the Carlisle Circus interface and, further down towards the city centre, the Catholic/Nationalist Carrick Hill neighbourhood. The prospect of housing there being allocated to Catholics/Nationalists was therefore troubling to Unionists. *The Irish News* revealed that McCausland, DUP MP Nigel Dodds and City Councillor Brian Kingston met representatives from Oaklee Homes on two occasions at the Clifton Street Orange Hall, close to the proposed housing development. The plans for housing were submitted in 2011, but weeks after the meeting they were withdrawn. A spokeswoman later confirmed that the meeting was requested by the DUP and that no minutes were recorded (Young 2016a, 2016b). In a 2013 development brief produced by DSD for the area, key parameters instead included that 'development fronting Clifton Street should provide for non-residential uses' (DSD 2013c: 11).

These were not the only accusations of gerrymandering in electorally sensitive North Belfast. Nationalist and Unionist politicians were unable to agree even on housing need figures. This was another point of contention around housing for the Girdwood site and elsewhere in North Belfast. Whilst the Housing Executive uses council boundaries for North Belfast to calculate waiting lists, the DUP insists that parliamentary constituency boundaries should be used. These take in large Unionist estates in Newtownabbey and Rathcoole on the outskirts of the Belfast Urban Area, as well as the Shankill, skewing the numbers towards a more equal picture of social housing need between Protestants/Unionists and Catholics/Nationalists in North Belfast (Hansard 2014a: 27). McCausland referred to the parliamentary constituency boundaries in his treatment of housing need in North Belfast, saying, 'the latest figures I have received from the Housing Executive, from 31st December 2013, again speak for themselves with 1,994 Protestants and 1,988 Roman Catholics on the waiting list in the North Belfast Constituency' (2014).

McCausland insisted that the claim of a housing crisis in Catholic areas was 'untrue', a 'manufactured myth' (2014). This perspective is echoed by some Protestant/Unionist residents and community workers, one of whom referred to 'a myth about housing need in North Belfast' (author fieldnotes 2015). Another said, 'if you take in all the demographics of North Belfast up to Glengormley, there's a need for [Protestant] houses in North Belfast as well. What they've done is, narrowed it down to a certain geographical area' ('Alex', interview with author 2016).

On the other hand, Housing Executive, activist and academic reviews on housing in North Belfast come to the opposite conclusion (CAJ 2006; ECNI 2017a, 2017b; NIHE 2000, 2017a, 2017b; Northern Ireland Human Rights Commission 2015; PPR 2007; Wallace 2015: 82).[9] Using NIHE council boundaries from March 2014, rather than the parliamentary constituency boundaries that McCausland used, the waiting list for North Belfast was measured at 1,310 Catholics and 494 Protestants (NIHE 2017b). And while not legally binding, the Office of the High Commission on Human Rights at the UN made recommendations regarding the housing situation in North Belfast. Visiting the area, UN High Commissioner for Children and Young People Koulla Yiasouma called for urgent action on the ongoing housing crisis, saying that these 'levels of homelessness and families living in hostels should not be happening in Northern Ireland' (PPR 2015a). Regardless of how one manipulates the figures, there is visible and genuine housing need among the Catholic/Nationalist population.

Some inferred that the continued failure to prioritising housing provision was a form of gerrymandering based on sectarianism. One Nationalist community worker remarked, 'the rationale would be if you built more houses, they would all be Nationalist houses there, and then it would be Nationalist votes' ('Maurice', interview with author 2016). Another related an anecdote:

> There was a lot of protesting ... about [the refusal to build housing], but in reality, it seems there was nothing we could do ... it was a strange period, 'cos ... if we're saying where McCausland was DSD minister, he was doing things like check how many Catholics worked in the Housing Executive in North Belfast, so he was creating this climate almost of fear, and he had some civil servants running scared. ('Thomas', interview with author 2016)

It was confirmed that McCausland had commissioned and published a religious breakdown of Housing Executive staff working in North Belfast, despite

---

[9] NIHE statistics from 2011 listed 619 Catholics and 220 Protestants on the waiting list; in its 2012 report *Equality Can't Wait*, PPR breaks down NIHE statistics further, noting that a new category of 'Undisclosed' had been used for monitoring. Their estimated perceived housing stress was 1,013 Catholics and 293 Protestants at that time.

warnings that the information was sensitive and could potentially put staff at risk (McCaffrey 2012a).

A *Detail* investigation into housing also found that over ten months, the DUP arranged a series of unpublicised meetings with the Housing Executive, attended only by other DUP members and focusing on North Belfast. The NIHE Board was not informed. Housing Executive officials asked for minutes of meetings but these were not circulated, and no official record was taken for three of the meetings. When *The Detail* asked the DSD for the number of meetings between McCausland and the NIHE regarding North Belfast, they were told that 'Minister for Social Development Nelson McCausland facilitated meetings ... on 30th September 2013 and 7th October 2013 respectively to discuss a range of housing issues including housing needs in North Belfast'. However, when they asked the same question of the Housing Executive, they replied that there had been nine meetings between 19 September 2013 and 1 April 2014 (McCaffrey 2014).

Within these meetings, dispute arose over the religious breakdown of housing waiting list figures and over social housing developments which would see people relocated outside the parliamentary constituency boundaries. Fellow DUP member and MP Nigel Dodds was reported as 'accusing NIHE officials of pushing people out of Belfast'. During the 16 September meeting, an A3 map of the North Belfast constituency was 'laid out on a coffee table' to allow DUP politicians to ask questions of Housing Executive officials. There were unattributed 'allegations of gerrymandering' (McCaffrey 2014).

North Belfast around that time was increasingly on an electoral knife edge – a 2011 election analysis showed the DUP with 37.1 per cent of the vote and Sinn Féin with 31.9 per cent. Sinn Féin had increased its vote by 1.3 per cent from the 2007 election (Russell 2011: 14). In theory, fulfilling Nationalist new-build housing need would be disastrous for the DUP's slim lead over Sinn Féin in North Belfast. Perhaps based on these electoral trends, the 2015 election saw a 'Unionist pact' where all the Unionist parties (the UUP, TUV and PUP) agreed not to stand for election in North Belfast, leaving the path clear for the DUP. Again, this drew allegations of gerrymandering from Nationalists, although one Unionist community worker pointed out that Sinn Féin had tried to do the same thing, but the SDLP refused to cooperate (author fieldnotes 2015).

The wrangling over policy and planning discussed in this chapter both exemplifies the formal and informal mechanisms of power in governance, and how these relate to the production of space and delivery of policy. Sinn Féin's and the DUP's rise to power in the devolved Assembly as 'ethnic champions' resulted in a continual tug of war over political legitimacy and access to physical and symbolic resources. Yet, in the case of the Girdwood development, consensus had to be reached to ensure the site moved forward. Resources were therefore 'shared out' rather than 'shared' – and the eventual Girdwood Conceptual Masterplan is a perfect example. This diluted compromise was the product of political deal-making to ensure no one lost out and no one won.

This differs slightly from the zero-sum resource competition and territoriality described in Chapter Three, where a lack of consensus stalled the process completely. Instead, a 'disagreed agreement' resulted where the two parties had to negotiate some sort of limited compromise. The DUP succeeded in holding territorial control of North Belfast, but the 60 houses allowed Sinn Féin to 'save face'. Furthermore, the Community Hub would be a 'shared space for all', something that everyone could agree on while ignoring the underlying sectarian contestations. The Community Hub looked good on paper and was the only major investment opportunity that had emerged post-economic crash.

The agreement on the Hub must also be seen in the wider context of political dynamics around social housing policy at the time. Unpicking those nuances allows us to see the strategies that actors of power use to shape space and discourse and underline division. These cannot be seen as isolated events but rather are indicative of 'well-maintained, well-functioning power relations' (Flyvbjerg 1998: 84). Different narratives were employed around rights to resources, and we see a 'tension between emotional and rational discourses' whereby there are competing rights rather than objective ones (Bradley and Murtagh 2007: 36). In the context of Northern Ireland, this is concerning given the importance of the legal framework embedded in the peace process, particularly equality of opportunity.

In April 2014, Lord Mayor Máirtín Ó Muilleoir of Sinn Féin broke ground on the Girdwood Community Hub's construction, shovel in hand for the cameras. He said that Girdwood would be 'iconic in bringing communities, now and in the future, together in a shared, welcoming space' (Belfast City Council 2014). People shook hands, politicians mugged for photographers and laudatory newspaper articles were published. Work commenced on the construction of the Hub.

CHAPTER SEVEN

The Trouble with 'Community'

Paramilitaries and the Peace Industry in Northern Ireland

After billions of pounds of investment in peacebuilding programmes,[1] after a series of community relations strategies that envisioned 'a spirit of genuine partnership' and a society 'free from sectarianism' (NIO 2006: 1–2), places like North Belfast remain blighted by paramilitarism, economic malaise and deep division. For a place envisioned as a 'shared space' and a beacon of reconciliation, funded with PEACE III money, the Hub site was not delivered with the commitments and mechanisms of peacebuilding at its core. The failure to transform the site speaks to the failure of politicians to deliver on a long list of promises: the commitments of the Agreement; the recommendations of the Dunlop Report, which envisioned a joined-up, coordinated community sector; or the commitments of the 2015 *Fresh Start Agreement* to dismantle paramilitary control of geographic areas.

Where previous chapters have focused 'top-down' on the political elite, this one provides context on the 'bottom-up' landscape of community development and paramilitary influence. It explores the various permutations and contradictions inherent in the notion of 'community' in Belfast. It also critiques the role of paramilitaries within their geographic 'communities'. I offer the latter with the caveat that both community development and paramilitarism are complex and polarising phenomena with their own academic literature (see for example, Mulvenna 2017 and Edwards 2017 on paramilitarism). My own analysis relates to what I observed and learned through desk research, fieldwork and life in Belfast.

---

[1] The SEUPB's PEACE programme alone invested £1.995 billion from 1995 to 2013, with future investment of £270 million ring-fenced for the period between 2014 to 2020 (Planning for Spatial Reconciliation Research Group 2016: 24).

Rhetorical Fluff: The Language of Community

The language of 'community' and 'community development' is omnipresent in peacebuilding rhetoric but so often left undefined and, more importantly, unchallenged. As Edwards notes, 'more rhetorical fluff attaches to "community" than most other words in the social science lexicon (with the possible exception of "empowerment" and "equity"). We still seem to have a romantic conception of community; all unitary values and communitarianism' (1997: 831).

It is a familiar word which connotes some measure of happiness, which suggests a sense of solidarity, rootedness and shared experience. Of course, this may be true to some extent in some situations. But the word 'community' *per se* never seems to be used in an unfavourable way. We talk about community engagement, community empowerment and community voice as a matter of course. Reference is often made in academic literature to 'communities of place', 'communities of identity' or 'communities of practice' (Amit and Rapport 2002; Cohen 1985). However, simply sharing the same neighbourhood, identity or beliefs does not in itself automatically constitute community (Somerville 2011: 10).

In Northern Ireland, the word 'community' is often used as a broad description of a seemingly homogenous geographical area and ethnonational group: in the highly polarised territories of working-class Belfast, the two go hand in hand. One might refer to the 'Lower Shankill community', or an 'interface community'. Nationalist or Unionist politicians describe standing up for their respective 'communities'. The media refers to the 'two communities'. Community development workers speak on behalf of 'the community'. Paramilitaries proclaim to 'defend their community'. Policymakers talk of 'building successful communities' rather than 'segregated communities' (Leonard 2014). The word features heavily in policy documents – used 461 times, for example, in the 116-page community relations strategy *Together, Building a United Community*. All this feel-good community talk can be exhausting. It is never defined and its nuances are often ignored.

Community groups in multiple neighbourhoods of Belfast all claim to represent their 'community'. Elements of Republican and Loyalist paramilitary groups continue to exercise a level of influence despite the ceasefires and subsequent decommissioning: they also claim to represent their 'communities'. This is despite the heterogeneity of people within these 'communities', many of whom are not connected to either community groups or paramilitaries. In the many usages of the term, a critical commentary is typically missing on how 'communities' are perceived by their inhabitants, and how individuals are connected, divided and constrained *within* these bounded areas. How the notion of 'community' and 'community development' mobilises people and sets them against one another, shapes space and legitimises division within that space – but can also be deployed in positive ways. As UUP MLA Michael Copeland observed: '"Communities" is a funny word that appeared only three or four years ago. We had communities before we called them communities. We had relationships across those communities before there was an industry in reinforcing those communities' (Hansard 2014b).

The term 'community' is problematic but it is used by political and community development elites for a reason. The discourse of sectarianism drives people to group into 'communities'. Claiming particular spaces as communities preserves homogeneity rather than diversity; this is an effective political tool as it symbolically unites people against an 'Other' and encourages attachment to place. However, it is important to note that even apparently homogeneous 'communities' are stratified by 'geography, social composition and the experience of individuals' (Shirlow and Murtagh 2004: 68). The two 'monolithic' blocs of Protestant/Unionist and Catholic/Nationalist are comprised of a wide variety of political ideologies and identities – or none – regardless of religion or ethnicity (Anderson and Shuttleworth 1998: 194). This runs contrary to the idea that the two blocs have 'fixed' ethnic and religious beliefs, crystallised over hundreds of years of tribal quarrel.

Indeed, in a speech made at the Girdwood Community Hub, community worker George Newell put forth: 'What is community cohesion? We don't have a community, we are diverse but we are divided – along ethnic lines, personality clashes, paramilitary lines, economic lifestyles. If cohesion means sticking together, our community isn't about that' (author fieldnotes 2016).

In Lundy and McGovern's seminal 2005 study of Ardoyne, several respondents also found the language of 'community' frustrating and inaccurate. As one respondent put it:

> People describe Ardoyne as a Republican or Nationalist community. There are people in Ardoyne who are not Nationalist, never mind Republican. We are not a Catholic community. The number of practising Catholics is probably twenty-odd percent at best. It's a divided community with different opinions … there's divisions there that aren't healed yet. But you have got all these kind of labels stuck on to a community, so you need to come away from that. We are all these different individuals, we share common things at different times, but not always. (40)

There is no unequivocal support and no homogenous 'community' in any area of Belfast, even those that were or are under paramilitary control. People hold opposing paramilitary and political allegiances or hold no allegiance at all. As Shirlow notes, 'the violent cultural and political acts which aid the reproduction of segregation should not be read as supported by all residents of segregated communities' (2006b: 227). Some residents disagree with the power paramilitaries hold in their areas: the 'community policing' that sees people kneecapped or killed, the extortion and racketeering, the control of the drug trade. Some have seen loved ones and friends killed by 'their own side', either by mistake or because of feuding or informing (Lundy and McGovern 2005: xiii). There are further divisions between the churches and paramilitaries, and community groups that see themselves as more socialist or revolutionary. Some of the most noticeable divisions are between groups affiliated and not affiliated with the Catholic Church (Shirlow and Murtagh 2004: 62). There are also typical neighbourhood grievances: personal disputes within and between families and clashes of personality (Lundy and McGovern 2005: 40). One community worker noted that 'community relations work and politics are vulnerable to personalities in roles' (author fieldnotes 2017). Yet this heterogeneity of experiences does not seem to be expressed from the top-down by political, community development or paramilitary elites. It is more expedient for these groups to claim to represent a homogenous and undefined 'community' and to attempt to symbolically unite this community against an 'Other' than to encourage diversity of opinion.

The concept of 'community' is not unique to Northern Ireland, and this is certainly true in terms of neighbourhood heterogeneity. It is also true in terms of approaches to urban regeneration. There has been a well-documented 'turn to community' in urban planning and policymaking centred around the language of 'community empowerment' and 'community engagement' (Docerty et al. 2001; Duffy and Hutchison 1997; Haughton 1999; Mitchell 2011; Sterrett et al. 2005). From the 1990s onwards in the United Kingdom, a 'Third Way' approach to urban regeneration emerged, driven by the concepts of 'civil society', 'community engagement' and 'participation' (Mitchell 2011: 99). This approach focused on 'building capacity' among local activists and developing 'social capital' within neighbourhoods to facilitate partnerships between the public sector, private sector and community/voluntary groups (Haughton 1999: 10). This rhetoric became central to funding bids for regeneration projects and inward investment (Cento Bull and Jones 2006: 769).

Over the following years, the language of 'community' has continued to permeate planning and development discourse. At its best, this involves genuine community engagement through participatory planning; however, more often it becomes a box-ticking exercise, or lip service to 'social responsibility' from large firms (Jacobs 1961; Jacobs 1992). At worst, places are destroyed or made unaffordable for former residents (what some term 'gentrification') (Fullilove 2004). Throughout, the issue of who truly represents a community, who belongs and who speaks for it remains salient.

The Peace Industry

Community development as we know it in Northern Ireland evolved over the course of the Troubles. Indeed, 'community development' was not a new phenomenon – even before the conflict, residents' groups and credit unions had been part of the local landscape, particularly in Catholic areas neglected by the Unionist government (de Baróid 2000: 12). Then in the 1980s, as part of the 'ballot box and Armalite'[2] strategy, the Provisional IRA started to direct their agenda towards political and social demands rather than outright violence. Their political arm, Sinn Féin, boasted a strong organisational structure within Catholic/Nationalist areas that supported advice centres and grassroots initiatives. At the same time, the British government deployed a counterinsurgency strategy based on 'normalisation' and began to engage with Nationalist community groups around economic and social regeneration. Engaging with the British state brought greater access to resources whilst consolidating an emergent Nationalist/Republican power base in these areas (Bean 2007: 14). However, this power was reliant on access to British state funding. Community groups originally founded on revolutionary politics thus became facilitators between the state and Sinn Féin and the Nationalist community. The structural relationships between the two blocs grew stronger (Bean 2007: 29).

Whilst Nationalist areas had a history of and infrastructure for community organisation, this did not, barring the churches and Orange Order, exist to the same extent in Protestant/Unionist areas. As a result, a sense of solidarity and common purpose was lacking in the latter. One Unionist community worker remarked, 'I think sometimes when you look at the word "community," I feel Nationalist communities are more intertwined with each other, they support each other much more than the Protestant communities do at times' ('Alex', interview with author 2016). This has underlined the sense of being 'on the back foot' to Nationalism described in earlier chapters for some Protestants/Unionists.

Post-ceasefire, Northern Ireland saw an influx of capacity- and peacebuilding funds from the European Union, the United States and various philanthropists. Some community groups assembled in response to funding opportunities that required 'community participation' or 'cross-community' reconciliation, others to provide stop-gap services in their own areas or to advocate around quality of life and social justice issues (Docerty et al. 2001: 2236). Community development became a full-fledged sector, 'upheld as a rational and accountable instrument'

---

[2] This approach was famously expressed by Danny Morrison at the 1981 Sinn Féin *ard fheis*: 'Who here really believes we can win the war through the ballot box? But will anyone here object if, with ballot paper in this hand and an Armalite in this hand, we take power in Ireland?' (English 2004: 225).

to promote inclusion and deliver social justice (Shirlow and Murtagh 2004: 58). This echoed the rhetoric of a 'Third Way' and 'citizen participation' that developed earlier in the UK. Community development workers are portrayed as gatekeepers to neighbourhoods and conduits for local voices, capable of representing their needs and delivering relevant programmes in a fair and competent manner. This presupposition is certainly true for some groups. There have been many notable successes in Northern Ireland at the grassroots level, facilitated by determined individuals working for the benefit of their area. This includes cross-community and trauma-informed reconciliation work as well as relationship-building and empowerment within neighbourhoods. Furthermore, as in other cities and countries, the sector is filling the gap in services where the public sector has withdrawn: from suicide intervention and mental health services to workforce development training to food banks (Northern Ireland Council for Voluntary Action (NICVA) 2014).

During my fieldwork, I made connections with multiple community development workers and was struck by their sense of purpose and conviction. It is demanding work. Because the groups' responsibilities are so varied, one might be called at any time of day to mediate trouble between young people at the interface, run afterschool programming or a neighbourhood crèche, connect people to housing resources, lobby for policy change at Stormont or organise cross-community trips to sites of historical interest. Over the years, I tagged along on trips to other community centres (to learn best practices for Girdwood), family fun days at the interface, Orange Order celebrations and dozens of meetings between community groups across the ethnonational divide. Despite their differences, the groups that operated around the Girdwood site wanted a development that would benefit the residents of the area. Some of this was lost at the political level and some of it was lost in arguments around the table, fuelled – again – by competing notions of 'needs' and 'rights'. But everyone generously opened their world and work to me as an outsider. I was welcomed into every setting and by the end of my fieldwork, I found it difficult to reconcile some of the broader structural sectarianism with the everyday community work I had observed. Yet to understand the story of Girdwood requires accounting for all the complex dynamics within and between the community development sector in Northern Ireland and those it claims to represent.

Northern Ireland has a wide variety of community development groups that deliver a range of programmes, from 'single-identity'[3] work to cross-

---

[3] 'Single-identity' is a term used to refer to community work that takes place among either Catholics/Nationalists or Protestants/Unionists exclusively to 'shore up' and affirm a sense of cultural identity. It tends to occur more often among the latter group, for example, studying the place of Unionists in Northern Irish history through their contribution to the first and second world wars. It seems to be a reaction to

community initiatives, from employment training to arts workshops to childcare. In Belfast, the density and diversity of these are remarkable given the city's relatively small size: at the time of my fieldwork, there were 337 registered in Belfast alone, and probably scores of smaller unregistered groups (NICVA n.d.). This is due in part to the phenomenon of territorialism, which continues to characterise neighbourhoods. In cities across the world, one finds different neighbourhoods arranged based on ethnic, religious and kinship ties. In this sense, Belfast is not exceptional. However, the legacy of recent conflict, paramilitary and political control, coupled with historical parochialism, has produced a remarkable range of geographically defined neighbourhoods.[4] All of these have at least one community group and sometimes multiple groups working in the same area.

Within these places, there are even smaller micro-neighbourhoods. This became apparent during my fieldwork, as I got to know the dynamics of the particular area around the site of the Girdwood Community Hub. In Lower Cliftonville, for example, those who live along the interface on Cliftonpark Avenue consider themselves a different micro-group from those on Brucevale Avenue, one minute down the road, or on the Antrim Road on the other side of the Girdwood Barracks, and again from those on Manor Street, two minutes in the opposite direction up the Cliftonville Road.

This speaks to the lingering influence of territorialism, which has exacerbated segregation and both inter- and intra-communal division. In some ways, these micro-geographies are an assertion of power on the part of both community groups and paramilitary associations. Multiple community groups exist within one geographical 'community', and they all claim to represent that 'community' as a homogenous whole. This contrasts with the idea of CEPs set out in the Dunlop Report in Chapter Three, which attempted to solve the problem of fragmentation and factionalism in North Belfast through partnerships. Over two decades later and despite the Dunlop Report's prescriptions, the community development landscape remains parochial and piecemeal. The CEPs ultimately failed due to territorialism and contest over 'representation' between different

> the enduring sense of loss and the persistent preponderance of educational underattainment and unemployment among young Protestants in deprived areas. It also feels like a counteraction of the sense of historical narrative and cultural traditions that Catholics/Nationalists typically enjoy (e.g., indigenous history and language, traditional Irish music and dance).
> 4 'Nationalist North Belfast' alone, for example, is comprised of dozens of distinct areas. Within a few square miles lie Carrick Hill, the New Lodge, Newington, Sailortown (now essentially defunct, a victim of motorway development), Lower Cliftonville, the Bone – made up of only a few streets but perceived as different from neighbouring Ardoyne – continuing up the roads and up the mountain to Ligoniel and Whitewell.

community groups. The idea of a unified community leadership threatened the micro-powers that had been assembled through tight control of place. Belfast thus remains fractured by hamlet-scale community leadership.

Community development has been hamstrung by this wider landscape of parochialism. For instance, duplication of services is a major issue within the community sector and a waste of resources. It is a consequence of the sectarianised system in Northern Ireland in which resources are doled out to 'both sides' in a zero-sum equation. On both sides of the divide, most areas have their own separate facilities: leisure centres, youth groups, childcare centres, housing advice centres, health centres, etc. These are often within close proximity to other similar facilities: for instance, as the Planning for Spatial Reconciliation Research Group notes, 'the Grove Health and Wellbeing Centre located on the York Road, is only 1.6 miles from the Carlisle Wellbeing and Treatment Centre located on the Antrim Road, which in turn is located only 1.7 miles from Shankill Wellbeing and Treatment Centre' (2016: 75).[5] In North Belfast, there are four main council-funded leisure centres – Ballysillan, the Grove, Loughside and Valley – all located in mainly Protestant areas. There is also a leisure centre on the Shankill Road, which has a swimming pool. There are no leisure centres in Catholic areas of North Belfast – the nearest swimming pool is on the Falls Road in West Belfast – and this has been a point of contention.[6] This is partly because of readings of sectarianised space, where some people are still unwilling to venture into areas deemed to belong to the 'Other'. But people are also unwilling to lose out – 'separate but equal' is the expectation. A gain for one side is a loss for the other, so trade-offs and carve-ups and share-outs must occur.

Duplication of services also puts pressure on multiple groups within the same area to compete for funding, rather than streamlining resources within a community. As one Nationalist community worker stated:

> Some people will tell you that they are so focused on the work that their organisation does, they think that they're the only people doing it. Now, that's because they're doing things which makes their organisation look good, as opposed to a shared vision of all the people in a geographical area, or all the people in a community of interest ... no one has a shared sense of purpose. So they all compete – and it's not to say that they're

---

[5] It is also worth noting that these are all in close proximity to the Girdwood Community Hub, which was built, in part, to promote health and well-being.
[6] The swimming pool idea seemed to be a sticking point for many people I spoke to. In 2020, I came across an article that described plans for a 'community swimming pool' at Girdwood and found this kind of humorous. A contact in Belfast later confirmed that a swimming pool was indeed in the works.

not doing social good, but they're all doing social good in a fractured way. ('Maurice', interview with author 2016)

Another community worker observed:

> The community sector might end up arguing with each other rather than putting their finger on what the real problem is – it's a problem with resources and distribution of resources and who controls them, and what is the philosophy behind that there, and how do people actually view how resources should be used in communities such as this? ('Liam', interview with author 2016)

It recalls the dynamics between CEPs which complicated the initial phase of the Girdwood development in 2006, whereby various groups competed to undermine each other rather than cooperate on a broader vision for the site and for North Belfast. This dynamic would also emerge, to varying extents, in the last phase of the Hub development as different groups jockeyed for a role in the process. However, this issue is not unique to Northern Ireland. As Edwards notes, 'there has always been competition for resources in urban policy in the sense that the requests for resources from local authorities and voluntary agencies ... have always exceeded the available funding' (1997: 826). This is becoming particularly difficult for the community development sector as funding cuts continue their relentless march and resources are increasingly stretched thin.

Community groups must also shrewdly negotiate the political landscape in order to sustain their funding. Some community and voluntary sector workers point to 'a damaging colonisation of the sector by party-political interests' (Ketola and Hughes 2016: 37). Some evidence suggests that favouritism exists whereby funding is channelled to particular groups (see Chapter Five), and that links between Sinn Féin and the IRA, and between the DUP and UDA, may influence funding priorities. Anecdotal evidence points to funding being cut for groups who speak out or have alternative views to the 'party line' of the dominant parties (Cochrane and Dunn 2002: 85; Mitchell 2011: 8). Dependence on funding can therefore silence dissent and maintain the status quo; indeed, Ketola and Hughes found that, 'due to funding dependency, some organisations have lost the ability to challenge government's distribution of resources, even when they believe that the distribution of resources is politically driven' (2016: 37). The day-to-day negotiations of community development work and funding constraints can therefore be messy and frustrating, influenced by a range of factors within a fundamentally divided political system.

The issue of representation and legitimacy has become contentious within post-Agreement community work. 'The claiming has to stop. A lot of it is just power plays', remarked one observer (author fieldnotes 2017). They continued:

> Despite what community groups say – 'they are representing the people' – they only represent certain people. There is still a large amount of people who aren't represented, who aren't participating or who are not engaged, who don't know what's going on with Girdwood. Who aren't in the right channels or who have different beliefs than the Shinners, for example.

Shirlow and Murtagh's influential study of Ardoyne highlights the dangers of presuming all community groups are representative of their areas. They found that despite 60 community groups operating in the North Belfast neighbourhood of Ardoyne, 'the vast majority of respondents neither knew nor were involved with community groups' (2004: 64). While this may not be typical of all areas, it is worth noting that levels of engagement are not always what they seem and that community agents can 'claim' to represent places with no real basis. This was reflected in a DSD survey of residents in the CEP areas, which had a response rate of around 15 per cent from residents from each zone. Their knowledge of and awareness of CEPs varied from 7 to 65 per cent. The researchers noted that the size of an area may have been a factor, but regardless there was 'tremendous' variability in knowledge (Murtagh et al. 2009: 15).[7] Some groups had made little or no effort to engage beyond small local elites. Others were overly based on family networks, or controlled by particular political parties or paramilitary groups, which excludes other people from participating (Liggett 2017: 99).

Residents can be otherwise marginalised, or apathetic, or find community groups irrelevant to their lives. Still others might utilise services like youth groups or credit unions in their daily lives but have no connection with other types of community development or political activism. Yet politicians, paramilitaries and community workers alike continue to employ the rhetoric of speaking for 'the community' and what 'the community' wants to legitimise their decisions.

---

[7] Two CEPs, New Lodge and Greencastle, had an awareness rate of at least +50 per cent. Ardoyne and Upper Ardoyne had rates around a third and above. All other CEPs were below 20 per cent (Murtagh et al. 2009: 15). The authors understood the New Lodge group as having been the most active through media and the Greencastle CEP operationalising the highest share of volunteers.

Paramilitarism in Northern Ireland: 'They Haven't Gone Away, You Know!'[8]

Paramilitaries draw upon the rhetoric of 'community' in their attempts to exercise power over areas. While the rhetoric around the Girdwood Hub promised a shared space open to all, the lingering presence of paramilitary groups in the surrounding neighbourhoods calls these promises into question. The space cannot be truly transformed, or shared, if paramilitarism is still tolerated alongside it. The continued existence of paramilitary power in Northern Ireland further highlights the chasm between the rhetoric and reality of peacebuilding, 25 years on from the Agreement.

All the main paramilitary groups from the conflict remain in existence, including the UVF, RHC, UDA, PIRA and Irish National Liberation Army (INLA). This means Sinn Féin is still linked to the Provisional IRA Army Council; a report by the Police Service of Northern Ireland (PSNI) and MI5 confirmed that the Army Council oversees both Sinn Féin and the IRA with an overarching strategy (2015: 4). According to the same report, 'the UDA, UVF and INLA have continued to recruit and all of the paramilitary groups maintain a relatively public profile in spite of being illegal organisations' (2015: 1). But paramilitarism involves a complex landscape that defies stereotype. There are many different factors as to why people become involved. For instance, some families have taken part in paramilitary groups for generations; involvement is perceived as an inherited duty to past sites of struggle. For some socio-economically marginalised young people, entry into a paramilitary group is seen as a pathway to opportunity and social standing, in the same way that gangs function in other places (Howell and Griffiths 2018; Hallsworth and Brotherton 2011; Kintrea et al 2008). And those engaged in criminality also operate under the guise of 'paramilitarism', although their activities may not be sanctioned by other branches of the paramilitary organisation in question (Independent Reporting Commission 2021: 9).

Some paramilitary groups still purport to be fighting, although they are in the minority. These are mostly small, angry subgroups of Republican 'dissidents' who reject the peace process. In areas under 'dissident' control, masked gunman patrol housing estates and there are instances of 'kneecappings' or 'punishment beatings' of young people. These groups plant explosive devices (which mercifully seem to fail more often than not) and stage intermittent attacks on PSNI and prison officers (which have not always failed, resulting in the murders of several officers) (Marijan and Brennan 2016; Morris 2016b;

---

[8] An oft-quoted remark about the Provisional IRA made by leader Gerry Adams at a rally in 1995, after a ceasefire but before the decommissioning of arms (McKittrick 1995).

BBC News 2012b; McDonald 2011). These elements have a particular foothold in Derry. In 2019, Northern Ireland was rocked by the murder of a young journalist, Lyra McKee, who was shot by dissident elements during rioting in the Creggan area of the city (Givetash 2019).

However, with the exception of the dissidents, the nature of paramilitarism has changed. There are no more 'tit-for-tat' cycles of sectarian attacks, common during the conflict. Violence in general has dramatically decreased, and 'the degree of support for progress among some key figures in both Republican and Loyalist groups is notable' (Alderdice et al. 2016: 7). For instance, many former and current paramilitaries have moved away from violence to engage in peacebuilding and the community development sector. They are often regarded as gatekeepers 'because their influence in communities enables them to deliver outcomes' (Alderdice et al. 2016: 10). Debate has occurred on the effectiveness of former and current paramilitaries' role in community development work. On the one hand, they typically have deep local knowledge, authority and connections – and thus the ability to 'influence, restrain and manage' expectations and, to some extent, behaviour (PSNI and MI5 2015: 2). Marijan and Brennan observe that 'post-ceasefire paramilitary peacekeeping', whereby former combatants are invited to steward parades or to restrain and mediate interface violence, can be positive: they can undermine 'spoiler' elements and facilitate or encourage support for policing (2016: 3). As gatekeepers, former or current paramilitaries can therefore use their influence in neighbourhoods to shape positive outcomes (Alderdice et al. 2016: 10).

For instance, one summer I attended an Orange Order parade that ended in North Belfast, just past a contentious interface in Ardoyne. In past years, rioting had occurred along this interface as the parade passed, and in response, the Parade Commission had ruled that the Orangemen[9] could not complete the traditional route. The decision had been met with widespread anger and sustained protest. The atmosphere was tense – would the scene break into violence, as it had before? Parade stewards and community workers moved among the crowd. There was no violence, and I suspected this was because those who controlled the area, including paramilitaries, had decided against the optics of a riot. Several journalists and photographers looked disappointed as the parade dispersed peacefully.

These gatekeepers can be both an 'asset and a liability' to their areas (Community Foundation NI 2017: 9). Critics have alleged that they can prevent cross-community work, and interface violence can be 'switched on' or 'ratcheted up' by those with paramilitary connections to attract funding. One DUP MLA described a situation in which 'somebody who one night

---

[9] Orangemen are members of the Orange Order. There are some examples of women's Orange lodges but the Order is definitively male in its make-up.

is out organising the petrol bombing is on the [television] screen the next night as a conflict transformation worker' (Foley and Robinson 2004: 33). It is impossible to generalise, however, as there are individuals with alleged links to paramilitary groups who use their credibility, influence and knowledge to ease violence, encourage support of the PSNI and deliver services to those most hard to reach in marginalised areas (Shirlow and McEvoy 2008; Independent Reporting Commission (IRC) 2021: 12).

Often, and sometimes paradoxically, paramilitaries claim to fill the role of 'community protectors', maintaining law and order by 'informal policing' of theft, joyriding and drug-dealing (Hamill 2010; Knox 2001: 207). In this way, they maintain power, even though the context of violent conflict has ceased. It is a new manifestation of old power roles. A Nationalist community worker near the Girdwood site remarked:

> There are threats from paramilitaries in these areas, no doubt about it, you know, threats to young people who step out of line, as far as they're concerned, their attitude towards drugs; [the paramilitaries] claim to be dealing with drugs, punishing drug dealers. Many people think that they're actually, you know, involved in drug dealing themselves or they're taxing these drug dealers or involved in other types of activities, and it's really all about money and it's about power rather than politics. ('Liam', interview with author 2016)

Indeed, some factions of paramilitary groups have become criminal organisations engaged in extortion, armed robbery and drug dealing, large-scale smuggling, money and food laundering (PSNI and MI5 2015: 2; Alderdice et al. 2016). 'Anything involved with money they're into it', remarked one Loyalist source in a BBC *Spotlight* documentary (2016a). In 2021, Northern Ireland ran a public service campaign warning people not to turn to paramilitary money-lending operations; residents have been forced to hand over benefit payments or engage in illegal drug transport or prostitution to pay back loans with exorbitant interest rates (NIE 2021).

The PSNI and MI5 record that violence and intimidation are still used to exercise coercive control at an individual and community level (2015: 1). A Unionist community worker recalled a campaign of intimidation by paramilitaries 'where they were trying to get into the community centre ... and that was quite a challenging and difficult time ... I thought I was gonna have to walk away from my job and my home' (author fieldnotes 2016). According to a Housing Executive representative, intimidation increased from 2015 to 2016, the year the Girdwood Hub opened. In 2015, there were 600 forced evictions due to intimidation, two-thirds of them by paramilitaries and usually on an intra-community basis. This trend increased year on year through 2018 in Northern

Ireland; since then there has been a decline (IRC 2021: 34; Hawthorne 2016). But punishment beatings and 'kneecappings' are still common occurrences in areas policed by paramilitaries: in February 2018, there was a spate of three reported punitive attacks in three days in Belfast, including one near Girdwood, in the New Lodge (McDonald 2017; *Belfast Telegraph* 2018). A newspaper article in March 2018 reported that such punitive attacks had surged by 60 per cent in the past four years (McDonald 2018a). In a 2016 investigative documentary about the Lower Shankill, too, anonymous residents spoke of punishment beatings, attacks on homes and forced exile of people still happening on a regular basis. The victims are those who defy the UDA, and most often young people (BBC *Spotlight* 2016b).

The first dedicated strategy by the Assembly to tackle paramilitarism was *A Fresh Start*, released in 2015. The document, according to its Sinn Féin/DUP authors, 'signals our resolve to engender the sea change so longed for by our community – a new beginning, an opportunity to move forward with a real sense of hope and purpose' (OFMDFM 2015: 6). This rhetoric is curious, as is the title itself, considering that the Good Friday Agreement was supposed to be the 'fresh start' for Northern Ireland to move forward. Over a decade after the Agreement, it seemed that the power-sharing government had failed to deliver a new beginning, societal transformation or political progress.

The 'fresh start' promised by the DUP and Sinn Féin provided for an independent panel, the IRC, to draw up recommendations for the disbanding of paramilitary groups (NIE 2015: 17). The panel consisted of former Chief Human Rights Commissioner Monica McWilliams, solicitor John McBurney and former Alliance leader Lord Alderdice. The panel has changed slightly in composition over the years but at the time of writing has continued to release annual reports on paramilitarism in Northern Ireland. Year on year, they find that paramilitary groups continue to exert coercive control in communities; in 2021, the IRC said that paramilitaries remained a 'clear and present danger'. This may have been due in part to the resurgence of street disorder linked to Protestant/Unionist/Loyalist opposition to trade barriers between Northern Ireland and the rest of the UK because of Brexit (see Epilogue).[10]

One IRC report noted that the PSNI engage with paramilitary representatives around issues like parading disputes, flags and anti-social behaviour, 'even though they are members of proscribed organisations' (Alderdice et al. 2016: 10).

---

[10] In photos that briefly made world news, a hijacked bus burned and crowds threw stones at police in Unionist areas; rioters as young as 13 and 14 were arrested. Individual Loyalist paramilitaries were reported to have stoked tensions and engineered the scenes of violence in the streets, supporting and encouraging young people in their behaviour (Al Jazeera 2021).

It suggests this engagement 'undermines a culture of lawfulness' (Alderdice et al. 2016: 21). One of the authors, McBurney, remarked:

> It has become almost an expediency to deal with some of these senior figures to try and quell problems that have arisen in the community. That creates a situation where they seem to be the 'go to' people. And that has an effect on the notion of normal law and order in the communities when police officers are seen to be engaging with people in those communities who are known to be senior paramilitary figures. (BBC *Spotlight* 2016b)

The PSNI does not deny engagement with paramilitary figures. A senior police figure said in the same documentary:

> I don't want to do anything to legitimise paramilitary groups but there also needs to be a pragmatism around how and when police engage with community representatives who may still have some sort of paramilitary trappings associated to them or are believed to be so. But let me be clear, we will never be so close to these people that we can't do our job. (BBC *Spotlight* 2016b)

Yet, police and government attempts to consult with paramilitary representatives do appear to legitimise the organisations, granting them an unofficial role in managing and policing neighbourhoods. This in turn 'validates and reifies' paramilitary leadership in what should be a post-conflict context (Marijan and Brennan 2016: 3), underlining new manifestations of old patterns of conflict.

Paramilitaries have other relationships within the community development sector and with political elites. This is not unique to Northern Ireland: in Lebanon, for instance, Randa Nucho notes that these actors are involved 'at every level of governance and [entangled] in the provision of public services, infrastructure and planning' (2016: 3). It is widely recognised in Northern Ireland that several political parties have direct links to paramilitaries despite their official denials (Knox 2001: 212). But like many things in Northern Ireland, it is simply not talked about; it is assumed knowledge that one picks up through being part of a place. During my research, I found it odd that this tacit knowledge is rarely expressed or explored in academic literature. It felt like paramilitarism was simply unacknowledged in polite conversation, that it didn't exist within the walls of the university.

On the one hand, Northern Ireland is such an intimate place that many overlapping connections and roles are to be expected. But it also demonstrates that old patterns of conflict have merely been expressed in new forms; politics, paramilitarism and community development remain intertwined to varying extents. This subverts the rhetoric of all these strategies that talk about fundamentally transforming the way power is exercised and resources allocated in society.

The controversy of funding Charter NI as outlined in Chapter Five is, perhaps, the public face of this phenomenon. Chief executive Dee Stitt was allegedly the commander of a UDA unit involved in drug-dealing, racketeering and intimidation of local residents, including an assault on a community worker (BBC *Spotlight* 2016a). That community worker spoke to the DUP and the PSNI but claimed they did not take any action. Later, Stitt was awarded £1.7 million in funding for Charter NI and was pictured next to DUP First Minister Arlene Foster (Manley 2016).

This is emphatically not to say all those involved with Charter NI have links to the UDA. However, in an Assembly debate, Alliance MLA Stewart Dickson alleged:

> The DUP has had a clear agenda of trying to direct funding to Charter over the last number of years … that, in itself, is of significant concern, but the interface between Charter and the UDA should ring alarm bells. Alliance welcomes people with a paramilitary past playing a positive and constructive role in society. However, when people with a paramilitary present are doing so and, indeed, are managing public funds that have been awarded through a closed system, there is clearly a problem. (Hansard 2016a: 4)

SDLP MLA Claire Hanna added that 'we are supposed to be giving money to people who are consistently good examples to their communities. Toy soldier Dee Stitt is absolutely not that. If you will not face down that man, how can we have any confidence that you will face down hundreds of other paramilitaries?' (Hansard 2016a: 16).

Closer to Girdwood, links have been alleged between the UDA and the Lower Shankill Community Association (LSCA), who helped engage residents in the Girdwood development process.[11] In 2016, a *Spotlight* documentary suggested that the LSCA was being used as unofficial headquarters of the UDA's C Company and known UDA members are alleged to have frequented the building. A member of the UDA claimed that whilst carrying out legitimate community work, the offices were also being used as 'UDA headquarters, C Company headquarters,

---

[11] This is not to say that the volunteers and staff at the LSCA are involved in the UDA. The organisation facilitates a variety of community work: they run workforce development training, education and youth programmes, hold monthly neighbourhood meetings and maintain relationships with the PSNI and Housing Executive. They also take part in cross-community initiatives. I was always welcomed into their offices and enjoyed ducking in to say hello on my long walks up and down the Shankill Road.

that's where it all happens from' (BBC *Spotlight* 2016b). Less than 24 hours after the *Spotlight* documentary aired, DUP Minister for Communities Paul Givan was pictured with DUP MP Nigel Dodds in the offices of the LCSA (Morris 2016a). The purpose of the meeting was to discuss the Building Successful Communities programme (see Chapter Six) taking place in the Lower Shankill and Lower Oldpark. SDLP leader Colum Eastwood said the visit was 'at best, an incredible lapse in judgement and, at worst, has provided succour to those intent on maintaining a stranglehold on that community' (Monaghan 2017).

This suggests that paramilitaries are, to some extent, actors of power in post-Agreement Belfast – and in the areas around Girdwood. Reminiscing about how the area used to function, community volunteers in the Lower Shankill area said, 'we tell the paramilitaries what to do now … the paramilitaries used to tell us what to do, but they realised we're not going away'. Yet the paramilitaries haven't gone away either – according to another resident, recruitment continues (author fieldnotes 2016). The estate is still festooned with UDA, UFF and Ulster Young Militants plaques – installed in 2015 – and UDA flags flutter from many of the bungalows.

In adjacent Lower Oldpark, the LOCA has refused to work with the UDA, resulting in tension in the area. Before the opening of the Girdwood Community Hub, new UDA plaques similar to those in the Lower Shankill were installed directly across from the Hub in Lower Oldpark, on the corner of Summer Street and Cliftonpark Avenue. This functioned as a clearly visible demarcation for pedestrians and visitors coming down the street. I noticed them all of a sudden one day, on my customary walk down Cliftonpark Avenue. 'They appeared overnight … and that was just making a statement. It always has been seen as UDA territory' one resident said (author fieldnotes 2016). These intimidating territorial markers actively militate against the prospect of 'shared space' at Girdwood by asserting paramilitary presence across the street. One wonders what the SEUPB funders would think of the colourful display.

Meanwhile, on the Nationalist side of North Belfast, power struggles between different factions of Republicanism continue. The PSNI and MI5 note that the structures of the PIRA remain, 'in a much reduced form', including a leadership and Army Council. PIRA members are 'instructed to actively support Sinn Féin within the community, including activity like electioneering and leafleting' (PSNI and MI5 2015: 4). On the other hand, smaller dissident groups have carved out niches of control. In some areas, there is particular tension between Sinn Féin and so-called 'dissidents' – as one Unionist commentator put it, 'the dissidents are puttin' it up to Sinn Féin IRA[12] and Sinn Féin IRA

---

[12] 'Sinn Féin IRA' is a colloquial name for Sinn Féin used by some Loyalists, who do not distinguish between politicians currently in power and IRA combatants, whom they perceive as 'terrorists', from the Troubles.

Fig. 7.1

are puttin' it up to the dissidents, and each are vying to make themselves more relevant than the other' (author fieldnotes 2016). Near Girdwood, this is reflected in a proliferation of Republican Network for Unity and Óglaigh na h-Éireann[13] murals in the New Lodge, competing for space with Sinn Féin-endorsed ones on gable walls. The battle for control plays out in the competing murals. These territorial demarcations – murals, flags, plaques – serve as physical statements of power in neighbourhoods, so '[paramilitary power] is reinforced all day, everyday', as one interviewee noted ('Maurice', interview with author 2016).

While the Girdwood Community Hub itself was envisioned as 'shared space', the fact that it is surrounded by spaces which remained divided, marked and controlled by paramilitary groups is concerning. It recalls the flawed *Cohesion, Sharing and Integration* community relations strategy described in Chapter Five, which set out 'shared space' as a short-term goal before the long-term goal of 'tackling the multiple social issues effecting and entrenching community separation, exclusion and hate' (OFMDFM 2010: 7–8). This progression incorrectly assumes that superficial territorial fixes will address deeper causes of (and creators of) division and enmity.

[13] These are Republican groups that are not allied with Sinn Féin.

A video produced by the Girdwood Youth Forum[14] and cross-community group North Talks Too underlined that the root causes of division continue to be exacerbated by paramilitary elements, precluding shared space: 'We already have a bad image of each other, and paramilitaries, they encourage people, like "stay away from each other 'cause they're dangerous" ... The reason why others are scared to go into other areas is to do with paramilitaries ... Because [paramilitaries] wanna be in control, they're just making things worse' (Bluebird Media 2016). Despite 25 years of peacebuilding and billions of pounds of funding, territorial disputes, paramilitary influence and duplication of resources continue to shape the post-Agreement landscape and the opportunities available to residents. One outcome is that the language of 'community' is used by elites to paper over the diversity of opinion within geographical areas. Another outcome is that paramilitaries, politicians and community groups are linked to varying extents. Even if they are engaged in legitimate peacebuilding work, this can serve to reify old power dynamics and subvert the rule of law. Such influences in the broader community development landscape point to the existence of the same power blocs and senses of territorialism that prevailed during the conflict, even if these are expressed in different ways.

---

[14] The Youth Forum was organised late in the Girdwood development process, ostensibly to promote youth engagement. It was made up of local young people from across the ethnonational divide.

CHAPTER EIGHT

'Shenanigans and Skullduggery'

Community Engagement and Argument at Girdwood

The final phase of development, the construction of the Girdwood Community Hub, experienced several ups and downs. After the Masterplan was finalised, Belfast City Council established the Girdwood Community Hub Forum, made up of community groups across North Belfast. The groups closest to the site were North Talks Too, a cross-community forum of Lower Shankill, Lower Oldpark and Lower Cliftonville, and the Ashton Centre in the New Lodge. However, as in the first phase of development back in 2006, a sense of parochialism and competition beset some interactions between groups as they jockeyed for a seat at the table. These competing claims to legitimacy occur in redevelopment processes everywhere as questions of ownership and community voice are debated. Relationships between community groups and the council were also sometimes fractious. The council had several unwelcome surprises up its sleeve: for instance, it announced that a private operator from England was going to be managing the site, along with other leisure centres in Belfast. It also gave the Community Forum last-minute notice that the council had underspent the EU funding by over £1 million – and they had three days to figure out how to spend it before the deadline. As one community worker put it, 'shenanigans and skullduggery' abounded.

The process felt divorced from the needs of the surrounding area. Politicians and civil servants had not learned from the mistakes of the previous attempts to develop the space. As PPR pointed out, there was again no consultation with the surrounding area to identify pressing social issues and target the Hub accordingly. All in all, the development process seemed rushed, as if building *something* on the space was better than nothing at all, regardless of who was involved or what the outcomes were. And in the run-up to the opening, it felt like time and money were running out.

Finally, the pernicious issue of territorial claim dogged the process up until the final days before opening. The removal of the old barracks walls felt momentous: where ugly sheet metal had once stood, new visual space was opened up and the area made whole. But community consultation among

Protestant/Unionist residents still pointed to the desire for a boundary. The issue then became, naturally, that with a new boundary, the Catholic/Nationalist side had easier access to the site than the Protestant/Unionist side. At the micro-level, tit-for-tat territoriality and contests over access were still very much alive, if illogical, up to the final stages of the Hub development.

How Can It Be 'Shared Space' When You're Wrangling Over the Whole Planning Process?[1]

After it won the SEUPB funding bid in 2011, Belfast City Council established the Girdwood Community Hub Forum. This involved a variety of community groups from around North Belfast, including: the North Belfast Interface Network; the North Belfast Partnership Board; the Ashton Centre (also referred to as Ashton Community Trust); the LSCA; the LOCA; and the Cliftonville Community Regeneration Forum (CCRF) (North Talks Too 2014b: 11).

In the years 2014–2017, when my fieldwork took place, four main community groups emerged in negotiations around the Girdwood site and with the city council. The LSCA, LOCA, CCRF and the Ashton Centre are all located in the neighbourhoods directly surrounding the Girdwood site (Lower Shankill, Lower Oldpark, Lower Cliftonville and New Lodge, respectively). Each group operates separately, but common concerns include working with hard-to-reach young people and the long-term unemployed and supporting the physical and social regeneration of the local area. They deliver various services: the CCRF and LOCA have housing officers and advice drop-ins, the LSCA and Ashton run skill-building and literacy programmes, and the LOCA and Ashton offer crèche services. The CCRF and LOCA, located on either side of the interface wall on Cliftonpark Avenue, were also funded by the International Fund for Ireland (IFI) to deliver the 'Bridging the Interface' programme together, which aimed to engage with young people and build relationships across the divide (IFI 2012).

The LOCA is perhaps the most fragile of the community groups around Girdwood. At the time of my fieldwork, it had few staff and no youth worker. Lower Oldpark is an enclave of about 400 houses, estranged from the Shankill by the Crumlin Road and surrounded by Catholic/Nationalist areas (Cliftonville, Ardoyne, New Lodge). Over the years, many of its homes had been abandoned and blighted. It was heavily impacted by the 2000 Loyalist feud, with the murder of Samuel Rocket[2] and a number of forced evictions

---

[1] Nationalist community worker (author fieldnotes 2016).
[2] Samuel Rocket, 22, was understood to have had links to the UVF. It is alleged that, during the 2000 Loyalist feud, he received assurances from members of C Company

by the UDA (BBC News 2000; Wood 2006: 250). Because of its geographical and symbolic isolation, there is an accompanying sense of threat and fear there, exemplifying the lack of confidence and sense of decline found in other Unionist areas. In response to the state of dereliction and blight, Lower Oldpark has been a beneficiary of significant infrastructural improvement in line with housing-led regeneration policy (see Chapter Six); along with Lower Shankill, it was part of DSD Minister McCausland's *Facing the Future* housing strategy and Building Successful Communities programme, had 26 new homes built by Clanmil Housing Association and also received a £110,000 refurbishment of its playpark adjacent to the interface barrier (DSD 2013b; LOCA 2012).

In 2009, the LOCA, CCRF and LSCA formed a partnership named North Talks Too (North Talks Too 2015: 3). They felt their communities were 'being left behind' by the council's bid for the Girdwood site (North Talks Too 2014a: 1). North Talks Too's key objectives were building relationships across the divide and ensuring the 'transformation of interface communities in Lower Shankill, Lower Oldpark and Lower Cliftonville' through 'substantial social, economic and physical investment' (North Talks Too 2014a: 2). Their work was founded on the idea that community representatives can create the structures for cross-community contact and empowerment between and within their respective areas.

Together, North Talks Too ran a series of cross-community trips, including to sites of historical interest on both sides of the ethnonational divide. In 2011, they organised the 'first ever' family fun day on Cliftonpark Avenue, once one of the most dangerous interfaces in Belfast. As one of their informational pamphlets said, 'the smoke at the interface now comes from BBQs, not petrol bombs' (North Talks Too 2015: 7). However, one community worker related that the first fun day had two barbecues – one for each side. The children played together but the adults didn't mix. The next year they put the two barbecues together on the Lower Oldpark side and people on the Cliftonville side complained, 'Why did they get it?' (author fieldnotes 2017). This anecdote is a small but significant (and kind of humorous) example of the zero-sum, 'themmuns vs our ones' perspective explored earlier. A gain for one side is perceived as a loss for the other, precluding the concept of 'shared space' or shared resources. Regardless, the cross-community aspect of North Talks Too's work has helped to lessen tensions around this formerly volatile interface.

Just around the corner from the Cliftonpark Avenue interface, two minutes' walk through the shadow of the barracks' metal perimeter, sits the New Lodge neighbourhood. New Lodge's primary community group is the Ashton Community Development Trust, located in the Ashton Centre. Ashton is arguably the largest

---

UDA that he would be safe to visit UDA-controlled Lower Oldpark, where his girlfriend lived. Instead, he was shot dead in front of his infant daughter and girlfriend (BBC News 2000; Sutton 2002).

and best-resourced community group in the area, funding a wide range of services and social enterprises including New Lodge Youth Centre;[3] KinderKids day care;[4] training and skills programmes;[5] the Bridge of Hope therapeutic and counselling services;[6] and the FabLab,[7] which teaches digital fabrication to a cross-community catchment of users, many of whom are marginalised from traditional employment (Murtagh et al. 2015: 5). Ashton is also the lead partner for the Lower North Belfast Family Support Hub, which works with vulnerable families to connect them to services. Its annual income and spending are over £6 million and it has won multiple best-practice awards for its work (Charity Commission for Northern Ireland 2021; Ashton Community Trust 2017a). Most of Ashton's 160-odd employees are from the local area, making it the largest social economy project in Northern Ireland (Ashton Community Trust 2017a).

Because of Ashton's reach and relative success in funding bids, other groups seem, at times, to regard it with a mix of jealousy and resentment. Its business model contrasts with some of the smaller groups, who struggle to make ends meet year on year. Furthermore, because the Ashton Centre works primarily within the New Lodge area, it is perceived by some Protestant/Unionist groups as being exclusively Catholic/Nationalist.

---

[3] Management of the Centre was handed over to Ashton from the Belfast Education and Library Board in 2012. The Centre is open seven days a week and offers sports, educational activities, arts and crafts, cooking and gardening; as well as programmes focused on health, well-being and leadership (Family Support NI 2017). The Education and Training Inspectorate deemed the centre as 'meeting very effectively the educational and pastoral needs of the young people; and has demonstrated its capacity for sustained self-improvement' (Ashton Community Trust 2014: 1).

[4] KinderKids was founded in 2000 as a social enterprise of Ashton Community Trust; there are three centres in North Belfast accommodating 200 children and employing 70 staff. The childcare service is both a driver for training and employment and a resource for working parents (Ashton Community Trust 2017b).

[5] For instance, Ashton offers an event management training programme which has partnered with the MAC Arts Centre, and childcare, hospitality, construction, food and hygiene training programmes among others (Ashton Community Trust 2014, 2017e).

[6] Bridge of Hope works with those affected by the conflict and poor physical and mental health. Tools include life coaching, transitional justice programmes, personal development courses and weekend residentials (Ashton Community Trust 2017c: 5). Bridge of Hope was nominated for an 'Innovation and Creativity' award by the Advancing Healthcare Awards NI (Ashton Community Trust 2017d).

[7] The FabLab provides 'state-of-the-art computer-controlled machinery that includes a 3D printer, a laser cutter, CNC router, full electronics station and a large scale vinyl cutter'. The equipment is used for skills development, training and manufacturing, particularly with a cross-community catchment of marginalised youth (Murtagh et al. 2015: 8). The programme is linked to the Massachusetts Institute of Technology (MIT).

North Talks Too, on the other hand, is cross-community, which lends it an edge in terms of funding applications. In the competitive landscape of community work, some groups form cross-community partnerships for better chances of accessing funding and thus numerous groups may be 'in conflict or in coalition' depending on the specific circumstances (Jacobs 1992: 163). This occurs often in Northern Ireland – and more broadly, in community development in general as people organise ways to better position themselves for limited funding and to reflect funders' priorities. The North Talks Too partnership echoed the 'shared ethos' of the proposed Hub; this lent it legitimacy and gave it a stronger front to approach the council and the SEUPB than if its members had done so as individual groups. And frankly, the council needed North Talks Too to 'show off' to the SEUPB that there was cross-community work going on as part of the 'shared' development. As a youth worker observed, 'it's not about "what can you do for us", it's about what we can do for [the government and the council] … presenting this cross-community consortium as something they can show off to SEUPB and fit in [to community relations strategy]' (author fieldnotes 2015). This is an interesting if somewhat cynical observation. It speaks to the lack of genuine transformation associated with the project ideals, suggesting that presenting the appearance of 'sharedness' to placate the SEUPB was more important to political elites than the outcome of the development itself.

Another underlying feeling in meetings of smaller groups like North Talks Too was fear of encroachment on 'their' project and their work, recalling the different claims to representation and competition for resources outlined in previous chapters. One community worker explained this dynamic regarding the plans for the Girdwood Hub. They had heard that:

> Some bigger groups might be coming in and trying to get involved, get a piece of the action, where there's opportunity for jobs, funding. So then there are the smaller groups being pushed out and the bigger ones taking over when the smaller have been involved in the whole thing and done all the grunt work, and the bigger ones are the ones with the connections and the money and strong partnerships. (author fieldnotes 2015)

For example, at a Girdwood Community Forum meeting about the proposed youth space, a North Talks Too representative said that they planned to run the space with a youth coordinator and a detached youth worker, implying that they would be the primary operators. A representative of the Ashton Centre replied that the youth space would be ideal to host their United Youth programme[8]

---

[8] The United Youth pilot programme engaged young people aged 16–24 not in education, employment or training. It focused on four areas: personal development involving social and emotional capabilities, citizenship, good relations and

since it delivered employability training for the most excluded young people in the area. They added that it would be important for Ashton's 'presence in the Hub'. The prospect of Ashton 'claiming' the youth space provoked argument; one meeting attendee said loudly, 'a couple of groups have no right to decide for all of North Belfast ... we've been working on this for five, six years now'. The tense exchange suggests that North Talks Too perceived Ashton as 'encroaching' on their terrain because of their better access to resources, and thus became defensive. This also demonstrates the point made in Chapter Three that fragmentation and competition for influence and power can impede a shared vision between actors in a particular space. The recommendations of the Dunlop Report for collective action within and between local communities have not worked in practice (NBCAP 2002: 76). Here, two local groups are both involved in working with young people; they have not overlapped but rather formed a site of contestation.

Who has the right to decide? It depends on which actors have the most resources and connections within the community development sector. As previously observed, the relationship between community groups and political parties is one factor – strong links with parties like Sinn Féin and the DUP are alleged to influence funding decisions and underline certain groups' control of areas. Paramilitary links to the community sector are another factor. However, power is exercised not only between the state and the community sector, but within and between community groups themselves. This concerns both control over resources and control over space. Groups may be dominant or subordinate depending on their access to resources, their strategic relationships and their individual and/or organisational capacity.

This was again illustrated during the development process when one of the groups in North Talks Too attempted to include a newly formed group, the TDK, in their work. TDK was a small group of residents representing the cross-streets of Thorndale, Duncairn and Kinnaird which lie directly next to Girdwood on the New Lodge/Brucevale side. They were an all-female group with a cross-community element, in that women from Lower Oldpark participated. The prospect of their inclusion was contentious. At one meeting in April 2015, the mood became tense as other community workers in the group closed ranks against the idea of letting someone else in. One community worker declared, 'I don't want TDK in North Talks Too. I've lost staff, I'm running around doing other people's jobs – I don't have time to catch them up on five years' worth of work. I'm not nurse-maiding anyone'.

But another member argued that the TDK was based closer to the site than anyone else, and they felt excluded. The CCRF maintained that they covered

---

employability. These reflected objectives in the Executive community relations strategy *Together, Building a United Community*; the programme was funded by the Executive (CES 2016: 10–11).

the same area as the TDK along Thorndike Avenue: they engaged with residents through surveys and brochures and knew most of the residents. In my many walks around the neighbourhood, I could not help but note how tiny the area under the TDK's remit was: there are only a handful of houses lining the three streets. One community worker insisted, 'I know more people there than [the head of the TDK] probably does'. However, the TDK stubbornly maintained that their area needed a voice. Casting blame on the nearby Ashton Centre, one member of the TDK stated, 'we don't have anyone … it's like there's a steel fence running down the middle of the Antrim Road' (author fieldnotes 2015).

One commentator later said it was all about power, and North Talks Too didn't want to have to share funding or influence with others. However, another community worker observed that after years of cross-community work, it would have been unfair for the TDK to come in at the last minute as an equal partner (author fieldnotes 2015). The TDK did not end up becoming part of North Talks Too, but began attending the bigger Girdwood Community Forum meetings that were held towards the end of the development process.

All these negotiations exemplify how contested representation can be in terms of community groups and claims to space. Parochialism and 'micro-politics' in each neighbourhood mean that there are diverse groups within small areas who do not see eye to eye (Shirlow and Murtagh 2004: 68; Liggett 2017). The issue of representation within micro-geographies, the heterogeneity within so-called 'communities' and the multitude of voices and claims to legitimacy that result occur in cities and neighbourhoods everywhere, as multiple parties vie for a seat at the table during redevelopment processes. But in Belfast, the inter- and intra-community competition that results can hinder strategic vision, the best use of resources and the pooling of best practices, particularly in the context of peacebuilding and 'shared space'.

'Have You Heard about Girdwood?': Building the Hub

As discussions at the community level wound on, work began on the Hub building itself. Construction started in April 2014, with a planned end date of June 2015. North Talks Too meetings were ongoing during this time, primarily around the question: 'How is this going to be a shared site?' I attended many of these meetings, which were held on a rotating basis at one of the community groups' offices.

The consensus in meetings was that 'shared space' would only happen if people were engaged from the outset. This would require identifying local needs and job opportunities, providing training to 'skill up' the surrounding population and creating a sense of 'ownership' across the divide. North Talks Too isolated three groups – young people, women in poverty and the long-term unemployed – to see how they could be moved into potential employment through the Girdwood site. Around the table, community workers discussed a five-point plan to promote engagement:

- Conducting a skills audit for potential jobs for the area;
- Creating training programmes based on the audit;
- Providing mentoring support for at least 15 residents;
- Recruiting at least 15 young people (five from each area) to a Youth Forum where they would carry out research on a shared youth space; and
- Distributing a promotional brochure across the three areas to raise awareness.

They also decided to circulate door-to-door resident engagement surveys to 1,200 households, aiming for a minimum sample size of 150. Given how long the development process had dragged on by this point (nearly a decade), a survey seemed to me well-intentioned but ultimately ineffectual. It also seemed too late to target the needs and the skillsets of the area given that construction was already ongoing on the plans set by the political elite. PPR had suggested doing a similar targeted engagement process back in 2006, and nothing had happened then, either. This was not the fault of community groups, but rather an indictment of the lack of EQIA, strategic vision or meaningful resident engagement on the part of Belfast City Council and government over the years.

In theory, the construction of the Hub had presented an opportunity to train local people through social clauses, something that came up in several North Talks Too meetings. Under the DSD's social clause initiative, those awarded contracts to undertake regeneration were required to provide local unemployed people with work experience (Clanmil Housing Group 2011). This is echoed in the Executive's 2013 community relations strategy *Together, Building a United Community*, which requires that 'all government contracts for work at interface areas and areas of contested space contain a social clause that provides training and employment opportunities and that members of the local population will be able to apply for these opportunities' (OFMDFM 2013: 5).

However, because Girdwood was an EU project, the construction contract was publicly tendered. Belfast City Council hired a firm from outside Belfast, O'Hare and McGovern, who already had its own employees. So, whilst jobs were created, people from the New Lodge, Cliftonville and Lower Shankill did not get them. 'The job opportunities in building the site is really just eye candy, it doesn't happen', one community worker said to me (author fieldnotes 2015).

An employment coach working in the North Belfast area attended one of the North Talks Too meetings in 2015. She had gone to a government-sponsored seminar for job-seekers titled 'Careers in the City' and Girdwood was not mentioned once, 'because [the government] don't know what they're doing'. For all the rhetoric about 'job creation' as an outcome of the Girdwood regeneration, this objective was not designed into the Hub from the outset.

Belfast Met, a regional college and one of the council's proposed anchor tenants for the Hub, was not required to have a social clause at all; at a December 2014 meeting, a council representative said it would be 'draconian' to require it of them. Ostensibly this was because of Belfast Met's financial difficulties. Earlier, concerns had been expressed as to the durability and viability of Belfast Met's involvement. It seemed that the council had shunted the college into the plans without much thought: including them in the Hub space was a convenient way to tick the 'educational opportunity' box. But in 2009, the organisation had been in financial crisis, with a deficit of over £6 million, and had made nearly 120 staff redundant as a result (McWilliams 2011). The Met had a three-year lease for the Girdwood Hub on a discounted rent. Some residents and community workers wondered what would happen after the three years had elapsed – if Belfast Met could afford to stay in the space or if would pull out of the Hub. Some questioned the value of Belfast Met as a substantive part of the development: from the outset its future sustainability at the Hub was uncertain. It seemed that something was better than nothing, but nothing was planned in a meaningful way.

In December 2014, I joined the CCRF on a visit to the building site. After months of walking past it, peeking through gaps in the fencing, this was admittedly exciting. It was a scene of constant activity: the bright sound of clanging metal, squat piles of bricks, a jumble of wooden planks and piping. The skeleton of the Hub was just taking shape. We piled into a trailer with two council representatives and the site manager, who passed out blueprints for the building. It was cold and our breath fogged as we huddled around a small table.

There was some confusion on the opening date. It had been scheduled for June 2015, but the contractor wanted more time, meaning it would be pushed back to August or September. This was not ideal, the CCRF agreed, since the Belfast Met semester was supposed to begin in September. There were concerns the space would not be ready. Belfast Met occupied an entire wing of the building, with two floors of classrooms, offices and storage. In addition to the Belfast Met wing, the blueprints showed a large foyer and reception area, two large 'multi-purpose spaces', one with basketball hoops and retractable bleachers, and a small café and kitchen. Towards the entrance was the youth facility. At 207.20 m2 out of a total 2,697.80 m2, it looked slightly underwhelming to me, particularly given the emphasis on youth engagement in community relations strategy at the time.[9] On the top floor were several

---

[9] *Together, Building a United Community*, released in 2013, listed 'children and young people' as one of its four key priorities (the others being a shared community, a safe community and cultural expression) (OFMDFM 2013: 1).

meeting rooms of different sizes, also for 'the community', as well as a gym, a spa and a sauna with a sweeping view of Cave Hill. The council representative was most excited about this, remarking on how beautiful it would be. Someone from the CCRF remarked drily under their breath, 'but will [residents] be able to afford it?'

We toured the space, slipping through a huge field of sleeching mud. It was difficult to envision the full development: the 3G pitch was still awaiting planning permission (in the end, construction wouldn't begin until summer 2015) and the indoor sports centre remained a pipe dream due to lack of funding.[10] We climbed up to a viewpoint – the same once used by the military at the barracks to surveil the area, soon to be a feature of the sauna. Orderly rows of terraced houses and intermittent church steeples stretched before us, invisible fault lines. We could see the city centre, the faint outline of the Harland and Wolff cranes and in the far distance the Castlereagh Hills. To the other side, Cave Hill jutted out. The light was odd and beautiful but the weather turned more fitful as we walked. The cold settled into my hands and fingers. I looked at the 60 houses that had been built at the far edge of the site. They took up very little of the available space and I couldn't help thinking of the people in North Belfast who remained in drafty temporary accommodation, in single-glazing houses or high rises plagued by damp and poor heating.

Three days earlier, North Talks Too had launched the results of the initial residents' survey at the Crumlin Road Gaol, adjacent to the Girdwood site.[11] The room was full. There were the requisite platters of sandwiches spread thin with margarine and pale, wobbly ham. There was the requisite weak tea and small talk. The survey questions were simple and straightforward. They were not coded by religion but compiled from a sample of 196 residents from across Cliftonville, Lower Oldpark and Lower Shankill:

- 'Have you heard about Girdwood?' – 78 per cent had, 22 per cent hadn't.
- 'Would you like to visit?' – 65 per cent would, 35 per cent wouldn't.
- 'Would you feel safe on the interface?' 66 per cent would, 22 per cent weren't sure, 12 per cent wouldn't.

There was also a list of potential activities for the Hub that people had suggested: dance classes, spin classes, weights, boxing, arts and crafts. And 62 per cent of people wanted a swimming pool. It was perhaps most striking that 22 per

---

[10] In 2022, the indoor sports centre was still being discussed (author fieldnotes 2022).
[11] Previous chapters have noted that as the Girdwood site stalled over housing, the Crumlin Road Gaol was redeveloped separately into a visitor attraction and conference and event space.

cent hadn't heard about the development at all and 35 per cent of the sample didn't want to visit (author fieldnotes 2014).

Considering that the Hub was already under construction and the Conceptual Masterplan already in motion, the survey seemed redundant. If resident engagement was a priority, it should have been included at the outset of the process. This is further evidence of the mismatch between policy and planning rhetoric and reality. Belfast City Council's application for the Hub had committed to 'enable and empower local residents to actively participate ... in the life and development of the Hub' (Cogent Management Consulting 2010: 52). Yet this was the first resident survey that had been carried out on the programming for the Hub, and it had been spearheaded independently by a community group.

The survey also found that 84 per cent of the sample agreed that the Hub should be shared 'by both communities' and 83 per cent believed the Girdwood site should be managed by local communities. In this regard, a new complication was about to arise. In December 2014, a few days before the survey launch, Belfast City Council had announced that the not-for-profit private social operator Greenwich Leisure Limited (GLL), based in London, would assume control of all Belfast leisure centres for an initial five-year contract (GLL 2014). The Girdwood Hub was included in that list.

At the survey launch, the council announced that GLL would be taking over the site. There was immediate uproar. Someone piped up: 'How will GLL deliver on peace and reconciliation?' Several people expressed concern that GLL had no experience or training with interface work or community relations – 'to them it's just a building, a leisure centre' – whereas the SEUPB money had been specifically provided for peacebuilding. The move to bring in an outside private operator also jarred with the council's rhetoric around shared community facilities and public space, a key element of the EU funding criteria (Cogent Management Consulting 2010: 17).

Another community worker asked, 'Why was no chance given to the community?' The council's news about GLL had come as a complete surprise to North Talks Too and other community groups in the area. Given the rhetoric of 'community engagement' and the involvement of the Girdwood Community Hub Forum with the council in the development process to this point, it was surprising that there had not been consultations, or even conversations, about who would be managing the site. One Community Forum member told me later that two years beforehand, the council knew that it was going to transfer ownership of leisure centres to GLL, but did not inform the Girdwood Community Forum until it had been officially decided (author fieldnotes 2015). The anger following the announcement may well also have been another manifestation by some community groups of territorialism and fear of encroachment on 'their' project; that is, the fear that their involvement in planning and service delivery would again be undermined by a competing actor.

Lastly, a resident at the launch asked about the impact on job opportunities. The council representative replied that while GLL was a social enterprise it would be bringing some of its own leisure staff to Girdwood. For local people there would be the café and kitchen and 'whole numerous things ... from the community level, people can run their own programmes'. The council representative was using a lot of words to say nothing – but I couldn't help feeling a bit sorry for him, stood there on his own in an ill-fitting suit, facing a roomful of angry community workers whose involvement had been undermined and a handful of bemused and frustrated residents. One local woman had the final say, shaking her head in frustration:

> I just think it's a terrible pity. This could've been the biggest feather in the council's cap if they did it for the people and not for the money – it could've been their biggest [public relations] project, could've been held up to other peacebuilding programmes as a standard. They are missing an opportunity to try now and do it right. The communities know what the communities want. It's a disgrace considering what the money was for because it's not going to the people. You could've done it right. (author fieldnotes 2014)

Perhaps in response to the scene at the meeting, the council hastily drew up a draft workshop proposal and issued it to around 20 groups across North Belfast, some of whom had already been involved in the Community Forum. The workshop was about the possibility of community management. Some thought the proposal was 'thrown together' and last-minute (LOCA and CCRF 2015). One community worker suggested slyly that this was a 'dirty deal by the council' – hypothetically, it would be clever to gather so many groups in one room as they would then become embroiled in argument over who should run the Hub. There was a palpable element of cynicism regarding the council's 'selling out' to GLL. At one meeting, I asked a community worker about new developments. His eyes lit up and his face stretched into a grin as he leaned forward.

> 'Shenanigans', he said.
> I raised my eyebrows.
> 'Shenanigans?!'
> 'And skullduggery', added his colleague. (author fieldnotes 2015)

A couple months later, I had another conversation about GLL with some of the community workers involved in the Hub. I was early for a meeting and walked into the kitchen. One of the community workers was preparing a lunch of hummus and burnt toast. They stuck the kettle on for me. We talked a little while we drank tea and the subject of GLL came up. They seemed indignant. On GLL's website, they were calling it the 'Girdwood Leisure Centre', and there was no mention at all of the historical context of the area or of the peace and reconciliation aspect. They were classing it like any other leisure centre. We discussed how disappointing it was that the Hub was being glossed over or diminished, when it had previously been held up as a landmark development funded by PEACE III.

'The True Spirit of Girdwood' and the Race to the Finish Line

As the development process continued through 2015, the relationship between Belfast City Council, the DSD and the various community groups grew distant and fraught. When I spoke to people in the field, common themes that came up were the piecemeal nature of the development, the inefficient use of resources and a general lack of leadership and vision. 'It's like a jigsaw and I'm not sure if anyone has the whole picture', said one community worker as we walked around the neighbourhood one afternoon (LOCA and CCRF 2015; Girdwood Community Forum 2015a). Another community worker cited the 'complete lack' of joined-up, strategic thinking at every level and in every department: 'As someone working on the ground, it would be nice to have a framework to work within, but instead everything is ad hoc, piecemeal' (author fieldnotes 2015). Government departments didn't work together, and in some cases there was real animosity. For example, three separate departments were involved in Girdwood within Belfast City Council: Properties and Management, Parks and Leisure, and Good Relations. According to one community worker, the departments didn't see eye to eye, so 'we're basically caught up in internecine war – well, low-level sniping' (author fieldnotes 2015).

The messy reality of the planning process was a far cry from the policy rhetoric that promised more cooperation among government agencies in regeneration. In multiple policy documents, a 'joined-up' government approach to decision-making seemed to be the new buzzword.[12] 2010's *Cohesion, Sharing and Integration* asserted that 'an isolated, piecemeal approach will not be effective in creating long-term, sustainable solutions' for neighbourhood renewal and development (OFMDFM 2010: 40). The subsequent community

[12] 'Joined-up thinking' was a hallmark of 2010's community relation strategy, *Cohesion, Sharing and Integration*, as well as strategic frameworks that informed the development of North Belfast, like 2001's *Regional Strategic Framework for Northern Ireland* and the 2007 *Strategic Regeneration Framework for North Belfast* (Neill and Gordon 2001: 41; Deloitte 2007: 21; OFMDFM 2010: 42).

relations strategy produced by the OFMDFM, *Together, Building a United Community*, further states that 'for us to be serious about taking down the barriers across our society, we must match our words and vision with strategic action and joined-up working' (2013: 60). This statement seems to acknowledge that rhetoric is empty without putting it into practice.

However, there was a pronounced 'silo effect' within government and redevelopment projects continued to be run in isolation. For example, in another report on the regeneration of North Belfast, PPR noted that the DSD had designed six Masterplans for North Belfast, including the draft Girdwood Masterplan, and released them all separately. They had launched the North Belfast Strategic Regeneration Framework at the same time, also separately. None of the plans was strategically targeted to solve inequality, and none was linked to neighbouring Masterplans (PPR 2008b: 3). Furthermore, during the last phase of the Girdwood Community Hub redevelopment (2014–2016), there was no tangible link between that site, the Crumlin Road Gaol, the (then-derelict) courthouse, the nearby Ulster University development, the York Street Interchange expansion or the wider regeneration of lower North Belfast, most of which were ongoing projects and located right next to each other. The Girdwood site was barely mentioned in policy documents on North Belfast and urban regeneration, despite its strategic importance and previous claims to international significance (Deloitte 2007; Belfast City Council 2015; DSD 2015; Campus Community Regeneration Forum 2015). It was a truly baffling state of affairs. In practice, then, it seemed the warnings of the Dunlop Report remained germane, that 'there is no sense of a strategic or shared vision for North Belfast and therefore no "big picture" to which individual communities can be directed for hope and inspiration ... There is a need to develop a long-term integrated strategy for community development in the area' (NBCAP 2002: 13).

Evidently, this has not been achieved. From the very beginning of Girdwood's development, policy rhetoric had also been heavily focused on 'community engagement' and 'community empowerment'. In practice, however, this was less obvious. One community worker related that they 'felt like they were always playing catch-up, that the government didn't have the money or inclination to engage with the community' (author fieldnotes 2015). Like many other projects in Belfast, it felt as though the government had to spend the money by a certain deadline. Genuine engagement with local people didn't fit with the agenda but rather 'jammed up the gears': 'They meet us and smile at us and give us cups of coffee but in the end it's only lip service', noted the same community worker. Another Unionist community worker talked about his experience of community consultation when a health centre was built in the Shankill. The policymakers came to the meeting with design options already drawn up: 'It was like, we built you a health centre, now what colour do you want it? A lot of it is an exercise in box-ticking' (author fieldnotes 2014).

While other chapters have addressed elements of alleged favouritism and close connections between community groups and the state, these observations also demonstrate that these relationships have their limits. While politicians claim to represent 'the community', this is a conditional statement; it only goes as far as convenience dictates. On the ground, there was a pervasive attitude of cynicism towards the government's approach to regeneration. One community worker opined that Girdwood was 'happening over people's heads – [the council] were doing it for their record and not for the right reasons'. 'It's all a wager for funding and politicking', another community worker remarked, continuing that, 'to [the government], shared space, they'd bring a group of Catholic school girls and Protestant school girls from Portadown,[13] pop them at Girdwood and call it shared space – it's all posturing and photo opportunities' (author fieldnotes 2014). This speaks to the continued clash between policy rhetoric and reality, suggesting a superficial approach to 'shared space' and 'community engagement' and an unwillingness on the part of government to work for genuine societal transformation.

By June 2015, the original planned opening date, the Girdwood Community Hub was still nowhere near being finished and the much-talked-about 3G pitch had yet to be built or allocated planning permission. Between the houses (which had been nearly completed but not yet allocated) and the Hub sat a sizeable swathe of empty land. The Morrow Gilchrist advisory service was undertaking preliminary proposals on behalf of the DSD for the mixed-use business units and the indoor sports facility, to be built at a later, unspecified date with unspecified funding (Girdwood Community Forum 2015b). There was no action on the proposed Protestant/Unionist housing on Cliftonpark Avenue. Meanwhile, the SEUPB funding deadline loomed.

It then transpired that the council had underspent the SEUPB money by £1.37 million. '[They] got a good going over from the EU top dogs', related one community worker who had been there for the meeting in June 2015. According to a North Talks Too meeting shortly after this revelation, the council had not told the community groups until the Tuesday, and they had until that Friday to figure out how to spend the money. Suggestions began to fly thick and fast – iMacs, Belfast Bikes, sporting equipment – but this was clearly a missed opportunity. All available funds had to be spent by 30 September, so the money could not go towards long-term projects like funding apprenticeships or events and programmes post-opening. And because construction was ongoing, the money could not go towards innovative employment measures for the site like vocational training rooms or social economy units. It was too late.

The collective feeling around the run-up to the opening – now planned for December 2015 – was that time and money were running out. In an October 2015

---

[13] Portadown is located 30 miles outside of Belfast.

meeting of the Girdwood Community Forum, a council representative proposed setting up a youth forum to engage young people with the space. This was a year after North Talks Too's youth forum had convened and disbanded because of lack of funding, and three months before the opening of the 'shared' youth space. Community workers in attendance reacted with bemused exasperation at the council's suggestion. Again, it was too late. To engage young people in the three months they had left, community workers suggested they plan short activity sessions so that young people could get a feel for the Hub, then offer youth outreach alongside drop-in hours at the local youth clubs. There was acknowledgement that time was tight. The goal, said the council representative, was that 'everyone in the room will feel like they own it and it has the true spirit of Girdwood – but right now we don't have much time to deliver'. They cautioned the Forum to be mindful of the limited financial resources available (Girdwood Community Forum 2015b).

Penny-pinching was a common theme in Forum meetings that autumn. It seemed that the Hub would be opening with a whimper instead of a bang. In a November 2015 meeting, the council said they expected £60,000 in funding for the Hub in the next financial year, with a quarter of that set aside for long-term outcomes. But in the first few months, from January to March 2016, there would be a gap between funding. This would impact programming for the Hub and necessitate 'shoestring' activities that could be done 'cheaply'. The council representative cautioned the Forum that they had to be realistic about what was possible.

Attendees passed a draft programme for January to March around the table. There was a 'core NEETS [not in employment, education or training] programme' run by the Ashton Centre as part of the United Youth programme, a 'young mums and tots' programme, and drama sessions for primary school children in the afternoons, both run by the CCRF. One representative noted that the organisations should be taken off the programme, since to a Unionist, it might seem to be controlled by Nationalists. All things considered, the programming was disappointingly simple and lacked any sense of innovation or excitement, especially given the initial potential of the site.

Looking back to the vision of the Dunlop Report for a 'centre for citizenship', or BDP's sketches depicting a vibrant new neighbourhood, or even the rhetoric around 'job creation' for the local populace, it seemed evident that the Hub had not delivered on any of these concepts. And since the council had failed to spend the entirety of the SEUPB funding, lack of resources was really no excuse. As noted in previous chapters, this could have been avoided by conducting an EQIA as part of the development process. In order to promote equality of opportunity – whether that be social housing, as explored previously, or tackling wider social issues like unemployment – it is necessary to identify which inequalities exist in a particular area. Yet, instead of mainstreaming equality as required by legislation and policy, the dynamic of political horse-trading and sectarianised decision-making in governance shaped the final design. Like the Assembly itself, it left much to be desired.

A final point of contention among community workers was the logistics of the youth space. In 2013, *Together, Building a United Community* had set out 'children and young people' as one of its four main priorities, in particular improving cross-community relations and working with young people in areas of 'community tension' (2013: 25, 37). One of the Community Hub's main selling points was promoting 'shared space', and in particular shared space for young people on an interface. But the execution was arguably muddled. There was only one youth space and it was a tiny room. In one meeting, Community Forum members asked the council what age group the space was intended for. How would difficult-to-engage teenagers develop a sense of ownership with small children using the same space, if each required different resources 'down to what's on the walls?' One youth worker said in frustration:

> I thought the youth space would be the first cross-community youth club in the city, a big deal. But what's the point of bringing Lower Shankill kids over to the youth space? What are they gonna get out of it? What's the draw for them when they have three snooker tables over at the Hammer [another youth club] in a much bigger room? (author fieldnotes 2015)

The council representative replied that Girdwood was unique because it was a shared space and promoted good relations.

Questions were raised about *how* this vision would be put into practice – and who would be responsible for it. Community Forum members asked about funding for youth workers around the site, who could facilitate engagement and bring hard-to-reach young people into the Hub. Previous discussions with young people had brought up the need for more detached youth workers who could offer support and help them back into education.[14] This also related to Belfast Met's programming and enrolment. However, the council had not earmarked funding to engage young people with the space. The danger in neglecting these concerns was not only 'anti-social behaviour' around the site, but a sense of exclusion from a building originally premised on shared space, education and employment opportunities.

In theory, the Hub could have been better targeted towards those young people categorised as NEETs, especially given Northern Ireland has the highest

---

[14] See Horgan, Conlon and Grey's 2010 study on NEETs: https://www.ark.ac.uk/pdfs/policybriefs/policybrief3.pdf.

proportion of NEETs in the UK (NISRA 2017: 2).[15] Unemployment levels remain high; as of 2017, North Belfast featured in the top ten parliamentary constituencies in the UK for unemployment, and in the top ten constituencies in the UK for unemployment claimants aged 18–24 (725 out of 3,030 total claimants) (ONS 2017; Powell et al. 2017: 12, 15). The global labour market has changed to support a technology-led, knowledge-based economy, but this is not reflected in North Belfast (except for places like the FabLab at the Ashton Centre). This has knock-on effects on mental health. A study published by the Princes' Trust showed that almost half of NEETs felt down or depressed 'always or often' and that one in five young unemployed people felt their confidence would not recover from being out of work; an earlier study suggested 35 per cent of NEETs had experienced suicidal feelings (Wilson 2016: 89). North Belfast has a higher concentration of NEETs than other parts of Northern Ireland as well as problems with unemployment, mental health, suicide and rising substance abuse (Hughes 2016; NISRA 2010, 2012).

With all this in mind, it seems neglectful that targeted outcomes were not put into place to make the youth space transformative. For instance, creating a social enterprise zone, designing programmes and projects around confidence- and skill-building or involving young people from the outset could all have contributed to better outcomes for marginalised youth. But party politics, competition around resources and service delivery and factionalism within the community development sector proved more important to shaping the space. Instead, the Hub offered a small youth space of undefined purpose. There was a playing field that would host Gaelic football (for Catholics) as well as soccer (for Protestants) – a rudimentary form of shared space.

Before it ran out of funding, the North Talks Too Youth Forum conducted a survey of 100 young people around the Girdwood area. The majority had not even heard of the Girdwood Hub (64 per cent had not vs 36 per cent who had) (North Talks Too Youth Forum 2015). I was passing by Kinnaird Close once, feeling awkward and exposed as the street turns into a dead end and you have to circle back round. I ran into a small group of young people. I asked, 'Do you know what they're building here?' One guy laughed derisively. 'Oh sure yeah, you know, it'll be mixed housing, you know they're taking all the peace walls down'. His friend let out a short, sharp bark of laughter. They nodded at me and loped away.

He wasn't entirely wrong – there was one small triumph, a glimpse of what could be if sectarianism and territorialism and clientelism and all the other 'isms' that shape space in Belfast no longer mattered. And that was the dismantling of the barracks' perimeter wall. On one walk in October 2015, I

---

[15] In August 2017, Northern Ireland had the highest 16–24 NEET rate (12 per cent) of the four countries that comprise the UK (NISRA 2017: 2).

Fig. 8.1

Fig. 8.2

turned down Brucevale from Cliftonpark Avenue and stood in total disbelief. It had been a few months since my last visit. All the green metal sheeting around the Girdwood site had been taken down. You could see clear into the space and far out across the city.

After years of walking past a formidable wall, it was truly remarkable to see the back of the New Lodge, the new-build housing and the neat roofs over in Lower Oldpark as one continuous stretch of land. The metal pillars that had propped up the sheeting were all that remained. I stopped again at the top of the street to admire the great gasping expanse of it. From this vantage point, you could almost pretend it was a 'normal' redevelopment project.

On another walk, I watched a lone worker taking the green metal sheeting down on the Cliftonpark Avenue side – a sight simultaneously ordinary and powerful. From this perspective, you could see from Lower Oldpark through to the Seven Towers of the New Lodge. This shared visual space, however, proved far more contentious. In community meetings, residents and representatives from Lower Oldpark had expressed uneasiness about the metal sheeting coming down. There was a sense of anxiety around this view they had never seen before. To all intents and purposes, the neighbourhood had been an enclave for decades, fenced in on every side by the Manor Street peace wall and by the barracks wall along Cliftonpark Avenue. According to North Talks Too meetings, residents felt vulnerable to attack from the New Lodge, suggesting that the deep-rooted sense of siege and threat had not yet been addressed. Discussions began about installing a temporary gate once the site was built. However, the CCRF's perspective was, 'we don't want another 20-foot wall built – we want people to see into the pitch, into the Hub'. They said they were opposed to a fence but it had to go ahead because of Lower Oldpark and Lower Shankill's views. The 'siege mentality', fear and suspicion of elements of Protestant/Unionist North Belfast continued to find expression through space, suggesting that territoriality and a sense of 'Otherness' remained a prime force in how space is perceived and shaped.

Although the development was meant to be open-plan and publicly accessible, community consultation on the Unionist side still pointed to the desire for a boundary. The DSD installed a perimeter fence and gates on the Cliftonpark Avenue side before the opening of the Girdwood Hub. However, the Antrim Road/New Lodge side still had open access to the site. The issue then became, naturally, that the Catholic/Nationalist side had easier access to the site than the Protestant/Unionist side. Representatives of the latter balked in a December 2015 Forum meeting. They argued that young Unionists would see the 'other side' accessing the development and feel excluded because of the big fence. Yet they had been the ones who asked for the boundary in the first place. A DSD representative, clearly miffed, challenged them: 'Why are we funding this? Now that we have the fence up, there's a change in opinion and that's concerning to me'. One Nationalist community worker remarked that the Protestant/Unionist side had 'shot themselves in the foot' – by asking for a fence, they ended up limiting their access, keeping them out of the development, losing out in the zero-sum game (author fieldnotes 2015). This back-and-forth is typical of the illogical nature of resource competition and calls into question what 'shared space' means in practice.

The final phase of planning for the Hub reflected the decision-making processes that had plagued the entire beleaguered development process. There was disagreement within the community development sector, and between community groups and the council, and an overall lack of 'joined-up' coordination. There was the introduction of a private leisure provider into the mix. There was mismanagement of every opportunity that the Hub had promised: employment, education, engagement for young people. There were missteps and misspent time and unspent budgets. It was truly a mess. Even as the Community Hub was readying itself to open, the original territorial considerations around access to the site had come back into play, tempering the hopeful dismantling of the barrack walls. The run-up to the grand opening of the Girdwood Community Hub felt confusing and uninspiring.

CONCLUSION

'Better' at Girdwood Community Hub
The Legacy of the Girdwood Development

We expect too much of new buildings and too little of ourselves.
(Jacobs 1961: 334)

Opening Day

After 11 years of contestation, stalemate and eventual compromise, after wrangling over service provision and delivery, the management of the site and the fencing around it, the Girdwood Community Hub was finally ready to open its doors. The launch occurred on 15 January 2016, eight months after it had originally been scheduled to open.

Walking down Cliftonpark Avenue, frost bloomed on the pavement. There was a dusting of snow on the thin black perimeter fence that had replaced the barracks walls. A new road curved through to the housing on the other side of the Hub. A trim blonde woman, towel slung around her shoulders, smiled from a large white banner that proclaimed: 'Girdwood Community Hub is now open! A range of options available from £13 a month: gym, spa, sports hall, community space, dance studio for fitness classes, birthday party room hire, educational and training courses, and much, much more!'

The Hub building was set back from the road, buffered by a parking lot. Architecturally, it was striking – all brick and glass with a large stone piazza. However, as a pedestrian, I found it intimidating and unfriendly and approached with trepidation. Inside, the foyer was filled with crowds of people chatting and networking. The familiar faces of community workers and politicians were out in full force. I spoke to a council representative and they told me about a 'Shared Space Charter' the Community Hub Forum was working on 'to ensure everyone felt safe and included'. I thought it sounded nice, but then, so did a lot of the rhetoric around the site.

The launch took place in the big multi-purpose room. A large PowerPoint screen and two sky-blue pop-ups with the GLL logo 'Better' flanked a podium. The space filled up quickly – about 200 people were in attendance. It was difficult to tell how many – if any – local residents were in the room. Next to me was a row of young rugby players in blue Belfast Met sports kits. I wondered if they were there because they wanted to be, or for a photo opportunity. I wondered if they were from the area. Outside the wide windows, a cluster of children peered into the building before losing interest in the crowd.

There were then, of course, the requisite speeches. The Sinn Féin Lord Mayor at the time, Arder Carson, called the Hub 'a significant stepping stone for North Belfast ... from its inception, a shared space that everyone can enjoy'. The phrase 'state-of-the-art' was mentioned countless times. The phrase most popular throughout the speeches, though, was 'community'. Carson said, for example, that he was a mayor for the community – all the communities – and that community was at the heart of what the city council does. That the Hub was designed 'by the local community, for the local community'. This, I thought privately, was not exactly accurate. And it smacked of using the 'rhetorical fluff' of 'community' to mask the continued division and poverty in the area. Suzanne Wylie, Chief Executive of Belfast City Council, stated in her speech that 'this is a place for the community, for all age groups, for all the communities. It's about community, it's about well-being, good relations, skills, jobs too'. I tried to silence the cynical voice in my head but couldn't help but speculate exactly how many new jobs had been created, since an EQIA had not been conducted and GLL was running the building, an independent contractor. I noticed that 'equality of opportunity' had not been mentioned; again, the idea of good relations took precedence over what should have been the cornerstone of policymaking.

Next up to the podium was Mervyn Storey of the DUP, who said that the building was an example of 'putting minds together, that we can still deliver for our communities', and that transforming contested space depended on engaging with local communities at 'every step of the way'. Again, I could not help but think of the dozens of community meetings fraught with confusion and contestation within and between groups and the council. Lastly, representatives from North Talks Too ascended to the podium, noting that 'it is an honour to represent our communities'. One added a special thanks to the OFMDFM for funding young people's and residents' engagement. I remembered someone else had said that the OFMDFM were never at meetings or involved in any aspect of the Girdwood plans, but that appealing to them was key for funding. Indeed, in the dozens of meetings that I attended, there was never a representative from the OFMDFM present.

Cynicism aside, there was a screening of a video made by local young people that was somewhat heartening. A teenage girl and her friend, self-conscious in front of the camera, said Girdwood 'gives us something to do, instead of standing out on the streets on a Friday or Saturday'. She went to an integrated school, so for her it was a neutral place to meet friends. Another remarked that if they don't want to go to their respective youth clubs, 'Girdwood is something different' – the perception seemed to be that the Hub was an in-between space to meet people of different backgrounds. In the last frame of the video, a young man leaned back, saying, 'It's the place to be, like'. His friend replied, 'Aye, it is', in a laconic voice (Prime Cut Productions 2016). It was funny and sweet. After the procession of speeches, I went to investigate the youth club, feeling like an interloper. It was even smaller than I'd anticipated. There were several beanbags and windows looking out onto the pitch (although the pitch would not be finished until March). Young people were playing guitar together, others were getting photographs taken. I had heard that North Talks Too would run the youth facility whilst GLL would manage the rest of the space. Despite having an entire wing to themselves, Belfast Met were curiously absent from the launch festivities.

Upstairs, the gym was filled with 'state-of-the-art' equipment, and floor-to-ceiling windows looked out over the pitch. On one side of the room, the Lord Mayor mugged for the camera with a pair of weights. On the other, a photographer arranged a group of young people by some machines. The adjacent spa was impressive, with white mosaic tiling and heated seats. Finally, I entered the wood-panelled, much-talked-about sauna with its sweeping views of the Belfast hills – on the launch day, they were masked by clouds of rain and sleet. One GLL employee mentioned the sauna was an extra charge on top of the membership, so 'not every Tom, Dick and Harry can come in'; one has to sign up to the spa package to get an access card. Of course, the vista – 'inspired by army gunner views', according to the *Irish News* – comes with a price (Archer 2016).

It seemed odd that GLL's role in the Hub was missing. It was barely mentioned in the speeches. One community worker said in passing that it would look funny, with all this talk of 'community', if the council said they had passed the Hub to an operator from England. At the end of the launch, a council representative introduced the GLL manager to the crowd, saying that 'Better[1] will be helping us out with the Girdwood site'. Another commentator later remarked that the council was 'embarrassed' that they had handed an EU peace and reconciliation project over to a private leisure provider (author fieldnotes 2016).

There was also the question of affordability for local residents versus those from outside the area who could drive to the centre, park in the parking lot and effectively bypass the interface. Initially, the price of a resident's monthly access package varied from £28.50 to £32.50 compared to £32.50 to £35.50 for non-residents (GLL 2017). Not much of a saving, then. In terms of 'shared space' from an economic standpoint, the price might well preclude access for

---

[1] 'Better: The Feel Good Place' is the GLL slogan (GLL 2017).

those around the site who lack disposable income. Conversely, it was hoped that perhaps the involvement of an external operator would 'neutralise' the site and counteract the sectarianism from which it was born, thus encouraging the 'shared space' which the SEUPB had originally funded. As one resident said to me, 'if people are going to the gym – people working out together, it's just a gym, identity doesn't matter' (author fieldnotes 2016).

As I left the Hub launch, I took a last look at the assembled crowd. There was a feeling of energy in the building, excitement and possibility. There were conversations taking place that never would have happened 30 years ago. This space, over the years, had symbolised pain and violence, fear and oppression. Innocent people were brutally interrogated in the barracks and had been murdered on the surrounding streets. A barrier had had to be constructed to separate two neighbourhoods; riots on Cliftonpark Avenue had been frequent and violent. The site had symbolised contestation over space and territory, and its initial redevelopment was surrounded by seemingly interminable arguments that stalled progress for years. In this context, the fact that a range of actors had come together, worked through a range of disputes, negotiated and come to a compromise cannot be denigrated. The space has changed for the better.

However, it is equally important to consider the possibilities for the site from the outset and the missed opportunities to not merely manage but to transform a divided and economically marginalised area; to target and tackle unemployment, poverty and housing need; and to challenge sectarianism and fear and territorialism on a fundamental level. To physically express the aspirational rhetoric of the Good Friday Agreement and the commitments to equality enshrined in the Northern Ireland Act. These were some of the benchmarks on which the rhetoric of the development rested, and the reality simply does not deliver. Instead, the final phase of the development took place in a context in which resource competition and fractious inter- and intra-community relationships remained commonplace and the blight of paramilitarism continued to stain neighbourhoods. Placing a building, however 'state-of-the-art', in the middle of this without any structural transformation is reductive. On these counts, the Hub development remains a white elephant.

Better than Nothing?

When asked about the impact of the Hub on the surrounding areas and residents, community workers and managers around the site initially expressed cautious optimism. One Nationalist community worker said, 'I'm not sayin' there are no benefits, there are … we're now able to use that site up there for events … I don't want to be niggardly about all this. That's good, I'd rather have it there than not' ('Liam', interview with author 2016). A community activist observed: 'Now, you balance it against what was there before. And you had an old British Army barracks that was going completely vacant … so going back, of course it's better than what was there before' ('Eamonn', interview with author 2017).

But is 'better than nothing' really the epithet one wants for North Belfast's biggest regeneration project? Initially, as outlined in Chapter Three, the Girdwood draft Masterplan anticipated a 'regeneration project of international significance', a symbol of 'hope and economic regeneration' and 'a benchmark for all new development which would follow' (BDP 2007b: 9). The subsequent bid for the Hub submitted by the council to the SEUPB, as explained in Chapter Six, also promised an 'iconic, state-of-the-art' development premised on 'shared space'. Both visions for the site assured the transformation of contested space; the provision of employment and training opportunities; and community engagement (Cogent Management Consulting 2010: 51, 54).

On all counts, this book argues that the Hub has not delivered. As a community worker remarked:

> It's like anything else, you don't wanna be too harsh or too critical, these things take time to develop their own momentum and dynamic, but you know, having said all that if you go back to sort of the very start, they were sayin' this was gonna be a place of international significance and which would bring massive benefits to the local community, the political and economic driver, and that is yet to be proven. ('Liam', interview with author 2016)

The eventual Girdwood Hub development was the 'best worst option': a fudge and unsatisfactory compromise that neither targeted social and economic need nor meaningfully transformed the interface. The reality of the process did not deliver on the initial vision for an internationally significant and locally important benchmark. It was essentially a political trade-off rather than a peacebuilding project, and promises were continually broken or ignored. Yet rhetoric around the site attempts to camouflage this through the feel-good aphorisms of 'community' and 'shared space'.

As in countless other societies and redevelopment processes, it is those on the ground who suffer the consequences of political disagreement. In the end, the socio-economic profile of this part of North Belfast has not changed – 'not an iota' – according to one commentator. An area community worker said that, looking back even before the Troubles to the present day, 'it's worse here, only different' (author fieldnotes 2017). There is still poverty, little opportunity for employment and a general sense of malaise (McDonald 2014). Instead of paramilitaries and soldiers, it is substance abuse and suicide that now make casualties of the population. It is often cited that more people have died by

Fig. 9.1 The proposed mixed-use facilities and indoor sports centre at Girdwood remain undeveloped.

their own hand in the years after the Good Friday Agreement than were killed in 30 years of conflict (Hughes 2016).

Lastly, housing supply remains in crisis. According to the NIHE data, 96 per cent of the social housing requirement in north Belfast in 2018–2019 was in the mostly Catholic areas of 'North Belfast One', with an average residual need of 1,041 homes in 2018/19. 'North Belfast Two', comprised of mostly Protestant/Unionist areas, saw an average residual need of 40 homes during the same period (Winters 2020). PPR found there were over four times as many children in predominately Catholic families from North Belfast on the waiting list, compared to those in predominately Protestant North Belfast (PPR 2021). The continuing lack of social housing provision in North Belfast shows that territorialism and sectarianism remain potent forces in development (PPR 2022). The Hub was not specifically targeted to address any of these urgent issues, despite the proposed project outcomes being 'a transformational project which addresses the pressing needs in the local area' (Cogent Management Consulting 2010: 55).

Six years after the Hub opened its doors, I had a chat with a Unionist community worker over Zoom. It had been a long time since we'd been in touch, but the pandemic had made video chat ubiquitous and I was delighted to hear from them. I asked, 'What's new with Girdwood?' Not much, as it turned out. The sports pitch was done, but the 'indoor sports centre' was still a pipe dream. The housing that had been promised at the Protestant/Unionist side of the complex and the 'mixed-use space' was still empty land. 'The development was never followed through to its logical conclusion, and there is no political will to finish the Masterplan', they said.

Now, however, there were new conversations taking place around building 'a world-class sport centre of excellence' and an indoor swimming pool at Girdwood. The community worker said that these conversations had been decided among politicians during the pandemic, and then put out to community groups after the fact:

> There's 4 million from SEUPB, 2 million from city council, 8 million from the Department of Communities. It all has to be spent by March 31. Here's how the government bully the little people: they already have this decided and they put it out to public consultation, but it has already been agreed. And they're bullying community groups to back it, saying, 'We have to spend this money by the 31st or hand it back to British Treasury'. (author fieldnotes 2022)

As they talked, I was powerfully reminded of the dynamics around the initial Community Hub, discussed in Chapter Six, described by another community worker as a 'fait accompli'.

While the optics of a swimming pool might be good for headlines, it will take more than a pool to effect a meaningful transformation of the surrounding area. In the course of my fieldwork, I remembered another commentator saying disdainfully: 'No more leisure centres. Belfast has enough of them, they've done that and it hasn't worked. No more swimming pools – they're hard to maintain. And these spaces do nothing for poverty and youth inclusion' (author fieldnotes 2015).

Indeed, in the years since its opening, the area around the Hub has become a hotspot for 'anti-social behavior', sectarian violence and attacks (Fitzmaurice 2020). Some of the houses around Girdwood have been severely damaged over the past few years. There seems to be a feeling that the site becomes unsafe after nightfall. As the community worker remarked over Zoom, 'put it this way – a lot of older people use the site [for exercise classes] … with the proviso they're home before 5. Once school is out, the atmosphere changes'. They added that Belfast Met still offer classes at the site, but some people have switched their night classes to other sites for the same reason.

In response to 15 consecutive nights of trouble around the Hub in 2020, a newspaper article quoted a community steward saying, 'this site was built on the ethos of shared space, the sad reality is that today many people refuse to use the complex as it is currently anything but that, and that must change' (Fitzmaurice 2020).

I was surprised by all this. In the hundreds of times that I'd walked the area before the Hub was built, I'd never felt particularly unsafe, even in the evening. It sounded like the gates around the site were an issue of concern – when open, youth from the New Lodge could cross freely to the Lower Oldpark side and vice versa, creating the potential for confrontation.

Girdwood has hosted some cross-community activity. North Talks Too runs some activities in the youth space. Young people play football, Gaelic football, hurling and rugby together on the sports pitch, although one football match between St Patrick's FC and Ballysillan Swift's FC made the news – there was sectarian abuse and violence, and one man was struck in the face (Scott 2021). In the wake of the incident, a sparring match between DUP and SDLP politicians also made headlines. DUP councillor Dale Pankhurst said, 'this sectarian attack highlights how Girdwood continues to be used as a site for attacks on both Protestants using the site and against local Unionist areas such as lower Oldpark' (McParland 2021).

In response, SDLP councillor Paul McCusker accused Councillor Pankhurst of adding 'fuel to the fire' rather than de-escalating the situation, and added, 'Leadership is about working together on these issues but he is not interested in this'. It's notable if not surprising that Pankhurst emphasised the attacks as a Protestant/Unionist issue, rather than condemning violence as a whole, and that the politicians bickered rather than uniting to address the violence. The same community worker I spoke to brought up the violence and suggested that there were recriminations around the way politicians engage with these issues – that politicians around the Girdwood complex need to be very mindful of the language they use, because people respond to it.

All of this calls into question the pervading policy rhetoric of 'shared space' found throughout the Girdwood development process and of the 'shared future' promised in the peace agreement. To truly create shared space or transform contested space, the structures and actors which reinforce sectarianism and division must be dismantled, and this epilogue shows that one building is not going to do that. The building was an opportunity, not a transformation of the imagined or physical boundaries between self and 'Other' that still run through society. The construction of place around Girdwood remains petrified and unshared.

'It could have been worse' was the resounding feeling among interview respondents in regard to the Girdwood site. But it also could have been better. It could have been an internationally significant development; it could have had a tangible and measurable impact on the very real social issues that North Belfast faces. It could have made a difference to a society emerging from conflict. But it really has only inscribed and reproduced the status quo in space, failing to tackle the underlying structures of segregation and sectarianism that still pervade society. The result is that £11.7 million of peacebuilding money was squandered on a 'state-of-the-art' white elephant. The result is 60 houses in an area where 938 are needed at the time of writing; an educational facility struggling with uptake; a privately operated gym in what should have been public space; empty land, devoid of investment, where 'mixed-use units' were once planned; and continued inequality, social exclusion and deprivation in all of the surrounding neighbourhoods.

'These Civil Wars Are Only Ever Over on Paper!'[2]

Contests over space are endemic to any society. Contestation can arise over the 'right' to space – how access to space is controlled and negotiated, who belongs and who is excluded. Boundaries, barriers and fear of the 'Other' shape spatial arrangements all over the world, from the West Bank barrier in Israel/Palestine to the Green Line in Cyprus; from the US's border wall to its racially segregated neighbourhoods. There are countless examples of places divided by ethnicity, race and class. And these dynamics can shape policy and planning in those places: as Bou Akar puts it, 'fear, threat, rumours and otherness provide as vital a ground for policy formation as statistics, censuses and other scientific findings' (2018: 5).

In the case of a divided society like Northern Ireland, space is filtered through the prism of difference and conflict is rooted in how space is imagined, claimed and perceived. In Northern Ireland, the rhetoric of 'themmuns getting more then us' prevails; as Hayward and Komarova put it, 'community members believe themselves to be competing against the "other" community for scarce resources and recognition' (2014: 782). These dynamics have not been challenged by political elites, but rather mobilised and exploited by them.

One way in which this has occurred is the use of discourse by political elites. The types of discourse which are made to function as 'true', the ways in which these are sanctioned and legitimised and the status of 'those who are charged with saying what counts as true' (Foucault 1980: 131) all shape policymaking and planning. Facts and opinions are contingent on what different actors in power put forth as true and real (Aughey 2002: 3). The political agent who can put the strongest case behind their interpretation of 'truth' is most decisive in framing political, economic, social and spatial reality (Flyvbjerg 1998: 117). This is evident in Northern Ireland, where actors of power decide what counts as 'truth', whose voices are heard and whose are silenced, which claims to territory

---

[2] Fiacc (1994: 87).

and identity are 'authentic', who deserves to belong, and who is entitled to resources (Murtagh et al. 2008: 43).

In turn, this impacts the way policy and planning is envisioned, performed and legitimised, and how sectarianism is ultimately reproduced in Northern Ireland. We can see this at play in the differing discourses around 'needs', 'rights' and 'truth' which emerged during the Girdwood redevelopment, particularly around social housing provision. For instance, the DUP's discourse around the possibility of Nationalists dominating the site both reinforced and responded to the fears of Protestant/Unionist residents. It played on residual feelings of territorial encroachment and loss experienced by the dwindling Protestant population in North Belfast, arguing these are commensurate with the Nationalist need for new-build housing. Instead of targeting inequality, the language of 'good relations' and 'differential deprivation' was deployed by Unionist elites to block social housing allocation on the site, in direct contravention of Section 75. No EQIA was conducted on the site, also a legal breach. On the other hand, the ways in which Sinn Féin initially fashioned support for conflict management – pragmatism, compromise with the DUP in the name of good relations, the view that equality was negotiable – ultimately fell flat. Their alleged backroom trade-offs on social housing also fell through. At different points in the Girdwood process, actors like PPR and the Equality Commission held Sinn Féin to account, pointing out the missed opportunities to advocate for Section 75 and just resource allocation. Their efforts to transform the basis of decision-making in the Assembly were ignored.

By contrasting theory and practice, rhetoric and reality, this book has set out the case of the Girdwood redevelopment as a microcosm of the difficulties of post-Agreement Northern Ireland. In theory, the Agreement promised a new future for Northern Ireland and, through a new legislative framework, the delivery of social justice and the protection of vulnerable groups. The subsequent Northern Ireland Act enshrined claim and promise into law. Section 75's robust emphasis on equal resource allocation was of particular note for Girdwood.

In practice, it has become evident that such aspirational rhetoric has not been reflected in the reality of governance. Power-sharing has not delivered the promises of the Agreement, nor the rule of law enshrined in the subsequent Northern Ireland Act. Rather, it has further institutionalised and formalised, rather than transformed, the dynamics of polarisation and political contestation that characterised Northern Irish society before the onset of the Troubles. The result, as Wilford and Wilson describe it, is a 'chopped-up' rather than 'joined-up' government (2006: 27). The rhetoric of transformation and the blunt reality of the failures around the Girdwood Hub speak to the promise of an internationally significant 'shared space' which instead became a parochial form of 'shared-out' resource competition.

Furthermore, the entire development process completely disregarded the equality legislation that was meant to form the cornerstone of post-ceasefire government policy and practice. This fact cannot be overstated. There should have been an EQIA conducted on the project, and Section 75 should have been mainstreamed into the planning process. There should have been more than 60 units of social housing on the 27-acre site. At multiple points in the process, different actors and agencies – from community workers to the NIHE to PPR to the Equality Commission, even the United Nations – called attention to the ongoing housing crisis in North Belfast. Yet sectarian logic and political intransigence won out over documented housing need. The result is that the mainstreaming of equality in governance envisioned by Section 75 and other peace legislation has been subverted and ignored. The result is that thousands of people in North Belfast remain homeless or in temporary accommodation, spending year after year on the waiting list. The result is clearly perpetuated social injustice in which the opportunity for positive space-shaping was lost.

The Girdwood case study calls into question whether Northern Ireland is truly a 'post-conflict' success story. Shirlow and Murtagh note in reference to Northern Ireland that 'democracy will have arrived when people no longer feel the need to defend the places they live' (2006: 4); yet the ethnic logic of segregation, control and territorialism still colours every aspect of governance, and, sometimes, daily life. Despite the promised ceasefire and decommissioning, paramilitary groups still hold power in certain areas and have alleged links to politicians and community groups. Despite billions of pounds of funding for policing reform, community capacity-building and investment, elements of the community development landscape remain fractious. Allegations of clientelism and favouritism within and between political and community development elites have flourished, as have charges of gerrymandering and sectarianism in policymaking and planning. It seems that despite sustained peacebuilding efforts, old patterns of conflict have merely been reproduced in subtle but no less insidious ways from the top down. As a result, Northern Ireland remains a fundamentally disagreed and dysfunctional place.

From start to finish, Girdwood's redevelopment process demonstrated the difficulties inherent in not only managing conflict in divided societies, but in fundamentally transforming contested spaces, attitudes and institutions. The 'story of Girdwood' is the story of the peace process gone awry. But it also serves as a reminder of the ways in which politics, power and planning shape all of our stories, and the neighbourhoods within which they take place. Cities are a testament to the actors of power who built them, but also evidence the power of the small-scale – those who continue to resist and push back through tactics great and small. We make what we can of our surroundings. We exist in a mutually reinforcing relationship with them. Sometimes, they bring us together, and sometimes they divide.

Epilogue

In the years since the Girdwood Hub opened its doors, the political context of Northern Ireland has experienced seismic changes, sat in stasis and changed again. I would be remiss not to address how the story of Girdwood predicated and predicted elements of this landscape. The same dynamics that delayed the Girdwood regeneration ultimately led to the collapse of the Northern Ireland Assembly, not once but twice. Further, these dynamics profoundly influenced Northern Ireland's place in the Brexit vote and its aftermath. However, at the time of writing, it seems that a sea change is occurring, and alternative politics are emerging among a frustrated polity – in Belfast, but also further afield.

The Assembly Collapses

As evidenced by the Girdwood Hub, policymaking and planning in Northern Ireland are based not on a robust democratic legislative framework, but on ethnosectarian trade-off and contestation. Yet Sinn Féin's willingness to compromise with their partners in power-sharing, the DUP, allowed this flawed system to float along, for the most part, in the post-Agreement period. Such an approach was indicative of managing problems as opposed to transforming them. This initially reflected elements of the Girdwood development process whereby Sinn Féin accepted the intransigence of the DUP in order to keep their place in government.

However, there are some issues that simply cannot be won; as one commentator observed, the DUP 'are not interested in the principles of equality of opportunity set out in Section 75 of the Good Friday Agreement' ('Eamonn', interview with author 2017). This situation led to increasing political angst for Sinn Féin and an increasingly shaky relationship with their electorate. Bean noted a 'specific disenchantment among [Sinn Féin] supporters caused by the structural limitations and Unionist hostility to fully implementing the "equality agenda"' (2014: 729).

The failure of Girdwood mattered little to the DUP, but for Sinn Féin it led to criticism from the neighbourhoods in which they held sway. The reality of Sinn Féin's decision-making in the devolved Assembly had drifted further and further from the rhetoric of – and more critically, the delivery of – social justice and 'equality of opportunity' on which they depended for electoral support. This was evidenced by their compromise on social housing in North Belfast at Girdwood and other sites, as well as their agreement to implement austerity measures from Westminster in 2015 (Agnew 2015). As political manipulation and expediency took precedence over everyday issues, the electorate became disillusioned. The 2016 Assembly elections served as a barometer for the Nationalist/Republican grassroots' shifting support. Sinn Féin's share of total votes fell for the first time in an Assembly election;[1] the results were, frankly, jaw-dropping. Gerry Carroll of People Before Profit[2] topped the polls in Sinn Féin 's traditional stronghold of West Belfast (BBC News 2016b, 2016c).[3] And it was because Sinn Féin voters, in particular, were not seeing the promises of 'equality' or 'the peace dividend' that the post-ceasefire Assembly was meant to deliver.

Following the 2016 election came the Renewable Heat Initiative (RHI) scandal and the subsequent collapse of the Assembly. RHI was a mismanaged renewable energy scheme that attracted allegations of incompetence and clientelism, particularly concerning the DUP and First Minister Arlene Foster, who had overseen the programme.[4] RHI was termed 'one of the biggest financial

---

[1] From the 2011 elections, Sinn Féin's share of first-preference votes fell by 2.9 per cent, and the sharpest declines were found in traditionally Republican strongholds – for instance, 11.6 per cent in West Belfast (Bertoldi 2016: 578).

[2] People Before Profit had canvassed largely on a left-wing, anti-Sinn Féin platform, arguing the latter had become 'an establishment pro-government party largely responsible for public sector cuts' (O'Driscoll 2016).

[3] Carroll received a massive 8,299 first-preference votes, almost a quarter of all votes, and the second highest total of personal votes in Northern Ireland (Doyle 2016).

[4] The RHI scheme was set up in 2012 by the Department for Enterprise, Trade and Investment (DETI), under then-DETI Minister Arlene Foster of the DUP. Following the model used in the UK, its aim was to incentivise the use of renewable heat technologies in businesses through the use of wood-pellet boilers (McAuley 2016; BBC News 2017b; McKeown 2017b). However, RHI went badly wrong. Key cost controls found in the UK scheme were omitted and Foster's energy team set the rate of payment too high – for every £1 spent on renewable heating systems, businesses received £1.60 in subsidies – with the result that claimants received more money the more fuel they burned (BBC *Spotlight* 2016c; Stewart 2016). Despite several instances of whistleblowers recording concerns about the scheme, DUP SPADs (special advisors/senior political advisors) in the OFMDFM and the Department of Finance ensured that it was extended (Nolan 2016; McAuley 2016). Auditors began an investigation and found evidence of gross overspend, fraud and a final cost to

blunders in the history of Northern Ireland', marked by a series of extraordinary oversights and of 'allegations of corruption, cronyism and incompetence; of cock-up and cover-up' set to cost taxpayers approximately £500m over 20 years (*Belfast Telegraph* 2016; Hansard 2016b: 25). It was also alleged that individuals connected to the DUP had benefited financially from RHI.[5] I remember reading the newspapers at the time with a mix of disbelief and strange affection for how typically ill-managed and outrageously nepotistic it all felt, how First Minister Foster continued to stoutly insist she was not at fault. In response to public outcry over the controversy – and Foster's belligerence – her partner in power-sharing, then-Deputy First Minister Martin McGuinness of Sinn Féin, resigned, thus collapsing the Assembly as of January 2017 (BBC News 2017a). His resignation letter highlighted that 'the equality, mutual respect and all-Ireland approaches enshrined in the Good Friday Agreement have never been fully embraced by the DUP' (McGuinness 2017).

Sinn Féin collapsed the Assembly ostensibly because of RHI. But it was really in response to the broader context of disillusionment among Sinn Féin's traditional constituencies. McGuinness had been advised that grassroots feelings were at breaking point (Mallie 2017). Anger around the RHI scandal was compounded by Sinn Féin's failures to stand up to the DUP on issues that directly affected Catholics/Nationalists, including not only the housing crisis but austerity measures and the DUP's intransigence on funding Irish language resources.[6] Sinn Féin's return to the rhetoric of 'equality' in line with the peace process was a considered electoral strategy: in evoking the Agreement's aims and objectives and charging the DUP with violation of its principles, Sinn Féin could regain political traction. This point was reinforced by one community activist, who noted:

> taxpayers of hundreds of millions of pounds (BBC News 2017a, 2017b; Hughes 2017). Foster rejected repeated calls to stand down as First Minister while an investigation took place over her handling of the scheme (*Belfast Telegraph* 2016a).

[5] In advance of claimants' information being made public, multiple DUP SPADs and MLAs revealed that family members, some connected to poultry businesses, had applied for the scheme before subsidies were capped. One former SPAD, Stephen Brimstone, was also confirmed as a claimant. He and other SPADs resigned when the scandal broke. There is no evidence of wrongdoing, as all participants entered the scheme legitimately. It is, perhaps, a coincidence that a number of claimants were linked to DUP officials by family connections or by poultry interests. However, a cynic might be forgiven for alleging some sort of underlying clientelism or favouritism given the context of mismanagement, unanswered questions and close DUP connections.

[6] In 2017, DUP minister Paul Givan cut a £50,000 Irish language bursary scheme days before Christmas with no explanation. This was in the context of ongoing frustration around the lack of legal protections for the Irish language as promised by the 2006 St Andrews Agreement (*Irish News* 2017a; Smyth 2017).

> I think there was, from [Sinn Féin's] own constituency base ... people were just pissed off, with being in government with the DUP, and the way the DUP acted with RHI, there was a certain arrogance that wasn't just sectarian ... there was also an arrogance of power, they could do whatever the hell they wanted without scrutiny or accountability. And Sinn Féin's approach a lot of this time, was to always play the bigger person – we'll compromise, we'll do it for the greater good, all this stuff. That runs very thin whenever what you're doing is actually compromising on core tenets of the Good Friday Agreement. ('Eamonn', interview with author 2017)

Given these dynamics on the ground, it was no longer in Sinn Féin's interests to compromise or negotiate in order to make the institutions function. It seemed that Sinn Féin's latent acquiescence to the DUP, their grudging partnership, had reached breaking point. The collapse of the Assembly was met with prolonged stalemate. Negotiations stalled around an Irish Language Act, provisionally promised in the 2006 St Andrews Act and at the time of writing still undelivered by the Executive.[7] The DUP balked at providing provisions for the Irish language without allocating equal resources for Ulster-Scots (a regional dialect used in some parts of rural Northern Ireland) (BBC News 2018). Again, a zero-sum approach to resource allocation was in play, although the demand for Irish services is considerably larger than for Ulster-Scots. For over three years, Northern Ireland was without a functioning government – at a standstill because of this disagreement.

Brexit and the Protocol

This power vacuum occurred during the Brexit referendum and subsequent negotiations. The same dynamics that hamstrung the Girdwood development so badly, and that led the Assembly to collapse, also left Northern Ireland divided by Brexit and wholly unprepared to take any kind of meaningful role in the ultimate negotiations. The DUP and Sinn Féin were predictably unable to agree on a bargaining position that made sense for Northern Ireland, instead settling into the old constitutional fault lines and demonstrating, once again, how political rationality can succumb to territoriality and the constitutional question writ large.

---

[7] An Irish Language Act would place Irish on an official parity with English, offering the option for the language to be used in the functions of public bodies, including courts and the Assembly; the appointment of an Irish language commissioner; the right to be educated in Irish; and bilingual signage. It is estimated that such an act would cost approximately £2 million per year (Conradh na Gaeilge 2017: 9, 11).

The EU referendum campaign in Northern Ireland boiled down to party political preferences and traditional constitutional allegiances. Under Arlene Foster (who remained the DUP's leader after RHI and the Assembly's collapse), and alongside conservative Brexiteers in England, the DUP's position was that Northern Ireland and the UK should leave the EU. Sinn Féin campaigned to remain. The UUP, unlike the DUP, advised voters to vote in favour of continued EU membership but not all UUP supporters heeded this advice. Ultimately, the majority of the electorate in Northern Ireland followed party lines: in all, 86 per cent of Sinn Féin and 92 per cent of SDLP voters supported Remain; 70 per cent of DUP and 54 per cent of UUP voters supported Leave (Coakley and Garry 2016; Murphy 2021: 412). Of course, the referendum was never going to be decided by Northern Ireland, but it served as a useful barometer and evidence that politicians used separate discourses to sway the electorate along lines of constitutional allegiance.

When Leave won the referendum, Northern Ireland found itself unprepared for the consequences. This time, it was not a development process at stake, as in the Girdwood case, but the tenets of the Good Friday Agreement itself that were imperilled by politicians' failure to agree on a way forward. As Evershed and Murphy note, Brexit represents an existential threat to the delicate balance that the Agreement is based upon, including open borders between the North and South of Ireland and a fluid approach to nationality and identity therein (2021: 1).[8] It is incompatible with some of the Agreement's core principles, and the framework of the Northern Ireland Act which codified those principles into law.[9] In the wake of the referendum, the future of Northern Ireland felt (and at the time of writing, still feels) more uncertain than it has in a long time – and these considerations were ignored by the political elite in the run-up to the vote.

Although the Northern Irish border featured little in the referendum discussions in the wider UK, it came to both 'dominate and complicate' the

---

[8] This was down to the Agreement's principle of consent, which technically empowers the people of Northern Ireland to decide the territory's constitutional future. It grants that a referendum can be held if there is appetite for it, but no change in Northern Ireland's constitutional status will be made without the consent of the majority. This served to reassure Unionists leery of the peace process while also allowing space for the aspirations of Nationalists to a future United Ireland. It 'finessed' the constitutional question in a vague and temporary way by placing it in the future – but people could live with that (Stevenson 2017: 112). In the meantime, the constitutional question played out at the micro-level in spaces like North Belfast.

[9] It also affects the language of the Agreement itself – within months of the Brexit referendum, a legal challenge was mounted (unsuccessfully) arguing that removing references to EU law and policy in the Agreement could potentially undo the tentative degree of toleration that had been achieved by the document (Hayward and Murphy 2018: 285).

subsequent EU-UK withdrawal negotiations (Murphy 2021: 405). Northern Ireland's shared border with the Republic of Ireland is rife with painful associations from the conflict and still holds symbolic weight for both Protestants/Unionists and Catholics/Nationalists. A major achievement of the peace process was that it took the border out of politics, foregrounding 'a more flexible and forgiving brand of sovereignty' (Stevenson 2017: 114). Although Unionists and Nationalists still cared about territory and identity, the border itself became a less potent site of political and cultural struggle. Achieving a sense of normalcy along the soft border was a part of the peace process that had, by all accounts, worked. And, critically, the open border between North and South was facilitated by the UK and Ireland's common EU membership. As Murphy put it, 'The single market is based on open borders and free movement of people and trade, so there was an easy and almost fortuitous way in which it enabled key aspects of the Belfast/Good Friday Agreement' (2021: 407). Leaving the EU would necessitate some type of border between Northern Ireland and the Republic of Ireland to control movement of people and goods. The idea of a hard border was floated and nixed. After much negotiation, the Northern Ireland Protocol was agreed between the EU and the UK in 2019: Northern Ireland remains part of the UK customs territory but is required to apply EU customs and align with the EU single market (Council of the European Union 2022). The Protocol was negotiated to ensure free movement of people and trade across the Irish land border post-Brexit. But the result is effectively a permanent customs and regulatory border in the Irish Sea between Northern Ireland and Great Britain, and a different trading relationship between the EU and Northern Ireland than that between the EU and the rest of the UK. This is an effect that has been vociferously opposed by Unionist politicians and Loyalist paramilitaries (Murphy 2021: 413). The same old dynamics of fear and threat have again reared their head.

In response to the Irish Sea customs border, the Loyalist Communities Council, an umbrella group that represents the views of the UVF, UDA and Red Hand Commando, wrote a letter to UK Prime Minister Boris Johnson and Ireland's Taoiseach, Micheál Martin, warning of 'permanent destruction' of the 1998 peace agreement without changes to the Protocol:

> Please do not underestimate the strength of feeling on this issue right across the Unionist family ... the Loyalist groupings are herewith withdrawing their support for the Belfast agreement until our rights under the agreement are restored and the protocol is amended to ensure unfettered access for goods, services, and citizens throughout the United Kingdom. If you or the EU is not prepared to honour the entirety of the Agreement then you will be responsible for the permanent destruction of the Agreement. (Carroll 2021)

Many of the towns outside Belfast and along the Irish Sea, like Newtownabbey, Carrickfergus and Larne, are controlled to some degree by stand-alone Loyalist paramilitary factions. For instance, the South East Antrim UDA, with over 2,000 members, is particularly notorious for violence, drug trafficking and criminality that other factions of the UDA have eschewed (BBC *Spotlight* 2021). As the controversy around the Protocol unfolded, posters sprang up in their territory on the roads that run from Belfast along the coast: 'No Irish Sea Border', 'Scrap NI Protocol' and 'EU Hands off Ulster'. Union Jacks lined the route by the water. There were issues at the ports where customs checks took place: in Larne, one port worker and their family were moved to alternative housing following a death threat from a Loyalist paramilitary organisation, and other threats on port staff led to a brief suspension of customs checks (Hewitt 2021).

Rioting broke out in predominantly Loyalist areas in response to the Protocol. In April 2021, Northern Ireland briefly made world headlines with images of a hijacked bus on fire and young people throwing stones, fireworks and petrol bombs at police. Nearly 90 police officers were injured and boys as young as 13 or 14 were arrested on rioting charges. There is evidence that some senior figures in the UDA and UVF allowed the trouble to proceed (Hirst 2021) and that it was criminally, not politically motivated. In particular, the South East Antrim UDA, whose criminal empire has been dismantled by the PSNI, seized the opportunity to hit back at the authorities (BBC *Spotlight* 2021). It seems that the Unionist/Loyalist appetite for violence is linked to these criminal elements rather than broader Unionist/Loyalist sentiment. In an interview, one Loyalist told Brennan, 'all these young ones going on about a return to violence don't know what they are talking about. I don't see any appetite for that. This new crowd of paramilitaries are more interested in their own wee rackets and lining their own pockets' (2021: 760).

The forces behind the sporadic rioting may be linked to a small subset of Unionist feeling. However, the broader reaction to the Protocol reflects the same obstinate dynamics as those that stopped adequate housing being built at Girdwood. They evidence the same dynamics that prevented the passing of an Irish Language Act as a condition of restoring the Assembly between 2017 and 2020. This is the latent perspective that shapes how Unionists feel about their place in the wider UK: the sense of fear, threat and insecurity, the oft-cited 'siege mentality' that defines Unionist political culture (Evershed and Murphy 2021: 12). Elements of Unionism ostensibly object to the Protocol because it means distinguishing Northern Ireland symbolically from the rest of the United Kingdom. It is a threat to their sense of identity and belonging. And in a context in which Unionism's electoral clout is disappearing and their position on the Protocol feels disregarded by Westminster, that mentality has been heightened (Murphy and Evershed 2019; Tonge 2019). It is the story of Girdwood at the macro-level.

The Assembly Collapses … Again!

Under the DUP and Sinn Féin, the Executive failed to produce any comprehensive plan for the impact of Brexit on Northern Ireland (Hayward and Murphy 2018: 284). Instead, the Assembly collapsed – again – because of the Protocol issue. This time, First Minister Paul Givan of the DUP resigned as a protest against the Protocol. The leader of the DUP, Sir Jeffrey Donaldson had been threatening to withdraw DUP ministers from the Assembly for months in response to customs checks, and the empty threats seemed to be losing them support among the hardline grassroots. When Givan resigned, Sinn Féin called for an early Assembly election in 2022.

Sinn Féin and the DUP have each to varying extents turned Brexit into a constitutional issue. The same community worker noted that, 'Because of the Protocol, the DUP is saying that Northern Ireland is considered separate from the UK, and that has loyalists "up in arms". And Sinn Féin never miss an opportunity to turn a crisis to their advantage – they have elevated the conversation around an All-Ireland border poll'. This is partly true; in theory, Brexit provides a political opening for a referendum on Irish unity. Sinn Féin Party President, Mary Lou McDonald has herself described Brexit as 'the opportunity of a lifetime' in this regard (Libreri 2020). But in practice, the materials risks posed by Brexit have seen Sinn Féin distancing themselves from notions of crisis as opportunity and mitigating rather than leveraging the difficulties of Brexit (Evershed and Murphy 2021: 8). Sinn Féin's 2022 election campaign, for instance, responded to 'bread-and-butter' issues like the high cost of living and the underfunded NHS, rather than ideological issues like Irish unity. This was a pointed rebuttal to the DUP's emphasis on the Protocol and symbolic Britishness.

For Unionists, however, the spectre of a border poll rankles. And the spectre looms larger with the results of the 2022 election. For the first time in Northern Ireland's history, Sinn Féin won the most seats in the Assembly (Sproule 2022). This means that, instead of the DUP, Sinn Féin will take the First Minister post. Although the difference between the First Minister and Deputy First Minister positions is only in name, that along with the increased number of seats in the Assembly provides a literal and symbolic boost for Sinn Féin. In response to the result, Party leader Michelle O'Neill said: 'Today ushers in a new era which I believe presents us all with an opportunity to reimagine relationships in this society on the basis of fairness, on the basis of equality and on the basis of social justice' (Landler 2022).

As in 2016, Sinn Féin is using the rhetoric of 'equality' as a considered approach. However, the First Minister cannot hold office without a Deputy First Minister, and the DUP have thus far refused to participate in government until their concerns about the Protocol are resolved. They have also refused to nominate a Speaker, meaning there can be no debates, no committees and no oversight of ministers, who are currently acting in a caretaker capacity with limited power (BBC News 2022). This leaves the Assembly unable to approve budgets, pass policy or sign off on much-needed healthcare reform (Carroll and O'Carroll 2022).

At the time of writing, it is unclear what the next steps will be if the DUP continue to refuse to take their place in the Assembly. It is also unclear what the results suggest for their electoral future. They now find themselves in an awkward position, having cultivated a hardline Loyalist polity opposed to any compromise on the Protocol (Brennan 2021: 758). The DUP have said themselves that they will not join the government without resolution on the Protocol. But polls suggest that the Protocol is not a priority for most voters outside of core Unionists – people are more concerned about the bread-and-butter issues that Sinn Féin campaigned on (Landler 2022). Finally, if the Protocol were overturned, it would violate the Good Friday Agreement and could prompt a bitter clash with the EU and the US. Whatever path they take, it seems the DUP miscalculated.

The DUP's missteps create space for a different political path outside of the traditional divides. There is, increasingly, room for hope. As Brennan and Edwards note, 'Recent elections have shown the beginning of cracks in the wider unionist/loyalist electorate block. People are increasingly shunning those Unionist politicians who have led them into poverty, paramilitary peacekeeping, and Protocol pessimism and opting for more progressive politics' (2022: 8). As one Unionist community worker observed in relation to the latest collapse, 'It's not the elites, again, it's the working class that suffer from these battles. Protocol or no protocol, it doesn't change the living conditions in spaces like North Belfast' (author fieldnotes 2022).

The DUP's focus on symbolic belonging and constitutional integrity is out of step with the concerns of most of the electorate. A series of events in the wake of the Assembly's collapse suggest that the emergence of another force in Northern Ireland is more fully at hand: people are tired of identity politics trumping rational decision-making time and time again.

In the run-up to the 2022 election, opinions on the ground leaned broadly away from constitutional issues and towards practical ones. The Assembly's collapse came at a time when political leadership was sorely needed around the rising cost of living and the funding of the NHS, not to mention the context of the global pandemic.[10] Citizens tended to be focused on these concerns and

---

[10] The National Health Service (NHS), the UK's healthcare system, is free at the point of service but buckling under lack of funding and staff.

articulated frustration with politicians' emphasis on identity issues. 'We're sick to the back teeth of this whole orange versus green, flags this, parades that. We're in a cost-of-living crisis, that's what the big priority should be', said one young person (McClements 2022). Another observed, 'Me and my siblings will vote for progression rather than religion' (O'Carroll 2022).

The election was notable beyond the 'Orange and Green' headlines – the Alliance party, which is centrist and non-sectarian, saw a huge surge in support, with 17 seats in the Assembly and its largest ever share of first preference votes (Associated Press 2022). Although a nascent trend, their rise in popularity suggests that perhaps voters are finally tiring of the sectarian back-and-forth, the lack of leadership seen in 2017–2020 and the implications of Brexit for people's everyday lives, not constitutional sympathies.

There is a growing body of research on the move away from constitutional politics and unambiguously Protestant/Unionist and Catholic/Nationalist identities (Coakley 2021; The Institute of Irish Studies and The Irish News 2022; McNicholl 2019; Tilley and Evans 2011; Tonge and Gomez 2015). This is supported by the 2020 Northern Ireland Life and Times survey, a barometer of opinion that shows 42 per cent of respondents answering 'neither' to the question, 'Generally speaking, do you think of yourself as a unionist, a nationalist or neither?' (NILTS 2020). The trend is not restricted to the younger generations but spread evenly across age groups (Hayward and McCall 2019: 144). Hayward and McCall posit that

> Many claiming a Neither identity may do so because the political institutions at Stormont do not appear to them to be particularly salient or reflective of social and economic realities in contemporary society. This is seen in the endless cycle of crisis talks, high-level interventions and repetitive 'agreements' on persistently divisive issues that never quite offer the breakthrough and progress that is hoped for. (2019: 151)

Indeed, a 2022 poll found significant consensus among Unionists (72.8 per cent), Nationalists (79.8 per cent) and Neithers (79.5 per cent) that: 'the next Executive should prioritise jobs, health and welfare over constitutional issues' (The Institute of Irish Studies and The Irish News 2022). It is difficult to judge how this might look in the long term, but it feels like people have had enough of the pettiness of identity politics, and that the latter is no longer mobilising or enthusing the electorate. As one scholar in Northern Ireland put it, 'for people now, stability counts more than symbolism. People want a more pragmatic approach' (author fieldnotes 2022).

During my time in Northern Ireland, I attended protests alongside thousands of other people in support of equal marriage and abortion rights and against austerity. I observed local social movements arise in response to climate change and fracking, homelessness in the North and South, and the direct provision system for refugees.[11] I saw coalitions like the Save the Cathedral Quarter campaign come together against irresponsible development plans and offer better visions for what Belfast could be (BBC News 2020b). Diversification of the electorate and new sites of political struggle have forged a space for politics to which traditional party politicians are ill-equipped to respond. Rather than the old identity politics, different political expressions are arising in response to the issues that matter in peoples' lives. As society has become more pluralistic, as these social movements have formed in response to both local and global issues, Stormont has failed to keep up. The gulf between civil society – 'street politics' – and the state is widening.

In some respects, the UK government has stepped into the vacuum left by the disagreed Assembly and addressed some of the issues that had for so long galvanised protest among cross-sections of the population. During the first Assembly collapse, between 2017 and 2020, Westminster brought Northern Ireland into line with the rest of the UK by legalising abortion and equal marriage. These were issues that had garnered widespread activism among the polity – and particularly among young people – but which Sinn Féin treated gingerly and the DUP rejected outright (Stewart 2019).

The British government also finally responded to the statis around protecting Irish language rights. According to a press release in 2022, 'following Executive failure to progress previous legislation through the Northern Ireland Assembly', Northern Ireland's Secretary of State introduced Identity and Language legislation in Parliament that will grant Irish official status in the North' (NIO 2022b). This occurred as the Assembly remained in limbo after the 2022 election result. The weekend before the announcement, the streets of Belfast had been choked with Irish language supporters clad in red: an estimated 17,000 people had turned out to demand protections for the Irish language.[12] The aerial shots of the march were a truly remarkable testament to the organising power of the movement for Irish, and how it had continued to grow in meaning and strength of feeling over the years. I remembered attending several of the organising meetings for An Dream Dearg back in 2017,[13] and helping to steward the first Lá Dearg march. Then, there were a

---

[11] Direct provision is a system that houses refugees and asylum seekers in temporary accommodation but does not allow them to work or participate in the wider community. In many cases people are trapped in the system, in limbo for months and years, isolated in overcrowded hotel rooms and hostels. Direct provision has been roundly criticised by human rights agencies as cruel, regressive and inhumane. See Gessen (2019).

[12] In 2022, an estimated 17,000 people took to the streets in support of an Irish Language Act. (Young 2022).

[13] An Dream Dearg is an advocacy group for Irish language rights.

few dozen people crowded into a meeting room and a few hundred people at the protest. Painted faces and placards held aloft, we went streaming down the Falls into Belfast City Centre in hopes that the Executive, or failing that, the British government would listen. Five years of continuous grassroots activism later, the same streets were packed with supporters. The future looks cautiously hopeful for those who have fought for Irish language rights.

While the British government has responded to these demands for rights-based equality more broadly, the issue of housing remains contested within the Northern Ireland Assembly. Here, too, though, there is some hopeful news. The former Mackie's factory site in West Belfast is a 30-acre piece of public land whose development process has been eerily similar to that of the Girdwood Barracks. Like Girdwood, Mackie's is located along an interface and, like Girdwood, the site offers space to address the ongoing housing crisis. Again, PPR has advocated for social housing to be built according to need. Again, politicians from both sides of the divide have deployed discourse that avoids the issue. And, again, no EQIA was conducted before the government released a Masterplan that privileged a 'greenway' – as PPR described it, a cycle path – over social housing (Winters 2021). The result is a huge expanse of publicly owned land with no plans for housing development. When asked about the lack of housing, a spokesperson for the Housing Executive said that 'Belfast City Council has secured PEACE IV funding to enable the creation of new shared spaces at that site. This programme will be delivered under the council's open spaces strategy'.

As at Girdwood, 'shared space' and 'good relations' have been used at Mackie's as a discursive tactic to supersede equality of opportunity. The language of 'shared space' also helped City Council to secure SEUPB funding for the site. The similarities are uncanny. In reference to the plan, PPR's Elfie Seymour commented that 'for too long "community balance" and "good relations" have operated as vetoes to progressing equality and these vetoes have been enforced by fearmongering, political deal-making and paramilitary threats' (Winters 2020).

This could have been Girdwood's epitaph. However, the Mackie's site might yet escape Girdwood's fate. A family in housing need demanded a judicial review against Belfast City Council, who had rezoned the land to prevent social housing development. The review found planning approval of a park and greenway at Mackie's 'unlawful'. Legal counsel for the applicant said the win was an 'important milestone in the long-standing campaign to use public lands for the public good, especially in a time of significant and chronic housing stress' (Corr 2022).

PPR has long been at the centre of that campaign. At the time Girdwood was redeveloped, PPR's work was an isolated example of what could happen if alternative politics were allowed room to grow outside of the traditional sectarian divide. In the interim, this alternative space has expanded. PPR continues to advocate for fair housing and to work with local residents in forging a different path than the ones that politicians have trod. The coalition Take Back the City (TBTC) was formed in 2021 around the issue of building homes and communities on publicly owned land, including the Mackie's site. In 2021, TBTC released an ingenious mapping tool, The State of Belfast, that charts the complexities of housing need and land ownership in Belfast. In partnership with residents and using a range of data, they have campaigned for a more creative and inclusive approach to building Belfast, starting with Mackie's. It remains to be seen whether this vision will bear fruit, but it will not be for lack of trying.

For all its faults and fault lines, the Northern Ireland I know has a sense of humour. It is a generous place. It is full of people who cross the typical categories of 'Orange and Green', and who transgress and defy the fixed identities of their politicians. This seems, increasingly, to be reflected by trends on the ground. As the Assembly has failed, and failed again, new voices and demands have sprung up – people are tired of the status quo. Groups like PPR, TBTC and An Dream Dearg, as well as many other local movements around social and economic issues, are organising for a different Northern Ireland. As Irish language activist Ciarán Mac Giolla Bhéin put it, 'The collapse of Stormont ironically led to a renaissance of politics; street politics re-emerged as movements representing those sections of society for whom the peace process had yet to deliver arose and poured out onto the streets demanding a fairer, more representative, rights-based society' (2022).

This, too, is a broader trend. On a global scale our societies continue to be in tension, with conflicting discourses of what is 'true' and 'real' drawn from fundamentally opposed political rationalities and social realities. Challenge and dispute over 'needs' and 'rights' are happening everywhere: in the US, for instance, as abortion rights are imperilled, as gun rights are challenged in the wake of mass shootings. Politicians use divisive discourses to appeal to people's deeper fears, and alternative actors – activists, advocates and organisers – continue to attempt to hold them to account. And in the midst of Brexit, broader crises like the COVID-19 pandemic, and national reckonings over racial equity and bodily autonomy, more people are taking to the streets. More people are questioning the cities we have built for ourselves and the sociopolitical dynamics and divisions they reflect. As we collectively emerge from the pandemic, there is a fragile feeling of possibility around building something new. We have an opportunity, now, to dismantle the walls that divide us.

Bibliography

Acheson, N. and C. Milofsky (2008) 'Peace building and participation in Northern Ireland: local social movements and the policy process since the "Good Friday" agreement', *Ethnopolitics* 7(1): 63–80.

Adams, R. (2006a) *Advisory Panel Working Methods*, February. Belfast, Northern Ireland.

—— (2006b) *Vision and Charter*, Girdwood Advisory Forum, April. Belfast, Northern Ireland.

—— (2006c) *Shared Future – Tourism, Heritage, Culture Arts and Leisure*, Girdwood Advisory Forum, 6 November. Belfast, Northern Ireland.

—— (2007a) *Living in the New Crumlin/Girdwood – A Discussion Paper*, Girdwood Advisory Forum, 7 March. Belfast, Northern Ireland.

—— (2007b) 'Proposal for New PRONI HQ Building at Crumlin Road Gaol/ Girdwood Park Site', communication by letter to Maria Eagle MP, 26 April. Print. Girdwood Advisory Panel Meeting Minutes (held by Elizabeth DeYoung).

—— (2007c) 'Foreword', in *Crumlin Road Gaol & Girdwood Barracks Draft Masterplan*, July. Belfast, Northern Ireland.

—— (2007d) 'Draft Masterplan Update', communication by letter to Advisory Panel, 23 August. Belfast, Northern Ireland. Print. Girdwood Advisory Panel Meeting Minutes (held by Elizabeth DeYoung).

Agnew, J. (1987) *Place and Politics: the geographical mediation of state and society*. Winchester: Allen & Unwin Inc.

Agnew, S. (2015) 'Welfare reform: "DUP and Sinn Féin have sold out Northern Ireland's most vulnerable"', *Belfast Telegraph*, 19 February. Available at: https://www.belfasttelegraph.co.uk/opinion/columnists/steven-agnew/welfare-reform-dup-and-sinn-fin-have-sold-out-northern-irelands-most-vulnerable-31006074.html (accessed 3 February 2017).

Al Jazeera (2021) 'Belfast protesters set fire to hijacked bus as violence continues', 8 April. Available at: https://www.aljazeera.com/gallery/2021/4/8/belfast-protesters-hijack-bus-attack-police-as-violence-continue (accessed 9 September 2021).

Alvesson, M. and D. Karreman (2000) 'Varieties of discourse: on the study of organizations through discourse analysis', *Human Relations* 53(9): 1125–1149.

Amit, V. and N. Rapport (2002) *The Trouble with Community: Anthropological Reflections on Movement, Identity and Collectivity*. London: Pluto Press.

Anderson, J. and I. Shuttleworth (1998) 'Sectarian demography, territoriality, and political development in Northern Ireland', *Political Geography* 17(2): 187–208.

—— (2003) 'Spaces of fear: communal violence and spatial behaviour'. Paper presented at the 'Cultures of Violence?' conference, Centre for Research in the Arts, Social Sciences and Humanities (CRASSH), University of Cambridge, 9–10 January. Available at: www.qub.ac.uk/c-star/pubs/Spaces%20of%20Fear%20Cambridge.pdf (accessed 14 March 2016).

Archer, B. (2016) '£11.7 million community hub opens on former Girdwood army base', *Irish News*, 16 January. Available at: http://www.irishnews.com/news/2016/01/16/news/-11-7-million-community-hub-opens-on-former-girdwood-army-base-384220/ (accessed 17 January 2016).

Aretxaga, B. (1997) *Shattering Silence: Women, Nationalism and Political Subjectivity in Northern Ireland*. Princeton: Princeton University Press.

ARK (1998) 'Northern Ireland life and times survey: political attitudes'. Available at: http://www.ark.ac.uk/nilt/1998/Political_Attitudes/index.html (accessed 13 October 2017).

—— (2001) 'Northern Ireland life and times survey: political attitudes'. Available at: http://www.ark.ac.uk/nilt/2001/Political_Attitudes/index.html (accessed 13 October 2017).

—— (2016) 'Northern Ireland life and times survey: community relations'. Available at: http://www.ark.ac.uk/nilt/2016/Community_Relations/ (accessed 8 February 2017).

Ashton Community Trust (2014) 'New Lodge youth centre goes from strength to strength', *Greater New Lodge CEP Magazine*, March. Belfast, Northern Ireland.

—— (2017a) 'Home: Ashton community trust online'. Available at: http://www.ashtoncentre.com/ (accessed 21 September 2017).

—— (2017b) 'KinderKids daycare'. Available at: http://www.ashtoncentre.com/services/childcare-family-support/kinderkids-daycare/ (accessed 21 September 2017).

—— (2017c) 'Ashton: Serving North Belfast for over 25 years', *Greater New Lodge Community Magazine*, December. Belfast, Northern Ireland.

—— (2017d) 'Bridge of Hope physiotherapy service shortlisted for prestigious healthcare award'. Available at: http://www.ashtoncentre.com/latest-news/bridge-hope-physiotherapy-service-shortlisted-prestigious-healthcare-award/ (accessed 21 September 2017).

—— (2017e) 'Training available'. Available at: http://www.ashtoncentre.com/training-available/ (accessed 21 September 2017).

Associated Press (2022) 'Sinn Féin celebrates an historic election win in Northern Ireland', 7 May. Available at https://www.npr.org/2022/05/07/1097417453/sinn-fein-wins-assembly-election-northern-ireland (accessed 8 May 2022).

Aughey, A. (2002) 'The art and effect of political lying in Northern Ireland', *Irish Political Studies* 17(2): 1–16.

Bairner, A. (2006) 'The *flâneur* and the city: reading the "new" Belfast's leisure spaces', *Space and Polity* 10(2): 121–134.

—— (2012) 'Between *flânerie* and fiction: ways of seeing exclusion and inclusion in the contemporary city', *Leisure Studies* 31(1): 3–19.
Bairner, I. and P. Shirlow (2003) 'When leisure turns to fear: fear, mobility, and ethnosectarianism in Belfast', *Leisure Studies* 22(3): 203–221.
Baker, A. (2012) 'What kind of crisis? Five underlying problems of Anglo liberal capitalism and their implications for Northern Ireland', *Social Justice Review: Labour After Conflict* 1: 8–16.
Ballynafeigh Community Development Association (BCDA) (2013) *A Shared Today: Belfast's Ballynafeigh Neighbourhood*. Belfast, Northern Ireland.
Barbour, R. (2008) *Introducing Qualitative Research: A Student Guide to the Craft of Doing Qualitative Research*. London: Sage.
Bardon, J. (1992) *A History of Ulster*. Belfast: Blackstaff.
Barnes, C. (2014) 'Sinn Féin expenses row: Caral Ni Chuilin forgot to say she paid relative £11,320', *Belfast Telegraph*, 22 December. Available at: http://www.belfasttelegraph.co.uk/sunday-life/news/sinn-fein-expenses-row-caral-ni-chuilin-forgot-to-say-she-paid-relative-11320-30855261.html (accessed 17 December 2016).
BBC News (2000) 'Funeral of third feud victim', 26 August. Available at: http://news.bbc.co.uk/1/hi/northern_ireland/896596.stm (accessed 27 September 2017)
—— (2001) 'Officers hurt in school protest blast', 5 September. Available at: http://news.bbc.co.uk/1/hi/northern_ireland/1526032.stm (accessed 20 November 2017).
—— (2008) 'I did "smash" Sinn Féin – Paisley', 9 March. Available at: http://news.bbc.co.uk/2/hi/uk_news/politics/7285912.stm (accessed 20 December 2017)
—— (2011a) 'Housing Executive to stick by Red Sky contract decision', 6 July. Available at: http://www.bbc.co.uk/news/uk-northern-ireland-1405352629614029.html (accessed 4 July 2017).
—— (2011b) 'Nelson McCausland vetoes Girdwood social homes', 29 July. Available at: http://www.bbc.com/news/uk-northern-ireland-14338142 (accessed 21 December 2016).
—— (2012a) 'Ebrington Barracks reborn', 14 February. http://www.bbc.com/news/uk-northern-ireland-17014694 (accessed 8 May 2018).
—— (2012b) 'David Black murder: new "IRA" group claims it murdered prison officer', 12 November. Available at: http://www.bbc.co.uk/news/uk-northern-ireland-20296702 (accessed 15 September 2017).
—— (2013a) 'Girdwood development: sixty new homes to be built on site', 6 June. Available at: http://www.bbc.co.uk/news/uk-northern-ireland-22797984 (accessed 16 October 2017).
—— (2013b) 'Timeline: Maze prison site development', 4 October. Available at: http://www.bbc.com/news/uk-northern-ireland-24395246 (accessed 21 December 2017).
—— (2014a) 'Gerry Adams: Unionists condemn use of swear word', 25 November. Available at: https://www.bbc.com/news/uk-northern-ireland-30186975 (accessed 5 May 2022).
—— (2014b) 'Spotlight: Research Services Ireland got £700,000 in Sinn Féin expenses', 26 November. Available at: http://www.bbc.co.uk/news/uk-northern-ireland-30204080 (accessed 1 May 2017).

—— (2015) 'Election 2015: DUP and UUP agree pact in four constituencies', 18 March. Available at: http://www.bbc.co.uk/news/uk-northern-ireland-31930496 (accessed 14 September 2017).

—— (2016a) 'NI Assembly election: leaders take part in BBC debate', 3 May. Available at: http://www.bbc.co.uk/news/election-2016-northern-ireland-36191435 (accessed 4 June 2017).

—— (2016b) 'Northern Ireland Assembly election: anti-austerity party picks up seats', 9 May. Available at: http://www.bbc.com/news/election-2016-northern-ireland-36235913 (accessed 28 December 2017).

—— (2016c) 'Northern Ireland election results', n.d. Available at: http://www.bbc.com/news/election/2016/northern_ireland/results (accessed 14 December 2017).

—— (2017a) 'Martin McGuinness resigns as NI Deputy First Minister', 10 January. Available at: http://www.bbc.co.uk/news/uk-northern-ireland-38561507 (accessed 8 August 2017).

—— (2017b) 'Timeline: renewable heat incentive scandal', 25 January. Available at: http://www.bbc.co.uk/news/uk-northern-ireland-38301428 (accessed 8 August 2017).

—— (2017c) 'NI election 2017 results', 9 June. Available at: http://www.bbc.co.uk/news/election/ni2017/results (accessed 9 June 2017).

—— (2018) 'SDLP: no deal leaves governments "embarrassed"', 13 February. Available at: http://www.bbc.co.uk/news/uk-northern-ireland-43037508 (accessed 13 February 2018).

—— (2020a) 'Londonderry: Ebrington hotel project delayed until summer 2021', 23 December. Available at: https://www.bbc.com/news/uk-northern-ireland-foyle-west-55423678 (accessed 5 January 2022).

—— (2020b) 'Tribeca Belfast: Council backs £500m plan for Cathedral Quarter', 22 January. Available at: https://www.bbc.com/news/uk-northern-ireland-51197944 (accessed 14 May 2022).

—— (2022) 'NI election 2022: Prime Minister to visit NI as DUP blocks assembly', 13 May. Available at: https://www.bbc.com/news/uk-northern-ireland-61427418 (accessed 14 May 2022).

BBC *Spotlight* (2012) 'North Belfast housing', 23 May. Transcript available at: https://subsaga.com/bbc/news/spotlight/2012/05/22/north-belfast-housing.html#transcript (accessed 16 February 2017).

—— (2016a) 'Clandeboye: community in fear', 16 March. Available at: http://www.bbc.co.uk/programmes/b072xj12 (accessed 18 March 2016).

—— (2016b) '04/10/2016', 4 October. Available at: http://www.bbc.co.uk/programmes/b07xtf2k (accessed 4 October 2016).

—— (2016c) '06/12/2016', 6 December. Available at: http://www.bbc.co.uk/programmes/b08402bs (accessed 6 December 2016).

—— (2021) 'Gangland: the murder of Glenn Quinn', n.d. Available at: https://www.bbc.co.uk/programmes/moootcry (accessed 18 March 2021).

Bean, K. (2007) *The New Politics of Sinn Féin*. Liverpool: Liverpool University Press.

Belfast City Council (2006) 'Gasworks redevelopment', presented to the NBCAU, 12 May. Belfast, Northern Ireland.

—— (2012) *Strategic Policy & Resources Committee: Girdwood Community Hub Update*, 20 January. Belfast, Northern Ireland. Available at: https://minutes3.belfastcity.gov.uk/documents/s33691/Girdwood%20Community%20Hub%20Update.pdf (accessed 4 May 2017).

—— (2013) *Belfast City Masterplan Review: Consultation Draft*. Belfast, Northern Ireland.

—— (2014) 'Details of Girdwood Hub revealed', *Belfast City Council*, 10 April. Available at: http://www.belfastcity.gov.uk/News/News-36297.aspx (accessed 17 July 2017).

—— (2015) *Belfast City Centre: Regeneration and Investment Strategy*. Belfast, Northern Ireland.

Belfast Telegraph (2012) 'SDLP fury over shared housing plan', 28 May. Available at: https://www.belfasttelegraph.co.uk/news/northern-ireland/sdlp-fury-over-shared-housing-plan-28753995.html (accessed 21 December 2017).

—— (2013) 'Maze site "will be shrine to peace"', 24 April. Available at: https://www.belfasttelegraph.co.uk/news/northern-ireland/maze-site-will-be-shrine-to-peace-29219532.html (accessed 21 December 2017).

—— (2015) 'Britain's secret terror deals: "truly disturbing" BBC Panorama allegations of collusion must be fully investigated, says Amnesty International', 28 May. Available at: http://www.belfasttelegraph.co.uk/news/northern-ireland/britains-secret-terror-deals-truly-disturbing-bbc-panorama-allegations-of-collusion-must-be-fully-investigated-says-amnesty-international-31261593.html (accessed 13 July 2017).

—— (2016) 'RHI scandal: Mike Nesbitt claims to have uncovered "smoking gun" of Arlene Foster's culpability in botched heating scheme', 13 December. Available at: http://www.belfasttelegraph.co.uk/news/northern-ireland/rhi-scandal-mike-nesbitt-claims-to-have-uncovered-smoking-gun-of-arlene-fosters-culpability-in-botched-heating-scheme-35291766.html (accessed 13 August 2017).

—— (2017a) 'RHI scandal: DUP MLA Jim Wells reveals four family members installed wood pellet boilers under scheme', 21 January. Available at: http://www.belfasttelegraph.co.uk/news/northern-ireland/rhi-scandal-dup-mla-jim-wells-reveals-four-family-members-installed-wood-pellet-boilers-under-scheme-35386151.html (accessed 21 January 2017).

—— (2017b) 'RHI scandal: DUP MLAs Carla Lockhart and William Irwin reveal family members have boilers under the botched green energy scheme', 23 January. Available at: http://www.belfasttelegraph.co.uk/news/northern-ireland/rhi-scandal-dup-mlas-carla-lockhart-and-william-irwin-reveal-family-members-have-boilers-under-the-botched-green-energy-scheme-35392405.html (accessed 23 January 2017).

—— (2018) 'Sinn Féin hit out over Belfast paramilitary shooting', 31 January. Available at: https://www.belfasttelegraph.co.uk/news/northern-ireland/sinn-fein-hits-out-over-belfast-paramilitary-shooting-36549387.html (accessed 31 January 2018).

Bell, D. (1990) *Acts of Union: Youth Culture and Sectarianism in Northern Ireland*. Basingstoke: Macmillan Education.

Bell, J. (2016) 'Social investment fund "flawed" and in need of root and branch reform: former public standards chair', *Belfast Telegraph*, 18 November. Available at: http://www.belfasttelegraph.co.uk/news/northern-ireland/social-investment-fund-flawed-and-in-need-of-root-and-branch-reform-former-public-standards-chair-35225953.html (accessed 8 August 2017).

Bell, J.B. (1993) *The Irish Troubles: A Generation of Violence, 1967–1992*. Dublin: Gill and Macmillan.

Benjamin, W. (1997) *Charles Baudelaire: A Lyric Poet in the Era of High Capitalism*. New York and London: Verso.

Berg, B.L. (2007) *Qualitative Research for the Social Sciences*. Boston: Pearson.

Bernard, H.R. (1988) *Research Methods in Cultural Anthropology*. London: Sage.

Bertoldi, F. (2016) 'Change beneath the surface: the 2016 Northern Ireland Assembly election', *Regional & Federal Studies* 26(4): 569–584.

Bew, P., P. Gibbon and H. Patterson (1996) *Northern Ireland 1921–1994: Political Forces and Social Classes*. London: Serif.

—— (2002) *Northern Ireland 1921–2001: Political Forces and Social Classes*. London: Serif.

Bew, P. and G. Gillespie (1999) *Northern Ireland: A Chronology of the Troubles, 1968–99*. Dublin: Gill and Macmillan.

Black, R. (2013) 'Why spend £10m on new leisure centre in Belfast when thousands wait for housing?', *Belfast Telegraph*, 27 November. Available at: http://www.belfasttelegraph.co.uk/news/northern-ireland/why-spend-10m-on-new-leisure-centre-in-belfast-when-thousands-wait-for-housing-29787572.html (accessed 18 March 2017).

—— (2015) 'Sinn Féin hit by storm of anger in "sectarian headcount" leaflet row', *Belfast Telegraph*, 5 May. Available at: http://www.belfasttelegraph.co.uk/news/general-election-2017/sinn-fein-hit-by-storm-of-anger-in-sectarian-headcount-leaflet-row-31195067.html (accessed 9 June 2016).

Bluebird Media (2016) *Girdwood Youth Forum*. Available at: https://vimeo.com/170781693 (accessed 14 July 2016).

Boal, F. (1995) *Shaping a City: Belfast in the Late Twentieth Century*. Queen's University Belfast, Institute of Irish Studies.

Boal, F. and R. Murray (1977) 'A city in conflict', *Geographical Magazine* 44: 364–371.

Bogaards, M. (2000) 'The uneasy relationship between empirical and normative types in consociational theory', *Journal of Theoretical Politics* 12(4): 395–424.

Bogaards, M., L. Helms and A. Lijphart (2019) 'The importance of consociationalism for twenty-first century politics and political science', *Swiss Political Science Review* 25(4): 341–356.

Boland, P., B. Murtagh and P. Shirlow (2016) 'Fashioning a city of culture: "life and place changing" or "12-month party?"', *International Journal of Cultural Policy* 25(2): 246–265.

Bollens, S. (2000) *On Narrow Ground: Urban Policy and Ethnic Conflict in Jerusalem and Belfast*. Albany: SUNY Press.

—— (2009) 'Intervening in politically turbulent cities: spaces, buildings, and boundaries', *Journal of Urban Technology* 16(2–3): 79–107.

Bou Akar, M. (2018) *For the War Yet to Come: Planning Beirut's Frontiers*. Stanford: Stanford University Press.

Bourdieu, P. (1990) *The Logic of Practice*. Translated by R. Nice. Stanford: Stanford University Press.

Bourdieu, P. and L. Wacquant (1992) *An Invitation to Reflexive Sociology*. Chicago: University of Chicago Press.

Bowcott, O. (2017) 'Unseated: the Sinn Féin MPs whose absence strengthens May's hand in Commons', *Guardian*, 13 June. Available at: https://www.theguardian.com/politics/2017/jun/13/sinn-fein-mps-house-of-commons-theresa-may-dup (accessed 19 December 2017).

Boyce G. and A. O'Day (eds) (2006) *The Ulster Crisis 1885–1921*. Basingstoke and New York: Palgrave Macmillan.

Bradley, C. and B. Murtagh (2007) *Good Practice in Local Area Planning in the Context of Promoting Good Relations*. Report for Belfast City Council Good Relations Research Programme, December. Belfast, Northern Ireland.

Brand, R. (2009) 'Urban artifacts and social practices in a contested city', *Journal of Urban Technology* 16(2–3): 35–60.

Breen-Smyth, M. (2008) 'Frameworks for peace in Northern Ireland: an analysis of the 1998 Belfast Agreement', *Strategic Analysis* 32(6): 1–23.

Brennan, S. (2021) 'From warrior regimes to illicit sovereigns: Ulster loyalist paramilitaries and the security implications for Brexit', *Small Wars & Insurgencies* 32(4–5): 747–771.

Brennan, S. and A. Edwards (2022) 'Alleviating the causes of direct and structural violence in Northern Ireland', *Peace Review* (0): 1–9.

Brett, D. (2004) 'Geologies of site and settlement', in N. Allen and A. Kelly (eds), *The Cities of Belfast*. Dublin: Four Courts, pp. 19–26.

Brewer, J.D. (2000) *Ethnography*. Buckingham: Open University Press.

Brinkerhoff, D. and A. Goldsmith (2002) *Clientelism, Patrimonialism and Democratic Governance: An Overview and Framework for Assessment and Programming*. Report, Abt Associates Inc.

Bruce, S. (2004) 'Turf war and peace: Loyalist paramilitaries since 2004', *Terrorism and Political Violence* 16(3): 501–521.

Bryan, D. (2000) *Orange Parades: The Politics of Ritual, Tradition and Control*. London: Pluto Press.

—— (2006) 'The politics of community', *Critical Review of International Social and Political Philosophy* 9(4): 603–617.

—— (2012) 'Titanic town: living in a landscape of conflict', in S.J. Connolly (ed.), *Belfast 400: People, Place and History*. Liverpool: Liverpool University Press, pp. 317–356.

Buchanan, C. et al. (2004) *Belfast City Masterplan*. Report for Belfast City Council, Belfast, Northern Ireland.

Buckland, P. (1981) *A History of Northern Ireland*. Dublin: Gill & Macmillan Ltd.

Building Design Partnership (BDP) (2007a) 'ARCrumlin sketchbook: Crumlin Road Gaol & Girdwood Barracks', presented to Girdwood Advisory Panel, 9 February. Belfast, Northern Ireland.

—— (2007b) *Crumlin Road Gaol & Girdwood Barracks Draft Masterplan*, July. Belfast, Northern Ireland.
Burgess, R. (1997) *In the Field: An Introduction to Field Research*. London: Routledge.
Burns, A. (2018) *Milkman*. London: Faber and Faber.
Burns, G. (2011a) 'Girdwood protest', *North Belfast News*, 28 September. Print.
—— (2011b) 'Girdwood protest continues', *North Belfast News*, 5 October. Print.
—— (2012) 'Site "was never going to solve North issues"', *North Belfast News*, 25 May. Available at: http://belfastmediagroup.com/site-was-never-going-to-solve-north-issues (accessed 16 July 2017).
Buro Happold (2005) *Crumlin Road Gaol Technical Feasibility and Development Potential Study*, March. Manchester, England.
Burrows, T. (2017) 'Legacy, what legacy? Five years on the London Olympic park battle still rages', *Guardian*, 27 July. Available at: https://www.theguardian.com/cities/2017/jul/27/london-olympic-park-success-five-years-depends (accessed 3 May 2022).
Burton, F. (1978) *The Politics of Legitimacy: Struggles in a Belfast Community*. London: Routledge and Kegan Paul.
—— (1979) 'Ideological social relations in Northern Ireland', *The British Journal of Sociology* 30(1): 61–80.
Byrne, J. (2009) 'Peace walls: a temporary measure', *History Ireland* 4. Available at: http://www.historyireland.com/20th-century-contemporary-history/peace-walls-a-temporary-measure (accessed 5 October 2016).
Byrne, J., C. Gormley-Heenan and G. Robinson (2012) *Attitudes to Peace Walls*. Report for Office of First Minister and Deputy First Minister. University of Ulster, Belfast, Northern Ireland.
Cadwallader, A. (2004) *Holy Cross: The Untold Story*. Belfast: Brehon.
Campbell, B. (2003) 'At the mercy of the mob', *Observer*, 1 December. Available at: https://www.theguardian.com/politics/2003/dec/01/northernireland.faithschools (accessed 21 November 2017).
Campus Community Regeneration Forum (2015) *Draft Campus Regeneration Plan*. Campus Community Regeneration Forum: Belfast, Northern Ireland.
Carroll, R. (2021) 'Brexit: Loyalist paramilitary groups renounce Good Friday agreement', *Guardian*, 4 March. Available at https://www.theguardian.com/uk-news/2021/mar/04/brexit-northern-ireland-loyalist-armies-renounce-good-friday-agreement (accessed 10 March 2022).
Carroll, R. and L. O'Carroll (2022) 'Sinn Féin celebrates victory but DUP warns over Northern Ireland protocol', *Guardian*, 7 May. Available at: https://www.theguardian.com/politics/2022/may/07/sinn-fein-celebrates-victory-but-dup-warns-over-northern-ireland-protocol (accessed 8 May 2022).
Carson, C. (1997) *The Star Factory*. New York: Arcade.
Cento Bull, A. and B. Jones (2006) 'Governance and social capital in urban regeneration: a comparison between Bristol and Naples', *Urban Studies* 43(4): 767–786.
Centre for Effective Services (CES) (2016) *Final Report: Evaluation of the United Youth Programme Pilot Phase, 2015–2016*, July. Department of the Economy, Northern Ireland.

The Charity Commission for Northern Ireland (2021) *Ashton Community Trust*. Available at: CharityDetails_104639_20220508144605.pdf (accessed 17 April 2022).

Charmaz, K. (2006) *Constructing Grounded Theory: A Practical Guide through Qualitative Analysis*. London: Sage Publications.

Cheek, J. (2004) 'At the margins? Discourse analysis and qualitative research', *Qualitative Health Research* 14(8): 1140–1150.

Chomsky, N. (2003) *Understanding Power*. New York: Vintage.

Clanmil Housing Group (2011) 'Social Clauses Initiative could create almost two thousand work placements', Clanmil Housing Group, 1 March. Available at: http://www.clanmil.org/newsdetail_front.php?id=202 (accessed 25 April 2016).

Clarke, P.W. (2003) 'The economic currency of architectural aesthetics', in A. Cuthbert (ed.), *Designing Cities: Critical Readings in Urban Design*. Malden: Blackwell, pp. 28–44.

Coakley, J. (2021) 'Is a middle force emerging in Northern Ireland?', *Irish Political Studies* 36(1): 29–35.

Coakley, J. and J. Garry (2016) 'Northern Ireland: the challenge of public opinion', *Queen's Policy Engagement*. Available at: http://qpol.qub.ac.uk/public-opinion-challenge-ni/ (accessed 22 May 2022).

Cochrane, F. and S. Dunn (2002) *People Power? The Role of the Voluntary and Community Sector in the Northern Ireland Conflict*. Cork: Cork University Press.

Cogent Management Consulting (2010) *Belfast City Council Girdwood Community Hub Economic Appraisal – Draft Final*. Report for the Special European Union Programmes Body.

Cohen, A. (1985) *The Symbolic Construction of Community*. Chichester: Ellis Horwood.

Committee on the Administration of Justice (CAJ) (2006) *Equality in Northern Ireland: The Rhetoric and the Reality*. Belfast: Shanways Press.

Communities NI (2020) *Knowledge and Use of Irish in Northern Ireland: Findings from the Continuous Household Survey 2019/20*. Report by NISRA and Department of Communities. Available at: https://www.communities-ni.gov.uk/system/files/publications/communities/knowledge-and-use-of-irish-in-northern-ireland-201920.pdf.

Community Foundation for Northern Ireland (CFNI) (2017) *The Paralysis of Parochialism: Research Project*, August. Belfast, Northern Ireland.

Conflict Archive on the Internet (CAIN) (2003) *RUC/PSNI Statistics: Table NI-SEC-05: Persons Injured (Number) Due to the Security Situation in Northern Ireland (Only), 1969 to 2003*. Available at http://cain.ulster.ac.uk/ni/security.htm#05 (accessed 3 March 2022).

Connolly, P., B. Kelly and A. Smith (2009) 'Ethnic habitus and young children: a case study of Northern Ireland', *European Early Childhood Education Research Journal* 17(2): 217–232.

Connolly, S.J. and G. McIntosh (2012a) 'Imagining Belfast', in S.J. Connolly (ed.), *Belfast 400: People, Place and History*. Liverpool: Liverpool University Press, pp. 13–62.

—— (2012b) 'Whose city? Belonging and exclusion in the nineteenth century urban world', in S.J. Connolly (ed.), *Belfast 400. People, Place and History*. Liverpool: Liverpool University Press, pp. 237–270.
Conradh na Gaeilge (2017) *Acht na Gaeilge: Pléchaipéis/Irish Language Act: Discussion Document*, 15 March. Conradh na Gaeilge. Available at: https://cnag.ie/en/get-involved/current-campaigns/irish-language-act.html (accessed 15 October 2017).
Conroy, J. (2001) *Unspeakable Acts, Ordinary People: The Dynamics of Torture*. Oakland: University of California Press.
Corr, S. (2022) 'Belfast housing crisis: family takes council to court fight over plans to rezone 25 acre Mackies site', *Belfast Live*, 25 May. Available at: https://www.belfastlive.co.uk/news/northern-ireland/belfast-housing-crisis-family-takes-24059482 (accessed 27 May 2022).
Cosstick, V. (2015) *Belfast: Towards a City Without Walls*. Newtownards: Colourpoint.
Coulter, C. (2014) 'Under which constitutional arrangement would you still prefer to be unemployed? Neoliberalism, the peace process, and the politics of class in Northern Ireland', *Studies in Conflict & Terrorism* 37(9): 763–776.
Council of the European Union (2022) *Agreement on the withdrawal of the United Kingdom of Great Britain and Northern Ireland from the European Union and the European Atomic Energy Community*. Available at: https://eur-lex.europa.eu/legal-content/EN/TXT/?uri=CELEX:02020W/TXT-20220222 (accessed 23 May 2022).
Cresswell, P. (2004) *Place: An Introduction*. Oxford: Wiley-Blackwell.
Cromie, C. (2013) 'Stormont MLA Robin Newton's family earn 800,000 of public cash – Stormont urged to tighten rules', *Belfast Telegraph*, 27 September. Available at: http://www.belfasttelegraph.co.uk/news/northern-ireland/stormont-mla-robin-newtons-family-earn-800000-of-public-cash-stormont-urged-to-tighten-rules-29614029.html (accessed 29 April 2017).
Crumlin Road Courthouse Ltd. (2006) *Communication by letter to North Belfast Community Action Unit*, 6 March. Print. Girdwood Advisory Panel Meeting Minutes (held by Elizabeth DeYoung).
Davidson, M. and L. Lees (2005) 'New-build "gentrification" and London's riverside renaissance', *Environment and Planning: A* 37: 1165–1190.
de Baróid, C. (2000) *Ballymurphy and the Irish War*. London: Pluto Press.
de Certeau, M. (1984) *The Practice of Everyday Life*. Translated by S. Rendall. Berkeley: University of California Press.
Deloitte (2007) *Strategic Regeneration Framework: North Belfast*. Report for Department of Social Development. Belfast, Northern Ireland.
Dempster, S. (2017) 'Charter NI: Speaker is alleged to have misled NI Assembly', BBC News, 10 October. Available at: http://www.bbc.co.uk/news/uk-northern-ireland-41574198 (accessed 10 October 2017).
Department of Communities (2017) *Building Successful Communities*. Available at: https://www.communities-ni.gov.uk/topics/housing/building-successful-communities (accessed 21 September 2017).
Department of the Environment (DOE) (2004a) *Belfast Metropolitan Area Plan (DBMAP) 2015 Draft Plan*. Belfast, Northern Ireland.

—— (2004b) *Belfast Metropolitan Area Plan (BMAP) 2015 Draft Plan: Technical Supplement I: Population and Housing (3)*. Northern Ireland Housing Executive. Belfast, Northern Ireland.

Department for Social Development (DSD) (2003) *People and Place: A Strategy for Neighbourhood Renewal*. Available at: https://www.communities-ni.gov.uk/publications/neighbourhood-renewal-people-and-place (accessed 15 April 2016).

—— (2006) 'Update statement from Roy Adams, Chair of advisory panel for the former Crumlin Road Jail and Girdwood Barracks', 20 October. Belfast, Northern Ireland.

—— (2008) *Public Consultation: Draft Equality Impact Assessment, Crumlin Road Goal and Girdwood Park Draft Masterplan*. Belfast, Northern Ireland.

—— (2009a) *Crumlin Road (Including Lower Oldpark): 'A New Quarter for the City'*. Report for Department for Social Development, RPS and Jon Rowland Urban Design. Belfast, Northern Ireland.

—— (2009b) *Lower Shankill: A New High Street Serving a Confident Community*. Report for Department for Social Development, RPS and Jon Rowland Urban Design. Belfast, Northern Ireland.

—— (2012) *Facing the Future: The Housing Strategy for Northern Ireland 2012-2017*. Belfast, Northern Ireland.

—— (2013a) *Northern Ireland Empty Homes Strategy and Action Plan 2013-2018*. Belfast, Northern Ireland.

—— (2013b) '25 million investment provides homes for 26 families in Lower Oldpark', *Belfast Telegraph*, October 24. Available at: http://www.belfasttelegraph.co.uk/debateni/press-feed/25-million-investment-provides-homes-for-26-families-in-lower-oldpark-mccausland-29698248.html (accessed 6 January 2017).

——(2013c) *Belfast: Northside Development Brief*. Produced for Deloitte, February. Available at: https://www.yumpu.com/en/document/read/39597527/bcc-northside-developer-brief (accessed 18 July 2023).

—— (2015) *Inner North Neighbourhood Renewal Partnership Revised Action Plan: March 2015-April 2016*. Belfast, Northern Ireland.

Derry City and Strabane District Council (2014) *Post Project Evaluation of City of Culture 2013*. Available at: https://warwick.ac.uk/about/cityofculture/researchresources/derry_eval.pdf (accessed 16 May 2022).

DeYoung, E. (2016) 'Lest we forget: observations from Belfast's Twaddell Avenue', *Streetnotes Section II: Mosaics of Spectacle and Resistance* 25: 179-193.

—— (2018) 'Recalling or suggesting phantoms: walking in West Belfast', in M. Svašek and M. Komarova (eds), *Ethnographies of Movement, Sociality and Space: Place-Making in the New Northern Ireland*. New York: Berghahn, pp. 85-107.

Dillon, M. and D. Lehane (1973) *Political Murder in Northern Ireland*. Harmondsworth: Penguin.

Dixon, P. (2002) 'Political skills or lying and manipulation? The choreography of the Northern Ireland peace process', *Political Studies* 50: 725-741.

—— (2011) 'Is consociational theory the answer to global conflict? From the Netherlands to Northern Ireland and Iraq', *Political Studies Review* 9(3): 309-322.

Docerty, I., R. Goodlad and R. Paddison (2001) 'Civic culture, community, and citizen participation in contrasting neighbourhoods', *Urban Studies* 38(12): 2225–2250.

Donnelly, K. (2011) *The Transfer of Former Military & Security Sites to the Northern Ireland Executive*. Report, Northern Ireland Audit Office. Belfast, Northern Ireland.

Doyle, S. (2016) 'West Belfast: massive vote sees Gerry Carroll top the poll', *Irish News*, 6 May. Available at: http://www.irishnews.com/news/assemblyelection/2016/05/07/news/west-belfast-massive-vote-sees-gerry-carroll-top-the-poll-511855/ (accessed 27 December 2017).

Duffy, K. and J. Hutchison (1997) 'Urban policy and the turn to communities', *Town Planning Review* 68: 347–362.

The Economist (2013) 'Civil wars: how to stop the fighting – sometimes', 10 November. Available at: http://www.economist.com/news/briefing/21589431-bringing-end-conflicts-within-states-vexatious-history-provides-guide (accessed 5 January 2015).

Edensor, T. (2010) 'Walking in rhythms: place, regulation, style and the flow of experience', *Visual Studies* 25(1): 69–79.

Edgar, D. and E. Flanagan (2022) 'DUP: NI First Minister Paul Givan announces resignation', BBC News NI, 3 February. Available at: https://www.bbc.com/news/uk-60241608 (accessed 8 May 2022).

Edwards, A. (2017) *UVF behind the Mask*. Kildare: Merrion Press.

Edwards, J. (1997) 'Urban policy: the victory of form over substance', *Urban Studies* 34: 825–843.

Electoral Office for Northern Ireland (2019) 'UK Parliamentary Election Result 2019 – Belfast North'. Available at: https://www.eoni.org.uk/Elections/Election-results-and-statistics/Election-results-and-statistics-2003-onwards/Elections-2019/UK-Parliamentary-Election-Result-2019-Belfast-Nort (accessed 19 November 2022).

Ellidge, J. (2016) 'On the joys of being lost in a new city', *CityMetrics*, 26 September. Available at: http://www.citymetric.com/horizons/joys-being-lost-new-city-2470 (accessed 29 September 2016).

Elliott, M. (2017) *Hearthlands: A Memoir of the White City Housing Estate in Belfast*. Newtownards: Blackstaff.

Emerson, R., L. Fretz and L. Shaw (1995) *Writing Ethnographic Fieldnotes*. Chicago: University of Chicago Press.

English, R. (2004) *Armed Struggle: The Secret History of the IRA*. London: Pan McMillan.

Equality Commission for Northern Ireland (ECNI) (2005) *Section 75 of the Northern Ireland Act 1998: Practical Guidance on Equality Impact Assessment*. Belfast, Northern Ireland.

—— (2010) *Section 75 of the Northern Ireland Act 1998: A Guide for Public Authorities*. Belfast, Northern Ireland.

—— (2012a) *Response to Department of Social Development Consultation: 'Facing the Future: Northern Ireland Housing Strategy 2012–17'*. Belfast, Northern Ireland.

—— (2012b) *Section 75 of the Northern Ireland Act 1998: A Guide for Public Authorities: An Outline Guide*. Belfast, Northern Ireland.

—— (2014) *Proposed Investigation under Paragraph 11 of Schedule 9 of the Northern Ireland Act 1998: Department for Social Development*, April. Belfast, Northern Ireland.

—— (2015) *Investigation Report under Schedule 9 of the Northern Ireland Act 1998 Department for Social Development: Housing Policy Proposals*, November. Belfast, Northern Ireland.

—— (2017a) *Equality in Housing and Communities: Draft Policy Recommendations*. Belfast, Northern Ireland.

—— (2017b) *Statement on Key Inequalities in Housing and Communities in Northern Ireland: Full Statement*, April. Belfast, Northern Ireland.

—— (2018) *Equal to the Task? Investigative Powers and Effective Enforcement of the 'Section 75' Equality Duty*, January. Report, Belfast, Northern Ireland.

Evans, J. and J. Tonge (2009) 'Social class and party choice in Northern Ireland's ethnic blocs', *West European Politics* 32(5): 1012–1030.

Evershed, J. (2018) *Ghosts of the Somme: Commemoration and Culture War in Northern Ireland*. Notre Dame: University of Notre Dame Press.

Evershed, J. and M. Murphy (2021) 'An bhfuil ár lá tagtha? Sinn Féin, special status and the politics of Brexit', *The British Journal of Politics and International Relations* 24(2): 243–258.

Family Support Northern Ireland (2017) *Ashton Community Trust – New Lodge Youth Centre*. Available at: http://www.familysupportni.gov.uk/listing/ashton-community-trust-new-lodge-youth-centre/ (accessed 21 August 2017).

Faul, Fr. D. and Fr. R. Murray (1972) *British Army and Special Branch RUC Brutalities: December 1971–February 1972*. Dungannon and Armagh, Northern Ireland.

—— (n.d.) *The RUC: The Black and Blue Book*. Dungannon and Armagh, Northern Ireland. Available at: https://cain.ulster.ac.uk/issues/police/docs/faul.htm (accessed 24 February 2022).

Feldman, A. (1991) *Formations of Violence: The Narrative of the Body and Political Terror in Northern Ireland*. Chicago: University of Chicago Press.

Fetterman, D.M. (2010) *Ethnography Step-by-Step*. Thousand Oaks: Sage.

Fiacc, P. (1994) *Ruined Pages: Selected Poems*. Belfast: Blackstaff.

Finlayson, A. (2007) 'From beliefs to arguments: interpretive methodology and rhetorical political analysis', *British Journal of Politics and International Relations* 9: 545–563.

Fitzduff, M. and L. O'Hagan (2009) *The Northern Ireland Troubles: INCORE Background Paper*. CAIN Web Service. Available at: https://cain.ulster.ac.uk/othelem/incorepaper09.htm#dates (accessed 5 May 2022).

Fitzmaurice, M. (2020) 'Girdwood residents subjected to 15 nights of trouble, community worker says', *Belfast Live*, 3 October. Available at: https://www.belfastlive.co.uk/news/belfast-news/girdwood-residents-subjected-15-nights-19040555 (accessed 18 December 2021).

Flynn, M.K. (2011) 'Decision-making and contested heritage in Northern Ireland: the former Maze Prison/Long Kesh', *Irish Political Studies* 26(3): 383–401.

Flyvbjerg, B. (1998) *Rationality and Power: Democracy in Practice*. Translated by S. Sampson. Chicago: University of Chicago Press.

Foley, F. and G. Robinson (2004) *Politicians and Community Relations in Northern Ireland*. Derry: INCORE.

Forester, J. (2001) *The Deliberative Practitioner: Encouraging Participatory Planning Processes*. Cambridge, MA: MIT Press.

Forum for Alternative Belfast (2009) *Missing City Map*. Belfast: Belfast Conflict Resolution Consortium.

Foucault, M. (1980) *Power/Knowledge: Selected Interviews and Other Writings 1972–1977*. Translated by C. Gordon. New York: Pantheon Books.

Fullilove, M. (2004) *Root Shock: How Tearing up City Neighborhoods Hurts America, and What We Can Do About It*. New York: New Village Press.

—— (2014) 'Jane Jacobs, Jim Crow and the madness of borders', in S. Hirst and D. Zahm (eds), *The Urban Wisdom of Jane Jacobs*. London: Routledge, pp. 122–135.

Gaffikin, F. and Morrissey, M. (1999) 'Understanding the contemporary city', in F. Gaffikin and M. Morrisey (eds), *City Visions: Imagining Place, Enfranchising People*. London: Pluto Press, pp. 3–33.

Gaffikin, F., M. Mceldowney and K. Sterrett (2010) 'Creating shared public space in the contested city: the role of urban design', *Journal of Urban Design* 15(4): 493–513.

Gallaher, C. and P. Shirlow (2006) 'The geography of loyalist paramilitary feuding in Belfast', *Space and Polity* 10(2): 149–169.

Geertz, C. (1973) *The Interpretation of Cultures: Selected Essays*. New York: Basic Books, Inc.

Gessen, M. (2019) 'Ireland's strange, cruel system for asylum seekers', *New Yorker*, 4 June. Available at: https://www.newyorker.com/news/dispatch/irelands-strange-cruel-system-for-asylum-seekers (accessed 7 September 2022).

Ghanem, A. (2009) 'Democratizing "ethnic states": the democratization process in divided societies – with a special reference to Israel', *Constellations* 16(3): 462–475.

Gieryn, T. (2000) 'A space for place in sociology', *Annual Review of Sociology* 26: 463–496.

Gilligan, C. (2009) 'Insecurity and community relations: vulnerability and the protests at the Holy Cross Girls Primary School in Belfast', in P. Noxolo and J. Huysmans (eds), *Community Citizenship and the 'War on Terror'*. London: Palgrave, pp. 32–50.

Girdwood Advisory Panel (2006a) 'Issues and aspirations', 4 April. Belfast, Northern Ireland.

—— (2006b) *Crumlin Road Gaol and Girdwood Park Development Brief*. Belfast, Northern Ireland.

—— (2006c) 'Crumlin Road Gaol/Girdwood Park Advisory Panel meeting minutes', 13 October. Belfast, Northern Ireland.

—— (2006d) 'Shared future: "living theme" feedback from breakout group discussion', 13 October. Belfast, Northern Ireland.

—— (2007a) Crumlin Road Gaol/Girdwood Park Advisory Panel meeting minutes, 20 April. Belfast, Northern Ireland.
—— (2007b) Crumlin Road Gaol/Girdwood Park Advisory Panel meeting minutes, 9 February. Belfast, Northern Ireland.
—— (2007c) Crumlin Road Gaol/Girdwood Park Advisory Panel meeting minutes, 18 May. Belfast, Northern Ireland.
Girdwood Advisory Panel Secretariat (2006) *Draft Masterplan Terms of Reference*, February. Belfast, Northern Ireland.
Girdwood Community Forum (2015a) 'Meeting minutes', 26 February. Vine Centre, Belfast, Northern Ireland.
—— (2015b) 'Community management working group meeting minutes', 21 October. Vine Centre, Belfast, Northern Ireland.
Givetash, L. (2019) 'Journalist Lyra McKee shot dead in Londonderry, Northern Ireland', NBC News. Available at: https://www.nbcnews.com/news/world/journalist-lyra-mckee-fatally-shot-during-northern-ireland-riot-n996241 (accessed 2 May 2022).
Gordon, G. (2017) 'DUP launches manifesto with "Sinn Féin victory warning"', BBC News, 20 February. Available at: http://www.bbc.co.uk/news/uk-northern-ireland-39030276 (accessed 20 February 2017).
Gormley-Heenan, C., J. Byrne and G. Robinson (2013) 'The Berlin Walls of Belfast', *British Politics* 8: 357–382.
Gormley-Heenan, C. and R. MacGinty (2008) 'Ethnic outbidding and party modernization: understanding the Democratic Unionist Party's electoral success in the post-Agreement environment', *Ethnopolitics* 7(1): 43–61.
Gray, D. (2014) *Doing Research in the Real World*. London: Sage.
Greenwich Leisure Limited (GLL) (2014) 'New operators of Belfast leisure facilities revealed', *GLL News*, 22 December. Available at: http://www.gll.org/b2b/newsitems/new-operators-of-belfast-leisure-facilities-revealed (accessed 17 September 2016).
—— (2017) 'Girdwood Community Hub: membership and pricing'. Available at: https://www.better.org.uk/leisure-centre/belfast/girdwood/memberships (accessed 27 April 2017).
Gregory, I., N. Cunningham, P. Ell, C. Lloyd and I. Shuttleworth (2013) *Troubled Geographies: A Spatial History of Religion and Society in Ireland*. Bloomington: Indiana University Press.
Guelke, A. (2019) 'Institutionalised power-sharing: the international dimension', *Ethnopolitics* 19(1): 92–95.
Gustafson, P. (2001) 'Roots and routes: exploring the relationship between place attachment and mobility', *Environment and Behaviour* 33(5): 667–688.
Hall, M. (1994) *Ulster's Protestant Working Class: A Community Exploration*. Newtownabbey: Island Publications.
—— (2015a) *A Process of Analysis (1): The Protestant/Unionist/Loyalist Community*. Belfast: Island Publications/FARSET.
—— (2015b) *A Process of Analysis (2): The Catholic/Nationalist/Republican Community*. Belfast: Island Publications/FARSET.

Hall, T., B. Lashua and A. Coffey (2006) 'Stories as sorties', *Qualitative Researcher* 3(1): 2–4.

Hallsworth, S. and D. Brotherton (2011) *Urban Disorder and Gangs: A Critique and a Warning*. London: Runnymede.

Hamill, H. (2010) *The Hoods: Crime and Punishment in Belfast*. Princeton: Princeton University Press.

Hanley, L. (2007) *Estates: An Intimate History*. London: Granta.

Hansard (2009) 'Committee for the Office of the First Minister and Deputy First Minister: Maze/Long Kesh Development Corporation', 14 October. Northern Ireland Assembly. Available at: www.niassembly.gov.uk/assembly ... / mazelong-kesh-development-corporation/ (accessed 21 December 2017).

—— (2010) 'Northern Ireland Assembly debate: Girdwood Barracks site', 9 February. Northern Ireland Assembly. Available at: https://www.theyworkforyou.com/ni/?id=2010-02-09.5.23 (accessed 15 December 2016).

—— (2011) 'Northern Ireland Assembly: official report 68(6)', 15 November. Available at: http://www.niassembly.gov.uk/assembly-business/official-report/reports-11-12/15-november-2011/#5 (accessed 15 December 2016).

—— (2012a) 'Personal accounts committee: inquiry into the transfer of former military and security sites to the Northern Ireland Executive' 25 April. Available at: http://www.niassembly.gov.uk/assembly-business/official-report/committee-minutes-of-evidence/session-2011-2012/april-2012/inquiry-into-the-transfer-of-former-military-and-security-sites-to-the-northern-ireland-executive-/ (accessed 14 October 2016).

—— (2012b) 'Northern Ireland Assembly: official report 75(6)', 12 June. Available at: http://www.niassembly.gov.uk/assembly-business/official-report/reports-11-12/ (accessed 21 December 2017).

—— (2014a) 'Northern Ireland Assembly: official report 92(3)', 24 February. Available at: http://www.niassembly.gov.uk/assembly-business/official-report/reports-13-14/24-february-2014/ (accessed 11 November 2016).

—— (2014b) 'Northern Ireland Assembly debate: social housing, North Belfast', 13 May. Available at: http://www.theyworkforyou.com/ni/?id=2014-05-13.5.1 (accessed 1 December 2015).

—— (2016a) 'Northern Ireland Assembly: official report 118(2)', 6 December. Available at: https://data.niassembly.gov.uk/HansardXml/plenary-06-12-2016.pdf (accessed 13 December 2016).

—— (2016b) 'Northern Ireland Assembly: official report 122(3)', 19 December. Available at: http://aims.niassembly.gov.uk/officialreport/report.aspx?&eveDate=2016/12/19&docID=286438 (accessed 22 December 2016).

Harris, R. (1972) *Prejudice and Tolerance in Ulster: A Study of Neighbours and 'Strangers' in a Border Community*. Manchester: Manchester University Press.

Harvey, D. (1996) *Justice, Nature and the Geography of Difference*. Oxford: Wiley-Blackwell.

—— (2009) *Social Justice and the City* (rev. ed.). Athens: University of Georgia Press.

—— (2012) *Rebel Cities: From the Right to the City to the Urban Revolution*. New York: Verso.

Haughton, G. (ed.) (1999) *Community Economic Development.* London: The Stationary Office with the Regional Studies Association.

Hawthorne, J. (2016) 'Engaging with communities at risk'. Paper presented at Leadership Academy Seminar Series, 26 January. Centre for Democracy and Peacebuilding and Institute of Irish Studies, University of Liverpool, London.

Hayward, K. (2008) 'The role of political discourse in conflict transformation: evidence from Northern Ireland', *Peace and Conflict Studies* 15(1): 1–20.

—— (2012) 'Negative silence: the unspoken future of Northern Ireland', *Nordic Irish Studies* 11(2): 21–38.

Hayward, K. and M. Komarova (2014) 'The limits of local accommodation: why contentious events remain prone to conflict in Northern Ireland', *Studies in Conflict and Terrorism*, 37(9): 777–791.

Hayward, K. and C. Mitchell (2003) 'Discourses of equality in post-Agreement Northern Ireland', *Contemporary Politics* 9(3): 293–312.

Hayward, K. and M. Murphy (2018) 'The EU's influence on the peace process and agreement in Northern Ireland in light of Brexit', *Ethnopolitics* 17(3): 276–291.

Heatley, C. (2004) *Interface: Flashpoints in Northern Ireland.* Belfast: Lagan Books. Available at: http://cain.ulst.ac.uk/issues/interface/docs/heatley04.htm (accessed 10 April 2016).

Hennessey, T. and R. Wilson (1997) *With All Due Respect: Pluralism and Parity of Esteem.* Report No. 7, *Democratic Dialogue.* Belfast, Northern Ireland. Available at: http://cain.ulst.ac.uk/dd/report7/report7a.htm (accessed 5 February 2017).

Hepburn, A. (1996) *A Past Apart: Studies in the History of Catholic Belfast 1850–1950.* Belfast: Ulster Historical Foundation.

Hewitt, R. (2021) 'Threat forces Larne port worker to move home', *Belfast Telegraph*, 1 April. https://www.belfasttelegraph.co.uk/news/northern-ireland/threat-forces-larne-port-worker-to-move-home-40262853.html (accessed 21 April 2022).

Higson, B. (2008) 'Anti-consociationalism and the Good Friday Agreement: a rejoinder', *Journal of Peace, Conflict and Development* 12: 1–17.

Hirst, M. (2021) 'NI riots: what is behind the violence in Northern Ireland?', BBC News NI, 14 April. Available at https://www.bbc.com/news/uk-northern-ireland-56664378 (accessed 21 April 2022).

Hocking, B. (2015) *The Great Reimagining: Public Art, Urban Space and the Symbolic Landscape of a 'New' Northern Ireland.* Oxford: Berghahn.

Holgersen, S. and G. Baeten (2017) 'Beyond a liberal critique of "trickle down": urban planning in the city of Malmö', *International Journal of Urban and Regional Research* 40(6): 1170–1185.

Horgan, G., A.M. Gray and C. Conlon (2010) *Young People Not in Education Employment or Training.* ARK Policy Brief No. 3, December. Belfast, Northern Ireland.

Howard, L.M. (2012) 'The ethnocracy trap', *Journal of Democracy* 23(4): 155–169.

Howell, J. and E. Griffiths (2018) *Gangs in America's Communities.* New York: Sage.

Hughes, B. (2016) 'More have died by suicide than were killed during Troubles', *Irish News*, 11 January. Available at: http://www.irishnews.com/news/2016/01/11/news/

more-have-died-by-suicide-that-were-killed-during-troubles-378739 (accessed 1 August 2017).

—— (2017) 'RHI: DUP advisers' relatives joined scheme shortly before payments capped', *Irish News*, 18 March. Available at: http://www.irishnews.com/news/2017/03/18/news/rhi-dup-advisers-relatives-joined-scheme-shortly-before-payments-capped-968679/ (accessed 18 March 2017).

Independent Reporting Commission (IRC) (2021) *Fourth Report*, December. Available at: https://www.ircommission.org/sites/irc/files/media-files/IRC%20Fourth%20Report%20web%20accessible_0.pdf (accessed 21 April 2022).

International Fund for Ireland (IFI) (2012) 'Launch of "Bridging the Interface Project" brings together North Belfast community groups', 16 June. Available at: https://www.internationalfundforireland.com/media-centre/96-press-releases-2012/485-launch-of-bridging-the-interface-project-brings-together-north-belfast-community-groups (accessed 26 June 2017).

The Institute of Irish Studies and The Irish News (2022) *Opinion Poll*. University of Liverpool. Available at: https://www.liverpool.ac.uk/media/livacuk/humanitiesampsocialsciences/documents/Institute,of,Irish,Studies,Irish,News,Poll,March,2022.pdf (accessed 8 May 2022).

Irish News (1993a) 'Victims of war without mercy', Special Investigation: Where Death Stalks Streets, 25 January.

—— (1993b) '25 dead in most dangerous street in the north', Special Investigation: Where Death Stalks Streets, 26 January.

—— (1993c) 'Records are made to be broken in despair', Special Investigation: Where Death Stalks Streets, 28 January.

—— (2017a) 'Paul Givan reverses cuts to Irish language scheme', 12 January. Available at: https://www.irishnews.com/news/northernirelandnews/2017/01/12/news/paul-givan-reverses-cuts-to-irish-language-scheme-882006/ (accessed 28 December 2017).

Irish Republican News (2012) 'Belfast housing plan linked to H-Block project', 31 May. Available at: http://republican-news.org/current/news/2012/05/belfast_housing_plan_linked_to.html (accessed 21 December 2017).

Irish Times (2005) 'British army to leave battered Belfast barracks', 23 February. Available at: https://www.irishtimes.com/news/british-army-to-leave-battered-belfast-barracks-1.1297061 (accessed 31 July 2017).

Jacobs, B. (1992) *Fractured Cities: Capitalism, Community and Empowerment in Britain and America*. London: Routledge.

Jacobs, J. (1961) *The Death and Life of Great American Cities*. New York: Random House.

Jacobs, J. and R. Fincher (1998) *Cities of Difference*. New York: Guildford Press.

Jarman, N. (1996) 'Week of 12 July, Torrens area', in N. Jarman (ed.), *On the Edge: Community Perspectives on the Civil Disturbances in North Belfast, June–September 1996*. Available at: http://cain.ulst.ac.uk/cdc/edge/jarman96a.htm (accessed 7 October 2017).

—— (1997) *Material Conflicts: Parades and Visual Displays in Northern Ireland*. Oxford: Berg.

—— (2002) *Managing Disorder: Responding to Interface Violence in North Belfast*. Belfast: Office of the First Minister and Deputy First Minister.

—— (2004) *Demography, Development and Disorder: Changing Patterns of Interface Areas*. Belfast: Institute of Conflict Research.

—— (2008) 'Security and segregation: interface barriers in Belfast', *Shared Space* 6: 21–34.

Jenkins, R. (1983) *Lads, Citizens and Ordinary Kids: Working-Class Youth Lifestyles in Belfast*. London: Routledge and Kegan Paul.

The Journal (2019) 'Sinn Féin's John Finucane shocks DUP with victory over Nigel Dodds in North Belfast', 13 December. Available at: https://www.thejournal.ie/sinn-fein-john-finucane-dup-belfast-4931417-Dec2019/ (accessed 7 May 2022).

Kelly, B. (2012) 'Neoliberal Belfast: disaster ahead?', *Irish Marxist Review* 1(2): 44–59.

—— (2013) 'Northern Ireland: the left, sectarian resurgence and the national question today', *Irish Marxist Review* 2(8): 48–56.

Keenan, D. (2013) '430,000 who throng Derry for *fleadh* see "a city transformed"', *Irish Times*, 18 August. Available at: https://www.irishtimes.com/culture/430-000-who-throng-derry-for-fleadh-see-a-city-transformed-1.1498092 (accessed 8 May 2018).

Kelleher, W. (2004) *The Troubles in Ballybogoin: Memory and Identity in Northern Ireland*. Ann Arbor: University of Michigan Press.

Kennally, D. and E. Preston (1971) *Belfast August 1971: A Case to Be Answered*. CAIN Web Service. Available at: http://cain.ulst.ac.uk/events/intern/docs/kennally71a.htm (accessed 8 March 2016).

Ketola, M. and C. Hughes (2016) *Independence of Purpose, Voice, Action: Independence of the Voluntary, Community and Social Enterprise Sector in Northern Ireland*. Report by Building Change Trust and Ulster University. Belfast, Northern Ireland.

Kintrea, K. et al. (2008) *Young People and Territoriality in British Cities*. Report, Joseph Rowntree Foundation, York.

Kitchen, R. and K. Lysaght (2002) 'Queering Belfast: Some thoughts on the sexing of space: working paper no 19', National Institute for Regional and Spatial Analysis. National University of Ireland, Maynooth.

Kleinfield, M. (2005) 'Destabilizing the identity-territory nexus: rights-based discourse in Sri Lanka's new political geography', *GeoJournal* 64: 287–295.

Knox, C. (2001) 'Establishing research legitimacy in the contested political ground of contemporary Northern Ireland', *Qualitative Research* 1(2): 205–222.

—— (2011) 'Cohesion, sharing, and integration in Northern Ireland', *Environment and Planning C: Government and Policy* 29(1): 548–566.

—— (2014) 'Northern Ireland: where is the peace dividend?', *Policy & Politics* 44(3): 485–503.

Komarova, M. (2008) 'Shared space in Belfast and the limits of *A Shared Future*: working paper no. 3', Conflict in City and the Contested State Working Paper Series. UK Economic and Social Research Council.

Landler, M. (2022) 'As Britain Turned Away From E.U., Northern Ireland Turned to Sinn Fein', *New York Times*, 7 May. Available at: https://www.nytimes.com/2022/05/07/world/europe/northern-ireland-sinn-fein.html#:~:text=%E2%80%9CToday%20ushers%20in%20a%20new,become%20the%20region's%20first%20minister (accessed 7 May 2022).

Lash, S. and J. Urry (1994) *Economies of Signs and Spaces*. London: Sage.

Lederach, J.P. (2015) 'Foreword', in V. Cosstick, *Belfast: Towards a City Without Walls*. Newtownards: Colourpoint, pp. 11–17.

Lefebvre, H. (1991) *The Production of Space*. Translated by D. Nicholson-Smith. Malden: Blackwell.

Leonard, P. (2014) *What Is a Community?* Short film. Available at: https://www.youtube.com/watch?v=MRzpOmpWZuU (accessed 12 October 2015).

Leonard, V. (2017) 'Catholics waiting six months longer to be housed than Protestants in Northern Ireland – report', *Belfast Telegraph*, 20 June. Available at: http://www.belfasttelegraph.co.uk/news/northern-ireland/catholics-waiting-six-months-longer-to-be-housed-than-protestants-in-northern-ireland-report-35844276.html (accessed 1 August 2017).

Libreri, S. (2020) 'Brexit "opportunity of a lifetime" for Irish unity: McDonald', *RTE*, 31 January. Available at: https://www.rte.ie/news/campaign-daily/2020/0131/1112204-sinn-fein-unity/ (accessed 23 May 2022).

Liggett, M. (2017) *Social Capital's Imagined Benefits in Ardoyne Electoral Ward*. PhD thesis, University of Liverpool. Available at: https://livrepository.liverpool.ac.uk/3009269/

Lijphart, A. (1971) 'Cultural diversity and theories of political integration', *Canadian Journal of Political Science* 4(1): 1–14.

Lofland, J. and L.H. Lofland (1984) *Analysing Social Settings: A Guide to Qualitative Observation and Analysis*. Belmont: Wadsworth.

Lord Alderdice, J. McBurney and M. McWilliams (2016) *The Fresh Start Panel Report on the Disbandment of Paramilitary Groups in Northern Ireland*, May. Report for Northern Ireland Executive. Belfast, Northern Ireland.

Low, S. and D. Lawrence-Zúñiga (2003) 'Locating culture', in S. Low and D. Lawrence-Zúñiga (eds), *The Anthropology of Space and Place: Locating Culture*. Oxford: Blackwell, pp. 1–48.

Lower Oldpark Community Association (LOCA) (2012) 'News and updates: re-naming the playpark'. Available at: http://www.locacentre.co.uk/news/view/re-naming-the-playpark (accessed 24 April 2016).

Lower Oldpark Community Association and CCRF (2015) 'Girdwood meeting minutes', 26 January. Vine Centre, Belfast, Northern Ireland.

Lundy, P. and M. McGovern (2005) *Community, 'Truth Telling' and Conflict Resolution. A Critical Evaluation of the Role of Community-Based 'Truth Telling Processes' for Post-Conflict Transition: A Case Study of the Ardoyne Commemoration Project*. Report for Community Relations Council. Belfast, Northern Ireland.

Lysaght, K. and A. Basten (2003) 'Violence, fear and the everyday: negotiating spatial practices in the city of Belfast', in E. Stanko (ed.), *The Meaning of Violence*. London: Routledge, pp. 224–244.

Mac Bride, D. (2008) *Good Practice in Conflict Transformation*. Report, Mac Bride International for Belfast City Council. Belfast, Northern Ireland.

Mac Giolla Bhéin, C. (2022) 'An Dream Dearg and the continued power of activism', *Slugger O'Toole*, 21 May. Available at: https://www.sluggerotoole.com/2022/05/21/an-dream-dearg-and-the-continued-power-of-activism/ (accessed 27 May 2022).

MacGinty, R. (1998) 'The Irish Peace Process - Background Briefing', CAIN Web Service. Available at: https://cain.ulster.ac.uk/events/peace/bac.htm (accessed 23 July 2023).

Mallie, E. (2017) 'How Arlene Foster helped nationalism find its teeth', *Irish Times*, 4 September. Available at: https://www.irishtimes.com/news/politics/how-arlene-foster-helped-nationalism-find-its-teeth-1.3208198 (accessed 5 September 2017).

Manley, J. (2016) 'Arlene Foster has "no regrets" over being pictured with a UDA commander', *Irish News*, 29 October. Available at: http://www.irishnews.com/news/2016/10/29/news/arlene-foster-has-no-regrets-over-being-pictured-with-a-uda-commander-760193/ (accessed 17 September 2017).

Marijan, B. and S. Brennan (2016) 'Paramilitary violence and policing in Northern Ireland', *CSI Insights: Selected Blog Posts from the SSR Resource Centre's the Hub*. Ontario, Canada: Centre for Security Governance.

Martire, A. (2017) 'Walking the street: no more motorways for Belfast', *Spaces and Flows* 8(3): 35–61.

Massey, D. (2005) *For Space*. London: Sage.

Matthew, R. (1961) *Belfast Regional Survey and Plan: Main Points*, 21 July. Available at Public Records Office Northern Ireland (PRONI), CAB B/163/2 BRS: 1.

—— (1962) *Belfast Regional Survey and Plan*. Belfast, Northern Ireland.

McAdam, N. (2015) 'Sinn Féin accused of surrendering to Tories over welfare reform', *Belfast Telegraph*, 19 November. Available at: https://www.belfasttelegraph.co.uk/news/politics/sinn-fein-accused-of-surrendering-to-tories-over-welfare-reform-34214858.html (accessed 19 December 2017).

McAuley, C. (2016) 'Renewable Heat Incentive scheme: whistleblower "ignored" after reporting abuse claims', BBC News, 9 November. Available at: http://www.bbc.co.uk/news/uk-northern-ireland-37925402 (accessed 8 August 2017).

McAuley, J. (1994) *The Politics of Identity*. Aldershot: Ashgate.

McCaffery, S. (2013) 'Is Stormont's £80m poverty fund deadlocked over cash going to Catholics or Protestants?', *The Detail*, 20 October. Available at: http://www.thedetail.tv/articles/is-stormont-s-80m-poverty-fund-deadlocked-over-cash-going-to-catholics-or-protestants (accessed 15 December 2016).

McCaffrey, B. (2012a) 'What really went on inside DSD when DUP demanded religious breakdown of Housing Executive staff', *The Detail*, 17 June. Available at: http://www.thedetail.tv/articles/what-really-went-on-inside-dsd-when-dup-demanded-religious-breakdown-of-housing-executive-staff (accessed 4 July 2017).

—— (2012b) 'McCausland challenged over special housing preference for Loyalist areas', *The Detail*, 18 June. Available at: http://www.thedetail.tv/articles/mccausland-challenged-over-special-housing-preference-for-loyalist-areas (accessed 15 December 2015).

—— (2012c) 'The DUP's full role in Red Sky row revealed', *The Detail*, 12 September. Available at: http://www.thedetail.tv/articles/the-dup-s-full-role-in-red-sky-row-revealed (accessed 4 July 2017).

—— (2014) 'Documents reveal DUP lobbying over North Belfast amid allegations of gerrymandering', *The Detail*, 13 May. Available at: http://www.thedetail.tv/articles/documents-reveal-dup-lobbying-over-north-belfast-housing-and-allegations-of-gerrymandering (accessed 6 September 2015).

McCall, C. (2002) 'Political transformation and the reinvention of the Ulster-Scots identity and culture', *Identities: Global Studies in Culture and Power* 9(2): 197–218.

McCartney, J. (2004) 'So now another estate has been cleansed of Protestants', *The Telegraph*, 29 August. Available at: http://www.telegraph.co.uk/comment/personal-view/3610190/So-now-another-estate-has-been-cleansed-of-Protestants.html (accessed 7 October 2017).

McCausland, N. (2012) 'Girdwood (2)', *Nelson's View*, 30 May. Available at: http://nelsonmccausland.blogspot.co.uk/2012/05/girdwood-2.html (accessed 6 January 2016).

—— (2014) 'North Belfast housing need (3)', *Nelson's View*, 24 February. Available at: http://theministerspen.blogspot.co.uk/2014/02/north-belfast-housing-need-3.html (accessed 6 January 2016).

McClements, F. (2022) 'Young NI voters swerve "that orange and green stuff"', *Irish Times*, 29 April. Available at: https://www.irishtimes.com/news/ireland/irish-news/young-ni-voters-swerve-that-orange-and-green-stuff-1.4864645 (accessed 6 May 2022).

McDonald, H. (2000) 'Sordid death of Top Gun', *Observer*, 1 October. Available at: https://www.theguardian.com/uk/2000/oct/01/northernireland.henrymcdonald (accessed 20 October 2017).

—— (2001) 'A hard lesson at Holy Cross', *Observer*, 9 September. Available at: https://www.theguardian.com/politics/2001/sep/09/northernireland.schools (accessed 9 March 2016).

—— (2011) 'Horror in Omagh as bomb kills Northern Ireland policeman', *Observer*, 3 April. Available at: https://www.theguardian.com/uk/2011/apr/02/omagh-booby-trap-bomb-policeman-killed (accessed 17 September 2017).

—— (2014) 'Peace and poverty for survivors of the Troubles', *Guardian*, 28 August. Available at: https://www.theguardian.com/uk-news/2014/aug/28/northern-ireland-peace-poverty-ira-ceasefire (accessed 1 August 2017).

—— (2015) 'Northern Ireland unionist parties agree pact as they seek more seats in May', *Guardian*, 17 March. Available at: https://www.theguardian.com/uk-news/2015/mar/17/northern-ireland-unionist-parties-dup-uup-agree-pact-win-more-commons-seats (accessed 17 September 2017).

—— (2017) 'Belfast couple shot in legs while protecting son from paramilitaries', *Guardian*, 13 January. Available at: https://www.theguardian.com/uk-news/2017/jan/13/belfast-couple-shot-in-legs-while-protecting-son-paramilitaries (accessed 17 September 2017).

—— (2018a) 'Northern Ireland "punishment" attacks rise 60% in four years', *Guardian*, 12 March. Available at: https://www.theguardian.com/uk-news/2018/mar/12/northern-ireland-punishment-attacks-rise-60-in-four-years#:~:text=Paramilitary%2Dstyle%20%E2%80%9Cpunishment%E2%80%9D%20shootings,figures%20obtained%20by%20the%20Guardian (accessed 11 April 2017).

—— (2018b) 'Anger over ruling that British army did not use torture in Northern Ireland', 20 March, *Guardian*. Available at: https://www.theguardian.com/uk-news/2018/mar/20/british-army-not-torture-northern-ireland-court-rules-hooded-men (accessed 7 May 2022).

McDowell, S. (2008) 'Debating the future of the Long Kesh prison site', in W. Logan and K. Reeves (eds), *Places of Pain and Shame: Dealing with 'Difficult Heritage' (Key Issues in Cultural Heritage)*. New York: Routledge, pp. 215–229.

—— (2012) 'Symbolic warfare in the ethnocratic state: conceptualising memorialisation and territoriality in Sri Lanka', *Terrorism and Political Violence* 24(1): 22–37.

McDowell, S. and C. Switzer (2011) 'Violence and the vernacular: conflict, commemoration, and rebuilding in the urban context', *Buildings & Landscapes: Journal of the Vernacular Architecture Forum* 18(2): 82–104.

McFarlane, C. (2011) 'The city as assemblage: dwelling and urban space', *Environment and Planning D: Society and Space* 29(1): 649–671.

McGarry, J. and B. O'Leary (2006a) 'Consociational theory, Northern Ireland's conflict, and its Agreement part 1: what consociationalists can learn from Northern Ireland', *Government and Opposition* 41(1): 43–63.

—— (2006b) 'Consociational theory, Northern Ireland's conflict, and its Agreement part 2: what critics of consociation can learn from Northern Ireland', *Government and Opposition* 41(2): 249–277.

MacGinty, R., O. Muldoon and R. Ferguson (2007) 'No war, no peace: Northern Ireland after the Agreement', *Political Psychology* 28(1): 1–11.

McGuinness, M. (2017) 'Letter of resignation', 9 January. Northern Ireland Executive Office. Available at: http://www.sinnfein.ie/contents/42984 (accessed 1 September 2017).

McKay, S. (2000) *Northern Protestants: An Unsettled People*. Belfast: Blackstaff.

McKenna, F. and M. Melaugh (2016) 'Violence – chronology of major violent incidents, 1969–1998', CAIN Web Service. Available at: http://cain.ulst.ac.uk/issues/violence/chronmaj.htm (accessed 8 October 2017).

McKeown, G. (2017a) 'Plans lodged for £15m Derry hotel at Ebrington Barracks', *Irish News*, 14 November. Available at: http://www.irishnews.com/business/2017/11/14/news/plans-lodged-for-15m-derry-hotel-at-ebrington-barracks-1186674/ (accessed 8 May 2018).

—— (2017b) 'RHI: timeline of a scandal', *Irish News*, 23 February. Available at: http://www.irishnews.com/news/2017/02/23/news/rhi-timeline-of-a-scandal-941046/ (accessed 3 September 2021).

McKinney, S. (2022) 'Work starts on Derry's new £15 million Ebrington Hotel'. *Irish News*, 21 January. Available at: https://www.irishnews.com/news/northernirelandnews/2022/01/21/news/work-starts-on-derry-s-new-15-million-ebrington-hotel-2566656/ (accessed 4 March 2022).

McKittrick, D. (1995) 'IRA has not gone away, Adams warns ministers IRA has not gone away', *Independent*, 14 August. Available at: https://www.independent.co.uk/news/ira-has-not-gone-away-adams-warns-ministers-ira-has-not-gone-away-1596152.html.

—— (2000) *Making Sense of the Troubles*. Belfast: Blackstaff.

McKittrick, D., S. Kelters, B. Feeney, C. Thornton and D. McVea (2007) *Lost Lives*. Edinburgh: Mainstream.

McLaughlin, D. (2012) 'Peace One Day concert attracts big crowd at Ebrington Square in Derry', BBC News, 22 June. Available at: http://www.bbc.com/news/uk-northern-ireland-18546598 (accessed 8 May 2018).

McNicholl, K. (2019) 'The Northern Irish identity: attitudes towards moderate political parties and outgroup leaders', *Irish Political Studies* 34(1): 25–47.

McParland, C. (2010) 'DUP and SDLP clash over Girdwood hate crime incidents', *North Belfast News*, September 10. Available at: https://belfastmedia.com/dup-and-sdlp-clash-over-girdwood-hate-crime-incidents (accessed 18 July 2023).

McWilliams, G. (2011) '£44m Belfast Met campus opens after much controversy', *North Belfast News*, 2 September. Available at: http://belfastmediagroup.com/44m-belfast-met-campus-opens-after-much-controversy/ (accessed 23 August 2017).

Melaugh, M. (2016a) 'The civil rights campaign – a chronology of main events', CAIN Web Service. Available at: http://cain.ulst.ac.uk/events/crights/chron.htm (accessed 8 October 2017).

—— (2016b) 'Internment – a chronology of the main events', CAIN Web Service. Available at: http://cain.ulst.ac.uk/events/intern/chron.htm (accessed 4 April 2017).

Melaugh, M. and F. McKenna (n.d.) 'Background information on Northern Ireland society – population and vital statistics', CAIN Web Service. Available at: http://cain.ulst.ac.uk/ni/popul.htm#3 (accessed 5 October 2017).

Middleton, J. (2010) 'Sense and the city: exploring the embodied geographies of urban walking', *Social & Cultural Geography* 11(6): 575–596.

Mills, T. (2014) 'NI education: poorer Protestant boys underachieving', BBC News, 3 April. Available at: https://www.bbc.com/news/uk-northern-ireland-26855040 (accessed 2 February 2022).

Mitchell, A. (2011) *Lost in Transformation: Violent Peace and Peaceful Conflict in Northern Ireland*. London: Palgrave Macmillan.

Mitchell, P., G. Evans and B. O'Leary (2009) 'Extremist outbidding in ethnic party systems is not inevitable: tribune parties in Northern Ireland', *Political Studies* 59(1): 397–421.

Monaghan, J. (2017) 'Housing Executive funding for community group at centre of UDA allegations trebles in three years', *Irish News*, 23 January. Available at: http://www.irishnews.com/news/2017/01/23/news/housing-executive-funding-for-community-group-at-centre-of-uda-allegations-trebles-in-three-years-899673/ (accessed 30 January 2017).

Moore, G., N. Loizides, N.A. Sandal and A. Lordos (2014) 'Winning peace frames: intra-ethnic outbidding in Northern Ireland and Cyprus', *West European Politics*, 37(1): 159–181.

Moriarty, G. (2021) 'The UDA killer nicknamed "Top Gun" behind a dozen sectarian murders', *The Irish Times*, 24 July. Available at: https://www.irishtimes.com/news/ireland/irish-news/the-uda-killer-nicknamed-top-gun-behind-a-dozen-sectarian-murders-1.4628830 (accessed 30 January 2017).

Morris, A. (2016a) 'UDA linked group to manage £1.7 million investment for east Belfast', *Irish News*, 30 September. Available at: http://www.irishnews.com/news/northernirelandnews/2016/09/30/news/uda-linked-group-to-manage-1-7-million-investment--714427/ (accessed 30 September 2016).

—— (2016b) 'Video: masked dissident republicans roam Belfast streets armed with rocket launchers', *Irish News*, 6 December. Available at: http://www.irishnews.com/news/northernirelandnews/2016/12/06/news/video-masked-dissident-republicans-roam-belfast-streets-armed-with-rocket-launchers-822430/ (accessed 15 September 2017).

Morrow, D. (2019) *Sectarianism in Northern Ireland: A Review*. Report for Ulster University. Belfast, Northern Ireland. Available at: https://www.ulster.ac.uk/__data/assets/pdf_file/0016/410227/A-Review-Addressing-Sectarianism-in-Northern-Ireland_FINAL.pdf (accessed 28 November 2021).

Mulholland, C. (2019). *Making Space for Each Other: North Belfast*. Planning for Spatial Reconciliation Group. Report, Queens University Belfast.

Mulholland, M. (2002) *The Longest War: Northern Ireland's Troubled History*. Oxford: Oxford University Press.

Mulvenna, G. (2017) *Tartan Gangs and Paramilitaries: The Loyalist Backlash*. Liverpool: Liverpool University Press.

Murphy, M. and J. Evershed (2019) 'Between the devil and the DUP: the Democratic Unionist Party and the politics of Brexit', *British Politics* 15: 456–477.

Murphy, M.C. (2021) 'Northern Ireland and Brexit: where sovereignty and stability collide?', *Journal of Contemporary European Studies* 29(3): 405–418.

Murtagh, B. (2002) *The Politics of Territory: Policy and Segregation in Northern Ireland*. Basingstoke: Palgrave Macmillan.

—— (2008) 'New spaces and old in "post-conflict" Belfast', Conflict in City and the Contested State Working Paper Series. UK Economic and Social Research Council.

—— (2011) 'Desegregation and place restructuring in the new Belfast', *Urban Studies* 48(6): 1119–1135.

—— (2013) 'Precarious spaces and urban change in post-conflict Belfast'. Paper presented at Precarious Peacebuilding: Exploring New Research Agendas conference, Stockholm, Sweden. Available at: www.pure.qub.ac.uk/portal/files/ … /Murtagh_Peacebuilding_Conferece_Sweden.pdf (accessed 7 November 2015).

Murtagh, B., P. Boland and P. Shirlow (2017) 'Contested heritages and cultural tourism', *International Journal of Heritage Studies* 23(6): 506–520.

Murtagh, B., B. Graham and P. Shirlow (2008) 'Authenticity and stakeholder planning in the segregated city', *Progress in Planning* 69: 41–92.

Murtagh, B. and G. Ellis (2011) 'Skills, conflict and spatial planning in Northern Ireland', *Planning Theory & Practice* 12(3): 349–365.

Murtagh, B. and K. Keaveney (2006) 'Policy and conflict transformation in the ethnocratic city', *Space and Polity* 10(2): 187–202.

Murtagh, B., L. Mullan and A. Grounds (2015) *Evaluation of the FabLab Project: Final Report*. Queens University Belfast: Institute of Environmental and Spatial Planning.

Murtagh, B., P. Shirlow and L. Copeland (2009) *North Belfast Community Action Unit: Evaluation of the Community Empowerment Partnerships*. Belfast, Northern Ireland.

Nagle, J. (2009a) 'Sites of social centrality and segregation: Lefebvre in Belfast, a "divided city"', *Antipode* 41(2): 326–346.

—— (2009b) 'Potemkin village: neo-liberalism and peace-building in Northern Ireland?' *Ethnopolitics* 8(2): 173–190.

Neill, W.J.V. and M. Gordon (2001) 'Shaping our future? the regional strategic framework for Northern Ireland', *Planning Theory and Practice* 2(1): 31–52.

Neville, S. (2009) *The Ghosts of Belfast*. New York: Soho Press.

New Lodge Six Time for Truth Committee (2002) *New Lodge Six Report of the Community Inquiry Report into the Killings of Jim McCann; Jim Sloan; Tony Campbell; Brendan Maguire, John Loughran, Ambrose Hardy*. Belfast, Northern Ireland.

Ní Cheallacháin, O. (2010) 'Northern Ireland and Israel-Palestine: spoilers and the politics of inclusion. A comparative analysis of peace processes', *Politikon (IAPSS)* 16(1): 50–65.

Nic Craith, M. (2001) 'Politicised linguistic consciousness: the case of Ulster-Scots', *Nations and Nationalism* 7(1): 21–37.

—— (2003) *Culture and Identity Politics in Northern Ireland*. London: Palgrave Macmillan.

Nolan, P. (2014) *Northern Ireland Peace Monitoring Report: Number Three*. Report for Community Relations Council. Belfast, Northern Ireland.

Nolan, S. (2016) *A Nolan Show Investigation*, BBC One, Northern Ireland, 16 December. Available at: http://www.bbc.co.uk/programmes/b088p3l6 (accessed 16 December 2016).

North Belfast Community Action Project (NBCAP) (2002) *Report of the Project Team (Dunlop Report)*. Belfast, Northern Ireland.

North Belfast Community Action Unit (NBCAU) (2005) *Gaol Times*, Volume 1(1). Belfast, Northern Ireland.

—— (2007) *Communication by letter to Phil Kelly, Leisure Services Manager, Belfast City Council. 17 April*. Belfast, Northern Ireland. Print. Girdwood Advisory Panel Meeting Minutes (held by Elizabeth DeYoung).

North Belfast News (2000a) 'Human rights for housing', 3 June.

—— (2000b) 'The Executive is our only hope – Adair', 1 April.

Northern Ireland Assembly (2016) 'Plenary terms', *Northern Ireland Assembly Online*. Available at: http://aims.niassembly.gov.uk/plenary/terms.aspx (accessed 14 July 2017).

—— (n.d.) 'History of the Assembly', *Northern Ireland Assembly Online*. Available at: http://www.niassembly.gov.uk/about-the-assembly/general-information/history-of-the-assembly/#8 (accessed 5 February 2017).

Northern Ireland Assembly Research and Library Services (2001) *New Targeting Social Need (TSN)*. Report, Northern Ireland Assembly, 21 August. Available at: archive.niassembly.gov.uk/io/research/0401.pdf (accessed 15 April 2016).

Northern Ireland Audit Office (NIAO) (2016) *Report by the Comptroller and Auditor General for Northern Ireland: Department of Enterprise, Trade and Investment Resource Accounts 2015–16*, 28 June. Northern Ireland Audit Office, Belfast, Northern Ireland.

Northern Ireland Council for Voluntary Action (NICVA) (2014) *A Review of PEACE III and Consideration for PEACE IV*. Available at: www.nicva.org/sites/default/files/ … /peace_iv_report_-_final_1_4.pdf (accessed 16 February 2017).

—— (n.d.) *Member Directory*. Available at: http://www.nicva.org/members?f[0]=field_constituency%3A39 (accessed 13 July 2017).

Northern Ireland Executive (2013) *An Agreement among the Parties of the Northern Ireland Executive on Parades, Select Commemorations and Related Protests; Flags and Emblems; and Contending with the Past*. Belfast, Northern Ireland. Available at: https://www.northernireland.gov.uk/haass.pdf (accessed 14 September 2017).

—— (2015) *A Fresh Start: The Stormont Agreement and Implementation Plan*. Available at: https://www.northernireland.gov.uk/publications/fresh-start-stormont-agreement-and-implementation-plan-0 (accessed 27 December 2016).

—— (2016) 'Northern Ireland Executive delivers £1.7million for East Belfast – Foster', 29 September. Available at: https://www.executiveoffice-ni.gov.uk/news/northern-ireland-executive-delivers-ps17million-east-belfast-foster (accessed 6 May 2022).

—— (2021) 'Ending the harm: about us'. Available at: https://www.endingtheharm.com/about-us/ (accessed 3 May 2022).

—— (undated) 'Social investment fund'. Available at: https://www.executiveoffice-ni.gov.uk/articles/social-investment-fund (accessed 2 December 2016).

Northern Ireland Housing Executive (NIHE) (2000) *The North Belfast Housing Strategy: Tackling Need*. Belfast, Northern Ireland.

—— (2006) 'NIHE housing needs assessment', Girdwood Advisory Panel, 12 June. Belfast, Northern Ireland.

—— (2017a) *Freedom of Information Request: North Belfast Residual Housing Need*. Made by N. Browne, PPR, 19 June 2017.

—— (2017b) *Freedom of Information Request: North Belfast Housing List by Religious Breakdown*. Made by Elizabeth DeYoung 14 September 2017.

Northern Ireland Human Rights Commission (2015) *Submission to the United Nations' Committee on Economic, Social and Cultural Rights: Parallel Report on the Sixth Periodic Report of the United Kingdom under the International Covenant on Economic, Social and Cultural Rights*. Belfast, Northern Ireland.

Northern Ireland Life and Times Survey (NILTS) (2020) Available at: https://www.ark.ac.uk/nilt/2020/ (accessed 23 May 2022).

Northern Ireland Office (NIO) (1998a) *The Belfast Agreement*, 10 April. Available at: https://www.gov.uk/government/publications/the-belfast-agreement (accessed 14 September 2015).

—— (1998b) *Northern Ireland Act*. Available at: https://www.legislation.gov.uk/ukpga/1998/47/contents (accessed 14 September 2015).

—— (2006) *The St Andrews Agreement*. Available at: https://www.gov.uk/government/publications/the-st-andrews-agreement-october-2006 (accessed 8 May 2016).

—— (2022a) *The Fourth Report on the Use of the Petition of Concern Mechanism in the Northern Ireland Assembly*. Available at: https://assets.publishing.service.gov.uk/government/uploads/system/uploads/attachment_data/file/1054277/PoC_report_4.pdf (accessed 5 May 2022).

—— (2022b) 'UK government acts on identity and language legislation for Northern Ireland', 25 May. Available at: https://www.gov.uk/government/news/uk-government-acts-on-identity-and-language-legislation-for-northern-ireland#:~:text=The%20Identity%20and%20Language%20(Northern,Scots%20and%20Ulster%20British%20tradition (accessed 27 May 2022).

Northern Ireland Statistics and Research Agency (NISRA) (2005) *Multiple Deprivation Measure*. Available at: www.nisra.gov.uk/archive/deprivation/nimdm2005fullreport.pdf (accessed 7 March 2016).

—— (2010) *Northern Ireland Multiple Deprivation Measure*. Available at: https://www.nisra.gov.uk/statistics/deprivation/northern-ireland-multiple-deprivation-measure-2010-nimdm2010 (accessed 7 March 2016).

—— (2011) *Census 2011 Short Stories: Religion*. NISRA. Available at: https://www.ninis2.nisra.gov.uk/public/census2011analysis/religion/index.aspx (accessed 23 May 2022).

—— (2012) *Census 2011: Key Statistics for Northern Ireland*. NISRA Department of Finance and Personnel. Available at: https://www.nisra.gov.uk/publications/2011-census-key-statistics-northern-ireland (accessed 3 October 2017).

—— (2017) *Quarterly Supplement to the Labour Market Report April–June 2017*, NISRA Central Survey Unit, 30 August. Available at: https://www.nisra.gov.uk/sites/nisra.gov.uk/files/publications/Quarterly-Supplement-to-the-Labour-Market-Report-April-June-2017.PDF (accessed 30 October 2017).

North Talks Too (2014a) *Building Relationships, Sharing Space*. Pamphlet distributed to residents. Belfast, Northern Ireland.

—— (2014b) *Outline of Girdwood Hub Community Management Feasibility Study: Terms of Reference*. Belfast, Northern Ireland.

—— (2015) *Peacebuilding on the Front Line*. Pamphlet distributed to residents. Belfast, Northern Ireland.

North Talks Too Youth Forum (2015) *North Talks Too Youth Forum*. YouTube. Available at: https://www.youtube.com/watch?v=7zfvtTuGVA4&t=22s (accessed 13 April 2016).

Northern Visions (NVTV) (2017) *Ó Líofa Go Lá Dearg*, 26 July. Documentary. Available at: https://www.facebook.com/AnDreamDearg/videos/1315096131920972/ (accessed 28 July 2017).

—— (n.d.) *The Rape and Plunder of the Shankill Revisited*. Documentary. Available at: http://archive.northernvisions.org/specialcollections/ogfeatures/the-rape-and-plunder-of-the-shankill-revisited/ (accessed 21 September 2016).

O'Carroll, L. (2022) '"It's a bit of a circus": the Northern Irish voters tired of polarised politics', *Guardian*, 1 May. Available at: https://www.theguardian.com/uk-news/2022/may/01/its-a-bit-of-a-circus-the-northern-irish-voters-tired-of-polarised-politics (accessed 5 May 2022).

O'Dowd, L. and M. Komarova (2011) 'Contesting territorial fixity? A case study of regeneration in Belfast', *Urban Studies* 48(10): 2013–2028.

O'Driscoll, S. (2016) 'People before profit win on Sinn Féin turf', *The Times*, May 7. Available at: https://www.thetimes.co.uk/article/people-before-profit-wins-on-sinn-fein-turf-9h86tsdmj (accessed 14 December 2017).

O'Duffy, B. and B. O'Leary (1990) 'Violence in Northern Ireland, 1969–June 1989', in B. O'Duffy and B. O'Leary (eds), *The Future of Northern Ireland*. Oxford: Oxford University Press, pp. 318–341. Available at: http://www.cain.ulst.ac.uk/issues/violence/bodbol.htm (accessed 6 October 2017).

Office of the First Minister and Deputy First Minister (OFMDFM) (2005a) *A Shared Future*. Northern Ireland Executive, Belfast, Northern Ireland.

—— (2005b) 'Press release prepared by the Office of the First Minister and Deputy First Minister (OFMDFM) on the publication of *A Shared Future: The Framework for Good Relations In Northern Ireland*', 21 March. Available at: http://cain.ulst.ac.uk/issues/community/sharedfuture/ofmdfm210305press.htm (accessed 6 December 2016).

—— (2005c) *Crumlin Road Gaol Planning Review: A Summary*, March. Belfast, Northern Ireland.

—— (2006) *Maze/Long Kesh Masterplan and Implementation Strategy*, May. Belfast, Northern Ireland.

—— (2010) *Draft Programme for Cohesion, Sharing and Integration*. Northern Ireland Executive, Belfast, Northern Ireland.

—— (2013) *Together, Building a United Community*. Northern Ireland Executive, Belfast, Northern Ireland.

Office of the First Minister and Deputy First Minister and Department for Social Development (OFMDFM and DSD) (2006) *Crumlin Road Gaol and Girdwood Park ... A Unique Development Opportunity*. Report, November. Belfast, Northern Ireland.

Office of the High Commissioner for Human Rights (OHCHR) (1966) *International Covenant on Economic, Social and Cultural Rights*, United Nations. Available at: http://www.ohchr.org/EN/ProfessionalInterest/Pages/CESCR.aspx (accessed 6 October 2017).

Office of National Statistics (ONS) (2017) *Dataset: Claimant Count for People Resident in Westminster Parliamentary Constituencies and Regions in the UK*, 14 September. Available at: https://www.ons.gov.uk/employmentandlabourmarket/peoplenotinwork/unemployment/datasets/claimantcountbyparliamentaryconstituencyexperimental (accessed 30 October 2017).

O'Hearn, D. (2008) 'How Has Peace Changed the Northern Irish Political Economy?', *Ethnopolitics* 7(1): 101–118.

O'Leary, B. (2001) 'The character of the 1998 agreement: results and prospects', in R. Wilford (ed.), *Aspects of the Belfast Agreement*. Oxford: Oxford University Press, pp. 49–83.

Ó Muilleoir, M. (2017) 'Sinn Féin will continue to oppose Tory-DUP cuts – Ó Muilleoir', 18 December. Available at: http://www.sinnfein.ie/contents/47644 (accessed 19 December 2017).

O'Neill, J. (2016) 'Nama: timeline of Northern Ireland property portfolio deal', BBC News, 14 September. Available at: http://www.bbc.co.uk/news/uk-northern-ireland-33507423 (accessed 4 July 2017).

O'Tuathail, S. (1971) *They Came in the Morning; Torture and Brutality in the North*. CAIN Web Service. Available at: https://cain.ulster.ac.uk/events/intern/pdfs/otuathail.pdf.

Participation and the Practice of Rights (PPR) (2007) *Unlocking the Potential: Crumlin Road Gaol and Girdwood Barracks*. Belfast, Northern Ireland.

—— (2008a) *Residents' Jury on Regenerating Girdwood Barracks and Crumlin Road Gaol. A Human Rights Based Approach. Jury Proceedings and Findings*, 28 May. Belfast, Northern Ireland.

—— (2008b) *Changing the Patterns of the Past: Putting People First in the Regeneration of North Belfast*, 1 August. Belfast, Northern Ireland.

—— (2009) *The Girdwood Gamble*. Belfast, Northern Ireland.

—— (2012) *PPR Response to DSD Consultation on Facing the Future; Northern Ireland Housing Strategy 2012–17*. Belfast, Northern Ireland.

—— (2013) *Equality Can't Wait: The Right to Housing*. Belfast, Northern Ireland.

—— (2015a) 'Local rights bodies back equality can't wait call for urgent action on inequality'. Available at: https://www.pprproject.org/local-rights-bodies-back-equality-can%e2%80%99t-wait-call-for-urgent-action-on-inequality (accessed 11 November 2016).

—— (2015b) 'Right to work and welfare', conference held 23 March at Duncairn Centre for the Arts, Belfast Northern Ireland.

—— (2021) 'Child homelessness and housing need in North Belfast: a look at the Housing Executive data. *Participation and the Practice of Rights*. Available at: https://www.nlb.ie/investigations/FOI/2021-08-child-homelessness-and-housing-need-in-north-belfast-a-look-at-the-housing-executive-data (accessed 27 May 2022).

—— (2022) 'Major social housing shortfall', *Participation and the Practice of Rights*. Available at: https://www.nlb.ie/campaigns/right-to-home (accessed 27 May 2022).

—— (n.d.) 'About PPR', *Participation and the Practice of Rights*. Available at: https://www.pprproject.org/about-ppr (accessed 18 October 2017).

Petty, J. (2016) 'The London spikes controversy: homelessness, urban securitisation and the question of "hostile architecture"', *International Journal for Crime, Justice And Social Democracy* 5(1): 67–81.

Planning for Spatial Reconciliation Research Group (2016) *Making Space for Each Other: Civic Place-Making in a Divided Society*. Report, Queens University Belfast.

Plöger, J. (2004) 'Strife: urban planning and agonism', *Planning Theory* 3(1): 71–92.

Police Service of Northern Ireland (PSNI) and MI5 (2015) *Paramilitary Groups in Northern Ireland*. Report for Secretary of State for Northern Ireland.

Potter, G. (2016) 'Public Records Office NI', *Future Belfast*. Available at: http://www.futurebelfast.com/property/2-titanic-boulevard-proni/ (accessed 10 October 2016).

Powell, A., J. Brown and F. McGuinness (2017) *People Claiming Unemployment Benefits by Constituency, March 2017 (Formerly Called Unemployment by Constituency)*. Briefing paper 7947, 12 April. London: House of Commons Library. Available at: http://researchbriefings.parliament.uk/ResearchBriefing/Summary/CBP-7947#fullreport (accessed 30 October 2017).

Power, P. (1972) 'Civil protest in Northern Ireland', *Journal of Peace Research* 9(3): 223–236.

Prime Cut Productions (2016) *Girdwood Arts Project*. YouTube. Available at: https://www.youtube.com/watch?v=cQLziTr84vY&t=28s (accessed 20 January 2016).

Public Accounts Committee (2012) *Report on the Transfer of Former Military and Security Sites to the Northern Ireland Executive and Ilex Accounts 2010–2011, Together with the Minutes of Proceedings of the Committee Relating to the Report and the Minutes of Evidence*. Belfast, Northern Ireland. Available at: http://www.niassembly.gov.uk/assembly-business/committees/2011-2016/public-accounts-committee/reports-2011-2016/report-on-the-transfer-of-former-military-and-security-sites-to-the-northern-ireland-executive-and-ilex-accounts-2010---2011/ (accessed 6 June 2017).

Purvis, D. et al. (2011) *A Call to Action: Educational Disadvantage and the Protestant Working Class*. Available at: https://www.yumpu.com/en/document/read/28757278/a-call-to-action-educational-disadvantage-and-the-protestant-nicva (accessed 8 May 2022).

Randa Nucho, J. (2016) *Everyday Sectarianism in Urban Lebanon: Infrastructures, Public Services, and Power*. Princeton: Princeton University Press.

Reidy, P. (2013) Not waving, not listening', *Index on Censorship* 42(4): 62–65.

Reynolds, L. (2005) *Full House? How Overcrowded Housing Affects Families*. Report for Shelter UK. Available at: https://assets.ctfassets.net/6sxvmndnpnos/6dU8FFbZ6RnSk6DbnDOMHb/61e30884aff47a789891b2dce54fcbc7/Full_house_overcrowding_effects.pdf (accessed 20 February 2022).

Rivera-Kumar, S. (2023) *Map of Girdwood Barracks Site*. Weitzman School of Design, University of Pennsylvania.

Rooksby, E. and J. Hillier (eds) (2005) *Habitus: A Sense of Place*. London: Routledge.

Rose, G. (1995) 'Place and identity: a sense of place', in D. Massey and P. Jess (eds), *A Place in the World? Places, Cultures and Globalization*. Oxford: Oxford University Press, pp. 87–132.

Rothstein, R. (2007) *The Color of Law: A Forgotten History of How Our Government Segregated America*. New York: Liveright.

Rush, K. (2022) *The Cracked Art World: Conflict, Austerity, and Community Arts in Northern Ireland*. New York: Berghahn.

Russell, R. (2011) *Northern Ireland Assembly Election 2011. Report for Northern Ireland Assembly Research Service*, 17 May. Belfast, Northern Ireland.

Rutherford, A. (2011) 'Disused Belfast army base sold for £1m less than its value ... and then re-sold by the buyer on the very same day', *Belfast Telegraph*, 22 November. Available at: https://www.belfasttelegraph.co.uk/news/northern-ireland/disused-belfast-army-base-sold-for-1m-less-than-its-value-and-then-resold-by-the-buyer-on-the-very-same-day-28683472.html (accessed 7 May 2018).

Sack, R. (1983) 'Human territoriality: a theory', *Annals of the Association of American Geographers* 73(1): 55–74.

Sartori, G. (1997) *Comparative Constitutional Engineering: An Inquiry into Structures, Incentives and Outcomes*. Basingstoke: Macmillan.

Schwartz, A. (2015) 'The problem with petitions of concern', *Q:POL – Policy Engagement at Queens*. Available at: http://qpol.qub.ac.uk/the-problem-with-petitions-of-concern/ (accessed 14 July 2017).

Scott, S. (2021) 'Girdwood Community Centre football match incidents being treated as hate crimes', *Belfast Live*, 5 September. Available at: https://www.belfastlive.co.uk/news/belfast-news/girdwood-community-centre-football-match-21486730 (accessed 17 April 2022).

Scraton, P. (2004) 'Speaking truth to power: experiencing critical research', in M. Smyth and E. Williamson (eds), *Researchers and Their 'Subjects': Ethics, Power, Knowledge and Consent*. Bristol: Policy Press, pp. 176–194.

Shaw, S. (2013) 'An ethnographic investigation into gender and language in the Northern Ireland Assembly', in I. Poggi, F. D'Errico, L. Vincze and A. Vinciarelli (eds), *Multimodal Communication in Political Speech: Shaping Minds and Social Action: International Workshop on Political Speech – Il Parlato Politico*. Heidelberg: Springer, pp. 39–53.

Shenker, J. (2015) 'Privatised London: the Thames Path walk that resembles a prison corridor', *Guardian*, 24 February. Available at: https://www.theguardian.com/cities/2015/feb/24/private-london-exposed-thames-path-riverside-walking-route (accessed 25 February 2015).

Shirlow, P. (2003a) 'Ethno-sectarianism and the reproduction of fear in Belfast', *Capital and Class* 80(1): 7–93.

—— (2003b) '"Who fears to speak": fear, mobility, and ethno-sectarianism in the two "Ardoynes"', *Global Review of Ethnopolitics* 3(1): 76–91.

—— (2006a) 'Belfast: the "post-conflict" city', *Space and Polity* 10(2): 99–107.

—— (2006b) 'Segregation, ethno-sectarianism and the "new" Belfast', in M. Cox, A. Guelke and F. Stephen (eds), *A Farewell to Arms: Beyond the Good Friday Agreement*. Manchester: Manchester University Press, pp. 226–237.

—— (2012) *The End of Ulster Loyalism?* Manchester: Manchester University Press.

Shirlow, P. and K. McEvoy (2008) *Beyond the Wire: Former Prisoners and Conflict Transformation in Northern Ireland*. London: Pluto Press.

Shirlow, P. and M. McGovern (1996) 'Sectarianism, socioeconomic competition and the political economy of Ulster Loyalism', *Antipode* 28(4): 379–398.

Shirlow, P. and B. Murtagh (2004) 'Capacity-building, representation and intra-community conflict', *Urban Studies* 41(1): 57–70.
—— (2006) *Belfast: Segregation, Violence, and the City*. London: Pluto Press.
Short, E. (2014) 'Houses given to tenants with zero points', *North Belfast News*, 6 June.
—— (2015) 'Barracks consultation "excludes" G'Gormley Nationalist population', *North Belfast News*, 24 January.
Sibley, D. (1988) 'Survey 13: purification of space', *Environmental and Planning D: Society and Space* 6: 409–421.
Simpson, M. (2004) 'Tears flow as families flee', BBC News, 26 August. Available at: http://news.bbc.co.uk/1/hi/northern_ireland/3602290.stm (accessed 7 October 2017).
—— (2013) 'Titanic Belfast has had more than 1m visitors since opening', BBC News, 30 July. Available at: http://www.bbc.co.uk/news/uk-northern-ireland-23504434 (accessed 4 September 2016).
Sluka, J. (1989) *Hearts and Minds, Water and Fish: Support for the IRA and INLA in a Northern Irish Ghetto*. London: JAI Press.
Smyth, C. (2016) 'Stormont's petition of concern used 115 times in five years', *The Detail*, 29 September. Available at: http://www.thedetail.tv/articles/stormont-s-petition-of-concern-used-115-times-in-five-years (accessed 8 August 2017).
—— (2017) 'Stormont file shows DUP minister was warned over Líofa cut', *The Detail*, 26 April. Available at: http://www.thedetail.tv/articles/nearly-three-quarters-of-young-irish-speakers-could-not-have-afforded-gaeltacht-course-without-liofa-bursary-scheme-minister-told (accessed 26 April 2017).
Smyth, M., M.T. Fay, E. Brough and J. Hamilton (2004) *The Impact of Political Violence on Children in Northern Ireland*. Belfast: Institute for Conflict Research.
Social Democratic and Labour Party (SDLP) (2010) *SDLP Response to the OFMDFM Consultation Document: A Programme for Cohesion, Sharing and Integration*. Belfast, Northern Ireland.
Solari, C. and R. Mare (2012) 'Housing crowding effects on children's wellbeing', *Social Science Research* 41(2): 464–476.
Somerville, P. (2011) *Understanding Community: Politics, Policy and Practice*. Bristol: Policy Press.
Southern, N. (2008) 'Territoriality, alienation, and Loyalist decommissioning: the case of the Shankill in Protestant West Belfast', *Terrorism and Political Violence* 20(1): 66–86.
Special European Union Programming Body (SEUPB) (2007) *PEACE III: EU Programme for Peace and Reconciliation 2007 – 2013 Northern Ireland and the Border Region of Ireland Operational Programme*. Belfast, Northern Ireland.
Sproule, L. (2022) 'NI election results 2022: what does Sinn Féin's vote success mean?', BBC News NI, 12 May. Available at: https://www.bbc.com/news/uk-northern-ireland-60786728 (accessed 15 May 2022).
Sterrett, K., M. Hackett and D. Hill (2012) 'The social consequences of broken urban structures: a case study of Belfast', *Journal of Transport Geography* 21(1): 49–61.

Sterrett, K., B. Murtagh and G. Millar (2005) 'The social turn and urban development corporations', *Planning Practice and Research* 20(4): 373–390.

Stevens, J. (2003) *Stevens Inquiry 3: Overview and Recommendations*. London: Metropolitan Police Force. Available at: www.cain.ulst.ac.uk/issues/collusion/stevens3/stevens3summary.pdf (accessed 5 January 2017).

Stevenson, S. (2017) 'Does Brexit threaten peace in Northern Ireland?', *Survival* 59(3): 111–128.

Stewart, L. (2016) 'Farmer "gets £1m of public cash to heat empty shed" – "catastrophic" blunder threatening to drain hundreds of millions from Northern Ireland's block grant', *Belfast Telegraph*, 5 July. Available at: http://www.belfasttelegraph.co.uk/news/northern-ireland/farmer-gets-1m-of-public-cash-to-heat-empty-shed-catastrophic-blunder-threatening-to-drain-hundreds-of-millions-from-northern-irelands-block-grant-34856610.html (accessed 17 September 2017).

Stewart, L. and D. Deeny (2016) 'Green light for Ebrington Barracks revamp', *Belfast Telegraph*, 9 January. Available at: https://www.belfasttelegraph.co.uk/news/northern-ireland/green-light-for-ebrington-barracks-revamp-34347545.html (accessed 8 May 2018).

Stewart, P. (2019) 'Northern Ireland strikes victory for equality', *Human Rights Watch*, 24 October, Available at: https://www.hrw.org/news/2019/10/24/northern-ireland-strikes-victory-equality (accessed 9 September 2021).

Strategic Investment Board (n.d.) 'Maze Long Kesh: securing the development of the Maze Long Kesh'. Available at: https://sibni.org/project/maze-long-kesh/ (accessed 21 December 2017).

Sutton, M. (2002) 'Appendix: statistical summary of death', in *Bear in Mind These Dead ... An Index of Deaths from the Conflict in Ireland 1969–1993*. Belfast: Beyond the Pale Publications. Available at: http://www.cain.ulst.ac.uk/sutton/book/#append (accessed 8 September 2017).

Svašek, M. and M. Komarova (2018) 'Introduction: spatiality, movement and place-making', in Svašek, M. and M. Komarova (eds), *Ethnographies of Movement, Sociality and Space: Place-Making in the New Northern Ireland*. New York: Berghahn.

Switzer, C. and S. McDowell (2009) 'Redrawing cognitive maps of conflict: lost spaces and forgetting in the centre of Belfast', *Memory Studies* 2(3): 337–353.

Taylor, S. (1997) 'Critical policy analysis: exploring contexts, texts and consequences', *Discourse: Studies in the Cultural Politics of Education* 18: 23–35.

Taylor, T. (2006) 'The Belfast Agreement and the politics of consociationalism: a critique', *The Political Quarterly* 77(2): 217–226.

The Telegraph (2002) 'Belfast ghettos', 12 January. Available at: http://www.telegraph.co.uk/comment/telegraph-view/3571797/Belfast-ghettos.html (accessed 16 October 2017).

Till, K. (1993) 'Neotraditional towns and urban villages: the cultural production of a geography of "otherness"', *Environmental and Planning D: Society and Space* 11: 709–732.

Tilley, J. and G. Evans (2011) 'Political generations in Northern Ireland', *European Journal of Political Research* 50(5): 583–608.
Todd, J. and J. Ruane (2010) *From 'A Shared Future' to 'Cohesion, Sharing and Integration': An Analysis of Northern Ireland's Policy Framework Documents*. Report for Joseph Rowntree Charitable Trust, October.
Tonge J. (2019) 'After Brexit, what's left for Northern Ireland's Unionists?', *Foreign Policy*, 21 December. Available at: https://foreignpolicy.com/2019/12/21/northern-ireland-unionism-irish-unity/ (accessed 31 March 2020).
Tonge J. and R. Gomez (2015) 'Shared identity and the end of conflict? How far has a common sense of "Northern Irishness" replaced British or Irish allegiances since the 1998 Good Friday Agreement?', *Irish Political Studies* 30(2): 276–298.
Toren, C. (1996) 'Ethnography: theoretical background', in J. Richardson (ed.), *Handbook of Qualitative Research Methods for Psychology and the Social Sciences*. Leicester: British Psychological Society, pp. 102–122.
Ulster-Scots Agency (n.d.) *A Wee Guide to Ulster Scots*. Available at: https://www.britishirishcouncil.org/sites/default/files/file%20attachments/Wee%20Guide%20to%20Ulster-Scots.pdf (accessed 5 May 2022).
Ulster Unionist Party (UUP) (2010) *Programme for Cohesion, Sharing, and Integration: Ulster Unionist Party Position*. Belfast, Northern Ireland.
—— (2011) *Response to the Social Investment Fund Consultation*, December. Belfast, Northern Ireland. Available at: https://uup.org/assets/images/featured/Ulster%20Unionist%20Party%20Response%20to%20Social%20Investment%20Fund%20Consultation%20Document.pdf (accessed 21 December 2016).
United Nations (UN) (1948) *Universal Declaration of Human Rights*, 10 December, Paris. Available at: http://www.un.org/en/universal-declaration-human-rights/ (accessed 3 August 2017).
Urban Initiatives (2004) *Titanic Quarter Development Framework: Final Report*. Report for Planning Service NI, August. Belfast, Northern Ireland.
Vergunst, J. (2010) 'Rhythms of walking: history and presence in a city street', *Space and Culture* 13(4): 376–388.
Walker, S. (2017) 'DUP leader would like to scrap Stormont's petition of concern', BBC News, 14 February. Available at: http://www.bbc.co.uk/news/uk-northern-ireland-38974716 (accessed 14 February 2017).
Wallace, A. (2015) *Housing and Communities' Inequalities in Northern Ireland*. Report for Centre for Housing Policy, University of York, June.
Weidenhoft Murphy, W. (2010) 'Touring the Troubles in West Belfast: building peace or reproducing conflict?', *Peace and Change* 35(4): 537–560.
Weiner, R. (1976) *The Rape and Plunder of the Shankill: Community Action, the Belfast Experience*. Belfast: Nothems Press.
Whiting, S. (2012) 'The discourse of defence: "dissident" Irish Republican newspapers and the "Propaganda War"', *Terrorism and Political Violence* 28(3): 483–503.
Whiting, S. (2016) 'Mainstream revolutionaries: Sinn Féin as a "normal" political party?', *Terrorism and Political Violence* 28(3): 541–560.
Whyte, J. (1991) *Interpreting Northern Ireland*. Oxford: Clarendon Press.

Wilford, R. and R. Wilson (2006) *The Trouble with Northern Ireland: The Belfast Agreement and Democratic Governance*. Report, TASC at New Island. Dublin, Ireland.

Wilson, T. and H. Donnan (1999) *Borders: Frontiers of Identity, Nation and State*. New York: Berg.

—— (2006) *The Anthropology of Ireland*. Oxford: Berg

Wilson, W. and C. Barton (2021) *Overcrowded Housing: England*. Report for the House of Commons, UK, 15 June. Available at: https://researchbriefings.files.parliament.uk/documents/POST-PN-0573/POST-PN-0573.pdf (accessed 20 February 2022).

Winters, R. (2020) 'Council plans for Mackie's site in west Belfast criticised amid calls for social housing', *The Detail*, 24 April Available at: https://thedetail.tv/articles/council-plans-for-mackie-s-site-criticised-amid-calls-for-social-housing-in-west-belfast (accessed 27 May 2022).

—— (2021) 'Call for Sinn Féin to apply its southern housing policies to west Belfast "housing crisis"', *The Detail*, 17 May. Available at: https://thedetail.tv/articles/call-for-sinn-fein-to-apply-its-southern-housing-policies-to-west-belfast-housing-crisis (accessed 27 May 2022).

Wood, I.S. (2006) *Crimes of Loyalty: A History of the UDA*. Edinburgh: Edinburgh University Press.

Wright, J. (2012) 'Chairperson's report', *Lower Oldpark Community Association Annual Review*. Belfast, Northern Ireland.

Yeginsu, C. (2019) 'Northern Ireland set to legalize abortion and same-sex marriage', *New York Times*, 21 October. Available at: https://www.nytimes.com/2019/10/21/world/europe/northern-ireland-abortion-same-sex-marriage.html.

Yiftachel, O. (1995) 'Planning as control policy and resistance in a deeply divided society', *Progress in Planning* 44: 116–184.

—— (1998) 'Planning as social control: exploring the dark side', *Journal of Planning Literature* 12(2): 395–406.

—— (2006) *Ethnocracy: Land and Identity Politics in Israel/ Palestine*. Philadelphia: University of Pennsylvania Press.

Yiftachel, O. and A. Ghanem (2004) 'Understanding "ethnocratic" regimes: the politics of seizing contested territories', *Political Geography* 23: 647–676.

Yiftachel, O. and H. Yacobi (2003) 'Urban ethnocracy: ethnicization and the production of space in an Israeli "mixed city"', *Environment and Planning D: Society and Space* 21: 67–693.

YouTube (2007) 'Old Shankill Road'. Available at: https://www.youtube.com/watch?v=UoqJckP6RUI (accessed 1 October 2015).

—— (2013) 'Original news footage of Holy Cross dispute', YouTube. Available at: https://www.youtube.com/watch?v=IEIX-I_Y8qw (accessed 21 April 2016).

Young, C. (2016a) 'Nationalist area housing plans scrapped after DUP directive', *Irish News*, 17 February. Available at: http://www.irishnews.com/news/2016/02/17/news/housing-group-scrapped-plans-because-of-dsd-directive-419827/ (accessed 27 December 2016).

—— (2016b) 'DUP meeting to discuss nationalist homes was held in Belfast orange hall', *Irish News*, 13 May. Available at: http://www.irishnews.com/news/2016/02/16/news/dup-meeting-to-discuss-nationalist-homes-held-in-orange-hall-418842/ (accessed 27 December 2016).

Young, C. (2022) 'Thousands turn out for Irish Language rally in Belfast,' *Irish News*, 23 May. Available at: https://www.irishnews.com/news/northernirelandnews/2022/05/23/news/thousands-turn-out-for-irish-language-rally-in-belfast-2718541/ (accessed 25 May 2022).

Young, D. (2015) 'Red Sky: DUP accused of putting party before public interest during angry clash over Nelson McCausland probe', *Belfast Telegraph*, 12 May. Available at: http://www.belfasttelegraph.co.uk/news/northern-ireland/red-sky-dup-accused-of-putting-party-before-public-interest-during-angry-clash-over-nelson-mccausland-probe-31216236.html (accessed 4 July 2017).

Index

Adair, Johnny 62
Adams, Gerry 44, 151n8
Adams, Roy 68, 70, 79, 83
Agnes Street 28
Agreement (1998) *see* Good Friday Agreement (1998)
Alderdice, Lord 154
Alliance Party 14, 100n2, 101–102, 106n11, 110–111, 128, 156, 204
Anderson, J. 80–81
Andersontown Road 27
Annalee Street 55
Antrim Road 35, 136–137, 147, 148, 167, 180
Ardoyne 59, 62n9–63, 68, 143, 147n4, 150
Aretxaga, B. 22, 26
Ashton Centre 161, 162–166, 167, 176, 178
Attwood, Alex 120
Avonbeg Street 55

Ballysillan 28, 133, 148
Basten, A. 29
BDP (Building Design Partnership) 10, 68, 78, 84–85, 123, 176
Bean, K. 49, 195
Belfast
 changing demographics 56–64, 102n5
 contested areas 1, 4, 7, 9, 14, 19, 38–39, 75
 effect of deindustrialisation 55–56
 identity politics 9–10, 13, 49, 55–64, 79n1, 85, 203–205
 territorialism 26–30, 55–64, 178–179
Belfast Agreement (1998) *see* Good Friday Agreement (1998)
Belfast City Council 173
Belfast Metropolitan College (Belfast Met) 2, 169, 177, 185, 189
black taxi tours 27, 32
Bogaards, M. 42
Bollens, S. 19
Bosnia-Herzegovina 41
Bou Akar, M. 17
Brand, R. 38
Brennan, S. 152, 201, 203
Brexit process 13, 101n4, 154, 195, 198–202, 207
 challenge to GFA 198–202
British Army 27, 36
Brucevale 128, 178–180
built environment *see* defensive architecture; housing crisis; political markers
Burns, Anna, *Milkman* 137
Burton, F. 26

Cameron, Pam 110–111
Carlisle Circus roundabout 3, 83, 136–137
Carrick Hill 137, 147n4
Carroll, Gerry 104, 196n3

247

Carson, Arder 184
Carson, C. 29
Castlereagh Hills 170
Catholic/Nationalist/Republican
    community 1
    community solidarity 145–146
    demographic changes 10n9, 59
    see also identity politics
Cave Hill 170
CCRF (Cliftonville Community
    Regeneration Forum) 162, 166–167,
    170, 176, 180
CEPs (Community Economic
    Partnerships) 65–68, 92, 117,
    147–148, 149
Charmaz, K. 21
Charter NI 156
Clausewicz, Carl von 5
Clifton Street 136
Cliftonpark Avenue 1, 3, 32–35, 55, 122,
    123, 128, 180, 183
Cliftonville, Lower 3, 4, 59, 68, 122,
    147n4, 163, 170
'community development' narrative/
    language 142–145, 161, 184, 191–192
    micro-neighbourhoods 147
consociationalism see power-sharing
    framework
Copeland, Michael 77, 143
COVID-19 pandemic 19, 52–53, 101n4,
    203–204, 207
exposed racial division 7, 19
Craig, James 56n3
Crumlin Road 32–33, 68
Crumlin Road Gaol 10, 33, 77, 119, 170,
    170n11, 174
Cunningham, Tim 92

de Certeau, M. 30
defensive architecture 9
D'Hondt system 42
Dickson, Stuart 106
'differential deprivation' narrative
    113–114, 121–122, 130–140, 192
Dixon, P. 127
Dodds, Nigel 101, 102, 137, 139, 157

Donaldson, Sir Jeffrey 202
Drumcree riots (1996) 60–61
DSD (Department for Social
    Development) 1n1, 52, 64, 78, 88, 93,
    115, 120–121, 130–140, 168
    Facing the Future 131–132, 135
Dunlop, Rev Dr John 64n11
Dunlop Report (2002) 64–68, 84, 90,
    114n1, 147, 166, 174
    'parochial agendas' 66–67
DUP (Democratic Unionist Party)
    5–6n6, 11–12n12, 44–45, 79n1,
    100n2–101, 123, 149, 166, 195
    housing 45, 48, 77, 113–114, 121–122,
        139–140
    rhetoric of 'differential deprivation'
        113–114, 121–122, 130–140, 192
    RHI scandal (Renewable Heat
        Initiative) 13, 196–197n4, 199
    see also power-sharing framework

Eastwood, Colum 157
Ebrington Barracks (Derry) 51, 52–53
ECNI (Equality Commission for
    Northern Ireland) 13–14, 43–44, 77,
    84, 86, 86–87, 131–132, 192
economic crash (2007) 72–73, 99–100,
    113, 115
Edwards, A. 142, 149, 203
Ellis, G. 6
EQIA (Equality Impact Assessment)
    86–89, 91, 113, 116, 119, 133,
    176–177
ethnocracy 45–48
ethnographic approach 21–26
European Union PEACE III funding
    1–2, 6n7, 12, 113–116, 128–129, 161,
    173, 191, 206
Evershed, J. 199

Falls Road 27n6–28, 55, 148
Feldman, A. 38
Finucane, John 102
flags (political markers) 5, 22, 31, 35,
    38, 158
Floyd, George 7

Flyvbjerg, B. 50, 121, 130
Ford, David 110
Foster, Arlene 101, 106, 156, 196–197n4, 199
Foucault, Michel 5
Frederick Street 136
Freedom Corner 27
Fullilove, M. 14–15

Gaffikin, F. 37
Geertz, C. 21
Girdwood Advisory Panel 24, 68–75, 77–95, 92–93, 113–140, 117, 120
Girdwood Community Hub 1–13, 113–140, 141, 143, 157, 158, 161–181
  legacy 183–193
Girdwood redevelopment 1–20, 4, 20, 51, 56, 68, 149
  contentious location 2–3
  snapshot of broader political dynamics 21–26, 68, 97, 192, 193, 196
  symbolism of 'New Northern Ireland' 3, 5, 10–11, 68–75
  see also Masterplan (Girdwood)
Girdwood Residents' Jury 92–95
Givan, Paul 157, 197n6, 202
Glen Road 27
GLL (Greenwich Leisure Limited) 171–173, 181, 183–185
Good Friday Agreement (1998) 3n3, 5, 6–7, 19, 24, 41–45, 85, 151, 181–188
  gap between rhetoric and reality 6–7, 24, 91–92, 151–159
  'good relations' rhetoric 44, 45, 192, 206
  handover of military sites 51–54
  influence of informal 'backroom' deals 50–54
  'New Northern Ireland' 3, 5, 10–11, 41–42, 74, 154
  normalisation of security arrangements 3
  'petition of concern' 42n3–43, 45n6, 48n9

post-agreement politics 8–9, 19, 24, 45–49
power-sharing framework 5, 41–45, 100
promise of economic 'peace dividend' 41, 69–72, 85, 94
two-party dynamic 5–6, 45–49, 100, 110
see also Northern Ireland Agreement (1998); power-sharing framework
Goodman, Michael 124
graffiti 31n11
Graham, Sir Alistair 106
'growth towns' development 57–58

Hanna, Claire 106, 156
Hansard 23n2, 110
Hayward, K. 44, 191, 204
Helms, L. 42
Higson, B. 100n2
Hocking, B. 52
Holy Cross dispute (North Belfast) 10, 56, 62, 63
housing provision 5, 6–7, 10–12, 13–14, 25–26, 32, 57
  'objective need' 11, 45, 81, 83, 90, 103, 106–107, 132
  religious composition of housing waiting lists 12n12, 139
Hughes, C. 104–105, 108, 149
Humphrey, William 120
Hutchinson, Billy 59–60

identity politics 9–10, 13, 49, 55–64, 79n1, 85, 203–205
INLA (Irish National Liberation Army) 24n3, 151
Intercomm 70n12–71
International Centre for Conflict Transformation (ICCT) 51–52, 126
IRC (Independent Reporting Commission) 154–155
Irish Language Act 197n6, 198, 201, 205–206

Jacobs, J. 18–19, 22, 30
Jenkins, R. 22, 23
Johnson, Boris 200–201

Kelly, B. 100–101
Kelly, Dolores 127
Kelly, Gerry 101, 124
Ketola, M. 104–105, 108, 149
Kingston, Brian 137
Kinnaird Terrace 178
Kitchin, R. 29
Komarova, M. 19, 50, 191

Laganside development 68, 72
Lawrence-Zúñiga, D. 14
Lebanon 17, 41, 110, 155
Lijphart, A. 41–42, 46
Lisburn Road 28
LOCA (Lower Oldpark Community Association) 162
Lofland, J. 22
Lofland, L.H. 22
Losty, Tim 68, 119
Low, S. 14
LSCA (Lower Shankill Community Association) 156n11–157, 162
Lundy, P. 143
Lysaght, K. 29

Mac Giolla Bhéin, Ciarán 207
McBurney, John 154, 155
McCall, C. 204
McCausland, Nelson 120, 121–123, 129, 130–138, 163
McClenaghan, Betsy 61
McClenaghan, Margaret 64
MacCormack, Inez 86
McCusker, Paul 190
McDonald, Mary Lou 202
McDonnell, Alasdair 127
McGee, J.J. 103n6
McGovern, M. 143
McGuigan, Philip 111
McGuinness, Martin 126, 197
McKeag, Stevie 32n13–33
McKee, Lyra 152

Mackie's factory site 206, 207
McWilliams, Monica 154
Magherafelt Barracks 51, 53
Maginness, Alban 92, 122
Malone Barracks 51, 53
Malone Road 18, 28
Manor Street 34, 83, 180
marching season 28, 35, 38
Marijan, B. 152
Marrowbone 68
Martin, Mícheál 200–201
Masterplan (Girdwood) 77–95, 117–118, 121–122, 123–130, 161–181, 187
  'community engagement' 117–119, 121–122, 161–181, 184
  conflict transformation centre 126
  housing provisions 123–130
  sectarian compromise 124–125
Matthew, Robert 57
Maze/Long Kesh prison 51, 53–54, 113–114, 126–127
memorial sites 22, 24, 31, 38
Mitchell, C. 44
Morrisey, M. 37
Morrison, Danny 145n2
Mulholland, C. 55
murals (political) 5, 22, 24, 38, 157–158
Murphy, M. 199, 200
Murtagh, B. 6, 37, 150, 193

NAMA (National Assets and Management Agency) 103–104n8
NBCAP (North Belfast Community Action Project) 10, 64–65, 67
NBCAU (North Belfast Community Action Unit) 65–69, 92–93, 93, 114n1, 116
NBCRA (North Belfast Civil Rights Association) 122n3
NEETS programme 176, 177–178
New Lodge 3, 4, 12, 59, 68, 123, 136, 147n4, 163–164, 180
Newell, George 143
Newington 147n4
Newton, Robin 103n6, 105n9
Newtownards Road 27

Ní Chuilín, Carál 79, 103n6, 124, 136
NIHE (Northern Ireland Housing Executive) 55, 80, 91, 120–121, 131, 138n9–139, 188
Nolan, P. 10n9, 109
Nolan, Stephen 111n14
North Talks Too 123, 159, 161, 165–166, 167, 170, 175–176, 178, 184, 190
Northern Ireland Act (1998) 3, 5, 13, 19, 24, 43, 186, 192
Section 75 9, 11, 12, 43–44, 48, 82, 83, 86, 115, 116, 132
Northern Ireland Assembly 5–6n6, 13–14, 19n14, 42, 45, 46n7, 48
A Fresh Start 106n10, 141, 154
A Shared Future 98, 99
alleged clientelism 102–108, 177, 193
alternative politics 195
backroom deals 113–140
Cohesion, Sharing and Integration 98–99, 158, 173n12–174
collapse 45n5, 48, 79, 99, 101n4, 195–207
duplication of services 148–149
ethnic/sectarian championing 97–111, 121–122
'peace industry' 107–108
sectarian head-counting 102
'zero-sum' approach 12, 25, 44n4, 46, 50, 51, 80–81, 97–111, 140, 148, 163, 181, 198
Northern Ireland Protocol 198, 200
Nucho, Randa 155

Ó Muilleoir, Máirtín 140
OFMDFM (Office of the First Minister and Deputy First Minister) 52, 53, 174, 184
Oldpark, Lower 2–3, 4, 12, 33, 62, 82, 120, 122, 123, 134, 163, 166, 180
O'Neill, Michelle 202
O'Neill, Terence 57
Orange Order parades 28n10, 136n8, 152n9
Ormeau Road 28–29

Pankhurst, Dale 190
paramilitary groups 141–159, 166, 201
ceasefires 41, 142
changing roles 152–159
community 'gatekeepers' role 141–159, 166, 193
community policing 143–144, 166, 193
place markers 5, 12, 22
participant observation, research methods 23–26
PEACE III funding *see* European Union PEACE III funding
People Before Profit 101, 196n2
plaques 157, 158
Plöger, J. 51
political markers 38–39
see also flags; graffiti; memorial sites; murals; plaques
post-agreement politics 6–10
power-sharing framework 5, 41–45, 46–49, 100, 109–111, 192–193
PPR (Participation and the Practice of Rights) 11n11, 13–14, 51, 77, 86–95, 107, 122, 124, 131, 161, 192, 206, 207
Unlocking the Potential 86–95
PRONI (Public Records Office of Northern Ireland) 10, 69, 78–79
Protestant/Unionist/Loyalist community 1, 145
ageing demographic 10n9, 56–57, 81
sense of decline 60–61, 134–135, 163, 192
'siege mentality' 37, 59, 61, 63–64, 82, 120, 128, 130, 180, 201
see also identity politics
Provisional IRA (PIRA) 24n3, 36, 149, 151–159, 157–158
'ballot box and Armalite' strategy 145n2
PSNI (Police Service of Northern Ireland) 27n8, 151, 154–155

Red Sky debacle 103–104n6
research methods 21–26
participant observation 23–26

RHI (Renewable Heat Initiative) 13, 196–197n4, 199
Ritchie, Margaret 114, 120
Robinson, Mary 94
Robinson, Peter 104n8, 126, 127
Rocket, Samuel 162–163n2
Roe Street 55
RUC (Royal Ulster Constabulary) 27n5, 36

Sailortown 147n4
St Andrews Agreement (2006) 79n1, 98n1, 197n6, 198
Sands, Bobby 27, 51, 126
Sandy Row 29
Sartori, G. 48
SDLP (Social Democratic Labour Party) 68, 98, 100n2, 115, 139
segregation
  array of boundaries 2–3, 29–30
  'ethnosectarian enclaving' 37
  gendered divides 29
  reproduction in housing policies 6–7
SEUPB (Special European Union Project Board) 113, 116, 141n1, 157, 162, 171
Seymour, Elfie 206
Shankill Road, Lower 3, 4, 28, 32, 36, 55, 58, 62, 68, 82, 122, 134, 163
Shirlow, P. 37, 143, 150, 193
Short Strand 27
Shuttleworth, I. 80–81
'Single-identity' terminology 146–147n3
Sinn Féin 5–6n6, 11–12n12, 77, 100n2, 123, 149, 157–158, 166, 195
  backroom deals on housing provisions 113–114, 121–122, 124, 127
  'dissident' association 122–123n4, 151
  see also power-sharing framework; Provisional IRA
Sluka, J. 25
Social Investment Fund (SIF) 105–106
Springfield Road 27

Sri Lanka 110
Stalford, Christopher 110–111
Stanhope Street 136
Stitt, Dee 106, 156
Storey, Mervyn 184
Stormont 5n5, 27, 79n1, 120
  see also Northern Ireland Assembly
Svašek, M. 19

TBTC (Take Back the City) 207
TDK (Thorndale, Duncairn and Kinnaird) 166–167
'telling', subtle markers to ethnoreligious identity 25
Thompson, William 94
Tiger's Bay 133
Titanic Quarter 73–75, 79, 126
Toren, C. 22
Torrens estate 60–61
'Troubles' 58–59, 145
  internment 36n18
  patterns of displacement and resettlement 58–59
  sectarian violence 35–36n17
Trump, Donald 49

UDA (Ulster Defence Association) 24n3, 27n5, 35, 61, 63–64, 83, 149, 151, 154, 156–157
UFF (Ulster Freedom Fighters) 62, 63, 157
United States 7, 14–15, 17–18, 49
  urban regeneration policies 7, 14–15
urban planning 192
  racially explicit planning 17–18, 92
  'redlining' policies 7, 18
urban renewal
  community 'engagement' 19
  negotiations 14–15
  spatial perspectives of citizens 15–17
  'Third Way' 144, 146
UUP (Ulster Unionist Party) 79, 98, 100n2, 199
UVF (Ulster Volunteer Force) 24n3, 28, 151

Westlink 15, 29
White City 55
Wilford, R. 192
Wilson, R. 192
Woodvale Avenue 28
Wylie, Suzanne 184

Yacobi, H. 17, 46
Yiasouma, Koulla 138
Yiftachel, O. 17, 46

www.ingramcontent.com/pod-product-compliance
Lightning Source LLC
Chambersburg PA
CBHW071820130326
41206CB00031B/2067